MAKING CITIES WORK

MAKING CITIES WORK

PROSPECTS AND POLICIES
FOR URBAN AMERICA

Edited by Robert P. Inman

PRINCETON UNIVERSITY PRESS PRINCETON AND OXFORD

Published by Princeton University Press,
41 William Street, Princeton, New Jersey 08540

In the United Kingdom: Princeton University Press,
6 Oxford Street, Woodstock, Oxfordshire OX20 1TW

Library of Congress Cataloging-in-Publication Data

Making cities work : prospects and policies for urban America / edited by Robert P. Inman.
p. cm.
Includes index.
ISBN 978-0-691-13104-7 (cl.: alk. paper) — ISBN 978-0-691-13105-4 (pb: alk. paper)
1. Cities and towns—United States.   2. Urbanization—United States.   3. Urban economics—United States.   4. Sociology, Urban—United States.   5. City and town life—United States.
6. Urban policy—United States.   I. Inman, Robert P.
  HT123.M285   2009
   307.760973—dc22   2008036268
British Library Cataloging-in-Publication Data is available

This book has been composed in Palatino.

Printed on acid-free paper. ∞

press.princeton.edu

Printed in the United States of America

10 9 8 7 6 5 4 3 2 1

Contents

Illustrations and Tables

Illustrations

Tables

Foreword

This book, *Making Cities Work: Prospects and Policies for Urban America*, and a companion conference held at the Wharton School, University of Pennsylvania, on May 4, 2007, honor the memory of Dr. Kathyrn Engebretson, past president of the William Penn Foundation, Philadelphia. Kathy was a graduate of Luther College (1977), received her MBA in finance from the Wharton School (1983), and then went on to earn her PhD from Wharton in applied economics and public policy (1996). She began her professional career in public finance in Denver, but soon returned to Philadelphia as vice president of Lehman Brothers, one of several senior financial management positions that she held in the private sector. In January 1991, Kathy joined the administration of then newly elected Mayor Ed Rendell as the city treasurer, and in that position was instrumental in helping to steer the city from the edge of bankruptcy to balanced budgets and finally to the city's first significant tax reductions in over fifty years. In 1997, Kathy joined the administration of President Judith Rodin at the University of Pennsylvania as vice president for finance and chief financial officer. In 2001, Kathy was appointed president of the William Penn Foundation, Philadelphia's largest regionally focused foundation, to lead its new efforts on policy-oriented grant making to address community needs. She held that position until her death in February 2005, at the age of forty-eight.

Kathy was a cherished friend of the Wharton School, the University of Pennsylvania, and the city of Philadelphia. Her accomplishments working with governmental, business, and not-for-profit organizations demonstrated how each sector can contribute to civic betterment. A volume and a companion conference on managing cities using the best practices from the public and private sectors therefore seemed a fitting tribute to Kathy's outstanding career. In her opening remarks for the conference, President Amy Gutmann of the University of Pennsylvania described Kathy as a pragmatic idealist. This volume aspires to that high standard, and I am extremely pleased that such an outstanding group of scholars agreed to participate in this project. The authors' chapters, originally presented at the Wharton Impact Conference, have been refereed and revised for publication here. Participants at the conference included other leading scholars, policymakers, financial managers, and foundation representatives.

Beyond the opportunity to honor the career of Kathy Engebretson, this project has proven timely for another reason as well. It has been almost forty years since James Q. Wilson and a similarly impressive list of urban scholars addressed the same agenda—the future of U.S. cities— in their book titled *The Metropolitan Enigma: Inquiries into the Nature and Dimensions of America's "Urban Crisis."* We have learned a lot since then, and it seems worthwhile to again survey our collective wisdoms and make these summaries available in a single volume. I am delighted that Princeton University Press agreed and is the publisher of the conference volume.

Robert P. Inman
January 28, 2008

Acknowledgments_____

The idea for this volume to honor Kathy Engebretson grew from conversations with Kathy's close friends, Mr. David Seltzer and Ms. Lisa Roberts. David and Lisa's commitment to this project from the beginning, and their good advice and encouragement along the way, were essential to its completion and publication here. Tim Sullivan and Heath Renfroe of Princeton University Press have been encouraging and supportive editors. Chris Trollen handled all conference and publication logistics with great skill and good humor, for which I am most grateful. Neither the conference nor this volume would have been possible without the generous financial support of the Poor Richard's Foundation, the William Penn Foundation, and the Wharton School. Finally, my deep thanks to the authors of the chapters presented here. Each is an outstanding scholar and very busy, but each was willing to step back to provide a valuable survey of their own portion of the research frontier for those courageous and optimistic enough, like Kathy, to work on the front lines of making city policy.

Robert P. Inman
January 28, 2008

Contributors

David Card is the class of 1950 professor of economics at the University of California at Berkeley, and a research associate of the National Bureau of Economic Research. Card was previously a professor of economics at Princeton University, and has had faculty appointments at the University of Chicago and Columbia University. He was coeditor of the journal *Econometrica* from 1993 to 1997, and coeditor of the *American Economic Review* from 2002 to 2006. Card coauthored the book *Myth and Measurement: The New Economics of the Minimum Wage* in 1995, and has written widely on many topics in labor economics, including immigration, discrimination, wage inequality, job training, and education. He is a Fellow of the American Academy of Arts and Sciences and the Society of Labor Economics. In 1995, Card received the American Economic Association's John Bates Clark medal for the best economist under the age of forty. In 2006, he shared the IZA Prize in Labor Economics with Alan B. Krueger. He was recently awarded the Ragnar Frisch Medal for the best article in applied economics published in *Econometrica* in 2005–2006.

Philip J. Cook, PhD, is ITT/Sanford professor of public policy, and professor of economics and sociology, at Duke University. He has served as consultant to the U.S. Department of Justice (Criminal Division) and the U.S. Department of the Treasury (Enforcement Division), and has served on a number of expert advisory panels of the National Academy of Sciences—including those dealing with alcohol abuse prevention, injury control, violence, and the school rampage shootings. He is an elected member of the Institute of Medicine and a fellow of the American Society of Criminology.

Janet Currie is a professor at Columbia University and the chair of the Economics Department. She is an affiliate of the National Poverty Research Center and the National Bureau of Economic Research, and is on the advisory board of the National Children's Study. Currie has also served on several National Academy of Sciences panels, including on the Committee on Population. Her most recent book is *The Invisible Safety Net: Protecting America's Poor Families and Children.*

Edward L. Glaeser is the Fred and Eleanor Glimp professor of economics in the Faculty of Arts and Sciences at Harvard University, where he has taught since 1992. He is the director of the Taubman Center for State and Local Government and the director of the Rappaport Institute of Greater Boston. Glaeser currently serves on the executive committee of the American Real Estate and Urban Economics Association, and has served as a consultant for the New Zealand Treasury, the.U.S. Department of Labor, and the Harvard Institute for International Development/U.S. Agency for International Development's Bolivia Project on housing market reform.

Joseph Gyourko is the Martin Bucksbaum professor of real estate and finance at the Wharton School of the University of Pennsylvania. He also serves as the director of the Zell/Lurie Real Estate Center at Wharton. Professor Gyourko received his BA from Duke University and a PhD in economics from the University of Chicago. His research interests include real estate finance, urban economics, and housing markets. He serves on the advisory board for the Brookings-Wharton papers on urban affairs series. A member and former trustee of the Urban Land Institute, he serves as an ex officio member of the Real Estate Roundtable's Research Committee.

Robert P. Inman is the Richard King Mellon professor of finance and economics at the Wharton School of the University of Pennsylvania. His research, focusing on the design and impact of fiscal policies, has been published in the leading academic journals in economics, finance, and law. He is the editor of two books, *The Economics of Public Services* and *Managing the Service Economy*. Inman has served as a consultant and adviser on fiscal policy to the city of Philadelphia, the states of New York, Pennsylvania, and California, the U.S. Department of Education, Housing, and Urban Development as well as the U.S. Department of the Treasury, the World Bank, and governments of the Republic of South Africa and Sri Lanka.

Richard J. Murnane, an economist, is the Thompson professor at the Harvard Graduate School of Education, a research associate at the National Bureau of Economic Research, and a member of the board of directors of MDRC, a research firm specializing in evaluations of policies aimed at improving the welfare of the disadvantaged. He has written several books, including *Teaching the New Basic Skills* and *The New Division of Labor* (both coauthored with Frank Levy), and many research papers explaining how changes in the U.S. economy have influenced the skills that Americans need to earn a decent living, and how schools, especially those in cities, need to change in order to prepare students to thrive in the twenty-first century.

Witold Rybczynski is the Martin and Margy Meyerson professor of urbanism at the University of Pennsylvania, where he is also founding coeditor of the *Wharton Real Estate Review*. He writes regularly on architecture and city planning for the *New York Review of Books*, and is the architecture critic for *Slate*. Rybczynski is the author of the prizewinning biography of Frederick Law Olmsted, *A Clearing in the Distance*; his latest book is *Last Harvest: How a Cornfield Became New Daleville*. He serves on the U.S Commission of Fine Arts in Washington, DC.

Kenneth A. Small, a professor emeritus of economics at the University of California at Irvine, specializes in urban, transportation, and environmental economics. He has advised the European Union, the World Bank, the National Research Council, and others on transportation policy. Small was honored in 1999 with the Distinguished Member Award by the American Economic Association's Transportation and Public Utilities Group. He recently coauthored *The Economics of Urban Transportation*. At Irvine, he previously served as chair of economics and an associate dean of the School of Social Sciences.

Jacob L. Vigdor is an associate professor of public policy studies and economics at Duke University and a Faculty Research Fellow at the National Bureau of Economic Research. He has written extensively on the topics of residential and school segregation, and on racial disparities in educational and economic outcomes.

1

Introduction

CITY PROSPECTS, CITY POLICIES

ROBERT P. INMAN

WHY CITIES? In this era of high-speed communication, videoconferencing, rapid transit, and high-definition radio and television, could we all not work and play at home? And could not home be anywhere, where the air is clean, the streets are safe, and the schools, including home schools, are excellent? What cities have always offered—proximity and easy access—may simply not be necessary today, thus giving us the freedom to locate wherever the environment, whether the metropolis or the mountains, is most conducive to our needs and tastes. In fact, however, cities are on the upsurge. In the United States, the share of the nation's population residing in cities of over a hundred thousand residents fell from 53 percent in 1960 to 41 percent by 1980, but rebounded to 44 percent by 2005.[1] Even more impressively, the United Nations projects that by 2020, over 55 percent of the world's population will reside in urban centers, with all the benefits and costs this will entail.[2]

Rather than reducing the economic importance of cities, new technologies have in fact made cities even more attractive places for work and play. Efficient production in the new economy appears to require more, not fewer, personal interactions.[3] When the market pays a premium for unique products and specialized services, then production adaptability will be essential for meeting customer demands. Adaptability requires give-and-take communication and proximity, and typically, the closer the better. The recent evidence suggests that most of the benefits of proximity are realized within one mile or less.[4] Cities provide these productivity advantages.

Efficient consumption, particularly of services, also favors dense locations. The provision of health care, education, legal, and financial services is best done in person. The same holds true for much of retailing and entertainment. Finally, and of no small importance to those between the ages of twenty to forty, cities offer a convenient way to meet new people with interests and tastes similar to their own.[5] As the low-cost supplier of proximity, cities have become critical locations for consumer spending.[6]

Finally, cities today retain their historical role as centers for economic and cultural innovations. For innovation, proximity is again the key. Seminars, exhibitions, and informal collegial interactions stimulate creativity while knowledgeable patrons, financiers, and an educated and demanding populace evaluates and rewards cost-saving innovations, promising new products, and provoking or appealing artistic change. Recent estimates, for example, show that doubling the density of employment in U.S. cities leads to a 20 percent increase in patentable innovations per capita.[7] So too, it appears, does density favor artistic innovations.[8] London and New York are the creative centers for contemporary art. Berlin, Paris, New York, and Los Angeles—and for a time Portland, Oregon, and Seattle—are the places offering the best new music. Los Angeles (Hollywood) and Mumbai (Bollywood) are where new cinema is produced, while New York is today's center for contemporary dance, and Paris, Milan, and New York for fashion. And while one might easily dispute its inclusion as part of Western culture, there is no doubt that country music would not be what it is today, or what it has ever been, had there been no Nashville, Tennessee.

This book, *Making Cities Work*, provides ten chapters by leading urban scholars that seek to understand what is required for a successful city in today's economy. The chapters here update the efforts of what had been a landmark survey at its time, 1968, when the future of U.S. cities was not so bright. Titled *The Metropolitan Engima: Inquiries into the Nature and Dimensions of America's Urban Crisis* and edited by James Q. Wilson, that book offered the first systematic overview of social sciences' understanding of how cities work for residents and firms.[9]

The tone of *The Metropolitan Enigma* was pessimistic. The observed decline of cities, and particularly the bleak economic prospects for cities' poorest residents, was seen as a consequence of larger economic, political, and social forces. Manufacturing jobs, the primary source of city employment, were leaving the city in search of cheaper land, and many residents, especially recent black in-migrants, could not follow. Federal highway expansion encouraged middle-class exit, however, further exacerbating central cities' economic declines. Economic decline led to weak city finances, while weak finances undermined educational opportunities for inner-city children. State and federal policies failed to fill the fiscal gap. Urban crime, particularly teenage crime, was a logical consequence of a weak economy, poor schooling, and the lack of city fiscal resources for a stronger police presence. Urban design theory favored large-scale public housing complexes that only made matters worse. The end result was a fundamentally dysfunctional social environment of concentrated poverty and limited economic opportunity. Seeing no future, it is then no surprise that families dissolved, single parenthood increased, and teenagers rioted. In 1968, cities were in decline.

The authors of *The Metropolitan Enigma* recommended a two-prong approach for easing the economic and social consequences of then failing central cities. First, spend more regional, state, and federal government money for city infrastructure and economic development. Second, relocate lower-income families into areas with better job opportunities, a richer fiscal base, and socially more functional neighborhoods. Both strategies are what we now call "place-based" strategies. The first favors city locations. If that didn't work, then the second approach was meant to help the less mobile escape their failing city for a more economically favored suburban residence.

Only the first strategy proved politically viable, and even then legislative coalitions for passage typically required funding for rural and suburban projects along with city funding. Figure 1.1 shows the relationship between real (2006 dollars) federal aid per resident in our largest cities (population greater than 150,000 residents in 2005) compared to federal aid to all other local governments, while figure 1.2 shows the relationship between real (2006 dollars) state aid per resident for the same set of large U.S. cities compared to each state's aid to all other local governments in the state. State education aid is excluded from the analysis.[10] Both the federal and state sample periods are from 1962 to 2002 in nine five-year intervals.

The relationship between large-city federal aid and other local government federal aid shows $1 of large-city aid is matched by $1 for all other local governments along a 45° line from the origin of figure 1.1. National politics ensures that if the residents of our largest cities get $1 of federal aid, so too do the residents of all other local governments.[11] At the state level, our large cities are treated worse, on average, than are small cities, suburbs, and rural communities, as seen in figure 1.2. Here, large-city residents receive a guarantee of $99 per resident (the intercept of the solid line in figure 1.2), but then share in additional state noneducation aid only at a rate of $0.31 for each $1 of state aid given to "other" local governments (the slope of the solid line). On average, our large cities received $185 per resident in noneducation aid over the sample period while all smaller local governments received $282 per resident. State policies seem to meet a "big-city obligation" with an average fixed payment of about $100 per resident, and then focus incremental spending on suburbs and rural localities at the rate of about three to one. Clearly, there has been no targeted spending on our largest cities as proposed by the authors of *The Metropolitan Enigma*. If

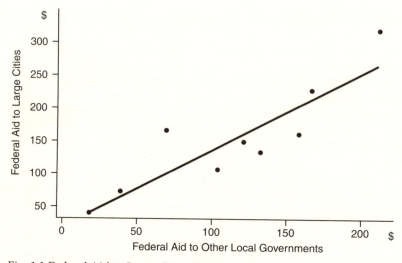

Fig. 1.1 Federal Aid to Large Cities (2006 Dollars)

anything, smaller cities and suburbs have been favored over the past forty years.

Nor is there compelling evidence that the federal and state monies that did go to our largest cities did much to revive their declining economies. The Urban Mass Transportation Acts of 1964 ($150 million) and 1970 ($1.3 billion) that helped cities directly were only modestly funded, while the more significant allocation ($11.6 billion) approved under the National Mass Transportation Systems Act of 1974 was for light-rail and only encouraged the further exit of the middle class to the suburbs. The Surface Transportation Acts of 1978, 1982, and 1987 did promise more funding for mass transportation, but in the end the appropriations fell far short of the promised authorizations. City public transportation ridership continued to decline and suburban-to-city car usage continued to increase. By the 1990s, the central focus of federal transportation policies was to ease suburban commuting costs with funding for more highways and even subsidized city parking for commuters.[12]

Federal housing policies for cities have emphasized the construction of moderate- and low-income housing, both in the central city and suburbs. The most successful of these programs was Section 8 of the Housing and Community Development Act of 1974, which offered rent assistance to lower-income residents. There were no restrictions on location. The flow of capital into lower-cost housing was also stimulated by the 1977 Community Reinvestment Act's aggressive pursuit of bank redlining practices. Finally, the Housing Act of 1990 provided funding to

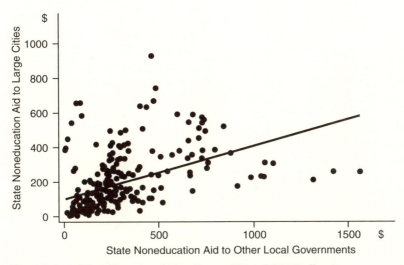

Fig. 1.2 State Noneducation Aid to Large Cities (2006 Dollars)

cities to upgrade—or knock down when appropriate—dysfunctional public housing and replace that housing with mixed-income housing complexes. The act also offered vouchers for the rental or purchase of housing by lower-income families displaced from public housing. The expanded supply of low-income housing has proven to be a mixed blessing, however. It did provide improved living space for the poor, but it has also concentrated the location of the poor in the central cities and inner-ring suburbs where this housing was built. As the chapters in this volume will stress, poverty concentration in cities has had significant adverse effects on city economies and therefore city residents, both poor and rich.

Federal efforts to stimulate inner-city economic development and job opportunities have included the Model Cities initiative within the Demonstration Cities and Metropolitan Development Act of 1966, the Comprehensive Employment and Training Act (CETA) of 1973, the Community Development Block Grant of 1974, the Urban Development Action Grants (UDAG, as section 199 of the Housing and Community Reinvestment Act) and the Targeted Job Tax Credit (TJTC) program both approved in 1977, and finally, the Empowerment Zone/Enterprise Communities (EZ/EC) program approved as part of the Omnibus Budget Reconciliation Act of 1993. Model Cities funding never exceeded $1 billion, and this limited budget was spread over 150 locations to ensure sufficient congressional support for budget approval.[13] CETA was a federally funded job creation program administered by the central cities. The funds were used by cities to hire low-skill workers for entry-level city jobs. No significant training occurred, and city funds were simply replaced by federal funds, which were then allocated as "free money" for tax relief and expanded city services largely benefiting middle-class city residents.[14] The UDAG and TJTC programs were both short-lived, and in their time proved ineffective in stimulating economic growth in cities' poorer neighborhoods. UDAG grants were subsidies to private developers and were largely capitalized into the price of city land.[15] TJTC subsidies lowered the effective wage for low-skilled workers, increased firm profits, and in end also enhanced inner-city land prices. Few, if any, new low-skilled jobs were created.[16] Current federal efforts at stimulating central city economies are now limited to funding for Empowerment Zones. Over the course of three rounds—1994, 1998, and 2001—the federal government has selected 122 cities to participate in the Empowerment Zone/Enterprise Communities program, but again federal dollars going to each community are modest ($100 million per community), and like its predecessors (UDAG and TJTC), most federal monies benefit developers and the owners of land rather than the residents in the favored, low-income neighborhoods.[17] Like most federal and state policies of the 1970s and 1980s, these place-based programs benefited those who owned the places and not the lower-income residents who lived there.

If not by these federal or state policies, how then have we moved from *The Metropolitan Enigma*'s pessimistic assessment for urban America to the more promising future now seen for the average U.S. city? Many cities whose futures looked so dim in 1968 are thriving today, or are at least on the mend. New York City, Chicago, Seattle, San Francisco, Oakland, Boston, Minneapolis, Saint Paul, Jersey City, and Des Moines had each lost population in the 1960s, but have gained population in the past ten years. Philadelphia, Newark, and Louisville have all slowed their population losses to a small trickle. Still, some large cities have continued their decline—for example, Detroit, Cincinnati, Cleveland, Milwaukee, Pittsburgh, Baltimore, and Saint Louis. These different economic fortunes of U.S. cities have occurred not because of differential availability or the success of federal or state policies. *What is it, then, about the successful cities that leads to growth and prosperity for their residents and firms, while other cities stagnate or decline?* This is the new urban enigma, and the central agenda of this book.

Edward Glaeser provides an overview of city growth and decline in chapter 2, clarifying in the process the necessary economic conditions for city prosperity. For once-declining cities such as New York and Boston, Glaeser stresses the need to reinvent the local economy—in these two cases, to make the transition from a manufacturing city to a service city. For small- and midsize cities the key to growth is finding a niche, a comparative advantage, in the new idea-driven, service-based economy. In most all instances of success, city growth occurs because of the presence of a college-educated workforce and the proximity of those skilled workers to each other. Only skilled workers have the ability to use and create new technologies, while workplace density enhances the productivity of those technologies through idea sharing. In Glaeser's analysis both conditions, skills and density, are necessary for local industries to remain competitive and grow.

For the skilled city to work, however, workers must interact, and that means converging on a common location to do business. Efficient transportation infrastructure and utilization (i.e., *pricing*) is essential for a productive city. This is the topic of chapter 3, in which Kenneth Small explores how to manage urban transportation. As Small emphasizes, for any transportation system and pricing strategy there is an equilibrium number of trips balancing the private benefits of travel in produced goods and services against the private costs, discomfort, and inconvenience of travel. That equilibrium can be inefficient, though. In particular, roadway congestion will discourage the efficient agglomeration of economic activities and undermine the productive potential of the city. In addition to skills and location, an efficient transportation policy becomes a third necessary condition for the economically efficient city.

What is not necessary for city efficiency and growth, although often an attractive by-product, are city amenities—good restaurants, theater, music, sports teams, and shopping—gathered in what Glaeser calls the "consumer city." In Glaeser's terms, a consumer city is a consequence of, not the cause for, the productive skilled city. This important point is amplified by the many valuable examples of "city spaces" offered by Witold Rybczynski in chapter 4. Cities have tried all manner of design strategies to lure suburban residents back and encourage city residents to do center-city shopping—such as walking or pedestrian malls, semi-malls with widened sidewalks and narrowed streets, transit malls accessible only by bus, and finally just plain mall malls. None have worked, unless there were first city residents in abundance wanting to shop in city stores.

Perhaps good design and attractive housing can entice residents back into the city? Here too Rybczynski's examples raise doubts. Using the concept of "community" or "campus" living, many cities encouraged the building of superblock complexes for middle- and upper-income families through subsidies and land assembly. But unless the city was already a successful location for firms and middle-class residents—for instance, Battery Park City in New York—those projects were never built. Finally, some cities have tried the "trophy building" strategy, hoping to mimic the success of Bilbao, Spain, with its new Guggenheim Museum by Frank Gehry. In most cases these buildings, even the attractive ones, are underutilized and stimulate little in the way of new economic growth for the city. Witness Lincoln Center in New York, the Getty Center in Los Angeles, and the Kimmel Center in Philadelphia. Rybczynski's important message is that successful city space only arises where there is a demand for that space. That means, first, being a competitive skilled city in the new service economy.

The path to being a skilled city is not an easy one, however, particularly for our once-dominant manufacturing centers such as New York, Chicago, Philadelphia, Boston, Pittsburgh, Buffalo, Detroit, Cleveland, Saint Louis, Milwaukee, and Birmingham. These cities must shed their old manufacturing exterior and develop a new service sector core. New York, Boston, Philadelphia, and Pittsburgh have succeeded. Buffalo, Detroit, and Saint Louis have failed. Cleveland, Milwaukee, and Birmingham may make it yet. In chapter 5, Joseph Gyourko's analysis of city housing helps us to understand an important structural barrier to a city's economic transformation. As the middle class exited these cities during the manufacturing downturn of the 1950s and 1960s, it left behind an attractive and still-productive housing stock. Because the middle-class demand was low, though this housing sold for less than its replacement cost. But it could still be rented to lower-income families, serving as a magnet for poor families to stay in or move into these older cities. As a consequence, the average share of our largest cities' population now living in poverty has grown significantly over the past four decades, from 12 percent in 1970 to 16 percent today (see figure 1.3). Our once-smaller cities with less older housing have experienced less of an increase in city poverty. Perhaps because of this draw of older housing, U.S. poverty is now largely urban poverty and particularly large-city poverty; compare the levels of the national and city poverty rates in figure 1.3. Poor families have low skills and place high demands on the city's middle-class tax base, both slowing or even killing the emergence of a new and more productive idea-based economy in these cities.

The United States has always attracted immigrants, and today is no different, both in terms of the number of immigrants and their decisions to locate in our largest cities (see figure 1.4).[18] In chapter 6, David Card helps us to assess the likely impact of new immigrants on city economies. High-skilled immigrants will surely aid their new cities' economies. Will low-skilled immigrants be a significant burden? While the average immigrant has lower than average human capital skills, the effect on average city wages is actually slightly positive. While high-skilled workers determine the long-run growth potential of cities—and thus high-skilled immigrants are important—low-skilled immigrants

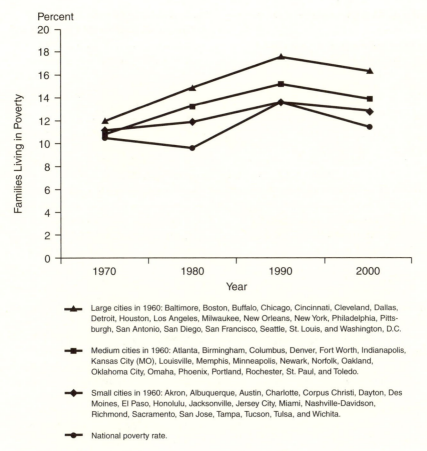

Fig. 1.3 City Poverty Rates

are valued productive inputs too. More low-skilled workers relieve high-skilled workers from routine tasks (e.g., washing test tubes), thus raising the productivity of high-skilled workers. More productive high-skilled workers lead to an expanding city economy and increasing demand for all city workers. As low-skilled immigrants are absorbed into this larger economy, native low-skilled workers are largely unaffected and do not exit the city. In fact, Card shows that average city wages rise. There is pressure on city housing costs from increased immigration, but it is modest and offset by rising average wages. City rent-to-income ratios are unaffected by immigration. Immigration's fiscal consequences for cities may be more significant, however, and especially so through immigrants' impact on the costs and quality of public education because of the learning needs of first-generation immigrant children. Just

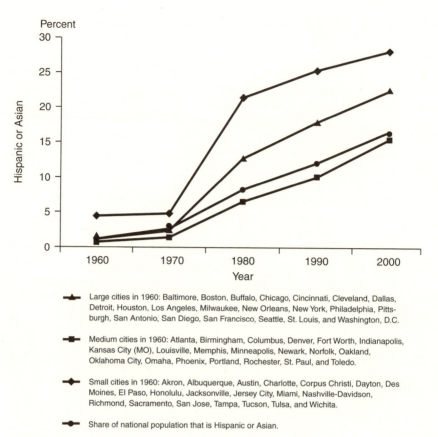

Fig. 1.4 Share of City Population That Is Hispanic or Asian

as middle-income families exit city public schools and perhaps the city itself when neighborhood poverty rates get too high, so too do they leave when the share of new Hispanic residents grows. Card estimates the "tipping point" to lie between 5 and 15 percent of a neighborhood's population. If there is a crucial adverse effect of the new immigration on city economies, Card concludes, it will most likely be in these unsettling effects on city neighborhoods and possibly the decisions of middle-income families to live within the city.

In chapter 7, Jacob Vigdor summarizes what we know about city neighborhoods and their impacts on the economic as well as life prospects of city residents. Untangling neighborhood effects from those of an individual's own unmeasured attributes and talents, however, is difficult. Vigdor steers us through these brambles, and four conclusions emerge. First, while racial segregation has declined substantially in the

forty years since the start of the civil rights movement, black-white economic inequality has not. There is no simple and enduring causal link
from spatial segregation to black-white economic inequality. Second,
neighborhood segregation has continued, though now not from legal
barriers but rather from an apparent misalignment of black and white
preferences for the racial mix of neighborhoods. When surveyed, whites
say they prefer neighborhoods with at least a few black families, but
their ideal neighborhood is never more than 20 percent African American. From the same surveys, a typical African American family says it
prefers neighborhoods that are 25 to 50 percent black. Thus, if a neighborhood were to become slightly more than 20 percent black, it could
easily "tip" into a predominantly black neighborhood; residential segregation can occur even without legally prohibited discrimination.
Third, some city families may have no choice as to where to live. The
decline of overt segregation allowed middle-class African American
families the chance to leave historically black neighborhoods for better
housing and better public services elsewhere in the city or the wider
metropolitan area. As a result, many black neighborhoods have suffered profound population loss and falling home values. The remaining
residents in these declining neighborhoods have become isolated, both
socially and economically. Fourth and surprisingly perhaps, the best
current evidence suggests that living in such a poor neighborhood does
not by itself greatly damage an individual's life prospects. Being poor
and having access to poor public services do significantly impact one's
economic future, but living next to other poor neighbors does not. It is
family and city resources that matter most. Chapters 8 through 11 make
this clear.

The consequences of family poverty are profound. From Janet Currie
in chapter 8, we learn that poor individuals have significantly worse
physical and mental health, poorer schooling outcomes, higher rates of
early teen parenthood, and greater rates of risk-taking behaviors, including increased criminal activity. These adverse results of poverty fall
not just on the poor. There are critical spillovers from city poverty to
high-skilled city residents in the form of higher rates of urban crime,
higher rates of city taxation, and less effective public schools.

In chapter 9, Richard Murnane clarifies the causes of poor performance by inner-city schools, and here too poverty concentration matters.
Children from lower-income families have unique educational needs
demanding increases in school resources. Immigrant children for whom
English is a second language compound these demands. Given the
challenges of such classroom environments, it is not hard to see that
attracting and retaining qualified teachers will be difficult for city
schools. All this leads to the exit of middle-class children to the suburbs

or private schools, thereby denying lower-income children a valuable classroom (and political) ally. An inadequate supply of skilled (or train-able) labor for city firms is one important consequence of failing city schools.

In chapter 10, Philip Cook's exploration of urban crime stresses the connection of poor schools and low earnings prospects for dropouts and even graduates to teenage crime. Peer pressure to engage in crimi-nal behaviors and the availability of illegal guns, both found in poverty neighborhoods, also contribute. The consequences for firms and middle-income residents are significant expected property losses and, perhaps more important, a rising threat to personal safety.

In chapter 11, I outline what is needed for city government to effec-tively combat city crime as well as provide quality schooling and other city services to residents and firms. Figures 1.5–1.7 show the large in-crease in city-financed spending for services most closely associated with increased city poverty: welfare, protection (police and fire), and public education. The implication is a significant rise in the tax rate for middle-class families, measured by the share of these expenditures in cities' median family income (see figure 1.8). Unless these tax dollars are managed to deliver equal or greater benefits for each dollar paid, firms and the middle-class families will leave for the suburbs or other cities, re-sulting in lost agglomeration economies and market productivity.

Cities are the centers of production and innovation in the modern U.S. economy, and for many, a center of consumption too. Yet U.S. cities face sizable obstacles because of roadway congestion, urban poverty, and low-skill immigration to maximizing their full economic potential. Federal and state governments are not likely to contribute new money toward removing these barriers to city growth. The place-based strate-gies of the past three decades have proven ineffective. Cities are on their own, and new approaches to city growth and prosperity are needed.

The authors understand these new realities. When making policy rec-ommendations, they focus on helping city residents and firms to be as productive as possible, and on ensuring city government is efficient and responsive. In contrast to past policies, the strategies proposed here are *people-* not place-*based* ones. Most can be implemented by cities alone, but none are free. Thus city government efficiency is essential. Only those policies that return more benefits than costs to city residents and firms should be adopted.

By this criterion, federal and state governments will be the most efficient providers of direct income transfers to poor city residents to meet national or state income standards, though city taxpayers should certainly be allowed additional payments to their poor residents if they wish. When recommending regional, state, or federal assistance for a

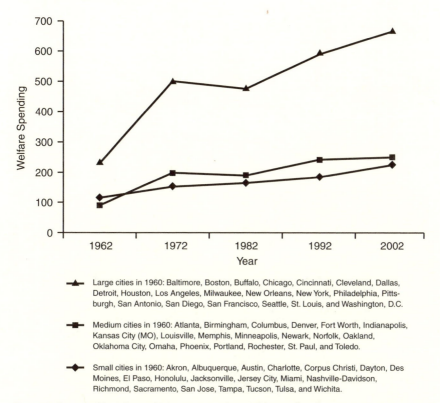

Fig. 1.5 City Welfare Spending per Resident (2006 Dollars)

city policy, there must be a clear and compensating benefit for the residents of the assisting government. Any call for outside aid must be accompanied by a demonstrable "win-win" policy emerging from clear regional, state, or national external benefits from improved city economic performance. Further, state and national urban policies should be coordinated, and since each city's economy and demographics differ, the political temptation to treat all cities equally, perhaps even adding in all suburbs, must be resisted. With any policy, the place to start and finish the policy debate is by answering this question: *Are all citizens—city, state, and national taxpayers included—better off with the policy than without?*

To lower the barrier caused by roadway congestion, Small recommends as an ideal a more efficient use of existing infrastructure through the expanded use of metropolitan-wide roadway tolls and access pricing for our denser downtown business districts, such as Manhattan, San Francisco, or Washington, DC. Pricing highways will do more to help

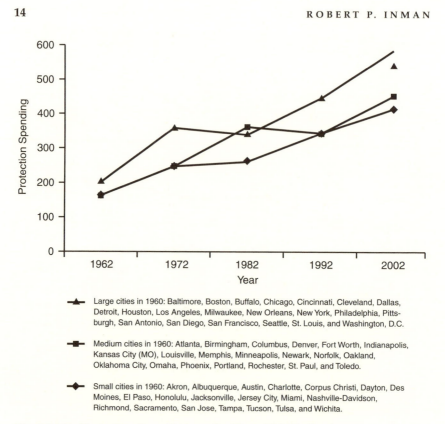

Large cities in 1960: Baltimore, Boston, Buffalo, Chicago, Cincinnati, Cleveland, Dallas, Detroit, Houston, Los Angeles, Milwaukee, New Orleans, New York, Philadelphia, Pittsburgh, San Antonio, San Diego, San Francisco, Seattle, St. Louis, and Washington, D.C.

Medium cities in 1960: Atlanta, Birmingham, Columbus, Denver, Fort Worth, Indianapolis, Kansas City (MO), Louisville, Memphis, Minneapolis, Newark, Norfolk, Oakland, Oklahoma City, Omaha, Phoenix, Portland, Rochester, St. Paul, and Toledo.

Small cities in 1960: Akron, Albuquerque, Austin, Charlotte, Corpus Christi, Dayton, Des Moines, El Paso, Honolulu, Jacksonville, Jersey City, Miami, Nashville-Davidson, Richmond, Sacramento, San Jose, Tampa, Tucson, Tulsa, and Wichita.

Fig. 1.6 City Protection Spending per Resident (2006 Dollars)

public transit than any infusion of new public money. To move toward the pricing ideal, Small proposes the franchising of existing access highways to private firms and the expanded use of niche, small bus services best competing by price and service quality. Rapid transit investments should focus on the expansion of high-speed bus not rail services, and new highway construction should be designed to ensure the efficient flow of passenger vehicles with perhaps isolated lanes for trucks. The objective is to move people to their destinations and back as efficiently as possible.

To lower the barriers arising from urban poverty and the high concentration of low-skilled immigrants, Currie and Murnane recommend a focus on the education and training for children and young adults beginning with prenatal health care, followed by nurse home visits to teach parenting skills to parents of children at risk, then high-quality preschool programs (e.g., Head Start), school-based breakfast and lunch programs stressing good nutrition, districtwide elementary school cur-

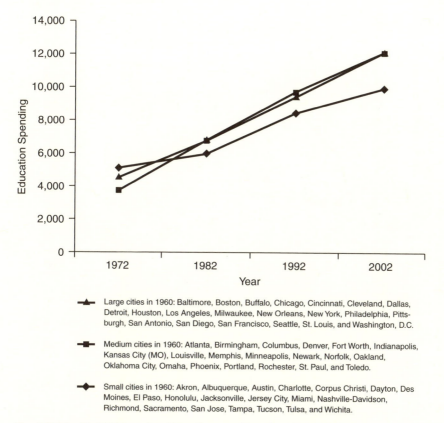

Fig. 1.7 City K–12 Education Spending per Resident (2006 Dollars)

ricula that emphasize mastery of basic reading and math skills and oral communication, volunteer programs providing adult mentors (Big Brothers/Big Sisters), secondary school curricula that prepare students for work with remedial training in basic skills if necessary, and finally, collaborative programs with business and local colleges to ready students for the challenges of full-time employment or higher education. These are all people-based programs. Separately, each has a proven track record of success. There is reason to think that there are program complementarities as well, particularly if grouped by preschool, elementary, and high school ages. Currie's and Murnane's chapters provide the evidence and examples of successful policy innovations. To the extent that the benefits of these programs reach more widely than the children, their families, and other city residents, then regional, state, or federal funding will be needed. It is the task of city

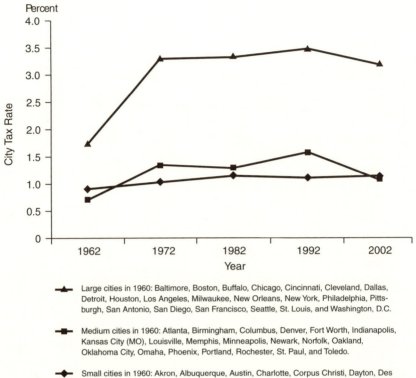

Fig. 1.8 City "Tax Rates" for Associated Poverty Spending (Percent of City Median Family Income)

officials, using the Currie and Murnane evidence, to make the case, however, and then leverage these outside funds with private city resident contributions of money and time.

To lower the rate of urban crime, Cook also suggests human capital policies, but he recognizes that some young adults will still find illegal activities attractive. What can cities do to deter youth crime? First, remove the means and temptation to commit crimes by removing from the street one of theft's high-value items: illegal guns. Locally enforced gun control lowers burglaries and murders. If illegal guns remain, then aggressively penalize their use. Both Boston and Chicago have adopted with success threatened crackdowns on drug gangs if there is any evidence of gang gun violence. Second, deter crime by raising the likelihood the crook will be caught and prosecuted. Police officers are a demonstrated deterrent to property crime, and new strategies such as "hot spot" policing add to their effectiveness. The Lojack technology is a proven deterrent to car thefts with significant positive benefits for all city residents; those spillovers might justify a city subsidy for adoption by city residents. One of the biggest limitations to controlling violent crimes is the reluctance of witnesses or surviving victims to testify against known assailants. Here Cook recommends more aggressive use of witness compensation and protection. Finally, incarceration has proven effective by removing habitual criminals from streets and neighborhoods. Jails are an expensive strategy, however, and their capacity needs to be used more efficiently. Cook proposes that the really bad guys should be kept in jail, but convicted criminals who have demonstrated an ability to function peacefully in society should be paroled and assisted with reentry. As with Currie's and Murnane's agendas for city human capital policies, each of Cook's crime prevention strategies has a proven record of success. But again, these strategies should be pursued only if city taxpayer benefits exceed taxpayer costs.

After lowering the barriers to growth, get out of the way. While recognizing city governments do provide important city services, Glaeser, Rybczynski, and Gyourko each stress the need for minimal government intrusion into the workings of the city economy. They detail examples where city policies have slowed city growth. Glaeser notes the adverse consequences for city growth of unfunded state government mandates to provide redistributive services to poor city residents. Such mandates shift the financing of redistribution from a broad-based tax to a local tax whose rate rises with the share of city residents who are poor. Local taxes are an inefficient way to finance national or state redistribution standards, particularly so given the importance of agglomeration economies in the new skilled city. Rybczynski underscores the inability of master planning to offer the best environment for city economic revitalization and growth. The new urban environment is best defined by market demand, not planners' preferences. Government should be responsive to the needs of developers and entrepreneurs by facilitating their compliance with safe building regulations as well as providing for complementary public spaces and amenities. Yet Gyourko cautions that city regulatory policies can be captured and abused. In cities with strong growth potential and hence high demand for city land, current residents can use building code and land-use regulations to restrict the supply of new construction. These supply restrictions raise the property values of current city residents, but they also choke off efficient city growth that benefits renters, less skilled workers in the building trades and services, and of course potential new entrants. The job of a mayor is to recognize these regulatory inefficiencies, fashion a pro-growth coalition, and then allocate the benefits of more efficient regulations among all city residents through city fiscal policies.

Finally, efficient fiscal policies may be how mayors can best help their cities reach full economic potential. Spending money to retain talented teachers and school administrators, hire additional police officers, provide neighborhood bus connections and express commuter bus services, and clear abandoned autos and properties while creating attractive neighborhood public spaces have each been recommended here as a potential high return use for public monies. Reducing the overall size of the public employee workforce through attrition as city populations decline, closing underutilized neighborhood fire stations, libraries, and recreation centers, and expanding the use of user fees are all nontax sources of new money that can help fund these new programs. Reforming, not raising, city taxes should be the city's primary revenue objective. Residential taxes should only pay for resident services, and business taxes should only pay for business services. Cross-subsidies from firms to residents deter city growth and, because of lost efficiency from reduced agglomeration economies, may even have a net negative impact on residential property values. The best tax on businesses is a land tax. To implement these reforms, however, a mayor must have sufficient institutional powers to say no to special interests. A mayor must have the ability to hire, reassign, and fire public employees as necessary. Second, a mayor must be able to set and protect an efficient budget—one where city taxpayer benefits exceed taxpayer costs—through agenda setting and sustainable veto powers. And a mayor needs the authority to competitively hire private firms to provide city-financed services when appropriate and feasible. Crime protection, transit services, infrastructure maintenance, housing and public space provision, and (perhaps more controversial) public education have each been suggested by the authors here as candidates for privatization. My chapter on city finances makes the general case for these reforms.

If there has been a single useful lesson from the past forty years of urban policies it is that federal and state officials are not the ones to be making decisions as to what is best for U.S. cities. National and state politics typically favor suburban economic interests, often to the detriment of productive cities. Facing significant fiscal burdens from concentrated urban poverty and hoping perhaps to join in suburban transfers, elected city officials had naturally turned much of their policy attention toward Washington and their state capitals. In this policy environment, local political success was determined more by how much outside money you attracted and not how well you spent the money you had.

Federal and state policies do have a role to play in helping our cities reach their full economic potential, but those policies should be targeted "contracts," not general handouts. As cooperative agreements, the chosen policy must benefit both city residents and residents of the funding government; urban policy must be a win-win situation. This is possible only when the city's economy provides a significant external benefit to the wider society. Two possibilities come to mind. First, as the primary provider of education and child care services, city government will typically be, because of economies of scale, the most efficient provider of any supplemental services required for poverty or first-generation immigrant children. *If* the city's state or national residents value these supplemental services, and *if* a city's government is the efficient provider, then a fully funded contract—not an unfunded mandate—with that larger government is appropriate. Second, as a key location for agglomeration economies often requiring personal interactions, cities need an efficient transit system to move workers into and around the city. Such a system may need large-scale infrastructure investments not easily supported by the private capital market. *If* public capital is needed, and *if* the benefits extend to firms and residents outside the city, then city investment aid may be warranted. Since the benefits of such assistance are likely to be regional, state or regional governments should fund the investment aid. In both instances, though, the city government qualifies for outside funding only if it is the efficient provider of the spillover benefits.

The appropriate new role of federal and state policies will therefore be a limited one. By necessity, then, successful cities today must be self-aware: What makes our city economy work, and how can we best use our own resources to promote the long-run economic fortunes of our residents and firms? Helping city officials to unravel this urban enigma and from this understanding to connect their city's prospects to effective city policies is the agenda of this book.

Notes

1. U.S. Census Bureau, *Statistical Abstract of the United States, 1974* (Washington, DC: U.S. Department of Commerce, 1974), table 23; U.S. Census Bureau, *Statistical Abstract of the United States, 2007* (Washington, DC: U.S. Department of Commerce, 2007), table 32.

2. United Nations, *World Urban Population, 1950–2000, with Projections to 2020* (New York: Department of Economic and Social Affairs, 2006).

3. See Sinai and Waldfogel (2004).

4. On the importance of urban density to firm productivity, see Beardsell and Henderson (1999). On the spatial decline of these productivity gains, see Strange and Rosenthal (2003).

5. See Black et al. (2002).

6. See Glaeser, Kolko, and Saiz (2001).

7. See Carlino, Chatterjee, and Hunt (2007).

8. Peter Hall (1998) provides an encyclopedic overview of cities as historic centers of cultural and artistic innovation.

9. Each chapter was written by the leading scholar of urban affairs at the time: John Kain on jobs, John Meyer on transportation, Dick Netzer on finances, Charles Tilley on race, Marvin Wolfgang on crime, Ted Sizer on education, Bernard Frieden on housing, Edward Banfield on urban riots, John Burchard on design, and Daniel Patrick Moynihan on poverty. The book received excellent reviews from leading journals in economics (*Journal of Finance*, December 1969), sociology (*American Sociological Review*, December 1969), and public administration (*Public Administration Review*, March–April 1970).

10. Some of the large cities in Maryland, Massachusetts, New Jersey, New York, Rhode Island, and Virginia also provide K–12 education, and thus receive state education aid. This aid is excluded from the analysis here.

11. There is no better analysis of how a program initially targeted for large cities is transformed by legislative politics into "money for everyone" than the study by Samuel Beer (1976) of the passage of General Revenue Sharing bill in 1972. More generally, see Inman (1989).

12. See Small (1985); Winston and Shirley (1998).

13. See Mollenkopf (1983); Judd and Swanson (1998).

14. For a careful review of CETA funding, see Barnow (1987). For a review of the incidence of city spending generally during this period, see Inman and Rubinfeld (1979).

15. See Mueller and Schwartz (1998); Mollenkopf (1983, 280).

16. See Mueller and Schwartz (1998).

17. For the argument, see Inman (1979). For the evidence, see Papke (1994); Boarnet and Bogart (1996); Bondonio and Engberg (2000); O'Keefe (2004).

18. Reported as the stock of Hispanic and Asian residents in our largest cities as a consequence of current and previous period immigration flows.

References

Barnow, Burt S. 1987. The Impact of CETA Programs on Earnings: A Review of the Literature. *Journal of Human Resources* 22 (Spring): 157–93.

Beardsell, Mark, and Vernon Henderson. 1999. Spatial Evolution of the Computer Industry in the USA. *European Economic Review* 43 (February): 431–56.

Beer, Samuel H. 1976. The Adoption of General Revenue Sharing: A Case Study in Public Sector Politics. *Public Policy* 24 (Spring): 127–96.

Black, Dan, Gary Gates, Seth Sanders, and Lowell Taylor. 2002. Why Do Gay Men Live in San Francisco? *Journal of Urban Economics* 51 (January): 54–76.

Boarnet, Marion, and William T. Bogart. 1996. Enterprise Zones and Employment: Evidence from New Jersey. *Journal of Urban Economics* 40 (September): 198–215.

Bondonio, Daniele, and John Engberg. 2000. Enterprise Zones and Local Employment: Evidence from the States' Programs. *Regional Science and Urban Economics* 30 (September): 519–49.

Carlino, Gerald, Satyajit Chatterjee, and Robert Hunt. 2007. Urban Density and Rate of Invention. *Journal of Urban Economics* 61 (May): 389–419.

Glaeser, Edward L., Jed Kolko, and Albert Saiz. 2001. Consumer City. *Journal of Economic Geography* 1 (January): 27–50.

Hall, Peter. 1998. *Cities in Civilization*. New York: Pantheon Books.

Inman, Robert P. 1979. Federal Policy and the Urban Poor. *Journal of Regional Science* 19 (February): 119–29.

———. 1989. Federal Assistance and Local Services in the United States: The Evolution of a New Federalist Fiscal Order. In *Fiscal Federalism: Quantitative Studies*, ed. Harvey S. Rosen, 33–77. Chicago: University of Chicago Press.

Inman, Robert P., and Daniel L. Rubinfeld. 1979. The Judicial Pursuit of Local Fiscal Equity. *Harvard Law Review* 92 (June): 1662–1750.

Judd, Dennis J., and Todd Swanstrom. 1998. *City Politics: Private Power and Public Policy*. 2nd ed. New York: Longman.

Mollenkopf, John Hull. 1983. *The Contested City*. Princeton, NJ: Princeton University Press.

Mueller, Elizabeth J., and Alex Schwartz. 1998. Why Local Economic Development and Employment Training Fail for Low-Income Communities. In *Jobs and Economic Development: Strategies and Practice*, ed. Robert P. Giloth, 42–64. Thousand Oaks, CA: Sage.

O'Keefe, Suzanne. 2004. Job Creation in California's Enterprise Zones: A Comparison Using a Propensity Score Matching Model. *Journal of Urban Economics* 55 (January): 131–50.

Papke, Leslie E. 1994. Tax Policy and Urban Development: Evidence from the Indiana Enterprise Zone Program. *Journal of Public Economics* 54 (May): 37–49.

Sinai, Todd M., and Joel Waldfogel. 2004. Geography and the Internet: Is the Internet a Substitute or a Complement for Cities? *Journal of Urban Economics* 56 (July): 1–24.

Small, Kenneth A. 1985. Transportation and Urban Change. In *The New Urban Reality*, ed. Peter E. Peterson, 197–225. Washington, DC: Brookings Institution.

Strange, William C., and Stuart S. Rosenthal. 2003. Geography, Industrial Organization, and Agglomeration. *Review of Economics and Statistics* 85 (May): 377–93.

Winston, Clifford, and Chad Shirley. 1998. *Alternative Route: Toward Efficient Urban Transportation*. Washington, DC: Brookings Institution.

2

Growth

THE DEATH AND LIFE OF CITIES

EDWARD L. GLAESER

AMERICA'S CITIES are remarkably dynamic. Some cities, both today and in the past, expand dramatically in a short period of time. Chicago's population expanded by 270 percent in the 1850s, and Las Vegas grew by 85 percent in the 1990s. Urban decline is slower, but population losses can also be striking. Saint Louis lost 12 percent of its population in the 1990s, and 59 percent of its population between 1950 and 2000. In this chapter, I will discuss the major factors that cause urban growth and decline, both historically and today.

First, in "The Demand for and Supply of City Space," I review the economic theory that allows us to make sense of urban growth and decline. The economic approach to urban growth starts with the view that urban change is driven by the choices of individuals who choose either to live in a place or not. Individual choices are driven by location-specific factors like income, amenities, and housing supply. Places become more attractive when the income and amenities rise, and when the costs of supplying housing services decline.

But income, amenities, and housing prices reflect the function of labor demand, the housing market, and government policy. High incomes reflect a greater willingness to pay for workers to be in a given locale, which must itself reflect higher productivity in that place. High local productivity reflects proximity to natural resources, especially waterways, and agglomeration economies, where productivity rises with the size or composition of a city. One example of such agglomeration economies are idea spillovers, where people are better at inventing new ideas if they are surrounded by a stock of smart people.

Housing prices reflect the combination of housing supply and demand. If housing is abundant, as in the case of Saint Louis and other declining cities, then prices are cheap. If the housing supply is restricted, as it is today in coastal California and an increasing array of other cities, then prices will be high. At any given point in time, the population of a city seems almost proportionate to the stock of housing in a city, and this means that a fixed housing supply will tend to mean a relatively fixed population. Indeed, the slow and steady population losses in places like Saint Louis can be attributed to the durable nature of the housing stock in that city (Glaeser and Gyourko 2005).

Some amenities are natural, like California's temperate climate, while others are constructed, like good schools and low crime. In some cases, growth itself can erode amenities by slowing commutes and crowding public services. Since there is every reason to believe that amenities are normal goods, meaning that people are willing to pay for more of them as incomes increase, we should expect to see amenities becoming an increasingly powerful force in city growth as Americans become richer (Graves 1980).

Urban productivity and amenities are particularly sensitive to changes in transportation technology. Since cities ultimately exist to provide proximity either to other people or fixed attributes of cities, we should expect changes in transport technology to have a strong impact on the demand for that proximity. Historically, cities grew because people wanted access to the great transport cost advantages created by access to waterways. In the twentieth century, the car remade urban America. We generally think that falls in transportation and communication costs tend to reduce the demand for urban proximity, but as I discuss in "The Rise of the Skilled City," there is some reason to believe that declining transportation and communication costs can also increase the demand for closeness by raising the returns to producing new ideas.

After providing an overview of urban theory, I turn to "America's Urban Origins," briefly surveying the growth of cities in the nineteenth century. In almost every case, the exact location of the urban area was determined by waterways, some of which were natural and others of which were humanly produced. Industry clustered around ports and rail yards to reduce shipping costs and exploit scale economies. Even in the nineteenth century, however, the concentration that formed for mundane reasons, like saving costs in butchering and shipping hogs, then came to facilitate the flow of new ideas and abet innovation.

In "Declining Transport Costs," I turn to the great trends in urban change between 1900 and 1975, where many of the older cities of the Northeast and Midwest began to decline even as the newer cities of the Sun Belt grew enormously. Urban growth during this epoch is best seen as reflecting changes in transportation technology. The general decline in the costs of moving goods eroded the erstwhile advantages of midwestern cities built around transport hubs, and allowed people to move to new areas with better climates, like California. The rise of the automobile led people and firms to move from city centers to suburbs. People also moved from cities that were built around walking and public transportation to newer areas, like Los Angeles, that could be built around the car.

"The Rise of the Skilled City" and "The Rise of the Consumer City" review the three most important urban growth phenomena over the past thirty years. Following this, "The Consumer City and the Skilled City" focuses on the increasing connection between skills and urban success. High levels of human capital, measured by the share of the population with college degrees in 1970, strongly predict income, population, and housing price growth since that time period. The connection with income is particularly strong, which tells us that the skills-growth connection is working primarily through an increasing link between urban productivity and proximity to skilled people. The relationship between skills and population growth is especially important in explaining the success of older cities in the Northeast and Midwest.

While the connection between skills and city growth is quite clear, its root cause is less obvious. One hypothesis is that the same reductions in transport and communications technology that led manufacturing to leave Detroit also increased the returns to innovation. If skilled cities have a comparative advantage in producing new ideas, then we would expect an increasing ability to export new ideas worldwide to increase the demand to live and work in skilled metropolitan areas. The rise of the skilled city suggests that local policymakers looking to improve their city's fortunes should make sure that their policies are oriented toward retaining and attracting the people at the top of the skill distribution.

In "The Rise of the Consumer City," I discuss the rise of cities that specialize in delivering high levels of consumer amenities. To a certain extent, this trend simply reflects a continuation of the growth of Californian cities described in "Declining Transportation Costs." The continuing decline in transport costs means that people have become freer to locate in places where they want to live instead of places where firms have a transport-cost related advantage in production. Nevertheless, there are also some dramatic changes between the first three decades of the twentieth century and the last thirty years.

Most notable of those changes has been the ability of some older urban areas to become more attractive places to live. Reductions in crime have meant that places like downtown areas in New York and Chicago have become nicer places to live. Big cities have an innate comparative advantage in providing amenities with high fixed costs like art museums and symphonies. The large scale of the urban market also improves the choices involved in consumption activities such as eating out and dating. While it would have been quite surprising in 1975 to find people who wanted to live downtown and work in the suburbs, that location pattern has become increasingly common.

The conclusion emphasizes the primary policy point of this chapter. People and firms are astonishingly mobile, and this severely limits the policy choices available to local governments. Attempts at redistribution can be counterproductive because high-income people just flee. The reality of constant urban change should be omnipresent in the thinking of local leaders who are making policy decisions for their communities.

The Demand for and Supply of City Space

The economic approach to city growth begins with the choices made by individuals about whether or not to live in a particular place. These choices are thought to be driven by the economic returns to living in a particular place (i.e., local wages), the noneconomic returns to living in a particular locale (generally called amenities), and the financial costs of living somewhere (i.e., housing prices). Rising population is usually attributed to increases in income or amenities, or decreases in housing costs.

The particular workhorse of the urban growth literature is the spatial equilibrium assumption, which plays the same central role in urban economics that the no-arbitrage equilibrium assumption plays in financial economics. This assumption essentially implies that people receive the same level of welfare in all of the different cities across the United States. It is not meant to be taken literally but rather is a convenient approximation that serves as a useful guide for empirical work. The spatial equilibrium assumption can create somewhat counterintuitive predictions, like the implication that if a place has a high real wage (i.e., income divided by the cost of living), then it must have low amenities. If high real incomes were not offset by low amenities, as the economic reasoning goes, then people would flock to the high real wage area and bid up housing prices.

The idea that urban growth reflects individual choices, which are themselves based on wages, housing costs, and amenities, does not provide us with a deep explanation of why cities succeed, since at least wages and housing costs are market outcomes, not innate characteristics of a place. Wages reflect the intersection of labor supply and demand in a given area, and if we are to understand why wages are high in some places and low in others, then we must understand why there are differences in labor demand across space. Why are firms willing to pay more for workers in New York than they are in Houston?

Differences in wage levels across space are thought to reflect differences in productivity. Indeed, in most neoclassic models of labor markets, wages are a direct reflection of labor productivity. Therefore, to understand the growth of a city that is driven by rising incomes, we must understand why productivity is increasing in that city. To understand why wages are higher in big cities than in less dense areas, we must understand why firms are more productive in big cities.

The urban economics literature argues that firms are more productive in cities because of the value of physical proximity either to other people and firms in that city, or productive features of that place. Historically, access to the port of New York increased the productivity of manufacturing firms locating in Manhattan. Today, Wall Street firms are more productive because of access to each other and the business service firms that cater to them. Another way of thinking about this is that urban proximity is valuable because it reduces transport costs for goods, people, and ideas.

The theoretical literature on urban productivity often starts with transport costs for goods—it is cheaper to buy inputs if they are being produced nearby. This creates a natural tendency for producers to cluster near one another to avoid the costs of shipping over long distances. The advantages of proximate production create an agglomeration economy, where each new firm raises the productivity of the existing firm and increases the incentives for yet another firm to come to the city. A virtuous circle can develop where an initial cluster of firms attracts more firms that want to buy or sell to these first firms, and then the new firms attract even more employment.

While reducing the transport costs for goods was once a critical element of urban success, over the twentieth century the price of moving goods declined enormously. The cost of moving people over short distances did not see the same decline, because lost time is the main component of the costs of moving people. Cities today serve to reduce the costs of connecting people, especially in the business service sector. Since many of these services involve face-to-face contact, the urban edge in eliminating distance still matters. The basic logic of the agglomeration of business services in San Francisco and Chicago follows the same logic behind the agglomeration of traditional goods producers. Firms that use business services locate in the city to have access to service providers, and the firms that provide services locate in the city to have access to their customers. The gains from eliminating transport costs continue to drive urban productivity, but now the relevant transport costs involve getting a lawyer to their client instead of getting a sewing machine to a garment factory.

The benefits that firms get from reducing the transport costs of their suppliers and customers can often be seen directly in the bottom line, but cities also increase access to new ideas, and these benefits are harder to quantify. New ideas always build on old ideas, and creativity almost never comes from a person working in splendid isolation. Instead, the process of generating knowledge generally involves constantly learning from others. By bringing people together, cities have historically fostered the production of new ideas. Silicon Valley today may be the famous example of a geographic locale where idea producers cluster together and consistently learn from one another (Saxenian 1994). This phenomenon is not new. The invention of Renaissance art in fifteenth-century Florence and skyscrapers in nineteenth-century Chicago were collaborative efforts, where individual innovators learned from their physically proximate competitors and created a chain of innovation.

The idea-producing function of cities used to be an interesting side product of people living close to one another to eliminate transport costs for goods. Today, idea production is increasingly the primary function of the most successful U.S. cities. The density of downtown New York originally served so that manufacturers could have ready access to each other and the harbor. Now that density serves to facilitate the flow of knowledge in the financial services industry—a sector where there are tremendous returns for having the best information.

It is possible, of course, that eventually improvements in information technology will make even this function of cities obsolete. But over the past thirty years, the decrease in transportation and communication costs has probably helped the idea-producing cities rather than hurt them. As the world has become flatter, the ability to export new ideas has grown and the returns to innovation have increased as well. As the returns to innovation increase, the returns to locating in urban places that specialize in innovation also increase. As the world has become flatter, the returns to becoming the smartest person in the world increase, and you can only become the smartest person by being close to other smart people. Improvements in transport and communication can therefore both increase and decrease the returns to locating in a dense area.

The demand for living in a city reflects both the economic returns from locating in that city as well as the nonmarket costs and benefits of that place. These nonmarket or quality-of-life attributes that help form demand for a particular place include weather, safety, schools, and traffic congestion. Weather is the most immutable urban amenity, but the demand for different types of weather can often change significantly. Air-conditioning, for example, made southern summers far more bearable. Higher incomes may have increased people's willingness to further economic returns in pursuit of a pleasant climate.

Most other amenities are formed by the interplay of government, private individuals, and density itself. For instance, historically disease was a great urban disamenity. Clustering people together may have made it easier to get goods from suppliers to customers, but it also made it easier for bacteria to spread across populations. The life expectancy in premodern London was substantially lower than in rural England due to the easy spread of infectious diseases in dense areas (Wrigley and Schofield 1983). Density also meant that water supplies were frequently polluted with human waste. Over the course of the nineteenth century, U.S. civic leaders gradually reduced the health costs of living in big cities by delivering clean water. This was a massive undertaking, requiring vast public expenditures (Cutler and Miller 2006).

If disease was the great scourge of premodern cities, crime has been a more common modern problem. Again, the connection between crime and cities is a natural product of density. If we are close enough for me to sell to you, then we are close enough for me to rob you. The urban tendency to attract poor people also contributes to the crime-cities connection, so poverty and crime are correlated (Glaeser and Sacerdote 1999). Again, the level of disamenity reflects the combination of government policy and private action. Since 1980, robust public policy responses have mitigated the extent of the urban crime problem.

Offsetting the urban disamenities of disease and crime are the urban amenities that are made possible by the large numbers in a city. Market size makes it possible to pay fixed costs for museums, theaters, and restaurants. New York City supports a remarkable number of entertainment venues, including art and natural history museums, theaters, and operas, that would be utterly infeasible in a smaller place. Many of these entertainment venues are luxury goods, in the sense that they cater to the rich, but as the nation as a whole gets richer, we would expect the demand for these particularly urban entertainments to increase.

A related urban advantage comes from the fact that large markets facilitate specialization. As Adam Smith wrote (1776, 24), "The division of labor is limited by the extent of the market." This effect is important in making cities more productive; in a big city, business service providers, like lawyers, are better able to reap the benefits of specialization. But urban specialization is also crucial on the consumption side. The diversity of urban restaurants is a classic example of Smith's dictum. Any large city will have a wide range of potential eating options; a small town will not. The ability of a large market to sustain diversity is true throughout the retail and consumer service sector, and this provides another attraction to places like New York.

Density is also valuable in cases where people want access to each other for social reasons. Cities have always been particularly attractive to young, single people because density means that there are other young, single people nearby. Cities essentially serve as marriage markets. A related fact is that two-earner families may find it easier for both adults to get good jobs in a big city than in a less dense area (Costa and Kahn 2003).

A final quality-of-life issue is commute modes and traffic. Today, more than 115 million Americans drive to work, and less than 10 million take public transportation or walk. For the drivers, the key issue is traffic congestion, which has risen dramatically in many metropolitan areas. One response to traffic in the urban core has been the decentralization of employment, which has tended to mean that people commute long distances from a suburban home to a suburban job, but that these commutes occur at high speeds. Another response to traffic is to use public transportation. Public transportation is a large transit mode in only a handful of the largest cities, like New York, but it plays a disproportionately large role in bringing poorer Americans to work. Indeed, one reason why poor people live disproportionately in central cities is that in those places, they can survive without a car for each adult (Glaeser, Kahn, and Rappaport 2007).

If demand for cities is fueled by economic productivity and amenities, the supply of city space is a reflection of housing availability. Figure 2.1 shows the almost perfect relationship between growth in population and growth in housing units across U.S. cities between 1980 and 2000. If homes are not being built, then the city will find it quite hard to grow. The housing supply itself is the product of both natural factors and government action, and when the supply is limited, for whatever reason, then urban growth will also be limited.

Most obviously, the housing supply reflects the availability of land. Cities in the middle of a flat plain will find it easier to build than cities on an island. The waterways that were so valuable for New York and Boston have also made it more difficult to build. In the nineteenth century, New York handled its need for space by building up, which is also possible but more expensive than just building out. Boston actually created more usable land by the massive engineering project of filling in its Back Bay. Today, the newer cities of the Sun Belt, like Houston, Atlanta, and Las Vegas, are unencumbered by water barriers and find it easier to just continue building out.

The growth of these cities also reflects their pro-growth regulatory environments. The more limited growth in coastal California since 1970 represents an increasingly restrictive regulatory environment (Glaeser, Gyourko, and Saks 2005). Starting in the 1960s, neighborhood groups and environmental activists have been increasingly able to raise hurdles for new development. Environmental impact reviews and large minimum lot sizes make it harder to build. In New York, development has

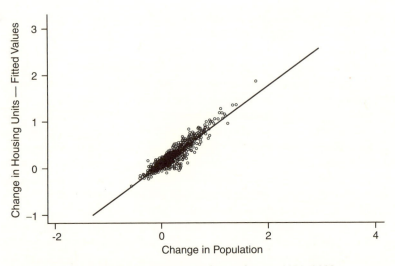

Fig. 2.1 Changes in Housing Units and Population, 1980–2000

also gotten more difficult, but it is the Landmarks Preservation Commission that is often the most effective tool of blocking taller building in well-to-do neighborhoods.

The housing supply doesn't just reflect the ability to build; it also represents the historical stock of past construction. Some cities, like Saint Louis, Detroit, and Philadelphia, have an abundant supply of homes because they once were more desirable than they are today. In these places, housing prices frequently can be lower than the cost of new construction because of the abundant supply. As a result, new construction will be rare, and we should expect increases in economic productivity or improvements in amenities to show up first in rising housing prices rather than larger population levels. Indeed, we should not expect the populations of such cities to start growing again until prices have risen above construction costs. The supply of homes is just one reason why the past matters, and for that reason I now turn to the periods of growth of America's older cities.

America's Urban Origins: Boston, New York, and Chicago

The American colonies began as distant outposts of Europe, and a connection to the Old World was critical. For this reason, American cities grew around transport hubs, and throughout most of history, the cheapest way to move goods long distances has been by boat. As a result, the twenty largest cities in the United States in 1900 were all on waterways. Eight were on the Atlantic, generally where rivers hit the sea. Three were on the Mississippi, three were on the Ohio, and three were on Lake Erie. Two were on Lake Michigan, and one was on the Pacific.

The oldest two of these cities were Boston and New York, which were founded in 1630 and 1624, respectively. In both cases, waterways were essential. Both Boston and New York have exceptional natural harbors and rivers that cut into the hinterlands. Those rivers made it possible to trade with inland natives and later colonial settlers. The Dutch East India Company originally surveyed New York, and even by 1624 Dutch fur traders had settlers on the tip of Manhattan. Its residents, from the beginning, were looking to make money. This did not make New York unique; almost every colonial incursion into the Americas was driven to a large degree by a desire for wealth.

In fact, the colonists coming to Massachusetts were one of the only examples of settlers who were driven primarily by nonpecuniary reasons. John Winthrop, Boston's first mayor, came from a prosperous English family. He came to Boston not because it seemed to have easy opportunities for amassing wealth but because he believed in a religious ideal that could only be realized far away from the English authorities. In a sense, Boston was America's first "consumer city," whose early growth was based on the desire for a different lifestyle, not economic productivity.

Since Boston was founded for religious rather than commercial purposes, it lacked a natural export industry. All cities must have something to export, because at the very least they need to be able to buy food produced in the hinterlands. Boston's problem was much more severe because its residents needed to buy manufactured goods, like guns and books, produced in the Old World. Yet Boston had little to export back to England that was valuable enough to cover the high costs of shipping. Since the climate of New England was pretty similar to that of England, Massachusetts didn't produce a lot of exotic products—like sugar or tobacco—that would have been hard to make back in the old country. The city essentially started out with a massive current account deficit that needed to be solved.

In the 1630s, Boston operated as a sort of colonial-era Ponzi scheme, where early settlers sold basic goods to later settlers who brought assets with them from England. Those assets were then used to pay for imported manufactured goods. This system could not last, and when the English Civil War cut off the flow of new immigrants to Massachusetts, Boston experienced an economic crisis. This crisis would be the first of many that Boston would have to face over the next 370 years, as the city's residents had to deal with the fact that it had no innate source of wealth.

Bostonians responded to this challenge by inventiveness rather than exit, and this illustrates the enormous urban strength that comes from possessing smart people who actually want to stay in the city. Many of the initial attempts to find a new export good were unsuccessful. Winthrop had tried to set the city up as a fur center, but competition for this commodity was extremely fierce. John Winthrop Jr. started an unsuccessful saltworks near Ipswich, Massachusetts (Bremer 2003, 332), and the Saugus Iron Works in 1646. While these efforts weren't complete failures, they weren't raging successes either. Instead, Boston's economic future was created by other entrepreneurs like George Story, Samuel Maverick, and John Winthrop's other sons, Stephen and Samuel—who established the source of Boston's financial well-being: trade in basic commodities with Spain, the West Indies, and the American South.

The new economic model was that Boston would export wood, fish, and meat to the Caribbean and southern colonies that could grow sugar and tobacco that were valuable enough to export across the Atlantic. The plantations of the Caribbean and the South could grow tropical commodities that were scarce and valued in the Old World. It made sense for them to specialize in those valuable goods, and for New England to produce basic foodstuffs. The income that Bostonians gained from selling south would provide them with enough gold to buy English goods.

While this model was ingenious and made Boston the largest city in the colonies for the rest of the seventeenth century, by 1740 Philadelphia surpassed Boston in population. By 1790, New York would pass Philadelphia. In their early years, these cities mimicked Boston's trade pattern by selling grain and other commodities to the southern colonies. The problem for Boston was that both New York and Philadelphia had an innate advantage at the trade that Bostonians pioneered. New York and Philadelphia are further south than Boston, and hence closer to the southern markets. In addition, both cities have a more fertile agricultural inland. Finally, both New York and Philadelphia have access to a better river network than Boston, thereby giving them better access to their hinterlands. Their success brought a fifty-year decline in Boston's fortunes from 1740 to 1790.

Boston did surge again in a second reinvention at the start of the nineteenth century. Boston's growth during this era was mercantile. As ships grew bigger and as Boston was freed from English trade restrictions, Bostonian clipper ships took increasingly long journeys connecting America with South Africa, Oregon, and China. New England whalers plied the waters of the Pacific Ocean. While Boston continued to have a less central port than New York, that disadvantage became relatively less significant as journeys got longer. Boston's one great advan-

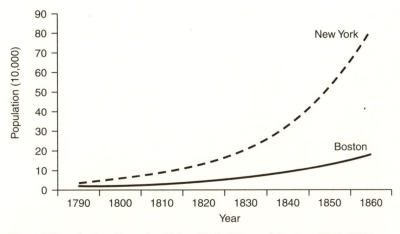

Fig. 2.2 Population Growth of New York City and Boston, 1790–1860

tage was a great stock of mercantile and sailing knowledge. Today, globalization has increased the returns to human capital, and the same thing happened in the nineteenth century. As the maritime networks became more global, Boston's superior sailors and merchants were able to use their human capital to reap higher returns. The importance of Boston's sail-specific human capital is directly demonstrated by the fact that the rise of steamships in the 1840s meant the end of the city's maritime empire and the need for a new reinvention.

Boston's success in the early nineteenth century should not blind us to the fact that New York was far more successful over the same time period. Figure 2.2 shows the population growth of both cities between 1790 and 1860. Even in the eighteenth century, it was clear that New York was the best harbor in the colonies. New York is more centrally located than Boston, and it has much more direct access to the sea than Philadelphia or Baltimore. Its harbor has less ice than the other northern ports, and its deep water gives it a major edge over Philadelphia. Finally, the Hudson is a deep river that runs 315 miles into upstate New York.

Even in the eighteenth century, New York was America's most important port, but technological changes in the nineteenth century greatly magnified its dominance over all of its rivals. In 1821, New York's exports were $13 million and Boston's exports were $12 million. By 1860, Boston's exports were $17 million and New York's exports were $145 million.

The great increase in the size of boats meant that shippers increasingly moved from a point-to-point shipping system to a hub-and-spoke one. In the eighteenth century, when three-hundred-ton vessels were the norm, smaller ships directly connected the different colonial ports with the Old World. In the nineteenth century, as ships increased to ten times that size, it made increasing sense to use fast, large clippers, like the Black Ball Express, to connect England with one port in the United States and then transfer goods to smaller coastal vessels for delivery to the different harbors. The switch to hub-and-spoke shipping was surely going to dramatically increase the importance of whatever port became the hub, and New York City, because of its geographic advantages, was the natural hub for the cross-Atlantic trade.

New York's increasing dominance as a port then attracted its major nineteenth-century industries: sugar refining, the garment trade, and book publishing. In 1850, New York was an industrial town with 43,340 people in manufacturing and 11,360 in commerce. These industries agglomerated in New York because of its port. Sugar refining, for example, was a direct outgrowth of New York's trade with the Caribbean. Sugar couldn't be refined at the initial point of production, because the sugar crystals would coalesce during a long, hot sea voyage and needed to be refined once again. But the large fixed costs involved in setting up a refinery meant that it made sense to refine sugar in a central place, and what place could be better than America's largest port. The garment trade as well grew in New York because of the city's role as a center for trade in both European textiles and southern cotton. Even book publishing owed its Manhattan locale to the enormous value associated with being the first American publisher to pirate British novels. Since New York was the dominant port, its publishers could get the books first.

The time path of New York's population shows that the Erie Canal, completed in 1825, did not make the city. The canal was certainly helpful, but New York was growing just as quickly before 1825 as it was after that date. Yet the canal was crucial for the cities of upstate New York, like Buffalo, Syracuse, and Rochester, that grew up along its path. The canal was also one of the two human-made waterways that enabled the growth of Chicago, as it connected the Hudson to the Great Lakes. The Illinois and Michigan Canal connected the Great Lakes to the Mississippi River system. With those two canals, the United States had a water network that cut through the continent running from New Orleans to New York. It was inevitable that great cities would form along that network and no inland city would be larger than Chicago, which occupied a key geographic spot along the network.

Chicago sits on the spot where the Illinois and Michigan Canal connects the Mississippi River to the Great Lakes. It is a natural place for cargo on canal loading boats to be transferred to lake traveling ships. This human-made geographic advantage would then be supplemented by a rail network that linked Chicago with the rich midwestern hinterland. The city would become the natural place for processing the exports of that hinterland and producing manufactured goods to be used by the farmers of the Midwest. At the end of the nineteenth century, Chicago's two largest industries were stockyards and clothes manufacturing.

The vast scale of Chicago's stockyards reflected the enormous productivity of corn production in Iowa and Illinois. Pigs are corn with feet. Since pork that is fed on corn can be slaughtered and salted to make ham, bacon, and sausage, pigs represent a cost-effective way of getting the calories in corn to consumers' tables. In the early nineteenth century, U.S. corn production was centered in Kentucky and southern Ohio, and as a result Cincinnati was America's Porkopolis. Corn production, however, was vastly more efficient in Iowa than in Kentucky. In 1889, Iowa's yield per acre was forty-one bushels, Illinois's yield was thirty-seven bushels per acre, and Kentucky's yield per acre was less than twenty-seven bushels. As Iowa and Illinois became more accessible by water and rail, corn growing shifted to the modern corn belt. Chicago then became the natural metropolis to butcher live hogs for shipment east.

Chicago brought food out of the Midwest, but it also supplied the Midwest. Cyrus McCormick invented the mechanical reaper in Virginia, and then moved to Chicago so he could be closer to midwestern farmers. Sears and Roebuck was another Chicago firm that thrived on its ability to sell to surrounding midwestern farmers. The clothing trade in Chicago was producing garments for Americans who were working the land.

As in the case of New York and Boston, the agglomeration of Chicago formed to reduce transport costs, but then turned into a hub of innovation. Gustavus Swift made it far more economical to ship dressed beef east by building refrigerated rail cars. The key idea was to put the ice on the top so it would drip down, instead of on the bottom. Late nineteenth-century Chicago also produced America's first skyscrapers. A cluster of innovators in building, including William Le Baron Jenney, Daniel Burnham, and Louis Sullivan, came together in this dense city and developed a new way of building together. The architects were not inventors working in splendid isolation. Chicago's density meant that they consistently had access to each other's ideas, which they regularly stole and improved.

The U.S. urban landscape in 1900 had cities spread throughout the hinterlands on all of our major waterways. This urban pattern was driven by the high costs of transportation and the desire to produce goods close to the agricultural market, which was tied to the soil. The cities were dense and getting denser, as the elevator and the skyscraper made it increasingly possible to build up. While public transportation allowed cities to build out, streetcars and subways still required walking to and from the station, so housing was still tightly clustered. Transportation innovation in the twentieth century would change that pattern dramatically.

Declining Transport Costs: The Rise of Los Angeles and the Decline of Detroit

When the twentieth century began, urban visionaries saw a future of vertical cities whose streets would be darkened by immense skyscrapers. Many of the great architects of this period tried desperately to find ways to humanize the great cities of the future. Le Corbusier thought that he could accommodate a natural human need for greenery by erecting sixty-story buildings that would be surrounded by gardens and connected by subways.

But twentieth-century Americans didn't accommodate a desire for foliage by living in vast skyscrapers surrounded by greenery. Instead, they came to live in vast suburban communities, where they got everywhere by car. Americans also moved in vast numbers to warmer locales. Lower-density Los Angeles, not tall New York, would be the great urban winner of this time period. About 90 percent of Manhattan households are in buildings with more than ten units, but only one-quarter of Los Angeles lives in such large buildings. Its growth, based on sun and sprawl, would be accompanied by a tremendous depopulation of the traditional cities of the Northeast and Midwest.

Los Angeles is in many ways the opposite of both New York and Chicago. Those older cities had their locations dictated by waterways. Easy access to the ocean, long rivers, and great lakes meant that building great cities in New York and Chicago made great economic sense. By contrast, little about the location of Los Angeles seems geographically determined. Southern California lies at the edge of the country, perched on the western seaboard, and Los Angeles didn't even start out with a port. The city wasn't a natural place to produce anything; it was just a beautiful spot with a great climate.

Los Angeles did eventually develop great export industries, like aerospace and entertainment, but the early pioneers in these industries often came to California for consumption reasons. D. W. Griffith, for example, moved to Los Angeles both because of the prospect of year-round movie production and because he had never really taken to northern weather. Donald Douglas, whose DC (Douglas Commercial) planes would become a bulwark of California aviation, left Cleveland

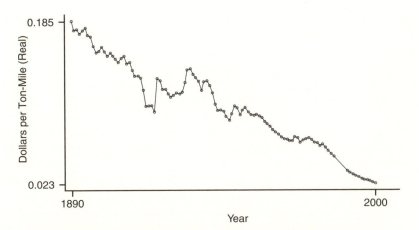

Fig. 2.3 Real Costs of Railroad Transportation over Time, 1890–2000.
Source: Historical Statistics of the United States, 1994, Bureau of Transportation Statistics Annual Reports, 1994 and 2002 (originally appeared
in Glaeser, Edward L., and Janet E. Kohlhase, "Cities, Regions and the
Decline of Transport Costs." *Papers in Regional Science* 83, no. 1 [2004]:
197–228).

in 1920 to return to Los Angeles because his family preferred warmer
weather. In successful cities, the agglomeration of smart people ends up
producing new ideas, and this certainly happened in both movie and
airplane production in Los Angeles. The big difference, however, between Los Angeles and Chicago or New York was that the initial force
driving the agglomeration had more to do with quality-of-life issues
than with transport-based productivity advantages.

The rise of consumer cities far from the great lakes was only made
possible by a radical reduction in transport costs over the twentieth century. In 1850, access to Los Angeles was so difficult that no climatic advantages could have made it into a great city. By 1950, Los Angeles was
distant yet accessible, and a great city had formed as the three thousand
miles that separate the East and West coasts had become less important.
Figure 2.3 shows the declining cost of moving a ton a mile by rail over
the last one hundred years (Glaeser and Kohlhase 2004). This 90 percent
decline in transport costs in some ways understates the full extent of the
death of distance, because it doesn't include the introduction of new
modes of transport like airplanes, trucks, and cars.

The internal combustion engine is the great force of urban change in
the twentieth century. The older forms of transportation required large
infrastructure, such as ports and rail yards, and cities were generally
built around that infrastructure. Since older forms of transportation

necessitated walking, cities were dense. Cars both require and permit the consumption of vast amounts of space. Cities built around cars must look totally different than those built around walking and public transportation. To make full use of the automobile and its tremendous speed advantages, people needed to move from the older cities to new places, like Los Angeles, that could be developed around the car.

Somewhat ironically, the mass-produced car is itself the product of the dense urban environments that it did so much to destroy. Detroit in 1900 bore a distinct resemblance to Silicon Valley in the 1960s. It was a hotbed of small entrepreneurs, many of whom were trying to improve the performance and production of cars. Detroit had two industries that came together to produce cars: engine production and maintenance, which was oriented toward Great Lakes shipping, and carriage production, which was based on abundant Michigan lumber. Henry Ford came out of the engine side of Detroit; he did his early work at Detroit Dry Dock. Billy Durant of General Motors came out of the carriage production business. Detroit initially had an abundance of small producers who could supply inputs to innovators. This extremely dense environment of smart people who could learn from one another and abundant suppliers who let an innovator start was perfect for experimentation.

Once Ford got his basic production process working, however, he quickly started to suburbanize manufacturing. Ford's massive River Rouge plant was a wholly integrated facility built outside the city. As Ford's need to innovate declined and his ability to supply his own industry increased, he chose abundant suburban land over access to other innovators and small-scale suppliers.

The Ford move to River Rouge was a sign of the great exodus of urban manufacturing that would be a central trend of twentieth-century urban change. Again, changing transportation technology was critical. In 1900, proximity to rail yards or the harbor was essential for industrial producers; by the mid-twentieth century, trucks made it possible to leave the city, and locate where land and labor was cheaper. In city after city, manufacturing decentralized to the point that few U.S. cities have much significant manufacturing left.

Indeed, over the late twentieth century, initial specialization in manufacturing was a robust predictor of urban decline. Figure 2.4 depicts the correlation between the change in the logarithm of population between 1950 and 1980, and the initial specialization of the city in manufacturing. This graph is shown at the city level and includes only places with more than one hundred thousand people in 1950. I am showing cities, rather than metropolitan areas, to emphasize the importance of the suburbanization of manufacturing. The figure reveals a −54 percent correlation. As a city had 10 percent more manufacturing in 1950, it lost 18 percent more of its population between 1950 and 1980.

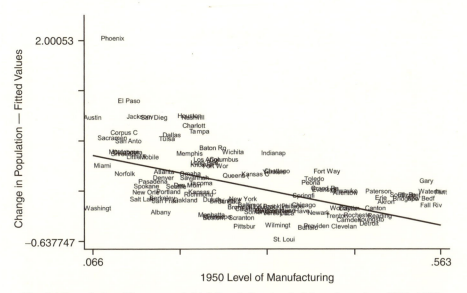

Fig. 2.4 Population Change on Initial Specialization in Manufacturing, 1950–1980

The decline of manufacturing cities is a part of the broader decline of almost all of America's older cities in the second half of the twentieth century. Table 2.1 shows the ten largest cities in the United States in 1950, and their population in 2000. Eight of the ten cities lost people over the fifty-year period, and many of them declined massively. Only New York and Los Angeles gained people, and New York's growth was less than 10 percent. Detroit lost almost 49 percent of its population, and Cleveland lost almost 48 percent of its population.

The decline of older, colder cities built around public transportation and the rise of the lower-density places in the Sun Belt is certainly the major urban transformation of the late twentieth century. Yet it is not the only major change that occurred. In the next three sections, I will discuss what are, in my view, the three major themes of urban change over the last thirty years: the rise of the skilled city, the rise of the consumer city, and the increasing importance of housing supply to urban growth and decline.

The Rise of the Skilled City since 1970

In 1975, every major city in the Northeast and Midwest looked troubled. New York and Boston appeared quite similar to Cleveland and Detroit. All of these cities had once thrived as centers of manufacturing, and in all of these places the exodus of manufacturing created economic

TABLE 2.1
Ten Largest U.S. Cities by Population, 1950 and 2000

		Population	
Ranking	*City*	*1980*	*2000*
1	New York City	7,891,957	8,008,278
2	Chicago	3,620,952	2,896,016
3	Philadelphia	2,071,605	1,517,550
4	Los Angeles	1,970,358	6,694,820
5	Detroit	1,849,568	951,270
6	Baltimore	949,708	651,154
7	Cleveland	914,808	478,403
8	Saint Louis	856,796	348,189
9	Washington, DC	802,178	572,059
10	Boston	801,444	589,141

Sources: Http://www.census.gov/population/www/documentation/twps0027.html, Population of the 100 Largest Urban Places: 1950; http://www.census.gov/population/ documentation/twps0027/tab18.txt; American Fact Finder at http://factfinder.census .gov/.

decline and social distress. Crime rates were uniformly high, and fiscal crises were ubiquitous. The demand for housing in these places was so low that in most of the cities, the majority of homes were priced below the costs of new construction in 2001 (Glaeser and Gyourko 2001).

Over the past thirty years, the fortunes of Rust Belt cities have diverged dramatically. Some places, like New York and Boston, have seen incomes and housing prices increase dramatically. Even population levels in their central cities have increased. Other areas, such as Cleveland and Detroit, have seen a continuing spiral of poverty and decline. In 1975, an observer could think that the United States was separated into a declining Rust Belt and a booming Sun Belt. But since 1975, the diversity within the older cities has been as striking as the gap between the Rust Belt and the Sun Belt.

On a statistical level, the most powerful variable that explains the heterogeneity in Frost Belt success since 1980 is the skill level of the city. Measures of human capital, like the share of the adult population with college degrees in 1980, can explain a significant amount of the heterogeneity in population, income, and housing price growth in colder areas since 1980. I use the college degree measure, but other proxies for

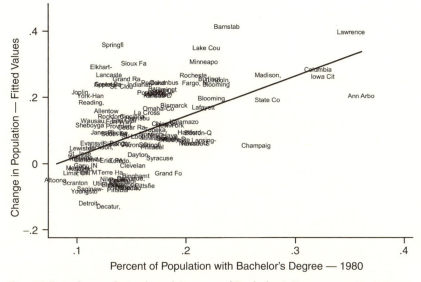

Fig. 2.5 Population Growth and Percent of Bachelor's Degrees, 1980–2000

skills, including measures that date from before World War II, have similar effects on growth (Glaeser and Saiz 2003). To show these correlations, I limit the sample to metropolitan areas in the Northeast and Midwest.

Figure 2.5 shows the 24 percent correlation between population growth between 1980 and 2000, and the share of the population with college degrees in 1980 in this sample. A 10 percent increase in the college-educated share is associated with roughly a 12 percent increase in population growth. Figure 2.6 shows the 64 percent correlation between median family income growth between 1980 and 2000, and the initial share of the population with college degrees. A 10 percent increase in the college-educated share is associated with roughly a 12 percent increase in income growth. Figure 2.7 depicts the 41 percent correlation between the Office of Federal Housing Enterprise Oversight repeat sales indexes change from 1980 to 2000, and the initial share of the population with college degrees. In this case, a 10 percent increase in the college-educated share is associated with a 2.2 percent increase in housing prices.

Tables 2.2 and 2.3 show these results in a regression setting. Table 2.2 gives results for metropolitan areas; table 2.3 provides results for cities. Regression (1) of both tables shows the relationship between population growth between 1980 and 2000, and the initial log of population, the logarithm of initial population density, median January temperature, and

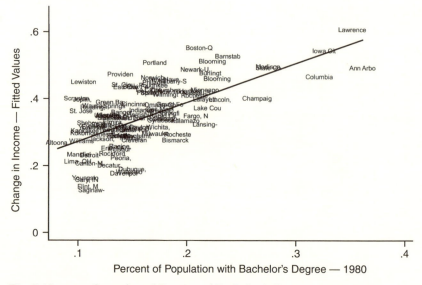

Fig. 2.6 Income Growth and Percent of Bachelor's Degrees, 1980–2000

the college education share. In table 2.2, the January temperature and college education share are both significant predictors of growth. A 10 percent increase in the share of the adult population with college degrees is associated with a 0.12 log point (approximately 12 percent) increase in population growth over the twenty-year period. The first regression of table 2.3 shows that initial skills have a smaller impact on city population growth than on metropolitan area population growth. A 10 percent increase in the share of the adult population with college degrees increases a city's population growth by about 4 percent over this time period. That effect is also quite statistically significant.

Regression (2) reproduces regression (1) for just those cities in the Northeast, Midwest, and South. The coefficient on the share of the population with a college degree becomes stronger when we restrict ourselves to these regions. The rise is modest in table 2.2 and quite significant in table 2.3. Among nonwestern cities, skills are an extremely potent predictor of population growth over the last twenty years. Regression (3) looks at just the western cities. In this case, the share of the population with college degrees is negatively associated with population growth for both the metropolitan areas and the city samples. I will return to the interpretation of this fact after discussing the other regressions in the two tables.

Regressions (4), (5), and (6) of both tables look at income growth using the same explanatory variables. Regression (4) shows that the col-

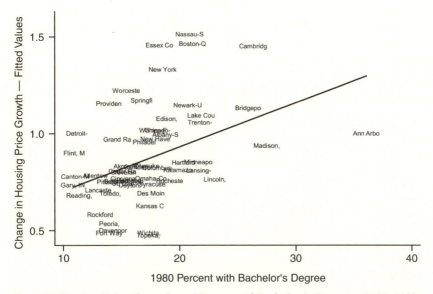

Fig. 2.7 Housing Price Growth and Percent of Bachelor's Degrees, 1980–2000

lege education share is a particularly powerful predictor of income growth. The effect is much stronger at the metropolitan-area level than at the city level. To a certain extent, this reflects the widely known rising returns to skill in the U.S. economy, but the connection between location-specific education and income growth persists even when we control for individual human capital measures (Glaeser and Saiz 2003).

In the 1970s, many of the highest-paid regions in the country were unionized, manufacturing places that weren't particularly well skilled. As figure 2.8 shows, the correlation between area-level incomes and area-level human capital is now quite tight. In this figure, our area income measures are estimated metropolitan area effects estimated in an individual-level wage regression containing only men between the ages of twenty-five and fifty-five, where we hold individual education and experience constant.

Regression (5) illustrates that the effect of human capital on income growth gets slightly stronger when we restrict our sample to the Northeast, Midwest, and South. In the Metropolitan Statistical Area (MSA) sample, the coefficient rises slightly when I restrict the sample to exclude the West. In the city sample, the coefficient rises slightly when I exclude the West. Regression (6) restricts the sample to cities in the West, and the effect of human capital on income growth is actually larger than it is for the entire United States. While skills don't predict population growth in the West, they certainly predict income growth.

TABLE 2.2
Population, Income, and Housing Value Growth at the MSA Level

	Change in population, 1980–2000			Change in income, 1980–2000			Change in housing value, 1980–2000		
	All Cities (1)	East, Central, and South Cities (2)	West Cities (3)	All Cities (4)	East, Central, and South Cities (5)	West West Cities (6)	All Cities (7)	East, Central, and South Cities (8)	West Cities (9)
Log of population, 1980	0.073 (0.016)**	0.052 (0.019)**	0.088 (0.053)	-0.031 (0.011)**	-0.012 (0.013)	-0.066 (0.024)**	-0.019 (0.018)	-0.025 (0.022)	-0.093 (0.044)*
Log of population density, 1980	-0.086 (0.013)**	-0.062 (0.017)**	-0.074 (0.037)	0.037 (0.009)**	0.009 (0.012)	0.060 (0.017)**	0.073 (0.014)**	0.085 (0.020)**	0.100 (0.031)**
Median January temperature	0.008 (0.001)**	0.008 (0.001)**	0.004 (0.003)	0.001 (0.000)	0.000 (0.001)	0.005 (0.001)**	0.001 (0.001)	0.000 (0.001)	0.007 (0.003)**
% of population with a BA or higher, 1980	1.296 (0.201)**	1.436 (0.213)**	-0.048 (0.619)	1.078 (0.129)**	1.182 (0.146)**	1.200 (0.279)**	0.419 (0.216)	0.041 (0.246)	1.769 (0.509)**
Constant	-0.508 (0.130)**	-0.466 (0.138)**	-0.350 (0.419)	0.247 (0.084)**	0.230 (0.095)*	0.302 (0.189)	-0.311 (0.140)*	-0.254 (0.159)	-0.024 (0.344)
Observations	255	207	48	255	207	48	255	207	48
R-squared	0.45	0.43	0.17	0.26	0.25	0.54	0.20	0.17	0.48

Standard errors in parentheses
* significant at 5%; ** significant at 1%

TABLE 2.3
Population, Income, and Housing Value Growth at the City Level

	Change in population, 1980–2000			Change in income, 1980–2000			Change in housing value, 1980–2000		
	All Cities (1)	East, Central, and South Cities (2)	West Cities (3)	All Cities (4)	East, Central, and South Cities (5)	West West Cities (6)	All Cities (7)	East, Central, and South Cities (8)	West Cities (9)
Log of population, 1980	-0.016 (0.0010)	-0.022 (0.011)*	0.000 (0.021)	-0.022 (0.006)	-0.001 (0.007)	-0.002 (0.011)	-0.020 (0.009)*	-0.025 (0.010)*	-0.016 (0.020)
Log of population density, 1980	-0.094 (0.011)**	-0.085 (0.012)**	-0.178 (0.027)**	0.023 (0.007)**	0.020 (0.007)**	0.009 (0.014)	-0.131 (0.010)**	-0.116 (0.011)**	-0.210 (0.025)**
Median January temperature	0.007 (0.001)**	0.006 (0.001)**	0.001 (0.002)	0.002 (0.000)**	0.001 (0.000)**	0.003 (0.001)**	0.004 (0.001)**	0.004 (0.001)**	-0.001 (0.001)
% of population with a BA or higher, 1980	0.386 (0.081)**	0.636 (0.082)**	-0.729 (0.160)**	0.335 (0.044)**	0.214 (0.051)**	0.558 (0.086)**	0.519 (0.072)**	0.702 (0.074)**	-0.225 (0.151)
Constant	0.787 (0.132)**	0.729 (0.139)**	1.914 (0.288)**	-0.183 (0.076)*	-0.127 (0.087)	-0.110 (0.155)	1.247 (0.117)**	1.128 (0.126)**	2.301 (0.272)**
Observations	921	653	253	903	652	251	921	653	253
R-squared	0.22	0.26	0.21	0.11	0.04	0.17	0.27	0.34	0.27

Standard errors in parentheses
*significant at 5%; ** significant at 1%

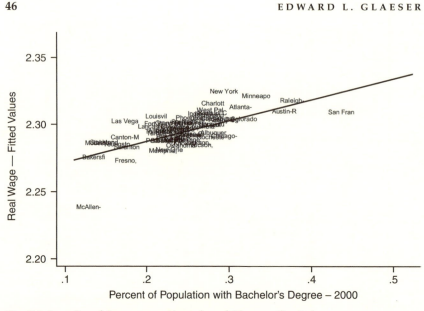

Fig. 2.8 Area-Level Incomes on Area-Level Human Capital

Housing price growth is a third measure of urban success, as the price of housing can be seen as the willingness of people to pay to live in a particular place. In regression (7), (8), and (9), we look at the correlates of housing price growth. Regression (7) shows that the connection between housing prices and skills is robustly positive for both metropolitan areas and cities. This rise in housing prices, though, does not offset the rise in incomes enough to create a decline in real incomes in more skilled cities (Glaeser and Saiz 2003). Since housing represents about 30 percent of expenditure, as a general rule a coefficient in a housing regression must be 10/3 times the coefficient in an income regression for real incomes to fall. At the metropolitan-area level, the coefficient on the skill variable is lower in the housing price change regression than it is in the income change regression. In the city-level regression, the coefficient on the skill variable is higher in the housing price change regression, but not by enough to suggest that real incomes actually declined.

Regressions (8) and (9) depict regional patterns that look quite different at the city- and metropolitan-area level. At the city level, the effect of human capital is greater outside the West. In the metropolitan-area level, the effect of human capital is actually greatest in the West. Much of this difference reflects the fact that the West has seen huge appreciation in prices in many places that were initially low skilled, but were in highly productive metropolitan areas.

Why is there such a robust correlation between skills and city success? Can our theories of the connection between skills and urban success explain the empirical patterns across regions? At a broad level, the tendency of skills to predict population growth might reflect a connection between skills and improvements in productivity, quality, or even the housing supply. Economic theory, however, tells us that if skill levels were driving population growth by boosting housing supply, then we should see declining housing prices in highly skilled areas, and that is obviously false. Moreover, there is no particular reason to think that skill levels should be related to more expansions of the housing stock, and every reason to think that more skilled people have been more effective in restricting new construction.

Yet there are good reasons to think that the rise of skilled places might reflect improvements in the quality of life. Skilled places do have less crime and richer tax rolls. Perhaps people are more willing to pay to have their children go to school with the children of better-educated parents. Still, economic theory gives us a good test to see if the connection between skills and growth represents an increased willingness to pay to have skilled neighbors. If the rise of skilled cities represented quality-of-life improvements, then we should expect to see real wages declining in skilled cities or equivalent, which would require that the rise in housing prices in these areas is a lot stronger than the rise in incomes.

A spatial equilibrium requires that high levels of quality of life be offset by low real wages. If this weren't the case, then people would start bidding up housing prices in places that offered both high real wages and a good quality of life. This logic suggests that places with an improving quality of life should have declining real wages as housing price increases outstrip nominal income increases. But research by both myself and Albert Saiz (2003) and Jesse M. Shapiro (2005) investigates the connection between area-level skills and the rise in real wages, and finds that real wages are rising, not falling, in places with high initial skill levels. Housing prices are rising, but they are not rising by enough to offset the rise in incomes, so it seems as if the rise in skilled cities is not ultimately about amenity levels.

Instead, the rise of the skilled city reflects an increasing connection between city-level productivity and skills. Since firms have the opportunity to leave high-wage areas, we tend to interpret rising wages in an area as evidence that the productivity of that area is rising, and wages in skilled areas have risen dramatically. The increasing connection between skills and incomes may reflect the highly innovative economies of skilled cities, or it may reflect the fact that working around skilled people is a good way to acquire skills. The wage and income data cannot distinguish between these hypotheses, but they do strongly suggest that skilled cities have become increasingly productive relative to unskilled ones, and this is the reason why colder cities like Boston and Minneapolis have thrived, while Cleveland and Detroit have not.

One variant on this hypothesis is that skills are especially crucial for the task of urban reinvention. According to this view, the differences between the cities of the East and the West suggest that skills are more important for the task of reconfiguring erstwhile manufacturing cities that were hit hard by improvements in transportation technology (Glaeser and Saiz 2003). This view follows a long tradition in economics that suggests that skills are particularly valuable during times of change—a view associated with the work of T. W. Schultz and Finis Welch.

There is, however, another explanation for why there are such regional differences: the housing supply. According to this perspective, highly skilled western cities restricted growth and low-skilled cities in that region did not, because skilled homeowners are more effective in blocking new projects than people with less education. Certainly, the leadership in the antigrowth movements in California came from the upper reaches of the educational universe, including the wife of Clark Kerr, the leader of the University of California system. Since the other regions of the country had much less growth overall, educated opponents of new construction had less scope to impact increases in the housing stock in the West. This view argues that skills increased productivity everywhere, but they didn't increase population growth in the West because of the association between skills and limits on new construction.

The evidence on income and housing price changes, at least at the metropolitan-area level, seems to support the notion that skills have impacted productivity everywhere. This tends to favor the housing supply interpretation of the lack of connection between education and population growth in the South. Still, this evidence is suggestive rather than conclusive, and there is little doubt that skills have been a key predictor of economic success in colder cities. Skilled places certainly have been more successful in reinventing themselves.

The statistical evidence is corroborated by a more fine-grained analysis of the economic revitalizations of New York and Boston. New York's economic success has become increasingly tied to its enormous strength in financial services. Today, roughly 40 percent of Manhattan's payroll is in the financial service sector. The rise of New York City finance post-1970 is a tribute to the ability of dense agglomerations of smart people to innovate. Just as in Detroit in 1900, each innovation creates the possibility for more new ideas along with a virtuous cycle of new ideas and productivity improvements.

In the 1960s, the groundwork was being laid for New York's finance-based resurgence. There was an increasing transfer of ideas about measuring and evaluating risk that moved from academia to practitioners. Highlights of this process included the use of the mean-variance frontier, the capital asset pricing model, and the Black-Scholes options prices formula. An increasingly quantitative body of financial professionals was able to look for situations where extra return made it sensible to move beyond the most blue chip of securities.

The increasing ability to evaluate risk made it possible for Michael Milken to sell high-yield debt (aka junk bonds) to investors who decided that the returns on these assets were high enough to offset the risks. The ability to sell high-yield debt made the takeover boom of the 1980s possible, because leveraged buyout specialists, like Henry Kravis, were able to borrow enough to buy large companies. This takeover boom was able to realize large returns by taking control of companies away from underperforming management. In the late 1980s, mortgage-backed securities emerged as a vast market, and the strength of this market again built on the ability to assess risk well. Modern hedge funds are essentially just the latest incarnation of the ongoing improvements in the ability to assess the mispricing of assets. Idea built on idea, as people in older, denser areas learned from each other and created an innovation engine.

The success of New York City finance was mirrored in other cities such as Boston and Minneapolis as well as regions like Silicon Valley, where skilled people worked close to one another and borrowed each other's innovations. In nineteenth-century Chicago and New York, the idea-producing capacity of cities was an interesting offshoot of the major urban business of producing manufactured goods, and then shipping them by rail and water. In the twenty-first century, idea production appears to have become the major business of many metropolitan areas, and skilled workers seem to be the most important element in the production of ideas.

One possible hypothesis is that the same decline in transportation costs that hurt Detroit saved New York. My work with Giacomo Ponzetto (2007) presents a model where the death of distance has two separate effects on urban economies. First, manufacturing firms leave urban areas to use the cheaper land and labor available elsewhere. Second, the increasingly global marketplace means that the returns to innovation have increased. In the 1950s, most good ideas would have been used primarily in regional or at most national markets. Good ideas today can be exported easily throughout the globe. Since urban density speeds the flow of new ideas, an increase in the value of innovation naturally strengthens those cities that specialize in innovation.

One way of thinking about the role of declining transport costs on innovation is that in an increasingly flat world, the returns to being the smartest person on the planet increase dramatically. But you can only become the smartest person on the planet by working around other smart people, and this increases the returns to locating in centers of intellectual agglomeration like Wall Street or Silicon Valley. As long as face-to-face contact delivers some edge, no matter how small, in the acquisition of knowledge, then increasing returns to knowledge will also increase the returns to the face-to-face contact that is provided by urban proximity.

One piece of evidence supporting the importance of this force is the increasing tendency of skilled people to live around other skilled people (Berry and Glaeser 2005). Figure 2.9 shows the relationship between the growth of the share of the adult population with college degrees between 1980 and 2000, and the initial share of the adult population with college degrees. As the share of the population with college degrees in 1980 increased by 10 percent, the share of the population with college degrees in 2000 increased by 3.3 percent. If having the best new ideas has become increasingly valuable, and if new ideas are produced by agglomerations of skilled people, then we shouldn't be surprised to see that skilled people are increasingly choosing to work near one another.

Of course, the tendency of skilled people to go to skilled cities is not the only factor in urban population growth over the last fifteen years. As David Card's chapter in the volume emphasizes, the population growth of many larger cities is tied closer to increasing numbers of immigrants coming to urban areas. Cities have had a long-standing comparative advantage in being a port of entry for immigrants. Ethnic enclaves and the ability to get by without multiple cars continue to make dense cities attractive for immigrants. The economic attraction of immigrants to cities like New York and Chicago also depends on the overall economic health of those cities, which itself depends on the idea-producing, skill-intensive sectors.

The rising importance of skills to urban success provides a key policy implication for local leaders hoping to generate income and population growth. Attracting and retaining skilled people is a critical task for local governments. Large-scale local redistribution that taxes the rich and firms will have the unfortunate side effect of pushing the skilled out of the city. The mobility of the skilled profoundly limits the ability of city governments to tax their richer workers.

There is some debate about how to attract the skilled. Some authors have advocated cultural policies that support the arts and funky downtowns. I am more convinced that skilled people respond to good schools, low crime rates, and general improvements in the quality of life. Such policies are likely to be beneficial, even if they don't attract the skilled. The impact that they might have on attracting smart people is just an extra reason to fight to improve local school districts or make private schooling options more feasible.

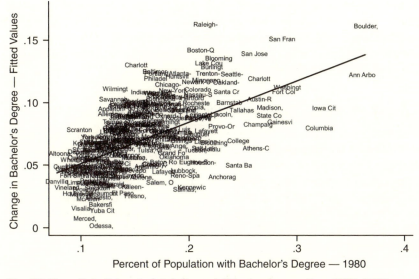

Fig. 2.9 Growth in Educated Adults and City Agglomeration, 1980–2000

The Rise of the Consumer City since 1970

The demand for any metropolitan area is driven by productivity and consumer amenities. Throughout most of U.S. history, productivity has trumped consumption. Nineteenth-century New York may have been fun, but it was a place marked by crime and disease. Gotham's growth reflected the enormous productive edge created by its harbor and rail yards along with the agglomeration that surrounded them. Only at the start of the twentieth century did a large swath of the population become sufficiently rich that they were willing to go to less productive places because they were more pleasant.

Over the past hundred years, Americans have become increasingly wealthy, and as a result increasingly willing to trade off a little bit of income for a more agreeable place to live. The rise of Los Angeles, and places with warm Januaries more generally, provides one example of the growth of the consumer city. But if climate were the only important consumer amenity, then this trend would be an intellectual curiosity rather than an important element in public policy. Since 1970, our wealthy, footloose population has been drawn to many different cities that offer different types of amenities. Beautiful architecture, museums, and a thriving restaurant scene all provide different places with amenities that then attract people and firms.

In this section, I first discuss the general evidence on growth and consumer amenities across metropolitan areas. I will then turn to the remarkable revitalization of many downtowns that have thrived even as they have become more pleasant places to live. Next, I turn to the policy implications of the rise of the consumer city.

Cross-Metropolitan Evidence on the Rise of the Consumer City

I have already discussed the role of sunshine in predicting urban growth, but it is worth remembering that the ability of January temperature continues to be a potent predictor of urban growth. Figure 2.10 shows the correlation between the mean January temperature and population growth between 1980 and 2000. The correlation coefficient between these two variables is 60 percent. As the January temperature increases by 10 percent, the predicted growth increase by 0.09 log points over this twenty-year period.

Of course, January temperature is only one of the amenities that can make living in a metropolitan area more attractive. Good schools, low taxes, and swift commutes are all factors that make an area more attractive (Gyourko and Tracy 1989). The spatial equilibrium concept discussed above provides us with a natural means of assessing the level of amenities in an area: high housing prices relative to income (Rosen 1979; Roback 1982) or, alternatively, low real wages. Following the re-

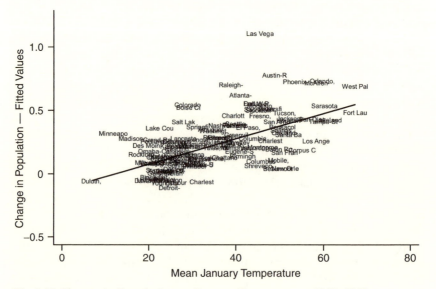

Fig. 2.10 Change in Population on January Temperature, 1980–2000

TABLE 2.4
U.S. MSA with Highest and Lowest Estimated Amenity Values

Highest	*Lowest*
Honolulu	Stamford, CT
Santa Cruz, CA	Norwalk, CT
Santa Barbara–Santa Maria–Lompoc	Anchorage
Salinas–Seaside–Monterey, CA	Rochester, MN
Los Angeles–Long Beach	Detroit
San Francisco	Midland, TX
San Jose, CA	Trenton, NJ
Santa Rosa–Petaluma, CA	Minneapolis–Saint Paul
Oxnard–Ventura, CA	Nassau–Suffolk, NY
San Diego	Bloomington–Normal, IL

Note: Estimated amenity value measured as residual from an OLS regression of log median house value on log median income in 1990.

Source: Originally appeared in Glaeser, Kolko, and Saiz (2001).

search I did with Jed Kolko and Saiz (2001), I regress the logarithm of housing prices on the logarithm of median family income at the metropolitan-area level in 1980. The raw coefficient is 1.04, so that a 1 log point increase in income is associated with a 1.04 log point increase in housing prices. The residual from this regression, which is essentially high housing prices unexplained by income, provides an index of the level of consumption amenities in a particular place.

To check the validity of this approach, table 2.4 shows the top and bottom ten metropolitan areas ranked by this consumption index. We generally think of urban amenities as including much more than the weather. Good museums, low electricity prices, and short commutes are all pleasant urban attributes that should push the consumption index up by either raising housing prices or depressing wages. Yet the top ten cities on the list are either in California or Hawaii. This list certainly suggests that California's temperate climate seems to be enormously valued by the market. Weather appears less critical in explaining the bottom ten cities on the list, some of which are cold (Rochester, Minnesota, and Anchorage) and one of which is hot (Midland, Texas). To my eyes, these lists seem to correspond generally with a reasonable view of what places have high and low amenities.

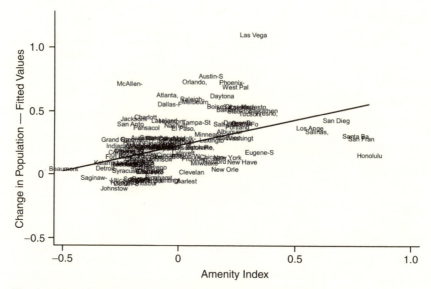

Fig. 2.11 Population Growth on Amenity Index, 1980–2000

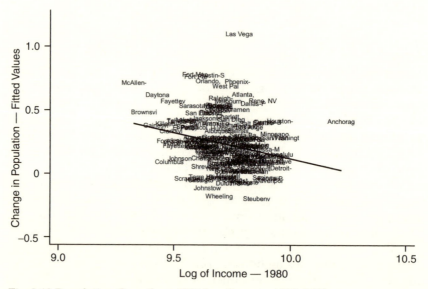

Fig. 2.12 Population Growth on 1980 Log Income, 1980–2000

Figure 2.11 shows the correlation between this amenity index and population growth between 1980 and 2000. A 1 standard deviation increase in the amenity index is associated with a 0.403 log point increase in population growth over this time period. People appear to be mov-

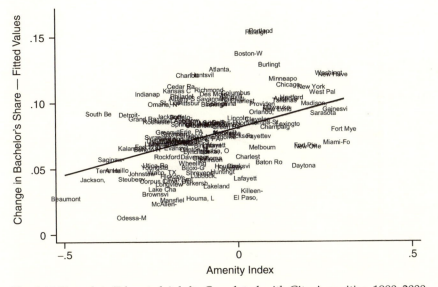

Fig. 2.13 Growth in Educated Adults Correlated with City Amenities, 1980–2000

ing toward high-amenity places. Figure 2.12 illustrates the correlation between the logarithm of income in 1980 and population growth over the next twenty years. Income is a plausible proxy for productivity, so a comparison of the two figures shows that amenity levels have been a stronger predictor than productivity of urban growth over the last twenty years.

One particularly important fact is that high-amenity places have seen their skill levels increase. Figure 2.13 shows the correlation between changes in the share of the population with college degrees and the amenity index for all U.S. regions except the West, as the rise of the immigrant population in the West makes this relationship quite different from the rest of the country. Places that seem to be more pleasant have increasingly attracted high-skilled people who are able to pay more to enjoy those amenities. It seems as if there has been increasing sorting across space between high-earnings individuals and highly attractive areas.

The connection between skill upgrading and consumer amenities suggests a crucial link between the consumer city and the skilled city. It is quite possible that improving consumer amenities may be the best way for a city to attract more skilled workers. As such, the right public policy question might not be whether to work for a consumer or skilled city but rather how to use a consumer city to create a skilled one.

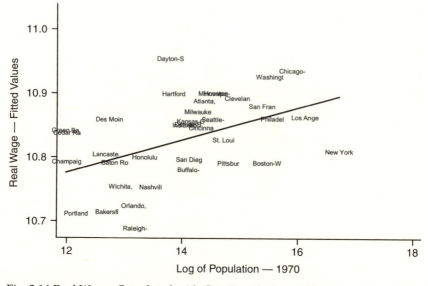

Fig. 2.14 Real Wages Correlated with City Population, 1970

Improving Amenity Levels in Large Cities

In 1970, the older, colder cities in the United States were not only facing economic distress but were also places that most people found unpleasant to live. Vast quantities of middle- and upper-income Americans had fled the old downtowns for suburban areas. Yet over the past thirty years, many of these cities have become more pleasant and have attracted people who want the unique amenities of dense, urban areas.

The rising amenity levels in big cities can be seen in real wage patterns. Since the Rosen-Roback framework tells us that people must be paid high real wages to compensate for low consumer amenities, I will look at real wage levels across cities to infer amenity levels. Figure 2.14 shows the correlation between real wages and the logarithm of city population in 1970. The real wage numbers were calculated using median family income from the U.S. Census and the American Chamber of Commerce local price level.

Figure 2.15 repeats figure 2.14 using year 2000 data. In 1970, big cities paid big real wage premiums, which economics tells us implies that these places had low levels of amenities. Thirty years later, there is no longer a real wage premium associated with living in a big city. Once firms needed to pay people a big real wage premium to locate in New York City. Today, workers no longer require such an incentive.

The improvement in the amenities of big cities is also seen in com-

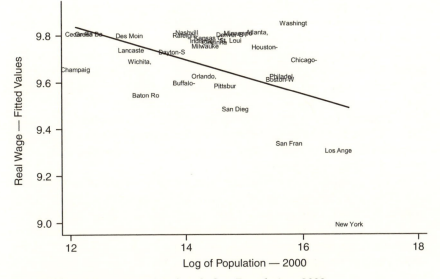

Fig. 2.15 Real Wages Correlated with City Population, 2000

muting patterns. Thirty years ago, there was almost no one who lived in a downtown area and commuted out to the suburbs. There has been a substantial increase in the prevalence of such commutes. The desire of people to live downtown and work in the suburbs is a remarkable testament to the ability of big cities to be attractive not only as places to work but also as places to live.

The increasing tendency of a small number of older downtowns to be consumer cities reflects two major forces. First, rising incomes have produced a class of people who are willing to pay for high-end urban amenities. In the 1970s and earlier, cities always had an edge in restaurants, museums, and entertainment venues, because of the advantages that come from scale. Theaters and museums use large buildings that can only be supported by large audiences, which are hard to find outside of big cities. As in every other area, concentrations of creative people create chains of innovation. The ideas in New York's theater industry or in Los Angeles's restaurants are the result of density-led innovation. Dense cities also provide the pleasures that just come from being around other people. It isn't an accident that some cities are referred to as marriage markets.

The large markets in these places have always made it possible to cover the fixed costs of specialized forms of entertainment. In the 1970s, however, there weren't a modest number of people who were willing to put up with the other costs of urban living in order to get those amenities. Thirty years later, there is an increasing crop of people with the resources to pay for expensive sky-rise apartments and private schools to be able to enjoy the consumption benefits of density.

The second major force in resurrecting urban downtowns has been a significant reduction in the amount of crime. City streets lose their luster when they are unsafe, as they were in the 1970s. Since that decade, in city after city, crime levels have fallen dramatically because of large-scale incarceration, improvements in policing, and possibly abortion (Donohue and Levitt 2001). Safer streets have made it easier for people to enjoy living downtown. Public spaces, no matter how beautiful, have little value if they are unsafe.

The rising importance of consumer amenities, and the ability of some downtowns to become attractive consumer cities, should lead local leaders to think that quality-of-life issues are a major ingredient in urban success. Indeed, it is quite reasonable to think that the best economic development strategy is to provide the amenities that will attract smart people and then get out of their way. Yet it is also worth remembering that there have only been a few older cities that have been able to thrive in this manner. For most Americans, good consumer cities mean car based living on large lots at the edges of metropolitan areas. This may mean that it will be quite hard for many metropolitan areas to thrive using the consumer city strategy.

There is a third, equally crucial post-1970 trend: housing supply has become an increasingly important element in urban growth and decline. It is impossible to understand why Houston and Atlanta are growing so much more quickly than coastal California without understanding the differences in land-use regulations between these areas. Given that the chapter by Joseph Gyourko in this volume addresses housing-related issues, though, I will not discuss them here.

The Consumer City and the Skilled City

In this penultimate section, I will look at the policy implications that come from the rise of both the skilled and the consumer city. While both trends are clear in the data, it is less clear how local leaders can respond to those trends. The skill base of a population is enormously sticky: it isn't easy for a mayor to snap their fingers and turn a low-skill city, like Cleveland, into a high-skill one, such as Boston. It is even more difficult to improve the local weather. Nonetheless, these two trends do give us some guide to government policy.

City leaders who are trying to make their city more prosperous cannot avoid the need to attract skilled residents. I believe that there are three key components to supporting the growth of skills. Perhaps most obviously, the education system is crucial. Good schools both create more educated graduates and attract more educated parents who want their children to have better schools. The problem with this advice is that fixing schools is a difficult problem, especially if more money doesn't translate automatically into higher school quality.

In many cases, changing the structure of the school system is at least as important as spending more on schools. One great advantage of big cities is that their size abets competition, which increases productivity and spurs innovation. Yet our public schools are usually organized as one big citywide monopoly, which eliminates any of that urban edge. Surely it makes sense to follow the path that some big cities have taken toward allowing more competition across schools and more parental choice within school districts. Charter schools also seem to hold some promise. It also appears sensible to be friendly toward private and parochial schools, which can provide high-quality schooling for some education-oriented parents, who are so important to attract to urban areas.

A second element of attracting skilled people is to avoid redistributive policies that target the rich and drive them away. The skilled population is extremely mobile and when they are punitively taxed, then they will flee. City governments have increasingly recognized that they do not have captive populations, and there has been a decline in the tendency to try to run a local welfare state. While it is hard to attract the skilled, it is awfully easy to repel them, and city governments at the least need to consistently ask whether their policies are stopping skilled people from coming to their city.

The final element in being pro-skill is to improve consumer amenities. As I noted in the last section, skilled people have flocked to high-amenity cities. The increasingly wealthy residents of some older downtowns reflect, in part, declining crime levels and an increased willingness to pay for the high level of consumer amenities that can only be provided in a big urban area. Furthermore, since cities are dense, they can offer short commutes, which are particularly valuable to skilled people with a high value of time.

What are the policies that can produce a consumer city? Certainly the most significant job of the city is safety. Crime was the great destroyer of urban amenities in the 1960s and 1970s. Keeping police strong and effective is a critical ingredient in maintaining a consumer city.

There are other forms of public infrastructure that can also help to create the consumer. Some of the urban renewal projects, like Boston's Faneuil Hall or New York's South Street Seaport, have created successful playgrounds for both tourists and local residents. If the costs of these projects are kept in check, and if they are well targeted toward the desired audience, then they can be part of a successful consumer city strategy.

Improvements in regulation are another essential ingredient in fostering consumer cities. In too many places, restrictions on land use make it difficult to develop exciting neighborhoods. Traditional barriers to combining workplaces and residences are often out of date and make it hard to reconfigure cities for a new reality where workplaces are shining glass towers rather than smoke-belching factories. Entertainment entrepreneurs don't need subsidies but they do need the freedom to innovate.

A final ingredient in successful consumer cities is transportation policy. People need to be able to speedily access entertainment venues if the city is to be fully enjoyed. Innovative policies, like congestion charges, offer one way to make sure that city streets are used more efficiently.

Conclusion

Urban change has been a major feature of American life for the last 375 years. Cities boomed in the eighteenth and nineteenth centuries to take advantage of waterways, and allow the wealth of the new world to be brought to the markets of the East Coast and the world in general. In the twentieth century, declining transportation costs made those cities seem obsolete. The car and truck ushered in a new era of booming Sun Belt cities built around the automobile.

Over the last thirty years, three new trends have arisen that challenge the view that sun always means success and cold always implies failure. First, the older cities that had a substantial stock of well-educated workers have managed to reinvent themselves as centers for idea-oriented industries, like finance and technology. As ideas get more valuable in an increasingly global economy, the returns for producing new ideas have risen, and proximity to smart people helps in producing ideas. Second, some of the older cities are now succeeding as places of consumption as well as production. Rising incomes and declining crime levels have meant that a select group of people are willing to pay for the attractions of older downtowns. Third, within the Sun Belt there has been a schism between the more temperate areas that have restricted construction and the places with hotter summers that have encouraged building. Both income and housing prices have risen strikingly as a result in those temperate areas, while population growth has been greatest in areas with hot summers.

There are two general policy lessons that follow from all of this urban change. At the local level, leaders must respect the mobility of their populations. They cannot set policies in the expectation that their firms or wealthy residents are fixed. This puts a strong brake on the ability of localities to redistribute income. They should set policies recognizing that they have the ability to attract potential entrepreneurs. This means that basic urban governance that improves the quality of life for urban residents becomes important as a way of attracting smart people who will then lead the economy.

At the national level, the strength of the forces that move cities suggests the futility of place-based policies meant to resurrect declining areas. Certainly, the urban renewal programs of the 1950s and 1960s have at best a mixed record. The obligation of the government is to people, not places. In many cases, people are best served by leaving areas that have passed their period of economic prominence. Economic efficiency would seem to be best served by a free market where people can choose where to live without the national government trying to intervene.

References

Berry, Christopher, and Edward L. Glaeser. 2005. The Divergence of Human Capital Levels across Cities. NBER working paper no. 11617. Cambridge, MA: National Bureau of Economic Research.

Bremer, Francis J. 2003. *John Winthrop: America's Forgotten Founding Father*. Oxford: Oxford University Press.

Costa, Dora, and Matthew E. Kahn. 2003. The Rising Price of Nonmarket Goods. *American Economic Review* 93, no. 2 (May): 227–32.

Cutler, David M., and Grant Miller. 2006. Water, Water Everywhere: Municipal Finance and Water Supply in American Cities. In *Corruption and Reform: Lessons from America's Economic History*, ed. Edward L. Glaeser and Claudia Goldin. Chicago: University of Chicago Press.

Donohue, John J., III, and Steven D. Levitt. 2001. The Impact of Legalized Abortion on Crime. *Quarterly Journal of Economics* 116, no. 2 (May): 379–420.

Katz, Lawrence, and Kenneth T. Rosen. 1987. The Interjurisdictional Effects of Growth Controls on Housing Prices. *Journal of Law and Economics* 30, no. 1 (April): 149–60.

Glaeser, Edward L., and Joseph Gyourko. 2001. Urban Decline and Durable Housing. NBER working paper no. 8598. Cambridge, MA: National Bureau of Economic Research.

———. 2005. Urban Decline and Durable Housing. *Journal of Political Economy* 113, no. 2 (April): 345–75.

Glaeser, Edward L., Joseph Gyourko, and Raven E. Saks. 2005. Why Have Housing Prices Gone Up? *American Economic Review* 95, no. 2 (May): 329–33.

Glaeser, Edward L., Matthew Kahn, and Jordan Rappaport. 2008. Why Do the Poor Live in Cities? The Role of Public Transportation. *Journal of Urban Economics* 63 (1): 1–24.

Glaeser, Edward L., and Janet E. Kohlhase. 2004. Cities, Regions, and the Decline of Transport Costs. *Papers in Regional Science* 83 (1): 197–228.

Glaeser, Edward L., Jed Kolko, and Albert Saiz. 2001. Consumer City. *Journal of Economic Geography* 1, no. 1 (January): 27–50.

Glaeser, Edward L., and Giacomo Ponzetto. 2007. Did the Death of Distance Hurt Detroit and Help New York. Mimeograph, Harvard University.

Glaeser, Edward L., and Bruce Sacerdote. 1999. Why Is There More Crime in Cities? *Journal of Political Economy* 107, no. 6 (December): S225–58.

Glaeser, Edward L., and Albert Saiz. 2003. The Rise of the Skilled City. *Brookings-Wharton Papers on Urban Affairs* 5:47–94.

Glaeser, Edward L., and Kristina Tobio. 2007. The Rise of the Sunbelt. NBER working paper no. 13071I. Cambridge, MA: National Bureau of Economic Research.

Glaeser, Edward L., and Bryce A. Ward. 2006. Myths and Realities of American Political Geography. *Journal of Economic Perspectives* 20, no. 2 (Spring): 119–44.

Graves, Philip. 1980. Migration and Climate. *Journal of Regional Science* 20 (2): 227–38.

Gyourko, Joseph, and Joseph Tracy. 1989. The Importance of Local Fiscal Conditions in Analyzing Local Labor Markets. *Journal of Political Economy* 97, no. 5 (October): 1208–31.

Roback, Jennifer. 1982. Wages, Rents, and the Quality of Life. *Journal of Political Economy* 90, no. 6 (December): 1257–78.

Rosen, Sherwin. 1979. Wage-Based Indexes of Urban Quality of Life. In *Current Issues in Urban Economics*, ed. Peter Mieszkowski and Mahlon Straszheim, 74–104. Baltimore: Johns Hopkins University Press.

Saxenian, AnnaLee. 1994. Social Networks and Open Exchange: Regional Advantages in Silicon Valley. *Firm Connections* 2, no. 5 (September–October).

Shapiro, Jesse M. 2005. Smart Cities: Quality of Life, Productivity, and the Growth Effects of Human Capital. *Review of Economics and Statistics* 88, no. 2 (May): 324–35.

Smith, Adam. 1776. *An Inquiry into the Nature and Causes of the Wealth of Nations*. London: Dent and Sons.

Wrigley, E. Anthony, and Roger S. Schofield. 1983. English Population History from Family Reconstruction: Summary Results, 1600–1799. *Population Studies* 37, no. 2 (July): 157–84.

3

Transportation

URBAN TRANSPORTATION POLICY

KENNETH A. SMALL

CITIES EXIST and thrive because they enable people to access each other. Thus they depend on a good transportation system, as confirmed by the strong impacts of transportation infrastructure on both economic growth (Gramlich 1994) and urban structure (Giuliano 2004). Furthermore, there is little doubt that at least in a city of any size, a healthy economy requires a transportation system that includes both private and public modes, since neither alone can possibly accommodate the enormous variety of trips that such an economy generates. Each mode involves important policy decisions about the extent of capital investment, the level of service provided, and the financing and pricing of that service.

Given its significance, it is no surprise that transportation is frequently a top concern to urban residents. Periodically this concern rises in prominence as one or another part of the system appears to be near breakdown. The high labor intensity of public transportation, combined with a variety of pressures toward more dispersed trip patterns, subject it to severe cost pressures that occasionally erupt in service cutbacks or unsustainable fiscal drains. Meanwhile traffic congestion on highways, inherent in urban life but never really accepted, continues its steady march toward an apparently intolerable future. The adverse environmental effects of traffic and the activities that support it just add to unease about the health of the underlying system, which depends so strongly on motor vehicles.

Often the reaction to both of these problems is to propose an infusion of funds into public transit. Whatever the wisdom of this approach for ameliorating the fiscal problems of transit, experience indicates that it can have at best a small effect on traffic congestion. It is highways that carry the overwhelming majority of urban trips in virtually all metropolitan areas, and so realistic planners typically look to highway capacity enhancements as the main weapon against congestion. Indeed, if one wants a simple explanation for why congestion is growing, it is not

TABLE 3.1
Demand Factors and Supply of Road Capacity: United States, 1980–2005

	1980	2005	Growth
All areas			
Adult population (age 15+) (millions)	175.3	235.7	34.5%
Registered motor vehicles (millions)	155.8	241.2	54.8%
Vehicle miles of travel (billions)	1,527.3	2,989.8	95.8%
Lane miles of major roads (thousands)*	552.2	724.6	31.2%
Urban areas			
Vehicle miles of travel (billions)	855.3	1,951.9	128.2%
Lane miles of major roads (thousands)*	219.9	351.5	59.9%

* "Major roads" are defined as expressways and other principal arterials.
Sources: U.S. Federal Highway Administration, (1997), tables MV-200, VM-201, HM-260; U.S. Federal Highway Administration (2006a), tables MV-1, VM-2, HM-60; U.S. Census Bureau (2006), table 11.

hard to find: for many decades, road capacity has grown far more slowly than the vehicle miles of travel—especially in urban areas. Table 3.1 shows some representative figures for the United States, covering 1980–2005.

Even as planners are busy projecting capacity needs (often requiring hopelessly infeasible levels of funding) and detailing apocalyptic scenarios in case the capacity is not forthcoming, many analysts are pessimistic about what can be accomplished through more road capacity. Since World War II, enormous capacity investments have been made; they have accommodated an impressive growth in population, mobility, and motor vehicle traffic in particular, but they have not stabilized congestion levels. Neither have transit initiatives, which have made only minor, if any, inroads into the decline of transit mode share. Improved signal timing, freeway ramp metering, carpool lanes, transit reorganization, and land-use policies all have their effects on congestion, but they are small. Anthony Downs (2004) draws a stark conclusion: congestion is here to stay because there is only one policy—road pricing—that can stop it, and the public will not support road pricing. In other words, public policy is at an impasse.

There is a consolation: congestion is self-limiting. It can exist only because people—lots of them—are willing to put up with it. Discourage them enough, and they will remove themselves from the upward pressure of highway use. An equilibrium is thus reached in which the cost of travel, including users' own time, becomes high enough that the demand is kept in check. The trouble with this solution is that it may be a quite unhappy equilibrium, disliked by those affected, politically potent and economically inefficient. Moreover, the functioning of the urban system, broadly conceived as an economic and cultural system aimed to provide enjoyment of life, is compromised.

I offer here a slightly less pessimistic view than that of Downs, focusing on some newer developments in transportation policy and analysis. Some of these make pricing more likely, while others broaden the comfort zone within which pricing and nonpricing innovations might work. While many of these developments are genuinely emerging trends, some are gleams in the eye of this beholder, representing possibilities that I believe are unleashed by the emerging trends but in nonobvious ways.

I first consider the developments related to highway congestion, and then those related to public transit. I conclude with observations about what transportation policy could look like, if things go well.

Highway Congestion

Let us begin with several recent or prospective developments affecting congestion and, more generally, the level of service that highways provide to private and commercial users.

Product Differentiation and Heterogeneous Preferences

Downs's thesis about the impossibility of serious congestion relief is formulated in the context of a homogeneous population. He postulates that people uniformly want to travel in dense areas at peak times, and have common political preferences against such possible ameliorative policies as regional land-use controls, the elimination of housing subsidies, or road pricing. This is of course an abstraction, and I believe a useful one. But recent events have highlighted another aspect of urban life: the heterogeneity of types of users and people's preferences concerning their travel conditions. Accounting for such variety changes the terms of the impasse described by Downs.

Decades ago, urban road managers realized that a highway system's efficiency might be increased by encouraging people to carpool, so that the same number of trips can be served in fewer cars. Thus began an extensive and still ongoing process of restricting certain expressway lanes to carpools. The hope was to stimulate more carpooling, which it does to a small extent. But the primary effect is to lower aggregate passenger travel times by offering faster service to those people, such as

some long-distance commuters to large employment centers, who choose
to carpool for other reasons. (To the dismay of planners, carpool lanes
have also attracted family members, especially parents carrying children,
who would not otherwise be using more than one motorized vehicle.)

The system of carpool lanes is not universally admired, especially
where there is insufficient carpool traffic to keep an entire lane well utilized. In a few cases, carpool lanes have been decommissioned and returned to general use. Joy Dahlgren (1998) notes the rather narrow
range of parameters that lead to carpool lanes meeting commonly applied criteria for success such as high utilization, high level of service,
and savings in aggregate travel time.

Yet interestingly, the system of carpool lanes has opened the door to
a broader notion of how differing levels of service can be offered to
people in different circumstances. In analytic terms, we could say that
with carpool lanes, cars are differentiated by the total value of time they
carry, on the presumption that each passenger values their time enough
so that the aggregate value in a carpool is typically larger than that of a
solo driver. This is a crude form of product differentiation, whereby two
otherwise similar products (expressway travel) are offered with different quality levels.

In other realms of economic life, product differentiation is much more
common and is usually accomplished by pricing. No one thinks twice
about the option to pay more for better theater tickets, faster computers,
nicer restaurants, or first-class seats on airplanes. But public services have
typically not been differentiated, and the provision of infrastructure for
highway travel, because it is typically provided by government agencies, has mistakenly been viewed as another public service—despite the
fact that highway travel lacks the features that normally define public
goods.

Recent events, motivated by quite other considerations, have expanded the idea of product differentiation on roads beyond carpools to
paying more for better quality, just as for other goods. I will explain in
the following subsections how this came about, so here let me just describe the outcome. In several U.S. metropolitan areas, beginning with
Orange County and San Diego (California) and Houston (Texas), express lanes were constructed or converted from carpool lanes, and then
offered not only to carpools but also to solo drivers willing to pay a toll.
In most cases the toll varied quite steeply by the time of day. In each
case the concept was presented as a modification of carpool lanes, either
as an explicit conversion for the purpose of making better use of spare
capacity in an existing carpool lane, or (in Orange County) as a substitute for previous plans to add a carpool lane. (In Orange County, this
change was not welcomed by neighboring Riverside County, where

most of the users live, although there was a sweetener: users of the congested corridor got four new express lanes instead of two.)

These early experiments were encouraged, if belatedly, by a federal program begun in 1991 to support innovative demonstrations of congestion pricing. Finding no takers for the actual implementation of pricing on an entire corridor, the U.S. Federal Highway Administration incorporated these "high occupancy/toll" (HOT) lanes into the program later in the 1990s. Indeed, HOT lanes were so much more popular than congestion pricing that the Congestion Pricing Pilot Program was renamed, changing "Congestion Pricing" to "Value Pricing"—a term originally coined to indicate product differentiation involving pricing, but one that has come to be used synonymously with (or euphemistically for) congestion pricing.

HOT lanes have spread to several other states, and are prominent components of a number of local, state, and federal transportation plans. Robert W. Poole Jr. and C. Kenneth Orski (2003) and Poole and Ted Balaker (2005) develop a nationwide proposal for networks of such lanes, including considerable investments in connecting interchanges so that users could avoid mixing with regular traffic when changing from one HOT route to another. (This feature also is levered off plans for carpool lanes, which in some states involve similarly expensive interchanges, but restricted to carpools.) Their proposal also incorporates bus transit vehicles.

HOT lanes have been joined by some additional instances of new toll roads that serve as congestion relievers. Toll roads have of course existed in many states, sometimes in urban areas, and have provided de facto product differentiation vis-à-vis nonexpress arterials. Recently, though, as urban areas have largely filled in their developed areas with expressway systems, new toll roads serve more often as alternatives not only to arterials but also to other urban expressways. An early example just outside the United States is Highway 407 in the Toronto metropolitan area, opened in 1997, which runs parallel to and just a few miles from the highly congested Queen Elizabeth Way. A more recent instance is E-470, a tolled half beltway connecting heavily developed suburbs north and east of Denver, Colorado, to each other as well as to Denver International Airport. Public opinion shows an increasing, if reluctant, acceptance of such ventures as sources of funding for needed capacity—acceptable because there are reasonably close substitutes that remain free.

The upshot of this activity is that people are becoming used to the idea of tolled facilities offering premium service. Furthermore, dramatic improvements in pricing technology, supported by aggressive corporate development within a dynamic and quite competitive industry, have made it possible to implement far more sophisticated pricing systems.

The market penetration of electronic toll payments has reached well over half on many toll roads, and HOT lane operators increasingly offer toll schedules that assume some sophistication on the part of the users. In a small number of cases, including HOT lanes in the San Diego and Minneapolis regions, pricing is "dynamic": that is, the price is varied in real time, depending on congestion levels in the adjacent lanes, in order to keep the HOT lanes busy yet congestion free. In what came as a surprise to many, users had little trouble adapting to dynamic pricing, and it works smoothly.

Thus, two prerequisites for road pricing—public familiarity and feasible charging technologies—have entered the public realm more or less by accident. In addition, transportation planners are by financial necessity becoming locked into systems that contain priced facilities. It is likely, then, that most current experiments will continue even though a priced facility is occasionally returned to free status, due, for example, to paying off a bond or political problems with a private operator (an example of which is described later).

Privatization

Financial pressures have induced state and local authorities to seek arrangements with private investors to hasten the process of building capacity. There are many institutional forms of private involvement in road finance, ranging from financing a publicly designed road to building and managing the road privately. All of them involve some form of privately provided finance recouped by toll revenues. Usually the arrangement is specified as a franchise that spells out the rights to operate a toll road for a specified period of time with some limitations on tolls, toll increases, or the rate of return to capital.

Private participation in road operations is significant for policy toward congestion for several reasons. First, private investors as well as the financial institutions supporting them through loans have a strong incentive to accurately forecast demand for the road. This raises the level of knowledge about the impacts of a given capacity expansion on the road network and helps steer investment away from projects that benefit only a narrow interest group.

Second, private firms have experience with price setting, and generally understand such important features as price sensitivity, public perceptions, marketing, and the roll of price differentiation. This is precisely the kind of knowledge needed to bring analytic models of price setting into a form that can be implemented practically.

Third, private road operators have a financial incentive to use pricing to manage congestion, which is also the goal of standard congestion-pricing theory. It is well-known in the academic literature that a private road operator, even one with a monopoly, will choose to differentiate prices by the time of day in a manner similar to that called for by standard congestion pricing recommendations (Small and Verhoef 2007, sec. 6.1.1). This is because the private operator can charge higher tolls if it can provide a high level of service by keeping congestion down. In fact, the pricing *structure* (i.e., the pattern of variation by the time of day or other factors determining congestion) will be virtually the same whether it is chosen to provide the greatest revenue or maximize public benefits as normally defined, although the *level* of prices may be substantially higher in the former case. For this reason, as private operators propose, bid on, or negotiate franchise agreements, they will tend to encourage public authorities to consider differentiated toll schemes that might otherwise be ruled out for simplicity, but that in fact can both increase revenue and help manage congestion.

The ability of private operators to capture the benefits of improved efficiency is so strong that even existing toll roads have begun to have their operating rights sold by state or local governments to private investors. Two large sales of this type occurred in recent years: the Chicago Skyway, owned by the city of Chicago, was franchised in 2005, and the Indiana Toll Road was franchised in 2006. These two road segments, which connect to each other, form parts of Interstate 80 and 90, two major east-west routes in the northern United States. Long-term leases were granted in return for up-front payments of $1.8 billion and $3.8 billion, respectively. Although the agreements do not specify time-of-day pricing, they do give the franchisees incentives to adopt road maintenance strategies that better match user preferences. It seems only a matter of time before the financial advantages of price differentiation by the time of day lead to proposals that include such differentiation.

Leasing an existing asset introduces some interesting issues of politics and public finance. The effect is usually to shift control over net revenues from a dedicated toll authority to a political authority, and to shift the timing of these revenues from gradual receipt over many years to a lump sum at the time of the lease. Whether and how this shift is accompanied by controls over spending the revenues can greatly affect transportation funding in current and future years.[1]

Another interesting feature of private highways is that in several cases, private firms have submitted unsolicited proposals for new highways. One notable example is the proposal by a consortium of Fluor Enterprises and Transurban for new HOT lanes on parts of the Washington Beltway and Interstate 395 in Virginia. These notoriously congested roads serve hundreds of thousands of Washington-area users, many of whom have influential positions in national government. Thus, direct consumer experience with private pricing proposals also constitutes experience by policymakers. What is especially relevant about unsolicited proposals is that the private firms are free to suggest pricing schemes that otherwise might never make it through a public bureaucracy.

Private participation in highway capacity, then, not only makes it possible to add capacity more quickly than could be done otherwise. It also brings with it a host of factors favoring the use of pricing for congestion management. Like the experiments in product differentiation described earlier, experiments with privately operated highways may break the impasse that makes congestion so intractable.

Public Attitudes toward Road Pricing and Privatization

Generally, the public does not like road pricing. Most people think that free travel on roads is a traditional and fundamental right (although in fact turnpikes played important roles in earlier centuries). The argument for pricing, moreover, is abstract and involves offsetting the welfare losses directly experienced by individual users with welfare gains in the form of toll revenues, which users may not trust will be spent wisely.

Nevertheless, the various experiments and demonstrations undertaken during the last two decades have resulted in considerable changes in attitudes among the affected users. Many people recognize that the private sector can deliver congestion relief sooner than the public sector and that paying tolls is the price of that accelerated schedule. In areas with HOT lanes, public acceptance has tended to rise over time, often reaching majority support. For example, before the HOT lanes opened in Orange County, about 65 percent of solo drivers approved of providing toll lanes to manage congestion; a year later, 69 to 82 percent of them approved, depending on whether or not they used the toll lanes. Before the project, a smaller proportion of solo drivers, 43 percent, approved of varying the tolls with the severity of congestion; a year later this rose to 60 percent of those continuing to use the free lanes and 73 percent of those using the toll lanes. (Carpoolers generally approved less of these concepts and did not show much change over time.) Approval of the concept of *private companies* operating toll roads rose among nearly all groups, to around 50 percent.[2]

Perhaps the most surprising political development in congestion pricing was the proposal by New York's Mayor Michael Bloomberg for a cordon toll of $8 during daytime hours for entry into Manhattan south of Eighty-sixth Street (except for circumferential travel on designated express arterials on the island's borders). Travel purely within the cordon would be priced at half that amount. This scheme, ultimately killed by the state legislature, attracted substantial funding under the U.S. Department of Transportation's "Urban Partnerships" program designed specifically to promote congestion pricing. Bloomberg's proposal touched off a political saga, which suggested that two significant factors in obtaining support were the availability of federal money and the use of fees to obviate increases in bridge tolls and public transit fares.[3]

Other states have also developed controversial proposals involving changes to highway finance and tolling. The governor of Indiana faced considerable hostility over a long-term lease of the Indiana Toll Road, which will lead to higher tolls. This hostility existed despite the fact that a high fraction of toll payers live in other states; nevertheless the lease did go through. Similar proposals for the New Jersey Turnpike and the Pennsylvania Turnpike have produced strong opposition. The extensive private investment program undertaken by Texas, with its first concession agreement in June 2006 for a new $1.35 billion road, has led to a backlash that seems certain to curtail the extent of planned privatization.[4]

An example illustrates how even successful instances of privatization can be reversed and yet still contribute to the growth in use of tolls to manage traffic congestion. The HOT lanes described earlier in Orange County were originally constructed and operated under a long-term franchise by a private consortium. As noted earlier, the deal creating these lanes was already unpopular in inland Riverside County, where most of its users reside. Two public relations snafus further eroded support for the private operation. First, the private operator made a clumsy attempt to reap a tax windfall by proposing to sell the lanes at a handsome profit to a newly created nonprofit organization, which would be eligible for tax-exempt bond financing. Press exposure revealed a less than fully arm's-length relationship between the seller and the proposed purchaser. Second, severe congestion on the regular (free) lanes of the corridor returned more rapidly than expected following its drastic decline on completion of the express lanes (which expanded capacity in the corridor by about 50 percent). When the California Department of Transportation attempted to add some new capacity under the guise of safety improvements at a merger point, the private operator invoked the noncompete clause in its franchise, which turned out to be one of the most restrictive ever written for a private highway—namely, it prohibited any such expansion and lacked the more common provision for compensation in case of overriding public need. The upshot was that the Orange County Transportation Authority bought out the express lane franchise in 2003. The sale price gave the private operator a healthy profit on its nearly eight-year ownership of the road, and the terms of the loan underwriting the public takeover ensure that pricing

will remain in place for many years. Indeed, as of January 2008, the
price has been raised several more times, making it one of the most
expensive roads per mile of travel in the United States, with a peak rate
of $10 for the ten-mile outbound trip between 3:00 and 4:00 p.m. on
Fridays.[5]

Still, the public is getting used to road prices being among the innovations they are likely to see as policymakers grapple with intractable
congestion. It will become increasingly hard to defeat pricing proposals
on purely ideological grounds, forcing discussion into a more objective
consideration of the actual effects. This enhances the possibility that
pricing proposals with especially high congestion-relief benefits will
get a hearing.

It is also important that analysts in federal, state, and local agencies
are gaining experience with road pricing. Many such agencies have at
least some staff with training in economics, and other staff members
have grown in their ability to understand and assess analyses of economic efficiency. It is now quite common, even routine in some agencies, for a menu of proposals in urban transportation to include pricing.
For example, the U.S. Federal Highway Administration (2006b, xi), in
one of a series of reports to Congress about the condition of the nation's
highway infrastructure and needs for investment, includes the following statement in bold type: "Congestion pricing has the potential to
significantly improve the operational performance of the Nation's highway system, while significantly reducing the level of future capital investment that would be necessary to achieve any specific level of performance." The report goes on to estimate that reduction in needed
capital investment at about $21 billion per year. Two decades ago, such
a statement by a highly visible public agency would have been considered impolitic.

Thus, both citizens and technocrats are giving pricing solutions a
hearing instead of dismissing them out of hand. This raises the chance
that a successful package can be constructed—one that improves efficiency by using price to lower congestion, but still provides overall
benefits that citizens understand and in which they have trust.

Goods Movement

The movement of freight within and through urban areas has long been
a critical part of the economies of urban areas, and a significant requirement of transportation facilities. Freight is increasingly important to
regional and national economies as trucking serves primary distributional roles for interregional and international shipments, often entering through water ports. The four largest U.S. ports alone—New Or-

leans, Houston, New York, and Los Angeles/Long Beach—handled 710 million tons of traffic in 2004; one-fifth of this, valued at $442 billion, involved international trade.[6] Much freight traffic originating at ports travels by truck and/or rail via the urban infrastructure to inland destinations, some of it passing again through urban hubs such as Chicago. (The Chicago region generates an estimated thirty-five hundred truck trips per day just connecting its own rail terminals, due to a shortage of connecting rail capacity.)[7]

Trucks impose considerable environmental and safety costs in the form of air pollution (especially particulates, which are the most clearly documented causes of severe health effects), noise, and collision damage to passenger vehicles. The explosion of port activity accompanying the recent expansion of global trade has accentuated these problems, and focused many residents and policymakers on finding alternatives to the large truck volumes found on some urban corridors, such as those serving the ports of Long Beach and Los Angeles.

One outcome of these factors is an interest in truck-only roads or lanes, frequently conceived as new capacity to be built for the dual purposes of congestion relief and channeling truck traffic to where it is less harmful (Poole 2007). Usually truck-only lanes are planned as toll facilities, either because they are proposed for accelerated investment or simply on the grounds of equity. The trucking industry typically has opposed special road charges aimed at it, but it has shown more flexibility toward truck-only toll lanes provided they are not made mandatory by prohibiting trucks from other highways. The outcome of attempts to deal with the special and growing needs of freight transportation could be another type of differentiated highway service, offering premium service for those freight movements for which the faster and more reliable travel are worth the payments.

Local distributional activity by trucks also creates significant problems for the urban transportation system, especially the congestion resulting from loading and unloading. Shippers' desires for rapid and predictable deliveries, combined with carriers' attempts to minimize labor costs, may lead to larger vehicles on dense city streets than would be efficient from an overall system point of view. Local businesses depend on such deliveries and often strongly resist efforts to regulate them in the interests of traffic management. This can greatly complicate the politics of congestion.

Highway Design Standards

The increased importance of product variety and differentiation casts doubt on some long-standing assumptions about design standards for highways. Furthermore, some standards that made sense when most travel was intended to be under free-flowing conditions are inappropriate to high-density urban settings where congestion must and should be common even under ideal policies.

Perhaps the clearest example of problematic design standards is the U.S. Interstate Highway System. Interstate highways are expected to meet nationwide standards for lane width, sight distance, grade, shoulders, and other characteristics (American Association of State Highway and Transportation Officials 2005). But simple economics suggests that where land costs, construction costs, and traffic volumes are high, one should trade off costly features like lane widths, shoulders, and long sight distances for more capacity whenever possible. In other words, those design features that provide better safety and ride quality at high speeds become less important relative to those that increase throughput at moderate (congested) speeds.

Another way to look at this is in terms of an equilibration of travel times across different types of highways. When the overall capacity of an urban traffic system is in heavy use, there will be a tendency for higher-quality roads to become congested more severely than others until their levels of service are equalized. This simple equilibrium concept is exposited in a highly stylized form by Arthur C. Pigou (1920) and more generally for urban traffic by Downs (1962). To the extent that it is valid, the extra expense incurred to improve design speeds on major roads has no payoff during congested periods, whereas anything to improve capacity has a huge payoff. In heavily congested urban areas, most people experience these roads under congested, not free-flow, conditions, and so the need for capacity should dominate the design process.

A simple example is lane width. The standard twelve-foot-wide lanes of U.S. interstate highways provide safety margins for roads carrying mixed traffic of cars and trucks at high speeds, and often under difficult conditions of weather and terrain. On most urban commuting corridors, trucks are fewer and it is practical to limit speeds to well below those of intercity travel. Indeed, urban expressway expansions are sometimes carried out by converting some shoulders into travel lanes and restriping all lanes to be narrower—sometimes to an eleven-foot width. But if the road has an interstate highway designation, exemptions are required, and these may be considered temporary until a fuller and more expensive reconstruction can be undertaken.

Even if pricing were in place to limit congestion, optimal speeds would be far from free-flow during much of the day. Theodore E. Keeler and Kenneth A. Small (1977) analyze the trade-off between capital expense and road capacity for congestion reduction, using the construction costs and speed-flow relationships estimated for the San Francisco Bay Area. They find that in the two main central cities of that area, San Francisco and Oakland, optimal speeds during the four busiest hours would be about fifty miles per hour with congestion pricing in place. Without pricing, the optimal speed would surely be lower. In today's most congested cities, with land costs much higher than those observed by Keeler and Small, the optimal speed for an expressway is probably lower still.

Many of the aesthetic and environmental objections to urban expressways are related to their size and visibility, which are magnified by designs permitting safe travel at very high speeds. To the extent that aesthetics carry extra weight in urban areas because they affect more people, those considerations also argue for reducing the free-flow speed for which roads are designed. Even speed itself is an environmental factor due to tire and engine noise, which become so severe that large expenditures are sometimes undertaken for sound walls and extra sound insulation on nearby homes. Lower-speed road designs could reduce these expenditures.

Peter Samuel (2006) documents a wide variety of innovative ways that capacity can be added to urban road networks in a more environmentally and aesthetically friendly manner. These include advanced intersection designs and tunnels. Tunnels carry urban express traffic in Oslo, Sydney, and other cities, and are now planned for the completion of missing links in the Long Beach Freeway near Los Angeles and the A86 ring road around Paris. In the Paris case, where the missing section will pass under the historic palace of Versailles, the planned car-only design permits high capacity with ten-foot lanes, low clearances, and a speed limit of forty-three miles per hour (Samuel 2006, 19). Tunnels are an attractive option for many urban motor vehicle movements, but the high cost of a large cross-section makes it especially important to plan for low speeds and limited vehicle sizes.

While exotic highway designs offer promise, conventional designs already exist for carrying substantial volumes at moderate speeds, in the range of forty to fifty miles per hour, while presenting a much less obtrusive public face. Lakeshore Drive in Chicago provides service at such speeds most of the time while preserving the Lake Michigan frontage as a mark of the city's beauty. Storrow Drive in Boston similarly offers substantial capacity at moderate speeds without ruining the landscape. Neither road meets interstate highway standards, nor do they allow urbanites to cross vast developed areas in an hour. Some older parkways, such as the Arroyo Seco in Los Angeles and the Merritt Parkway in Connecticut, similarly fall below some modern interstate standards and operate in an uneasy compromise, having historic as well as scenic value (the Arroyo Seco Parkway is a National Scenic Byway), but being overloaded and therefore under pressure for safety upgrades that make them more like conventional freeways.[8]

A few cities have moved to upgrade their major arterial streets to "superstreets," which provide a level of service closer to that of limited-access highways by means of turn lanes, traffic signal coordination, under- or overpasses at key intersections, and the like. The most essential (and expensive) component is improved intersections, for which a number of innovations have been proposed, including some that conserve on land consumption (Samuel 2006, 48–61). A key consideration of such proposals will be to demonstrate they are safer than conventional arterials, which have substantially higher accident rates than freeways.

Many of the roads built to such intermediate standards do not accommodate large trucks. Indeed, evidence suggests that accommodating trucks adds 30 to 60 percent to the cost of an urban road.[9] For tunnels, the savings are potentially larger because a given cross-sectional area can handle two to three times as many lanes for cars as for mixed traffic (Poole and Sugimoto 1995, fig. 1). A move to make lower-profile roads a larger portion of our high-capacity road network will undoubtedly raise objections from truckers, who like to maintain full routing flexibility. But trucks are a minority of traffic, especially during rush hours, and their needs add greatly to the aesthetic and environmental problems of the roads that carry them. It simply does not make sense to build the entire network around trucks. Instead, it is better to apply the principle of differentiated products, and offer some roads well suited to trucks and others well suited to handling massive peaked flows of passengers.

An important part of making future cities livable is to provide mobility through designs that are both aesthetically and economically sensible. An interesting by-product would be that even when supplying the same level of service, such roads would be perceived as only moderately rather than severely congested—simply because there would be a smaller gap between the actual and potential speed. The most common measure of time lost in congestion is precisely this gap (Schrank and Lomax 2007); by this measure, the quickest way to reduce congestion would be to lower the speed limit on all expressways. That of course would be perceived as artificial, but road designs that carry current traffic volumes in a more aesthetic manner might indeed be seen as providing better service (i.e., less deteriorated due to congestion) even if at the same speed as now.

Research on the comparative costs of high-capacity roads designed for different speeds and vehicle sizes is needed before any firm recommendation can be made. Equally pressing is a better understanding of their safety implications. But safety depends on many factors besides road designs, leading to a further question: If roads are designed to be safe only at moderate speeds, can we prevent people from choosing higher speeds, thereby compromising their own and others' safety? Attempts to retain the scenic character of the Arroyo Seco Parkway, mentioned earlier, have foundered partly on this problem. Rather than simply accept driver behavior as a given, we should consider what public policies might be undertaken, in conjunction with road design changes, to encourage compatible driver behavior. One such policy is to introduce visual clues that cause drivers to slow down. Another is to regulate speed (or other behavior) differently from how it is done today. I will now consider this latter approach in more detail.

The Regulation of Driver Behavior

Imagine a visitor from another planet with a highly organized society possessing technologies similar to ours. Governments on this planet provide a variety of transportation services, facing similar trade-offs between cost and quality as we do. They offer mass transportation in scheduled vehicles, and also more individualized transportation in vehicles carrying one person or a small number of people traveling together. The planet's residents undergo occasional tragic accidents, just as we do, but these incidents affect only a small proportion of trips and are accepted as one of the costs of living, albeit one they try constantly to reduce.

You might think this visitor would feel quite at home in any of Earth's developed countries. But the visitor is struck by a disparity that seems incomprehensible. Although our rail and air transportation is carefully organized with elaborate attention to coordination among vehicles, our personal vehicles are subject to no such control other than some rudimentary signal lights (roughly the same technology introduced on railroads in the early 1900s). Could it be, the visitor wonders, that Earth has substituted intensive driver training of all its citizens for the technological measures with which this other planet manages its many small vehicles? Inquiry reveals that no, we lack such training; indeed, the disparity of habits and methods used by our drivers is quite astounding. How could it be that with such advanced technology, we have failed to apply it to reduce the rate of accidents and traffic interferences that differentiate our highways from the smoothly functioning system familiar to our visitor?

The answer presumably lies in political attitudes, social norms, and the history of our highway transportation system. We in fact have the

technology to carry out many forms of driver regulation that would reduce accidents and improve traffic flow. Speed "governors" have been
used on certain commercial vehicles for decades. Controlled braking has
become standard equipment on many vehicles, and gap control between
vehicles is now offered on some models as an option to reduce rear-end
collisions. Mobile communications, used for toll collection as well as
driver information and guidance, would make it possible to activate
such devices according to a centralized traffic management plan.

Such centralized control would assuredly come at considerable cost.
But not necessarily more so than current systems, such as route guidance, that are rapidly gaining in open markets. Furthermore, the cost of
a centralized system of vehicle management is unknown because no
one has seriously proposed it. Drivers' choice of speed, acceleration,
lane movements, and expressive gestures (up to a point) have traditionally been viewed as part of freedom of movement, and controls on them
would likely be derided as "social engineering."

Yet it seems quite possible that such controls would permit just the
kind of more favorable trade-offs discussed in the previous subsection,
by which capacity could be increased while limiting the accompanying
land consumption and aesthetic impact, not to mention the pollution
and fuel consumption resulting from thousands of vehicles all trying to
gain an edge on each other in the competition for road space. Specifically, it seems the main factor preventing more widespread acceptance
of curved, narrow-lane highways is that they are considered unsafe. En-
forceable limits on speed and lane-change maneuvers would reduce or
eliminate this disadvantage while increasing the maximum throughput
possible on a given pavement.

Clearly, any such proposal today would face a skeptical reaction at
best. But might we see such a change in attitudes in the future, even in
a nation devoted to individual freedom? I think it is possible. People
accept considerable intrusion into their freedom of movement in the interests of security (airport check-in procedures), safety (drunk-driver
laws), and as already argued, optional premium service (tolled express
lanes). They also accept data collection on their movements when it suits
their convenience (mobile phones, credit card records, and electronic toll
collection). What is needed is a demonstration of direct, perceptible
benefits from accepting moderate limitations. One way to accomplish
this would be to construct optional, premium-service roadways available only to vehicles equipped so as to be part of a traffic management
system, including speed control.

An important by-product of such an innovation would be improvements in our record of motor vehicle crashes. Although large gains have
been made in terms of reducing crash rates (per vehicle mile traveled),

motor vehicle accidents remain one of the largest categories of costs of driving: $0.12 per vehicle mile by one estimate, or about one-seventh of the total short-run average variable cost for a typical U.S. urban work trip during rush hour, including the cost of travel time, unreliability, and vehicle capital.[10] Indeed, it appears that driving is the most danger-ous activity undertaken regularly by most people. A public relations campaign that demonstrates both the safety and congestion-relief bene-fits from a program of voluntary limitations on driver behavior could have considerable appeal.

Public Transit

Public transit in the United States plays a key role in supporting large employment clusters, serving lower-income populations, and facilitat-ing tourism. But it carries far fewer people than automobiles, and its share of trips has declined inexorably since the years soon after World War II. The main reasons for this decline appear to be rising incomes and the widespread decentralization of employment and residences; sec-ondary but still important reasons include strong federal support for the Interstate Highway System, tax and housing policies that favor single-family residences, zoning restrictions on high-density housing, tax poli-cies favoring free or highly subsidized parking at workplaces, low gaso-line taxes compared to most developed nations, and little explicit pricing of highways. John F. Kain (1999) and Small and José A. Gómez-Ibáñez (1999) describe these factors in more detail.

A lot of money has been put into transit service in the last half cen-tury. Much of it is motivated by a desire to use transit to lure drivers off congested highways. In the United States, these efforts have met with limited success. Yet even where successful in diverting auto users, the expansion of transit has not been the hoped-for solution to congestion. A primary reason for this is the existence of "latent demand" for peak-period road use in large and highly congested urban areas. Many people have been deterred by congestion itself from traveling when and where they would most prefer. Whenever new road space is opened up by a successful diversion to transit, some of the latent demand becomes again realized, tending to fill up the road space. The result is only small, if any, improvement in peak conditions, although there may be substan-tial benefits to the individuals involved.

There is little prospect that public transit will ever return to being a dominant force in urban transportation in the United States. Still, there are several ways in which its use can be expanded and its value can be raised. These changes in turn would raise the attractiveness of cities as places to live and visit, and would help marginally to ease the pressure of highway congestion.

Specialization

The same forces of differentiation discussed in connection with highway transportation affect public transit as well. People served by transit are different from each other. Probably transit's two most important markets are affluent suburbanites traveling to downtown business destinations and poor residents traveling within inner cities (Meyer and Gómez-Ibáñez 1981). This differentiation in markets creates a need for more differentiation of products.

That need is accentuated by the strong scale economies that characterize scheduled services in large vehicles, as demonstrated by Herbert Mohring (1972). These economies arise from two sources: the savings in operator costs if vehicles become more fully utilized, and the savings in user costs associated with accessing transit vehicles if service is increased. These user costs include walking or driving to transit stops, waiting for a vehicle, and making transfers between transit lines—all of which can be decreased, if more vehicles are in service within a given area, by increasing the spatial density of transit lines and the frequency of service on each line.

These scale economies arise from higher rider density within a given area. As a result, standard transit service is well suited for offering frequent and densely packed service in areas with high rider density, but is poorly suited to offer service where rider density is low.

Hence, product differentiation and scale economies lead to a common conclusion: transit operators should specialize. They should seek their strongest markets and pour intensive resources into them, including marketing resources and supportive political actions such as high-density zoning near large transit stations. Weaker markets should not be served at all, or should be served mostly using some model other than regularly scheduled vehicles.

Unfortunately, trends since the 1950s have been in the opposite direction (Wachs 1989; Garrett and Taylor 1999). Many transit agencies today are large, multijurisdictional conglomerates subject to bureaucratic and political pressures to homogenize their service. To a great extent, this is a by-product of the public takeovers of financially failing private firms following the precipitous decline in ridership in the 1950s and 1960s, as ownership of single-family homes and automobiles surged. Such takeovers were often accompanied by the consolidation of several transit systems into a single large one. The result has been metropolitan-wide transit authorities, which in order to achieve the necessary political sup-

port in widely dispersed jurisdictions, have tried to offer at least rudimentary service everywhere. This is just the opposite of specialization.

Abandoning low-density markets will raise strong protests, of course,
some of them pointing to inequities and harm to particular disadvantaged groups. Indeed, these markets frequently contain groups—
including poor, physically handicapped, and elderly residents who
cannot feasibly use private automobile—that society apparently deems
worth supporting even at a considerable cost. Finding a type of transit
appropriate to such groups has proven a challenge. Demand-responsive
transit, consisting of small buses or vans dispatched according to pre-
arranged requests, is one way, but it has been expensive, and in the
United States has largely become a service solely for the elderly and
handicapped. New dispatching algorithms may be helping these services, and have been demonstrated even for general use in a few sites in
Europe.[11] In many situations, shared-ride taxi service would be a relatively economical approach if institutional barriers can be overcome.

The point is that serving low-volume markets with standard scheduled service is costly and not an economical way to take care of special
needs. Even offering free or highly subsidized taxi service to target
populations would often be less expensive. Meanwhile, by focusing
service on those markets where demand is strong, transit operators can
take advantage of scale economies, and create the kind of frequent service and dense route coverage that can entice people to view public
transit as a real alternative to private automobiles, rather than as an occasional convenience.

The Role of Buses

A focus on high-density markets raises the question of the appropriate
type of transit vehicle. Large cities worldwide have, of course, found
rail transit to be a vital part of their transportation system. But does rail
transit make sense for the second tier of city sizes or, in the largest cities,
for service in lower-density suburbs?

Many studies over the last forty years have compared the costs of rail
transit with those of other modes providing similar service (Small and
Gómez-Ibáñez 1999). They have found that for nearly all situations in
the United States where rail transit does not already exist, buses can
supply essentially the same amount of service as rail at far less cost.
These arguments have been instrumental in a few cases in causing city
governments to scale back ambitious rail plans—for example, in Honolulu in the 1970s and Houston in the 1980s. Yet these decisions tend to
be reversed later (Houston opened a light-rail system in 2004). Meanwhile, many cities large and small, serving areas dense and not so dense,

have opted for rail systems. There are many reasons: pressures from private interest groups such as downtown landowners, the desire to enhance a city's public image, the advantages of rail in terms of comfort and convenience to users, and support from federal grants.

Recent innovations in the design of bus transit have to some extent overcome each of these reasons for preferring a more expensive rail system. These innovations are loosely known as "bus rapid transit," designating a variety of initiatives giving bus transit some of the characteristics usually associated with rail. These characteristics include specialized boarding stations, off-vehicle fare payment, fixed and well-publicized routes, real-time information at stations, restricted rights-of-way, preferential signal timing, low-emitting vehicles powered by electricity or natural gas, and marketing.

The prototype bus rapid transit system is that of Curitiba, Brazil, which carries close to two million passengers daily. Larger South American cities, including São Paulo (Brazil) and Bogotá (Columbia), have also built major systems—São Paulo runs four hundred buses per hour during the peak time and carries over thirty thousand passengers per hour (International Energy Agency 2002). There are also substantial long-standing exclusive buses operating in Ottawa and Pittsburgh, and a new line in Los Angeles with grade-level intersections that opened in 2005.

Several cities in the United States and Canada have recently designated new bus rapid transit lines as upgrades to existing bus routes. The early results on two Los Angeles lines showed increases in the average travel speed of roughly 25 percent, to about fourteen miles per hour on the busy Wilshire corridor (Levinson et al. 2003, sec, III.B); an express service (stopping only at selected locations) was subsequently introduced on Wilshire to provide a faster option. In Vancouver, three regular bus routes were upgraded to rapid bus transit status between 1996 and 2002, also achieving a reported overall speed of fourteen miles per hour in two cases (BRT at TRB! 2005). The move to bus rapid transit connects also to privatization: recent federal legislation has created the Public-Private Partnership Pilot Program, affectionately known as Penta-P, which will consider proposals for bus rapid transit from Houston and Atlanta.[12]

What these experiments have in common is an attempt to focus resources on a small number of bus lines in order to dramatically improve their level of service. This focus mimics what happens when a new rail line is built. It is also exactly what the specialized markets and the scale economies that characterize urban transit demand. Bus rapid transit therefore offers a promising prospect for making public transit an economical yet vital part of urban life in an advanced highway-oriented economy like that of the United States.

Subsidies

Two features of urban transit create a strong case for subsidizing it (Kerin 1992). The first is the scale economies characterizing transit costs when the user costs are included, as already described. When the average cost declines as a function of usage, each new user costs less than the average to the overall system (including other users), so it makes sense to encourage such users with fares set below the average cost. The other feature is the underpricing of peak-hour automobile travel, which is a substitute mode for public transit. This underpricing creates an inefficient amount of traffic congestion; thus setting transit fares below cost, especially during peak periods, may be desirable to entice drivers off congested highways. Small and Erik T. Verhoef (2007, sec. 4.5.1) provide a more formal treatment of these two arguments for transit subsidies.

Working against the case for subsidizing transit is the strong evidence that a large portion of transit subsidies has been absorbed in higher costs to transit agencies (Pickrell 1983; Lave 1991; De Borger and Kerstens 2000). Much of the higher costs have been in the form of higher wages, mainly for drivers through union negotiations. One might regard this type of higher cost as a transfer payment and so not strictly a social cost, although it is socially wasteful if it results in using higher-skilled workers than needed for the job. But to the extent that subsidy payments are funded by taxes with adverse effects on economic efficiency, even transfer payments exact a cost. Furthermore, some of the higher costs are in the form of less efficient operations, more administrative overhead, and a bias toward a higher-than-efficient ratio of capital to other inputs in producing transit services.

Hence, transit subsidies pose a dilemma: there are sound economic reasons for subsidies, yet too much of them may be wasted in unnecessary expenditures.

A possible resolution to this dilemma is offered by the tentative moves toward more pricing of highways, as discussed earlier. The quantitative evidence suggests that of the two rationales for transit subsidies just described, diverting drivers from congested roads justifies much larger subsidies than scale economies (Van Dender and Proost 2004; Parry and Small 2007). If congested roads are priced at the marginal cost, the rationale based on congested roads disappears. In a world with road pricing, it therefore may be possible to offer efficient transit service even while greatly reducing current transit subsidies.

Small (2004) provides an example of how a virtuous circle can magnify the positive effect that road pricing has on transit use, using congestion charging in central London as a case in point. An immediate impact of road pricing is, of course, to divert drivers to public transit as a substitute mode. This then creates a cycle of new impacts. First, the new riders provide new fare revenue for the transit operator. Second, the transit operator can now economically expand service offerings to handle the new ridership, which in turn reduces user costs for existing riders. Third, new riders are attracted by better service offerings, creating additional rounds of service improvements and diverting yet more drivers from congested roads. (This latter diversion is not necessarily a net social benefit, since now those roads are priced and so the diversion entails lost revenue; but it does support the goal of reducing road congestion.) At the same time, where transit vehicles share street space with cars, reduced congestion improves service quality and substantially reduces labor costs. Over a longer period, the changes in transit use can also encourage land-use changes in the form of transit-friendly development, thereby extending the number of people for whom transit is an attractive service.

Congestion pricing on roads thus supports not only the goal of congestion relief but also that of transit finance. Furthermore, road pricing makes it economical to increase transit service; this stands in contrast to attempts to increase transit service as a mechanism to divert auto drivers, which tends to falter by inducing a realization of latent demand, as described earlier. One could say that rather than looking to transit to solve the problems of highway congestion, a task to which it is inadequate, we should turn to road pricing as a way of resolving the financial dilemmas of public transit. Happily, it does this as a by-product of its main function, which is to efficiently reduce road congestion.

A more prosaic solution is to structure subsidies to minimize the adverse effects on operating costs. "User-side subsidies" are one way to do this: that is, calculate subsidies based on the number of users rather than on the costs of serving them. This is equivalent to giving the subsidies in the form of a payment to the users—for example, a stated amount per ride. The operator then has an incentive to provide service valued by the users in order to attract them, and no incentive to increase the costs.

Privatization

Transit operations have recently been subjected to numerous experiments aimed at using the private sector to improve performance. Here, I discuss the main categories and a few examples; Christopher A. Nash (2005) and Matthew G. Karlaftis (2007) offer more thorough reviews.

A simple form of privatization is contracting out. The public authority retains control over what services are offered, but some of those services are delegated to private firms under specific contractual terms. For example, London Transport contracted with private bus operators as part of British bus deregulation during the 1980s. This approach has also been used in Santiago, Chile (Gwilliam 2005), and in Bogotá, Columbia (Estache and Gómez-Lobo 2005). Contracting out has been used extensively in the United States since the late 1970s (Frick, Taylor, and Wachs 2007), Australia since the early 1990s, and many other nations. Most such contracts have proceeded relatively smoothly, although there are some notable exceptions such as Melbourne, Australia, where financial failures and poor service have been attributed by at least one observer to poorly structured incentives in the contracts (Mees 2005).

Going somewhat further, the public authority can franchise some of these services by licensing private firms to operate them under less specific guidelines. Performance goals may be mandated or encouraged through incentives, including the prospect of favorable consideration for later renewal of the franchise. Such franchises are usually controversial; they allow more room for private initiative than contracting out, but they also are subject to contract disputes, strategic renegotiations, and the abandonment of obligations by a financially failing firm.

Most examples of franchising in public transportation have been for regional rail service, notably in the United Kingdom and Sweden. Starting in 2003, however, the London Underground has franchised the maintenance and upgrading of its infrastructure and vehicles to two private companies—over the strenuous objections of the mayor of London and his commissioner for transport, and also leading to some safety problems.[13] As with many franchising arrangements, a big motivation for the London Underground private initiative was to accelerate a capital improvement program that, by all accounts, was urgently needed due to years of underfunding during public operation.

Going further still, the public authority can simply turn over certain transit-service markets to private industry. The industry may be regulated like other public utilities or it may be opened to free entry on the assumption that competition will produce a desirable result just as for other goods in a largely market economy. Just as with other businesses serving the public, regulatory oversight of such things as safety and financial disclosure can be maintained. Urban bus transit in Great Britain outside of London was deregulated in the 1980s, as was transit service in New Zealand in the early 1990s.

Because of scale economies, it is likely that just one or a few firms in a given area will provide service, even in a privatized system. Will the mere threat of entry cause incumbent firms to act competitively? The limited empirical evidence suggests not. For instance, Andrew Evans (1988) describes the experience in Hereford, England, where transit service was deregulated beginning in 1981. There was a brief period of intense competition, but then the dominant firm drove out all its rivals except in one small segment of its market. The fares ultimately returned nearly to the levels that prevailed prior to the experiment, although the service levels remained substantially higher—perhaps a remnant of the effectiveness of the threat of competitive entry.

Many researchers have investigated whether private or public firms operate more efficiently. The results are ambiguous (Karlaftis 2007). It appears that the key to efficiency is well-structured management incentives, and that these can be achieved under either public or private ownership, at least in some circumstances. The United States is somewhat behind the rest of the world in undertaking the more thoroughgoing types of privatization of public transit, which may be a problem because some observers have argued strenuously that U.S. institutions cause the country's public transit operations to be especially inefficient (Winston and Shirley 1998). As experience accumulates, it should be possible to use private firms in appropriate ways to improve the efficiency of transit.

Conclusion: A Road Map for Urban Transportation Policy

Policymakers can take advantage of the shifting terrain on which urban transportation operates through a number of steps. Taking any of them will help. Taking all of them would inaugurate a revolutionary change that would greatly improve urban life.

1. *Encourage innovations in highway pricing.* In some cases, the direct benefits of a specific measure are not large. For example, models of priced express lanes suggest that when the express lanes are kept operating at free-flow speeds, the net benefits are small compared to letting the same lanes operate as general-purpose lanes (Small and Yan 2001; Verhoef and Small 2004). But such express-lane innovations are typically improvements over the actual situation preceding them, which usually involved less capacity or express lanes restricted to carpools. Moreover, these innovations are leading to more thoroughgoing proposals, including proposals to price all the lanes in a corridor.

2. *Expand highway pricing to an entire corridor or area.* The same evidence just mentioned suggests that a fully priced corridor offers much greater benefits than a partially priced one. This remains true even if the price is set lower than optimal to meet political goals (Small, Winston, and Yan 2006). The cordon pricing of an entire downtown business dis-

trict, along the lines of London and Stockholm, also may be possible in a few U.S. cities with dense downtowns, such as Manhattan, San Francisco, and Washington, DC.

3. *Seek better trade-offs between efficiency and public appeal for pricing schemes.* Small, Clifford Winston, and Jia Yan (2006) study a series of pricing policies for a freeway corridor with express lanes. The pure express-lane policies tend to have small net benefits, whereas optimal congestion pricing has large benefits but high prices that inhibit public support. They offer a policy that prices all lanes, at differential rates, with the lower-priced lanes at a low rate designed to strictly limit the direct costs incurred by users. This type of policy may be the compromise needed to enable pricing to extend beyond just a few selected express lanes.

4. *Encourage private participation in highways with good franchise terms.* Private highway finance has entered the United States in a big way, but most of it is for conventional toll roads. If franchise terms are made flexible, bidders will find ways to use flexible pricing to everyone's advantage. Innovative private operations will involve firms taking on demand risk, so it is important to give them enough pricing flexibility to have some control over this risk. Regulation is still needed, but with a soft touch—allowing latitude for price differentiation while regulating overall revenues (or profits) to avoid the abuse of monopoly power.

5. *Pursue highway designs that emphasize high capacity at moderate speeds and with an environmentally friendly footprint.* Urban road designers should be allowed to sacrifice free-flow speed and the ability to handle large vehicles in favor of the high throughput of passenger vehicles. If curves or lane widths present safety hazards at high speeds, they should be encouraged to offer options in which electronic speed control on these corridors is used in return for fast and reliable service.

6. *Encourage niche transit.* Private entrepreneurs have proven adept at finding profitable transit markets, even when it is illegal for them to do so (Cervero 1997). Public transit authorities should be forced to encourage such competition with their systems, rather than to outlaw them or drive them out of business using predatory tactics, as happened in Los Angeles in the early 1980s (Teal and Nemer 1986).

7. *Break up large metrowide transit providers by spinning off those serving lower-density areas.* Low-density transit service is a drag on the finances of big-city transit operators. There may be reasons to subsidize such service, but any such decision needs to be taken on its merits and not as part of a quid pro quo for keeping the larger operator afloat. Services for low densities and populations with special needs should look quite different from regular transit service, typically involving small vehicles with flexible scheduling, and therefore need not be provided by the same agency.

8. *Configure federal capital-grant programs to encourage bus rapid transit.* Currently the U.S. Department of Transportation is doing just this, but it is a political decision that can easily change. Legislators tend to like big visible projects to showcase their accomplishments, and rail has served this purpose, yet at great expense. Meanwhile, many U.S. bus operations are starved for funds. Bus rapid transit offers a solution by making visible and attractive improvements at a modest cost.

9. *Use open-ended user-side subsidies to improve incentives for public providers to control costs.* Transit policy is caught on the horns of a dilemma, in which needed subsidies are hijacked through union wage increases and/or operator inefficiencies. One way to lessen this tendency is to make the subsidies proportional to ridership, thereby forcing the agency to do everything it can to keep riders happy.

Notes

The author is grateful to Robert Inman, Charles Lave, Robert Poole Jr., and Martin Wachs for helpful comments on earlier drafts of this chapter. All responsibility for the contents lies with the author.

1. The Chicago Skyway lease provided up-front funds to the city of Chicago for general use. For the Indiana Toll Road, authorizing legislation places the proceeds in a ten-year highway improvement fund. The governor of Pennsylvania proposed to place proceeds from a lease of the Pennsylvania Turnpike in a transportation endowment fund of an indefinite lifetime, whose earnings would support transportation improvements.

2. These numbers are estimated from Sullivan (1998 figures 6-1, 6-3, 6-12). Updates (Sullivan 2000) show that these approval ratings subsequently dropped substantially, probably due to some controversial actions of the private toll operator described later.

3. See Schaller (2006); Bindrim (2007); Congestion Pricing Deadline (2007). For more details on the proposal, see Grynbaum (2007).

4. The Texas legislature voted overwhelmingly in May 2007 for a series of limitations including a two-year moratorium on new franchise agreements and restrictions on the terms that can be offered. About the same time, a multibillion-dollar agreement for the extension of a toll road north of Dallas was reopened to allow a competing bid by the public toll road authority in the region. See Texas Toll Moratorium Hodgepodge (2007); "Price Check" Bid Upsets Cintra's Texas SH 121 Deal (2007).

5. The toll schedule is available at http://www.91expresslanes.com/toll schedules.asp. Generally the inbound peak tolls, which occur during the morning, are only about half as large as the outbound peak tolls.

6. U.S. Census Bureau (2006, tables 1043, 1061).

7. McCarron and LaBelle (2002, 1).

8. The Arroyo Seco Parkway, opened in stages between 1938 and 1953, was

originally considered a model of safety with its eleven-foot lanes and speed limit of forty-five miles per hour. Renamed the Pasadena Freeway after various upgrades, it now carries nearly five times its original design volume and, with its original tight curves but a speed limit of fifty-five miles per hour, is one of the most accident-prone of Southern California freeways. A community task force in the 1990s spearheaded the freeway's designation as a National Scenic Byway and recommended a return to the original speed limit. See Loukaitou-Sideris and Gottlieb (2003).

9. Meyer, Kain, and Wohl (1965, 204–6) present data suggesting that a cars-only expressway would cost 77 percent of a mixed-traffic expressway (as calculated by Keeler and Small 1977, 8). Dehnert and Prevedouros (2004) find that an underpass at an arterial intersection costs 61 percent of one that accommodates trucks, mainly due to shorter length and lower clearance.

10. The cost estimates are from Small and Verhoef (2007, table 3.3). The rate of motor vehicle accidents per million vehicle miles declined from 11.7 in 1980 to 3.7 in 2004, during which time the rate of traffic fatalities (within thirty days of an accident) fell from 0.033 to 0.014 (U.S. Census Bureau 2006, tables 1080, 1082).

11. Computer-aided demand-responsive bus scheduling through a travel dispatch center was implemented through the European Union's SAMPLUS research program in several areas, including at least one that is open to all residents of a moderate-density urban site: Porto Romana (with a population density of thirty-six hundred square kilometers) in the Florence metropolitan area. The Porto Romana service uses flexible routes with predefined stop points and reported an operating cost of 1.69 per trip, not including the dispatch center (Mageean and Nelson 2003). Other demonstration sites had much higher costs per ride, possibly because of a lower density of users.

12. See Federal Transit Gets Back on the PPP Track (2007). The interest in bus rapid transit is now worldwide; see, for example, the thirteen articles in the *Journal of Public Transportation, Special Edition: BRT* (2006). Sydney, Adelaide, and Brisbane in Australia have reported travel-time savings of 37 percent and higher, substantial patronage growth, and perhaps even a positive effect on adjacent property values from introducing bus rapid transit on specific corridors (Currie 2006).

13. See Tubes Untangled (2004); Small and Verhoef (2007, sec. 6.3.4).

References

American Association of State Highway and Transportation Officials. 2005. *A Policy on Design Standards: Interstate System*. 5th ed. Washington, DC: American Association of State Highway and Transportation Officials.

Bindrim, Kira. 2007. Congestion Pricing OK If No Fare Hikes: Poll. NewYork-Business.com, June 19.

BRT at TRB! Bus Rapid Transit Presentations at the 84th Annual TRB Conference. 2005. *BRT Quarterly* 3.01.05:1–4. Tampa, FL: Center for Urban Transportation Research, University of South Florida.

Cervero, Robert. 1997. *Paratransit in America: Redefining Mass Transportation*. Westport, CT: Praeger.

Congestion Pricing Deadline. 2007. *New York Times*, editorial, June 25.

Currie, Graham. 2006. Bus Rapid Transit in Australasia: Performance, Lessons Learned, and Futures. *Journal of Public Transportation, Special Edition: BRT* 9 (3): 1–22.

Dahlgren, Joy. 1998. High Occupancy Vehicle Lanes: Not Always More Effective Than General Purpose Lanes. *Transportation Research* 32B:99–114.

De Borger, Bruno, and Kristiaan Kerstens. 2000. The Performance of Bus-Transit Operators. In *Handbook of Transport Modelling*, ed. David A. Hensher and Kenneth J. Button, 577–95. Amsterdam: Pergamon.

Dehnert, Gregory, and Panos Prevedouros. 2004. Urban Intersection Congestion Reduction with Low Clearance Underpasses: Investigation and Case Study. *ITE Journal* 74:36–47.

Downs, Anthony. 1962. The Law of Peak-Hour Expressway Congestion. *Traffic Quarterly* 6:393–409.

———. 2004. *Still Stuck in Traffic: Coping with Peak-Hour Traffic Congestion*. Washington, DC: Brookings Institution Press.

Estache, Antonio, and Andrés Gómez-Lobo. 2005. Limits to Competition in Urban Bus Services in Developing Countries. *Transport Reviews* 25:139–58.

Evans, Andrew. 1988. Hereford: A Case Study of Bus Deregulation. *Journal of Transport Economics and Policy* 22:283–306.

Federal Transit Gets Back on the PPP Track. 2007. *Public Works Financing* 213 (February): 7.

Frick, Karen Trappenberg, Brian Taylor, and Martin Wachs. 2007. Contracting for Public Transit Services in the United States: Evaluating the Tradeoffs. In *Privatisation and Regulation of Urban Transit Systems*, ed. Andreas Kopp, forthcoming. Proceedings of Roundtable 138, European Conference of Ministers of Transport. Paris: Organization for Economic Cooperation and Development.

Garrett, Mark, and Brian Taylor. 1999. Reconsidering Social Equity in Public Transit. *Berkeley Planning Journal* 13:6–27.

Giuliano, Genevieve. 2004. Land Use Impacts of Transportation Investments. In *The Geography of Urban Transportation*, ed. Susan Hanson and Genevieve Giuliano, 237–73. New York: Guilford Press.

Gramlich, Edward. 1994. Infrastructure Investment: A Review Essay. *Journal of Economic Literature* 32:1176–96.

Grynbaum, Michael M. 2007. New York Pitches "Congestion Pricing" to Federal Officials. *New York Times*, June 26.

Gwilliam, Ken. 2005. Bus Franchising in Developing Countries: Some Recent World Bank Experience. Revised keynote paper presented at the eighth International Conference on Ownership and Regulation of Land Passenger Transport, Rio de Janeiro, Brazil, June 2003. Available at http://siteresources.worldbank.org/INTURBANTRANSPORT/Resources/bus_franch_gwilliam.pdf.

International Energy Agency. 2002. *Bus Systems for the Future: Achieving Sustainable Transport Worldwide*. Paris: International Energy Agency and Organization for Economic Cooperation and Development.

Journal of Public Transportation, Special Edition: BRT. 2006. Vol. 9 (3): 1–257.

Kain, John F. 1999. The Urban Transportation Problem: A Reexamination and Update. In *Essays in Transportation Economics and Policy: A Handbook in Honor of John R. Meyer*, ed. José A. Gómez-Ibáñez, William B. Tye, and Clifford Winston, 359–401. Washington, DC: Brookings Institution Press.

Karlaftis, Matthew G. 2008. Privatisation, Regulation, and Competition: A Thirty-Year Retrospective on Transit Efficiency. In *Privatisation and Regulation of Urban Transit Systems*, ed. Andreas Kopp, forthcoming. Proceedings of Round-table 138, European Conference of Ministers of Transport. Paris: Organization for Economic Cooperation and Development.

Keeler, Theodore E., and Kenneth A. Small. 1977. Optimal Peak-Load Pricing, Investment, and Service Levels on Urban Expressways. *Journal of Political Economy* 85:1–25.

Kerin, Paul D. 1992. Efficient Bus Fares. *Transport Reviews* 12:33–47.

Lave, Charles A. 1991. Measuring the Decline in Transit Productivity in the U.S. *Transportation Planning and Technology* 15:115–24.

Levinson, Herbert, et al. 2003. *Bus Rapid Transit*. Transit Cooperative Research Program report no. 90 (vols. 1 and 2). Washington, DC: Transportation Research Board.

Loukaitou-Sideris, Anastasia, and Robert Gottlieb. 2003. Putting Pleasure Back in the Drive: Reclaiming Urban Parkways for the 21st Century. *Access* 22:2–8. Available at http://www.uctc.net/access/access.asp.

Mageean, Jenny, and John D. Nelson. 2003. The Evaluation of Demand Responsive Transport Services in Europe. *Journal of Transport Geography* 11:255–70.

McCarron, John, and Jim LaBelle. 2002. *Critical Cargo: A Regional Freight Action Agenda for Jobs, Economic Growth, and Quality of Life in Metropolitan Chicago*. Chicago: Metropolitan Planning Council. Available at http://www.metro planning.org/resources/images/criticalCargo.pdf.

Mees, Paul. 2005. Privatization of Rail and Tram Services in Melbourne: What Went Wrong?" *Transport Reviews* 25:433–49.

Meyer, John R., and José A. Gómez-Ibáñez. 1981. *Autos, Transit, and Cities*. Cambridge, MA: Harvard University Press.

Meyer, John R., John F. Kain, and Martin Wohl. 1965. *The Urban Transportation Problem*. Cambridge, MA: Harvard University Press.

Mohring, Herbert. 1972. Optimization and Scale Economies in Urban Bus Transportation. *American Economic Review* 62:591–604.

Nash, Christopher A. 2005. Privatization in Transport. in Button, Kenneth J., and David A. Hensher (eds.)In *Handbook of Transport Strategy, Policy, and Institutions*, ed. Kenneth J. Button and David A. Hensher, 97–113. Amsterdam: Elsevier.

Parry, Ian W. H., and Kenneth A. Small. 2007. Should Urban Transit Subsidies Be Reduced? Working paper 06-07-23, Department of Economics, University of California at Irvine, May. Available at http://www.economics.uci.edu/docs/2006-07/Small-23.pdf.

Pickrell, Don H. 1983. Sources of Rising Operating Deficits in Urban Bus Transit. *Transportation Research Record* 915:18–24.

Pigou, Arthur C. 1920. *The Economics of Welfare*. London: Macmillan.

Poole, Robert W., Jr. 2007. The Case for Truck-Only Toll Lanes. *Public Works Management and Policy* 11:244–49.

Poole, Robert W., Jr., and Ted Balaker. 2005. Design and Evaluation of Nationwide Deployment of Urban Area HOT Networks. March. Washington, DC: Science and Technology Policy Institute, Institute for Defense Analyses. Available at http://www.ida.org/stpi/pages/IDAHOTNetworksReport.pdf.

Poole, Robert W., Jr., and C. Kenneth Orski. 2003. HOT Networks: A New Plan for Congestion Relief and Better Transit. Policy Study 305. Los Angeles: Reason Foundation. Available at http://www.reason.org/ps305.pdf.

Poole, Robert W., Jr., and Yuzo Sugimoto. 1995. Congestion Relief Toll Tunnels. *Transportation* 22:327–51.

"Price Check" Bid Upsets Cintra's Texas SH 121 Deal. 2007. *Public Works Financing* 216 (May): 4–6.

Samuel, Peter. 2006. Innovative Roadway Design: Making Highways More Likeable. Policy Study 348. Los Angeles: Reason Foundation. Available at http://www.reason.org/ps348.pdf.

Schaller, Bruce. 2006. *Battling Traffic: What New Yorkers Think about Road Pricing.* Center for Rethinking Development, report no. 3, December. New York: Manhattan Institute. Available at http://www.manhattan-institute.org/html/rdr_03.htm.

Schrank, David, and Timothy Lomax. 2007. *The 2007 Urban Mobility Report.* College Station: Texas Transportation Institute. Available at http://mobility.tamu.edu/ums/report/.

Small, Kenneth A. 2004. Road Pricing and Public Transport. In *Research in Transport Economics, Vol. 9: Road Pricing: Theory and Evidence*, ed. Georgina Santos, 133–58. Amsterdam: Elsevier.

Small, Kenneth A., and José A. Gómez-Ibáñez. 1999. Urban Transportation. In *Handbook of Regional and Urban Economics, Vol. 3: Applied Urban Economics*, ed. Paul Cheshire and Edwin S. Mills, 1937–99. Amsterdam: North-Holland.

Small, Kenneth A., and Erik T. Verhoef. 2007. *The Economics of Urban Transportation.* London: Routledge.

Small, Kenneth A., Clifford Winston, and Jia Yan. 2006. Differentiated Road Pricing, Express Lanes, and Carpools: Exploiting Heterogeneous Preferences in Policy Design. *Brookings-Wharton Papers on Urban Affairs* 7:53–96.

Small, Kenneth A., and Jia Yan. 2001. The Value of "Value Pricing" of Roads: Second-Best Pricing and Product Differentiation. *Journal of Urban Economics* 49:310–36.

Sullivan, Edward. 1998. *Evaluating the Impacts of the SR 91 Variable-Toll Express Lane Facility: Final Report.* San Luis Obispo: California Polytechnic State University. Available at http://ceenve.calpoly.edu/sullivan/sr91/sr91.htm.

———. 2000. *Continuation Study to Evaluate the Impacts of the SR 91 Value-Priced Express Lanes: Final Report.* San Luis Obispo: California Polytechnic State University. Available at http://ceenve.calpoly.edu/sullivan/sr91/sr91.htm.

Teal, Roger F., and Terry Nemer. 1986. Privatization of Urban Transit: The Los Angeles Jitney Experience. *Transportation* 13:5–22.

Texas Toll Moratorium Hodgepodge. 2007. *Public Works Financing* 216 (May): 6–7.

Tubes Untangled. 2004. *Economist*, March 27, 57.

U.S. Census Bureau. 2006. *Statistical Abstract of the United States: 2007*. Washington, DC: U.S. Census Bureau.

U.S. Federal Highway Administration. 1997. *Highway Statistics Summary to 1995*. Washington, DC: Federal Highway Administration.

———. 2006a. *Highway Statistics 2005*. Washington, DC: Federal Highway Administration. Available at http://www.fhwa.dot.gov/policy/ohpi/hss/index.htm.

———. 2006b. *Status of the Nation's Highways, Bridges, and Transit: Conditions and Performance*. Washington, DC: Federal Highway Administration. Available at http://www.fhwa.dot.gov/policy/2006cpr/.

Van Dender, Kurt, and Stef Proost. 2004. Optimal Urban Transport Pricing in the Presence of Congestion, Economies of Density, and Costly Public Funds. Working paper, Department of Economics, University of California at Irvine.

Verhoef, Erik T., and Kenneth A. Small. 2004. Product Differentiation on Roads: Constrained Congestion Pricing with Heterogeneous Users. *Journal of Transport Economics and Policy* 38:127–56.

Wachs, Martin. 1989. U.S. Transit Subsidy Policy: In Need of Reform. *Science* 244:1545–49.

Winston, Clifford, and Chad Shirley. 1998. *Alternate Route: Toward Efficient Urban Transportation*. Washington, DC: Brookings Institution Press.

4

Space

THE DESIGN OF THE URBAN ENVIRONMENT

WITOLD RYBCZYNSKI

THE UNITED STATES is a large society with a steadily growing and highly mobile population—a demographic condition that has had a dramatic effect on the fortunes of its cities. For example, in 1900, the five largest cities were New York, Chicago, Philadelphia, Saint Louis, and Boston. A hundred years later, only New York and Chicago remain on the list. Los Angeles, which barely figured in the top twenty-five in 1900, is now in second place; Houston is number four, and Phoenix, which in 1900 had barely five thousand inhabitants, has just edged out Philadelphia for fifth place; meanwhile, Boston has dropped to the twenty-third rank and Saint Louis is no longer in even the top fifty. If growth does not— or cannot—occur in one city, it moves to another.[1] According to a recent survey, for instance, from 1990 to 2000 the metropolitan areas of Las Vegas, Charlotte, North Carolina, Austin, Texas, Portland, Oregon, and Atlanta increased their share of college-educated twenty-five to thirty-four year olds, at the expense of Washington, DC, Philadelphia, New York, and Los Angeles (Dewan 2006, A1). The competition between cities appears to be a zero-sum game.

A person's decision to settle in a particular city is influenced by many factors, including employment opportunities, the presence of good schools, and the cost of living. Only slightly less important is the quality of urban life. Unlike housing prices, crime levels, and transportation infrastructure, which can be measured, the environmental quality of a city, which involves ephemeral attributes such as comfort and charm, is difficult—probably impossible—to quantify. Yet there is little doubt that today quality is a crucial urban variable. It has been well documented that in a postindustrial society, a warm climate, adjacency to recreational water, and proximity to wilderness areas are sought-after urban amenities (Wolf 1999, 15–34). The physical urban environment— what's there—likewise plays a role in attracting prospective employers and employees to cities (Florida 2004, 231–32).

Lively public spaces, appealing parks and streets, attractive build-ings, and accessible amenities are not accidents; they are the result of ef-fective design. The last few decades have seen many concepts in city de-sign, such as downtown stadiums, redeveloped waterfronts, and signature museums and concert halls. The design of the urban environ-ment is not a science, however. As cities compete with one another, new concepts often turn into fads. Ideas proliferate before they are tested, and it becomes evident that not all the new ideas are successful, or at least not in all situations.

This lesson of the urban design experiences of the last forty years can be summed up in a pithy observation: "In the long run, it is the demand-side pressures that forge the shape of cities" (Skaburskis 2006, 233). Architects and city planners suggest many different, sometimes ingenious solutions to perceived problems, but it is the marketplace that decides which will succeed and which will fail. Multifamily urban housing, for example, has been proposed in many forms—low-rise clus-ters, mid-rise deck housing, and high-rise towers—but the majority of U.S. households still prefer single-family homes. Since suburbs and ex-urbs have generally proved congenial to commercial home builders, these areas have grown accordingly. Some of this growth is the result of cities' restrictive policies with regard to construction and development. On the other hand, in the last decade, as baby boomers have aged, a small though significant segment of the residential market has shown a definite desire to live in denser surroundings, with concentrated ameni-ties. This has seen growth in smaller communities—especially college towns—and selected big-city downtowns. Municipalities that have provided an attractive physical environment as well as opportunities and incentives—rather than obstacles—to builders and developers have benefited from this reverse migration.

A Little History

Any discussion of design in U.S. cities must begin with a caveat: histor-ically, their design has been governed more frequently by expediency than by artistry. Although towns such as New Orleans, Saint Augustine, Savannah, Williamsburg, Annapolis, and Philadelphia were carefully and often imaginatively conceived by their colonial governors, the new American republic generally spurned elaborate urban plans.[2] The streets of U.S. cities founded after 1776, with the notable exception of the fed-eral capital of Washington, DC, were laid out as utilitarian grids.[3] Grids were not only convenient to replicate and easy to survey but also suited a growing democracy, since they did not privilege one property owner over another.[4] Entrepreneurs filled in the empty blocks with houses and warehouses, shops and workshops, stores and saloons—depending on the demands of the market. Civic buildings took their places in a similarly undifferentiated fashion—houses of worship, city halls, and courthouses were casually interspersed among private residences and places of business (Greenberg 2006, 32–33).

There were attempts at civic beautification, such as the great urban parks of the second half of the nineteenth century and the City Beautiful movement of 1900–1910, but on the whole, the appearance of U.S. cities remained the product of economic and social circumstances, not governmental intervention. This started to change in 1908, when the city of Los Angeles introduced zoning ordinances that differentiated between residential and industrial uses (Weiss 1987, 81). Two events helped to popularize zoning nationwide: in 1916, the largest U.S. city, New York, adopted comprehensive land zoning; and in 1926, the U.S. Supreme Court upheld the constitutionality of municipal land-use regulations (Rabin 1989, 103–7). With the active encouragement of the federal government, within a decade almost every state passed laws that enabled local governments to enact citywide zoning ordinances.

The introduction of zoning was prompted chiefly by concerns about health and safety, yet it had the effect of giving city government wider powers over design, since zoning affected not only what could be built and where but also how. Rules about building materials, build-to lines, setbacks, and open space changed the appearance of U.S. cities. The New York City zoning ordinance of 1916, for example, included regulations that required the upper floors of tall buildings to be stepped back to reduce the shadowing of the streets and adjacent buildings, thereby producing the characteristic ziggurat form of that period. Henceforth, while city governments rarely directly controlled the design of buildings (except for public ones), they did so indirectly—through zoning.

Land-use controls were only the beginning. The two decades following the passing of the national Urban Renewal Act in 1948 was a period of extreme activism by U.S. municipal governments. Impatient with the marketplace, which had produced neighborhoods of dense tenement housing, city planning departments—assisted, encouraged, and often funded by the federal government—intervened directly and sometimes drastically in the design of cities. This was the period of slum clearance, urban renewal, public housing, and interstate highway construction. It was also the period of powerful city planning agencies, led by forceful planning officials such as Robert Moses in New York City, Edmund Bacon in Philadelphia, and Edward Logue in New Haven and Boston. In time, federal funding for urban megaprojects was discontinued, but the idea that municipal governments could and should involve themselves directly in the design of cities took root. Over the last four decades, city administrations have undertaken a number of planning and design initiatives to influence public and private development. What follows is an overview of these schemes, both their successes and failures.

Public Spaces

The design of the urban environment starts with the organization of streets. The detailed design of urban streets, which originated in Europe centuries ago, includes a well-established hierarchy of alleys, lanes, streets, avenues, boulevards, and drives. There are widely accepted norms about the relationship between street widths and building heights as well as rules about tree planting and sidewalk dimensions (Duany Plater-Zyberk and Company 1999). Despite this long tradition, beginning in the late 1950s U.S. city planners and architects believed that an entirely new approach to street design was required to accommodate the widespread use of motor vehicles (both private cars and trucks). In short, separate people and cars. This view was expressed by the architect and planner John Burchard (1968, 230) in his chapter on urban design in *The Metropolitan Enigma*: "There should be substantial areas in a city, some even up to a half mile square, into which no automobile should ever intrude unless beneath the ground."

The separation of pedestrians and car traffic was pioneered by the planner Victor Gruen (1964, 217–20) in 1956 in the widely admired Fort Worth, Texas, downtown plan, which proposed a bilevel solution to traffic: pedestrians above, vehicles below. Although the Fort Worth plan was not carried out due to public opposition to its high cost, the concept nevertheless had a powerful influence on planners nationwide. Several North American cities adopted design solutions that separated pedestrians from traffic, creating weather-protected downtown pedestrian circulation systems, either one level above the street or one level below. Streets in the air, or *skyways*, were built in Minneapolis, Saint Paul, and Calgary; *underground concourses* appeared in Dallas, Houston, and Montreal. Have they been successful? There is no doubt that in cities with climatic extremes, such as Minneapolis and Houston, heated and air-conditioned spaces attract people, but do they necessarily produce more economic activity? In a Montreal midwinter, it is possible to go from one's office to a restaurant in shirt sleeves, but since people have to eat lunch somewhere, shirt sleeves or not, it is unclear that this convenience generates more business.[5] Is the marginal convenience of weather-protected pedestrian circulation worth the cost? Advocates say yes, although critics point out that dividing pedestrian traffic between outdoor sidewalks and indoor skyways and concourses is a self-defeating strategy that not only dilutes shopping traffic in both areas but also has an adverse effect on the vitality of city streets (Barnett 2003, 238).

The vertical separation of cars and pedestrians, whether by tunnels or bridges, is extremely expensive, as evidenced by Boston's infamous Big Dig, which as of 2006 cost more than $14.6 billion. Although burying a previously elevated interstate highway freed up thirty acres of downtown land for development, it is hard to see this as a cost-effective strategy. Since tunnels are so expensive, depressed or elevated highways have been more common solutions, although both have a negative effect on the city, creating unsightly intrusions and physical barriers in city neighborhoods. Multilane surface streets are also an intrusion, but if properly designed, with tree-planting strips and separated lanes for local and high-speed traffic, their local impact can be minimized. There have been at least three cases—San Francisco, Portland, Oregon, and Toronto—where 1960s-era downtown expressways were later demolished and replaced by surface streets.

Beginning in the late 1950s, many downtowns adopted a less expensive solution to separating cars and pedestrians than tunnels or bridges: closing selected streets to vehicular traffic and turning them into *pedestrian malls*. This strategy has the advantage of leaving existing rights-of-way and private property boundaries undisturbed. These pedestrianization programs were part of a strategy for rejuvenating downtown districts, which had declined as people—and businesses—moved to the suburbs. The theory was that suburbanites, having become used to walking in shopping centers, would be attracted to car-free environments downtown.

Pedestrianized streets are of three types: pedestrian malls, semimalls, and transit malls. Pedestrian malls are streets closed to all vehicular traffic (except for emergency vehicles). Semimalls are streets whose sidewalks are widened and whose roadways are narrowed, usually to two lanes without parking. Transit malls are similar to semimalls, except that the traffic lanes are restricted to buses. The detailed design of malls, semimalls, and transit malls can vary. In minimal makeovers, streets are closed with portable barriers, and planters and benches are placed in the old roadway. More elaborate schemes incorporate decorative brick paving, trees, landscaping, fountains, lighting, sculptures, kiosks, sidewalk cafes, and in some cases, sheltered walkways. The conversion costs have varied from less than one hundred thousand dollars to several million (Garvin 1996, 142–51).

The first pedestrian shopping street in the United States was Burdick Street Mall in Kalamazoo, Michigan, built in 1957. Three blocks long, it was extended to a fourth block in 1974. It is estimated that during the 1960s and 1970s, more than two hundred North American cities undertook pedestrianization programs.[6] These projects were influenced by European examples such as the Lijnbaan, a pedestrian shopping street in downtown Rotterdam, whose center had been almost completely destroyed by wartime bombing, and the pedestrian-only town center of Vällingby, a new satellite city outside Stockholm (Garvin 1996, 142). U.S. pedestrianization schemes differed significantly from their European models, however. European pedestrian areas encompassed entire districts, while U.S. pedestrianization was typically only a portion of a single street. European malls were either laid out over medieval plans, with picturesque squares and curving streets, or were designed from scratch, while U.S. malls were usually simply converted streets in a rectangular grid. There were other differences. Since European town centers included high-density housing, retailers had a captive market, whereas U.S. downtown storekeepers had to attract shoppers from a distance. European pedestrian malls were typically part of vibrant city centers, while most U.S. malls were built in declining downtowns. In the 1950s and 1960s, European downtown shops did not have to compete with suburban shopping centers, unlike their U.S. counterparts. Lastly, car ownership was much lower in Europe than in the United States (especially in the immediate postwar era), meaning that people who came downtown traveled by mass transit, so the provision of parking was not an issue. In U.S. cities, where most people traveled by car, parking as well as convenient drop-off and pickup were major concerns for prospective shoppers.

For all these reasons, the separation of pedestrians and cars in U.S. downtowns rarely provided the anticipated benefits; pedestrianization in many cases actually discouraged shoppers. Businesses suffered, stores relocated, and car-free pedestrian malls became magnets for vagrants. The problem, as Jane Jacobs (1961, 269) wrote at the time, was that "planned pedestrian street schemes, *if* they throw formidable borders for moving and parked cars around inherently weak and fragmentary preserves, *can introduce more problems than they solve.*"

Store owners in pedestrian malls, who saw traffic decline as businesses moved elsewhere, called for streets to be reopened to cars. Like many failing pedestrian malls, the Burdick Street Mall in Kalamazoo reopened to limited vehicular traffic in 2000; Chicago reopened its State Street pedestrian mall to traffic; and Philadelphia, which turned a downtown section of Walter Street into a transit mall, followed suit after business on the street declined drastically. Only about thirty pedestrian malls remain in operation in the United States today. In the cases of transit malls in Louisville, Portland, Oregon, and Denver, extraneous factors such as free mass transit along with new downtown convention centers and shopping malls contribute to their survival (although retail on Denver's Sixteenth Street Mall has not flourished). Pedestrian malls have been more successful in Burlington, Vermont, Charlottesville, Virginia, Ann Arbor, Michigan, and Boulder, all—not coincidentally—college towns. College communities have large populations of young people living in close proximity to downtown; many college students do not own cars; and lacking 9:00 to 5:00 jobs and family obligations, students have plenty of free time to populate a mall's cafés and bars.

The other context in which pedestrian malls have succeeded is in temperate-climate cities whose main industry is tourism. Lincoln Road Mall in Miami Beach is one of the oldest fully pedestrianized streets in the nation. Although the eight-block-long mall (crossed at intervals by regular streets), designed by architect Morris Lapidus in 1960, was not an immediate success, it blossomed in the late 1980s when Miami Beach became a fashionable tourist destination. Today, Lincoln Road is an active shopping street, with stores, restaurants, nightclubs, theaters, and movie houses. (Parking lots and structures are in close vicinity.) It should be noted, however, that the users appear to be predominantly tourists (the portions of Lincoln Road that are not pedestrianized have fewer tourist shops). Freemont Street Experience is a five-block-long pedestrian mall in downtown Las Vegas, another leisure city with a warm climate. The Fremont mall, which opened in 1995, is unusual in being covered by an open steel canopy, which serves as an armature for a spectacular light show that turns the street into a huge casino lobby.

The lesson of the pedestrianization experiment is that the best solutions for accommodating pedestrians in a U.S. downtown remain crowded sidewalks next to vehicular streets. Every successful urban shopping street in the country has maintained this traditional arrangement: Manhattan's Madison and Fifth avenues, Boston's Newbury Street, Philadelphia's Walnut Street, Charleston's King Street, Chicago's North Michigan Avenue, Los Angeles's Rodeo Drive, and the crowded shopping streets around San Francisco's Union Square. This is also the arrangement that was adopted in downtown Fort Worth. Having rejected the vertical separation of pedestrians and cars in 1956, that city did not jump on the pedestrian mall bandwagon. Fort Worth, with its busy streets and sidewalks—and plentiful free parking—is a particularly successful example of downtown revival, and is generally considered to be much more vibrant than neighboring Dallas, whose dreary underground concourses have not been an animating force. Traditional streets and sidewalks have also been adopted by recent urban redevelopment schemes in downtown Albuquerque and Bethesda, Maryland.

One of the most successful *new* downtown districts is Reston Town Center in Reston, Virginia, whose first phase was completed in 1990. The plan is modeled on early suburban planned cities such as White Plains, New York, Stamford, Connecticut, and Evanston, Illinois. Mid- and low-rise buildings line sidewalks in a more or less conventional grid, relieved by an occasional park. Victory, a new development on the northern fringe of downtown Dallas, likewise combines pedestrian malls, plazas, and a park with vehicular streets and traditional boulevards in a way that may become a model for future high-density, mixed-use development (Dillon 2006, 82).

Successful streets must be designed. City planner Allan Jacobs (1993, 270–92) lists a number of qualities required for a "good" street: wide sidewalks, shade trees, benches, and sunlight, which all contribute to a comfortable pedestrian environment. According to Jacobs, city streets should be defined by buildings, architecture should engage the eye, and street-level buildings should incorporate a high degree of transparency— shop windows, entryways, balconies—so that they are interesting to look at. The quality of construction and the design of curb details, paving, and street furniture are also important (although banners, planters, fancy streetlights, and elaborate graphics are not required). Equally essential is effective maintenance and, above all, cleanliness, but also care and repair as well as good policing. The last two management issues have been successfully addressed in many cities by the formation of business improvement districts.

The other lesson of pedestrianization is that "taming the motorcar" is best done not by physical separation, which is both expensive and ineffective, but through management. Policies such as charging tolls for access to the central city (currently practiced in London and being considered by New York City), and providing on-street parking as well as off-street parking in the form of parking structures, reduce traffic and congestion, and go far in improving the pedestrian's experience of the city.

A close relative of the pedestrianized street of the 1960s is the *pedestrian plaza*. "The city could profit from a considerable number of squares or plazas," suggested Burchard (1968, 230–31) in *The Metropolitan Enigma*, voicing the conventional wisdom of the time, "with well-designed linkages from one to the other, perhaps even through quite narrow pedestrian channels going through buildings and almost certainly on multilevels by which pedestrians could make the journey from one square to another without being aware of an automobile." In the 1950s and 1960s, pedestrian plazas were created in various ways. Many cities encouraged developers of high-rise office buildings to add plazas by granting "open-space bonuses" or increases in the floor-area ratio in return for setting towers back from the street. This was, in effect, a way to create public space on private land. Architects favored plazas since they provided a neutral setting that showed off their buildings. To that end, plazas were generally paved, without trees or landscaping, their large surfaces relieved only by huge abstract sculptures, typically by Henry Moore or Alexander Calder.

Like the pedestrianized street, the plaza (as the name suggests) is a European import. Plazas originated in Mediterranean towns, where they continue to be an integral part of public life, but they are ill suited to U.S. cities, where life is generally more private. Nor are plazas well adapted to the North's climate, being windswept and cold in the winter, and unpleasantly hot in the summer. It is significant that the most famous U.S. plaza—Times Square—is hardly a square at all, but merely an expanded street intersection.

The largest U.S. city spaces are *public parks*. By the 1960s the great nineteenth-century public parks of New York, Philadelphia, Boston, Chicago, Washington, DC, Louisville, Denver, and San Francisco, and in scores of smaller cities, had fallen on hard times. They were run-down, poorly maintained, and often downright dangerous. Moreover, compared to pedestrian malls and plazas, parks were thought by city planners to be old-fashioned and thus not considered important urban amenities. One of the most encouraging trends of the last two decades has been the resurgence of urban parks, led by the restoration and revival of New York City's Central Park in the 1980s (thanks to the efforts of a privately funded conservancy). As a result of the public's interest in outdoor activities such as exercise walking, jogging, in-line skating, and bicycling, and a greater awareness of—and appreciation for—the natural environment, large urban parks have grown enormously in popularity and the intensity of use.

City parks take many forms: nature preserves such as Washington, DC's Rock Creek Park and Louisville's Cherokee Park, downtown green spaces such as New York's Bryant Park and Philadelphia's Rittenhouse Square, and linear parks such as Boston's Commonwealth Avenue and Fenway. Because of their popularity, public parks have become intensively used urban amenities. There are a number of newly built urban parks, notably Millennium Park in downtown Chicago, Crissy Field on the site of a decommissioned military air base in San Francisco, and Olympic Sculpture Park in Seattle. Major parks are planned along the Potomac in Georgetown, next to the New York waterfront, in Brooklyn, and on Governor's Island. These new parks are generally smaller than their nineteenth-century antecedents (since land is expensive and unbuilt urban land is in short supply), and they devote more space to active recreation such as jogging, bicycling, game playing, and picnicking.

Many of the new parks are next to water, reflecting a general trend for cities to use their waterfronts for recreation.

When Central Park was conceived in the late 1850s, one of the economic rationales for the investment of public money in park construction was the anticipated increase in real estate values. This increase did in fact occur, and the property values of lots facing the park—or in close proximity—rose (Rosenzweig et al. 1992, 268). This remains true today, not only of Central Park and other New York City parks, but also of high-profile urban green spaces such as Rittenhouse Square in Philadelphia and Commonwealth Avenue in Boston. These are high-income residential neighborhoods, but green space is an even stronger amenity in low-income neighborhoods. A recent study shows that one of the most important contributors to housing value in low-income neighborhoods is proximity to public open space, probably because private open space is in many cases restricted or minimal (Russo 2007). This relationship argues for the added significance of public parks as a cost-effective means of providing open space in higher-density areas.

Parks are recreational amenities, but they also have a social function. More than a hundred years ago, the great park builder Frederick Law Olmsted described this purpose: "Men must come together, *and must be seen coming together*, in carriages, on horseback and on foot, and the concourse of animated life which will thus be formed, must in itself be made, if possible, an attractive and diverting spectacle (quoted in Rybczynski 1990, 272; emphasis added)." Public parks are one of the few places in the city where people of different incomes and backgrounds mix (sports stadiums and arenas are other mixing place). At a time when social segregation is increasingly common not only in residential neighborhoods but also in retail and recreational environments, the mixing role of parks assumes greater importance.

Shopping Places

The failure of pedestrianized streets was a setback to city officials and planners attempting to revive faltering downtown shopping districts in the 1970s. For their next improvement model they looked closer to home, to what had become the most successful retail environment in the nation: the regional shopping mall. Shopping malls are sometimes called the "new downtowns," but they are really different than city centers, being designed and structured to a much higher degree (Rybczynski 1993a, 98–106). As urban researchers Bernard Frieden and Lynne Sagalyn (1992, 66) put it, "Developers believed that suburbanites had little nostalgia for downtown's hit-or-miss retailing, pushy crowds, dirty

streets, or dress-up shopping rite. Seeing the projections for rising incomes and standards of affluence, they assumed suburbanites wanted
something better, though more casual and informal, and they built a
shopping environment to match." The challenge for city planners was
to adapt this suburban solution to urban locations.

Suburban malls are built on cheap land, which means that they can
take up a lot of space, but urban land is expensive, which constrains the
design of *urban shopping malls* in two crucial respects. The rule of thumb
for developers of suburban malls is that shoppers will climb only one
story up or down, and hence suburban malls typically have a maximum
of two floors; only if the topography allows shoppers to enter the mall
at mid-level is it possible to add a third (Garreau 1991, 465). Urban malls
usually require four to six floors to pack the same floor space on to a
smaller lot. Expensive land imposes another constraint: since there is
insufficient space for surface parking lots, parking structures are required. Escalators and elevators can facilitate multilevel shopping, with
their costs amortized by the high levels of traffic in downtown locations
(although the two-story rule still applies, and upper floors in urban
malls are generally less popular and usually lease at a discount). On the
other hand, the high cost of building parking structures ($10,000 per car
space for a parking structure, compared to $1,000 per car space for sur-
face parking) is difficult for developers to justify economically (Barnett
2003, 52). The common solution in downtown malls is for municipalities to assume the cost of building and operating parking structures.
Despite the high up-front costs of building vertically, during the 1970s
and 1980s, developers were encouraged by city concessions and incentives to build a number of urban shopping malls: ZCMI Center in Salt
Lake City (1974), Water Tower Place in Chicago (1976), the Gallery at
Market East in Philadelphia (1977), Stamford Town Center in Stamford,
Connecticut (1982), and Horton Plaza in San Diego (1985).

The earlier success of the suburban shopping mall was the result of a
marketing strategy that grouped together national brand-name stores
in clean, hospitable environments. It also depended on access and convenience—that is, suburban shoppers were able to easily drive to malls
(which were always located next to highway interchanges) and park
their cars conveniently nearby in large, free parking lots. While urban
shopping malls more or less replicate the interior environment of their
suburban competitors, they rarely provide the same easy access and
convenience; shoppers have to navigate congested city streets, and
parking structures are rarely free, nor are they as convenient as surface
lots. As a result, the financial record of urban shopping malls has been
checkered. Frieden and Sagalyn (1992, 311–12) suggest that in many
cases, while urban malls are profitable for lenders (who incorporated

high-risk premiums) and merchants (the sales per square foot in urban malls are generally high), they have not always been profitable for developers, since the up-front and operating costs have been high.

What about the benefits of urban shopping malls to cities? On the plus side, urban shopping malls, which offer large retail spaces, attract national chains to downtown locations that they might not have otherwise chosen. National chains provide a direct benefit to urban shoppers—especially low-income ones—in the form of lower prices (compared to local neighborhood stores). The other direct benefit of malls to urban shoppers is security, in the form of (privately) policed, safe shopping environments. The economic impact of safety is difficult to quantify, but it undoubtedly explains the success of urban malls in troubled downtown districts. On the minus side, the inward-looking nature of most urban shopping malls often drains the surrounding streets of their pedestrian traffic and vitality.

Since the shops themselves—and the shopping experience—are similar to what one finds in the suburbs, it is doubtful that urban shopping malls have attracted large numbers of suburban shoppers to downtown. Neither do the lower prices, since these are lower only compared to local city retailers, and not to suburban malls. Instead, there is some evidence that pedestrian malls simply siphon customers from other downtown stores (Garvin 1996, 119–20). Nor do shopping malls promote development. In downtown Philadelphia, for example, although a three-block-long enclosed urban mall (the Gallery at Market Street, 1974–1983) is full of people, neighboring Market Street has remained largely blighted, with faltering retail and dollar stores.

The latest version of an urban shopping mall is in the Time-Warner Center in New York City, completed in 2004. This five-story mall benefits from high pedestrian traffic counts, although the upper levels contain only restaurants, not shops. The mall is designed to be outward looking, and its form at street level follows the curved shape of Columbus Circle. This being Manhattan, parking for shoppers was not required; the garage for the entire development has only 504 spaces. The shopping mall is relatively small (only forty shops, but including a midsize supermarket), and is part of a much larger project (2.8 million square feet) that includes residential condominiums, offices, a hotel, and a major performance space that effectively acts like an anchor, pulling people to the upper level of the mall. In other words, the retail space is only one part of a *mixed-use complex*.

The mixed-use program of the Time-Warner Center is a more successful arrangement than the retail-only urban malls of the 1970s, since it creates a situation where many different uses serendipitously support one another. Nevertheless, it is important to note that (unlike a suburban mall) the Time-Warner Center is not self-sufficient but relies on the proximity of a dense residential population on the Upper West Side, and the nearby stores on Broadway and Seventh Avenue. It also takes advantage of preexisting public infrastructure, not only Central Park and Lincoln Center, but also a bus and subway system. The Ferry Terminal Building in San Francisco is another mixed-use project that takes advantage of a thriving urban environment. In addition to being a ferry terminal (and being connected to BART, MUNI, and the historic cable cars), the building houses shops, restaurants, a farmers market, and two floors of commercial space. It is unlikely that such mixed-use projects would be successful in a failing downtown, or one that lacked actively used mass transit. Mixed-use complexes require lively and wealthy cities such as New York, San Francisco, Chicago, and Washington, DC (where a large, mixed-use complex is projected for the site of an old convention center). The largest urban mixed-use project to date is planned for Las Vegas. CityCenter is a sixty-seven-acre, $7 billion complex (under construction) that will have six towers housing a four-thousand-room hotel and twenty-seven hundred condominium units, and will include a convention center and half a million square feet of retail space.

Successful downtowns such as New York, Chicago, and San Francisco have attracted shoppers by capitalizing on the unique qualities that set cities apart from suburbs: density, bustle, crowded sidewalks, and heterogeneity. Another distinctive urban quality, particularly of older cities, is historic architecture, not only cultural monuments, but also— surprisingly—industrial buildings, especially waterfront industrial buildings. The first commercial developments that took advantage of industrial buildings' architectural quality were two retail centers that opened in renovated historic structures on San Francisco Bay: Ghirardelli Square (1964) and Fisherman's Wharf (1970s). These retail developments were followed by Quincy Market in Boston (1976), Pike Place Market in Seattle (1976), Harborplace in Baltimore (1980), South Street Seaport in New York (1983), and Navy Pier in Chicago (1995). What came to be known as *festival marketplaces* were typically located inside old buildings, although in some cases new structures were built. Unlike urban shopping malls, festival marketplaces are not inward oriented but take advantage of their surroundings, including water views. Although most festival marketplaces are centrally managed—just like suburban malls—they usually include local retailers as well as national chains. The atmosphere and organization creates a sense of place that emphasizes a regional identity. The shopping is usually linked to leisure activities such as eating, especially outdoor eating. In other words, the experience of a festival marketplace is different from that of an urban or suburban mall.

An alternative to the festival marketplace, especially for cities that do not have historic waterfronts, is the *lifestyle center*. Lifestyle centers are basically new pieces of urban fabric (incorporating one hundred thousand to more than one million square feet of retail space) loosely modeled on small-town main streets. Lifestyle centers are distinguished from traditional shopping malls—and festival marketplaces—by their design. These are not simply buildings but urban places, with vehicular streets and storefronts spilling out on to broad sidewalks. In addition, the mid-rise buildings (typically four to six floors) contain a mixture of uses: residential or commercial above street-level retail. The architectural style of lifestyle centers can be "traditional," as in City Place in West Palm Beach, Mizner Park in Boca Raton, Florida, and Santana Row in San Jose, California, or "contemporary," as in the town center of Reston, Virginia, Victoria Gardens in Rancho Cucamonga, California, Crocker Park in Westlake, Ohio, and the East Twenty-ninth Avenue Town Center in Denver's Stapleton. Lifestyle centers should not be confused with themed shopping places such as Universal CityWalk in Los Angeles, Downtown Disney in Anaheim, or La Encantada in Tucson, which are really open-air regional shopping malls, with retail as the single use.

In Rockville, Maryland, a suburb of Washington, DC, a fifteen-acre section of downtown that included an abandoned shopping mall (built as part of an urban renewal project of the 1970s) and a strip mall was converted into a lifestyle center called Rockville Town Square. The uses include 108,000 square feet of retail space at the street level, 644 residential units on three to five upper levels, 2,000 parking spaces, a 100,000-square-foot public library, and a community center. The planning incorporates automobile streets and is pedestrian oriented, with a landscaped town square as the central feature. The project is a joint venture of the city (which invested $90 million in infrastructure and parking garages), the county (which spent $30 million to build the library), a retail developer (who invested $40 million), and a residential developer (who invested $200 million) (Brenner 2006, C7). The presence of civic uses signals a growing trend in lifestyle centers: incorporating nonretail ground-floor uses such as theaters, libraries, and educational buildings.

Reston Town Center extends the lifestyle center concept to the scale of a full-fledged downtown. At 460 acres, this is the largest of the current generation of mixed-use town centers, with a projected residential population of six thousand people in seven-, fifteen-, and twenty-one-story buildings. Other uses include offices, a hotel, and extensive retail

on the ground level. Parking is underground, in above-ground structures, and on surface lots. Many of the apartment buildings have private inner courts. In other words, this is an updated version of practices
that were common—and successful—in the early 1900s. The residential
density will be relatively high (75 persons per acre), exceeding many established downtowns (Ward 2006, 71).

Lifestyle centers, with their lively mixture of uses and emphasis on
design, are expensive to build, require surrounding density to support
the retail operations, and depend on a relatively affluent population
that can afford upscale shops and high-end residential units. In that respect, the challenge to city planners attempting to revive cities less
affluent than Rockville or Reston, is how to integrate retail uses such as
big-box stores, which is where the majority of working Americans shop,
into the urban fabric. Municipal city planners have long resisted big-
box retailing in downtown locations, arguing that it represents a suburban form that has no place in the city (city merchants also resist big-box
stores, which threaten to reduce their profits). The big box is not merely
an architectural form, however; it is a form of retailing (just as that earlier "big box," the department store, represented a novel type of retailing in the mid-1800s) (Rybczynski 2003, 34–41). Consumers benefit
from the lower prices and greater choice offered by big-box retailers
such as Wal-Mart, Home Depot, Costco, and Ikea. There are architectural precedents for integrating big boxes into a high-density urban environment—not only traditional department stores but also merchan-
dise marts and city markets as well as nonretail big boxes such as post
office depots, armories, generating plants, and railroad stations. There
have been some attempts to locate big-box stores in urban surroundings, including recycling vacant industrial land, redesigning the stores
on more than one level, and downsizing the floor area (the average size
of a big box is two hundred thousand square feet) to a "small box"
(forty thousand square feet). The provision of parking—whether structured or surface—remains a major challenge.

Building Groups

Urban design is also concerned with the way that individual buildings
are grouped. For a long time the placement of buildings, whether
eighteenth-century row houses in Philadelphia or nineteenth-century
brownstones in New York, followed simple rules. Land was valuable,
so buildings left no setbacks on their sides, but were built touching each
other. Facades were built to a common line along the street, leaving a
small setback, and sometimes even hugging the sidewalk. Rear gardens
or inner courtyards provided private outdoor spaces. Even large build-

ings observed these rules. For instance, concert halls, such as Symphony Hall in Boston, Carnegie Hall in New York, and the Academy of Music in Philadelphia, were built close to the sidewalk and their neighbors. Special public buildings such as city halls and central libraries were sometimes freestanding, occupying an entire city block and set back from the street (as in Philadelphia, New York, and Boston). The City Beautiful–era civic centers are examples of groups of such buildings, often combined with public parks. Large art museums were frequently sited in parks (such as in New York, Philadelphia, Chicago, and San Francisco).

The other principle that governed the design of urban buildings was heterogeneity. Occasionally someone might acquire several adjacent lots and build a row of identical houses, but on the whole, urban growth was piecemeal, at the scale of the individual lot. This practice produced a pleasant architectural variety, in which the street itself acted as the unifying element. Urban design in the 1950s and 1960s abandoned this traditional approach on the assumption that the twentieth-century city required something totally different. This attitude was influenced by the visionary ideas of early European modernist architects such as the Italian futurist Antonio Sant'Elia, who imagined the "city of the future" as an interconnected, three-dimensional beehive, in which streets were replaced by multilevel bridges, parks by aerial platforms, and individual buildings by vast structures, which came to be known as *megastructures*. This concept was later revived in the 1960s in various projects by the French architects Candilis, Josic, and Woods, the American utopian Paolo Soleri, and the British architectural group Archigram (Barnett 1986, 157–72).

The chief challenge for putative megastructure builders, apart from assembling sufficiently large tracts of land and resolving the complex legal issues of overlapping ownership, was economic. Not only was the up-front cost of building a megastructure extremely high, it was difficult to phase in over time, and was inflexible once built. Thus, while a number of urban megastructures were proposed, notably a mixed-use project for Lower Manhattan (1967) and the first scheme for Battery Park City (1969) in New York, none were actually built. The closest that North American architects came to building megastructures was a series of single-owner institutional buildings in Canada: a college in suburban Toronto (Scarborough College, 1963–1969), and universities in suburban Vancouver (Simon Fraser University, 1963) and rural Alberta (University of Lethbridge, 1968). The only residential megastructure built was Habitat (1967), part of Montreal's world's fair.

While few megastructures were constructed, a related idea did find wide implementation: the *superblock*. A superblock was created by consolidating several properties into one large tract, usually covering one

or more city blocks. On such large sites, buildings did not have to be
lined up on the street as before. (The chief difference between New
York's Rockefeller Center, which covers three city blocks, and 1960s' superblocks is that in the older project, individual buildings maintained a
conventional relationship to the surrounding streets.) The spaces between buildings in superblock developments were treated either as
pedestrian plazas or parkland; in both cases, the buildings were delib-
erately isolated from the surrounding streets. Examples of superblock
projects include: residential developments such as Lafayette Park (1955–
1963) in Detroit and Society Hill Towers (1964) in Philadelphia; downtown office complexes such as Place Ville Marie (1960) in Montreal and
the Toronto-Dominion Centre (1963–1969) in Toronto; and civic building groups such as City Hall Plaza (1968) in Boston and the Federal
Center Plaza (1969) in Chicago.

Superblocks, like megastructures, were an attempt by architects and
planners to remake the city in a new image. This image was primarily
artistic, but as architect Jonathan Barnett (1995, 185) has pointed out,
"Designing a city is not like making a painting or a sculpture, it is not
an expression of individual will or private sensibility." Arranging apartment buildings to resemble a Piet Mondrian painting ignored too many
practicalities, which led to the ultimate failure of the superblock idea.
Pedestrians tended to avoid plazas because they were boring compared
to lively streets. The open spaces, in turn, became deserted and sometimes dangerous. Large portions of the city designed by a single architect
or a group of architects subscribing to the same architectural aesthetic
were visually oppressive (which is why filmmakers such as Stanley
Kubrick and Michelangelo Antonioni used superblock settings as sym-
bols of urban anomie). Since superblocks tended to concentrate buildings with similar functions (residential, commercial, and civic), they
produced environments that were inactive during large parts of the day,
unlike lively streets, where an office building might be next to a department store or an apartment building. Superblocks of office towers were
busy on weekdays, but deserted on weekends; residential superblocks
tended to be lifeless during the week.

During the 1960s and 1970s, superblocks were not used only for residential and commercial projects; a group of buildings around a plaza
was also the preferred solution for performing arts centers, such as Lincoln Center in New York and Place des Arts in Montreal. The layout of
these complexes was based on the college campus concept, although
the environments turned out differently. Instead of being crowded, the
cultural centers were vacant most of the time (except during evening
performances). Unlike the old practice of integrating opera houses and
concert halls into the city, performing arts centers were set apart and

isolated. Perhaps the most extreme example of such withdrawal is the Getty Center in Los Angeles, a campus of exhibition and research buildings that sits in splendid yet lonely isolation, overlooking Santa Monica and the rest of the city.

The Getty Center reveals another trend among cultural institutions: using signature architecture to attract the public. Ever since distinguished architects designed the first public art museums in the late nineteenth century, art and architecture have gone hand in hand, but today striking architecture—not planning—is given the leading role in contemporary urban renewal. After Frank Gehry built the widely acclaimed Guggenheim Museum in Bilbao, creating a destination for international tourists and spurring the revival of the old industrial Spanish city, U.S. cities looked to architects to create so-called *iconic buildings* (Rybczynski 2002, 138–42). The convergence of celebrity architects, media attention, and the public's attraction to unusual-looking buildings has produced a spate of striking art museums and libraries in Seattle (Rem Koolhaas), Milwaukee (Santiago Calatrava), Cincinnati (Zaha Hadid), Denver (Daniel Libeskind), Salt Lake City (Moshe Safdie), San Francisco (Herzog and de Meuron), and Bellevue, Washington (Steven Holl). Not all have been successful, however: the Bellevue Art Museum was forced to close due to a lack of funds; Seattle's Music Experience Project (Gehry) has not attracted the expected number of visitors; and Philadelphia's Kimmel Center for the Performing Arts (Rafael Viñoly) has not been successful as a public gathering space. Nevertheless, cities continue to build signature buildings, hoping to duplicate the Bilbao effect. Until the media gets tired of reporting on startling new buildings—or the public gets tired of visiting them—signature buildings will remain for many cities a hoped-for shortcut to re-creating the downtown as a cultural destination.

But there is no shortcut. The U.S. cities that have proved most successful at attracting tourists (other than Las Vegas and Orlando, which remain the prime destinations for leisure travelers) are those that have provided a wide range of attractions: waterfronts, parks, museums, restaurants, festival marketplaces, and active shopping streets. In other words, those cities where planning and urban management have been practiced at the neighborhood and district scale are the most successful. Perhaps the best examples of late twentieth-century urban planning are the restored *historic districts* that appeared in many U.S. cities. Beginning in Charleston, South Carolina, cities designated historic districts, using design guidelines for restoration and new construction. Restoration was often the result of public activism, and it depended on the involvement of citizens serving on design review boards. Restored historic districts include Society Hill in Philadelphia, Georgetown in Washington, DC,

Beacon Hill and Back Bay in Boston, Vieux Carré in New Orleans, and the West End in Seattle as well as districts in smaller cities such as Santa Barbara, Santa Fe, and Savannah. Historic districts have sometimes been the catalysts for successful urban renewal and redevelopment in adjacent neighborhoods. These old areas are distinctly pedestrian friendly. Although they generally do not have streets closed to traffic, the districts are small and intimate enough to be walkable, and their architecture is varied and visually stimulating.

Residential Neighborhoods

The most important influence on city design of the last two decades has been the belated discovery that the essential components for successful downtowns—so-called twenty-four-hour downtowns—are not office buildings, cultural centers, convention facilities, or sports stadiums but residents (Rybczynski 2000; Birch 2006). The marketplace has identified three specific categories of potential urban dwellers: young professionals (singles and couples), empty nesters, and retirees. In the case of a select group of what some economists have called glamour or playground cities, one can add a fourth residential category: suburbanites who want second homes downtown in order to take advantage of urban amenities such as concert halls, museums, and theaters (Kotkin 2005b). In global cities such as New York, and leisure cities such as Las Vegas and Miami, these pieds-à-terre may belong to interregional or even international owners. During the late 1990s and early 2000s, in the downtowns of New York, Boston, Philadelphia, Washington, DC, Chicago, and Miami, high-rise condominiums have been the chief form of new residential construction. The other popular forms of urban housing are industrial and commercial buildings adapted to residential use. Rehabbed industrial spaces, warehouses, and factories with tall ceilings, wide-open floor space, large areas of glazing, and exposed brick and concrete have turned out to be desirable residential products. So much so that cities without recyclable industrial buildings have built brand-new, so-called loft apartments. Government has played a key role in the adaptive reuse by providing historic tax credits and tax abatements for old buildings converted to residential use.

Judging from the experience thus far, new residential developments in cities have one serious limitation: they are expensive. Building dense housing, especially if mixed-use is involved, on costly urban land, incorporating special architectural features and attractive public amenities as well as renovated historic buildings costs a lot more than suburban development. It is affordable by the usual target buyers (young professionals, empty nesters, and retirees), but is generally too expensive for middle-income households.

The design of urban housing for middle-income families remains problematic. The demand for urban family housing is extremely small, due in part to the poor state of urban public schools, which has driven middle-income families to the suburbs. Moreover, except in select cities, there is still resistance on the part of U.S. home buyers with children to apartment living. The housing experiments of the 1960s and 1970s, aimed at developing alternative forms of medium-rise, medium-density housing, did not produce solutions that found a market; most families continue to prefer single-family housing in the form of detached or attached homes. One design solution to the mismatch between home buyer expectations and the current stock of urban housing might be the development of new, in-town garden suburbs. These would be higher density than conventional suburbs, and could be modeled on the early railroad suburb of Forest Hills Gardens (c. 1912) in Queens, New York. Still, because of the increase in land prices in desirable neighborhoods and the high costs of urban construction, it is likely that *any* urban housing solution will be beyond the affordability of the middle-income buyer (Stern 2007, 85–88).

The present lack of middle-class residents has led to cities with increasingly bimodal income distribution—that is, cities composed of the very rich and the very poor. Some urban scholars have decried the emergence of such "dual cities," with their skewed economies and potential for social conflict (Kotkin 2005a, 154). They criticize public investment in museums and other cultural amenities rather than schools and neighborhood improvement. It is unclear that all vibrant cities need a strong middle class, however. Global cities such as New York, or cities that depend to a large extent on international tourism such as San Francisco, may develop along different lines than Seattle or Denver. Or Los Angeles, which remains the U.S. city with the largest percentage of its economy in manufacturing, and is a magnet for immigrants. While nineteenth-century cities were all, to a greater or lesser degree, industrial cities, twenty-first-century cities no longer follow a single model. There are global financial centers, tourist cities, regional centers, and postindustrial manufacturing cities.

What about the urban poor? The postwar experience with building large public housing projects has been decidedly mixed. Most cities proved to be bad housing managers, the proper maintenance of housing projects was expensive (hence generally ignored), high-rise buildings were inappropriate for low-income families, and in any case, large concentrations of poor households turned out to be socially undesirable (Wachter and Schill 1998; Rybczynski 1993b). Lafayette Courts in Baltimore is a typical project of that period. It was built in 1955, and replaced dilapidated row houses with six identical high-rise slabs and seventeen low-rise buildings on a 21.5-acre superblock. The fate of Lafayette Courts followed an all-too-familiar pattern: deterioration, abandonment, and demolition. By the time the project was demolished in 1995, it was in poor physical shape—one-third of its 807 housing units were abandoned— and had become notorious as a center for drug dealing and violent crime (Rybczynski 1999, 17).

Housing vouchers have been proposed as a way of avoiding pockets of poverty by distributing poor families over a wider geographic area, although this approach is limited by the availability of inexpensive housing and the reluctance of landlords to rent to poor tenants. Another alternative is to guarantee a supply of low-income housing by requiring developers to mix social housing with market housing. One version of this, begun during the Clinton administration, was the so-called Hope VI program, which adopted new urbanism as a planning and design model, and built low-rise town houses in place of high-rise apartment slabs. These developments were built on the sites of demolished public housing projects, some of which were in central locations, and hence desirable to market buyers. The strategy was to make social housing indistinguishable in design and quality from market housing. So far, it is unclear if mixing income groups in public/private housing is an effective long-term solution, and whether it really reduces the isolation of the poor (Ambrose and Grigsby 1999). What is certain is that social housing built to market standards is expensive, with the result that these projects have been unable to provide large numbers of housing units for low-income families. In the case of the Hope VI project that replaced Lafayette Courts in Baltimore, for example, 110 senior apartments and 228 row houses replaced the original 807 housing units. Moreover, in 1999, most of the occupants were subsidized low-income tenants, and only 27 of the units had been sold to qualified low-income buyers (at subsidized prices, since the real cost was too high for low-income families). There were no market-rate units in the project (Rybczynski 1999, 20).

The goal of integrating people of different incomes, lifestyles, and values in close proximity flies in the face of U.S. urban history. Urban households of different incomes and social standing have traditionally lived in different neighborhoods: the top and bottom of the hill, the right and wrong sides of the track, uptown and downtown, old housing and new. There have been many reasons for this geographic separation, not only differences in the value of real estate that affect the cost of housing, but also differences in the types of housing (rental flats, row houses, single-family cottages, large houses, and mansions), different physical characteristics (the view or the proximity to green space), and different distances to employment.

Residential separation by income is also the result of the demand for different community amenities. For instance, a campus neighborhood might support art cinemas and used bookshops, while a middle-class neighborhood might favor multiplexes and drive-in banks. An upper-income neighborhood might look down on fast-food franchises and big-box retailers, preferring boutiques and exclusive shops, while a blue-collar neighborhood might support big boxes but not gourmet supermarkets or upscale coffeehouses. Parks might be especially important in a low-income neighborhood, but less so in a high-income area (where residences have their own private outdoor space). It is difficult to imagine all these contradictory features being combined in a single neighborhood. "Different from the utopian planners ideal, the creation of a surrogate form of extended family in contemporary society requires the provision of physical environments designed for the specific needs of a group of families pursuing similar life-styles," writes planner and architect Oscar Newman (1980, 17), "for example, residential environments exclusively for families with children, as different and separate from environments exclusively for young adults or for the elderly."

If spatial segregation in low- and middle-income housing is inevitable, perhaps even necessary, how will social integration be achieved? Public parks, sports facilities (basketball arenas, baseball parks, and football stadiums), and recreational sites (swimming pools and waterfront esplanades) have become the prime mixing places for city inhabitants. The role of city government in their provision is key.

Densification and Urban Infill

The densification of U.S. cities that began in the early 1900s, but had largely slowed in the succeeding decades, is recommencing. Existing residents often resist such densification on the grounds that it adversely affects their way of life (there is even talk of "vertical sprawl"). But densification is an organic part of how old cities, which cannot expand horizontally, have always grown. While densification does affect views and open space, it also results in more people on the street (hence usually a safer environment), more amenities, more choices, and higher property values. Densification produces a larger municipal tax base, which is important for those cities that lost population when they deindustrialized. It should be noted that thanks to smaller households and larger residential units, current population densities, even in the densest

U.S. cities, are still far below what they had been during the early 1900s
(Bruegmann 2005, 26–27).

The preferred locations for new residential development in old cities
have been downtowns and waterfronts. Downtowns are favored for
their ease of access to cultural, entertainment, and sports amenities; waterfront areas are attractive due to their views and recreational amenities. Thus, present densification tends to be highly selective and produces
an unbalanced sort of urbanism, in which some city neighborhoods are
underpopulated and poor, while others in the same city are growing
and wealthy (Rybczynski 2000).

Densification is encouraged by the presence of a range of urban
amenities, not only waterfront views and parks, but also access to mass
transportation, shopping districts, and cultural venues. Yet these amenities are not autonomous; they require population density in order to
achieve full realization. The pleasures of a waterfront esplanade, city
park, or shopping street, for example, depend on the presence of large
numbers of people. An empty esplanade, a deserted park, or an unin-
habited street are not only unattractive, they may even appear threatening and dangerous. So in the process of densification, which comes first,
the amenity or the people?

"Build it and they will come" is one answer. Large urban projects can
act as "pump primers" by attracting large populations in a relatively
short period of time. Since sufficient public amenities must be in place
from the beginning in order to attract buyers and tenants, the success of
such projects depends on developers who have the financial resources
to fund the considerable up-front investment. The project must have a
large enough critical mass to warrant such investments, and the developer must have the experience and skill to deal with a variety of uses.
The role of city government is likewise key, particularly in the land-
assembly phase and in facilitating community acceptance. Design is
also a critical factor, since the project must quickly establish that elusive
quality, "a sense of place." To prime a pump there must be water in the
well, however. It is essential that the surrounding city is part of a metropolitan region where there is steady growth and strong demand.
Densification is not a recipe to save a declining city.

The current densification of downtown Los Angeles, for instance, has
many supportive ingredients: scale, developers with experience and resources, and a growing metropolitan area. The much-admired Disney
Hall, designed by Gehry, serves to give a focus and identity to the
"new" downtown. Another large urban densification project, currently
being planned, is Atlantic Yards in downtown Brooklyn. The $4 billion
development covers twenty-two acres, and includes 6,400 units of
housing, 336,00 square feet of office space, 247,00 square feet of retail, a

hotel, a public school, a health care center, and eight acres of public green space. The magnet facility here is a publicly owned professional basketball arena seating eighteen thousand. While the Brooklyn proposal has engendered controversy due to the height of some of the buildings, it has the requisite ingredients for success: scale, an experienced developer, access to mass transit, an active demand for housing, and a strong regional real estate market.

Battery Park City in downtown New York is a successful example of densification on reclaimed waterfront land. The ninety-two-acre project comprises fourteen thousand residential units built on landfill where piers once stood. The plan could be described as "traditional" in terms of planning—that is, instead of a superblock approach, it extends the Lower Manhattan street grid (although the West Side Highway rudely interrupts this extension), and creates small blocks as the basis for phased development. With the exception of the huge World Financial Center, the results have been pleasantly heterogeneous and avoid the architectural uniformity that bedeviled urban renewal developments of the 1960s. The residential buildings at Battery Park City are medium-rise New York–style apartment blocks. Interspersed among them are a number of public parks and an extremely popular riverfront esplanade, which attracts visitors from outside the development and provides the requisite sense of place. Similar—though much smaller—waterfront residential developments have occurred in Portland, Oregon (River-Place), Memphis (Harbor Town), and Miami (Aqua).

Projects such as RiverPlace, Harbor Town, and Aqua are examples of a planning movement called *new urbanism*. New urbanism began as a strategy for densifying suburban developments by reducing the sizes of lots, narrowing streets, and emphasizing walkability and public amenities. Sometimes referred to as "traditional neighborhood development," this approach recognizes that successful neighborhoods are a function of buildings as well as public spaces, and architectural "codes" regulate not only the location, height, and setbacks of buildings but also architectural features such as materials, the sizes and proportions of openings, and features such as bay windows, porches, and balconies. The best executed of these suburban greenfields projects is Celebration, a planned community for ten thousand residents, outside Orlando, Florida. Celebration consists chiefly of single-family houses, but includes low-rise apartments and apartments above retail in the town center. The architectural styles, such as colonial, low country, and craftsman, are traditional, giving an overall impression of a U.S. small town built at the end of the nineteenth century (Rybczynski 1996).

The financial success of Celebration, and other neotraditional inner-suburb communities such as I'On and Daniel Island in South Carolina,

Kentlands and Lakelands in Maryland, and Laguna West in California, has encouraged developers to adapt this approach to urban locations. One example is Stapleton, a forty-seven-hundred-acre development on the site of the old Denver airport, which will have thirty thousand residents and thirty-five hundred new jobs when it is complete. While consisting predominantly of (dense) single-family housing, it includes apartments and condominiums. At about seven units per acre, compared to a typical suburban density of one unit per acre, and surrounded by existing urban neighborhoods, Stapleton has been able to develop more retail and commercial uses as well as employment than would be possible in a suburban greenfield site (Gyourko and Rybczynski 2000, 743). Another new urbanist infill project is Atlantic Station in Midtown Atlanta, a 138-acre brownfield site that will contain five thousand housing units (both high-rise apartments and single-family homes) and two million square feet of retail space as well as a mixed-use town center.

Not all cities have a sufficiently dynamic real estate market to attract large investments of capital, or sufficient vacant land for a large downtown development project. Such cities must depend on a piecemeal approach to densification. The process generally begins with an increased downtown population in the form of individual risk takers, such as small entrepreneurs and artists. These residents attract small-scale retail, which in turn attracts more residents, perhaps young professionals and empty–nesters. The growing demand encourages developers to undertake new projects, which bring with them more retail and entertainment venues, and so on. This slow process may take a decade or more. Examples are the Back Bay in Boston (in the 1980s), Old City in Philadelphia, and downtown Wilmington, Delaware. Although in most cases the initial decision to densify a neighborhood is taken by the market, not by public officials, the role of government is important, especially in the early phases. Facilitating the permitting process allows redevelopment to start at a small scale; tax abatements provide incentives in weak markets; and in later phases, streetscape and infrastructure improvements and parks attract more residents. Finally, constructing new public buildings (libraries, concert halls, and arenas), while it is unlikely to jump-start the process, is an important reinforcement in later stages.

Lessons

The experiences of the last forty years have taught important lessons concerning the design of urban spaces.

1. The old, well-tried solutions are best: crowded sidewalks, close mixtures of different uses, and large city parks. Don't ignore centuries of urban history.

2. Modern technology, whether it is the automobile or the Internet, does not automatically require the city to be "reinvented." In many cases, it is best simply to add another layer to the many layers of the past.

3. The most successful examples of urban design have involved adjustment rather than radical change: the refurbishment of historic districts, the reuse of disused industrial buildings, and the reconfiguration of obsolete waterfronts.

4. On the whole, the design initiatives of the "planning period" (1950–1970) have been less successful in providing what consumers want than those of the "market period" (1970–2000). The design of the urban environment—buildings and neighborhoods—must meet the market test.

5. Urban amenities (parks, waterfronts, and streets) work best when they are intensively used. Conversely, amenities often fail in the absence of sufficient numbers of users. Densification of the urban environment is the key to vital city life. Densification can be achieved through either large-scale development projects (where strong markets already exist) or gradual, piecemeal development (where markets need to be created).

6. While the government-initiated planning projects of the 1950s and 1960s often failed, the role of government in supporting the urbanization process remains important, particularly in the provision of public spaces, the regulation of building, and the design and maintenance of public amenities. Government efforts should facilitate and complement consumer choices.

In the conclusion to his chapter in *The Metropolitan Enigma*, Burchard quotes the eminent city planner Martin Meyerson (1968, 23) on the challenge facing cities in the future: "The greatest need in our cities is not so much for a giant rebuilding program as for a giant upsurge of popular concern for and pride in the urban environment." Meyerson's point was that in a representative democracy, urban change required a supportive constituency. In 1966, what was hoped for was a political constituency that would support the expenditure of public funds on urban improvements such as urban renewal, highway construction, and public housing. Forty years later, the "supportive constituency" asserts itself in the form of individual choices channeled through the marketplace. It is up to public planning agencies to respond to—and support—this demand.

Notes

1. The relatively greater stability of European cities in the twentieth century was due in large part to the absence of significant national population growth.

2. An excellent discussion of colonial urbanism in America is contained in the first eight chapters of Reps (1965).

3. Detroit, Buffalo, Indianapolis, and Madison, Wisconsin, whose original plans were directly influenced by Washington, DC, were the rare exceptions.

4. Thomas Jefferson once designed a block subdivision that smoothed out the advantage of lots located near street corners by making them smaller than the lots farther from the corners (Reps 1965, 245).

5. Revealingly, the most dynamic and fast-growing commercial streets in Montreal in recent decades, such as St. Denis, St. Laurent, and Laurier, have been those unconnected to the underground system.

6. A partial list of cities that built pedestrian malls, semimalls, or transit malls in the 1960s and 1970s includes Louisville, Minneapolis, Denver, Philadelphia, Chicago, Los Angeles, Santa Monica, Miami Beach, Buffalo, Boulder, Iowa City, Kalamazoo, Madison, Salem, Massachusetts, Burlington, Vermont, Ithaca, New York, Battle Creek, Michigan, Portland, Oregon, Eugene, Oregon, Charlottesville, Virginia, Raleigh, North Carolina, Louisville, Kentucky, Rockford, Illinois, La Grange, Illinois, Oak Park, Illinois, Saint Charles, Missouri, Fresno, California, and San Jose, California. In Canada, the cities include Montreal, Ottawa, Toronto, and Regina, Saskatchewan.

References

Ambrose, Brent W., and William Grigsby. 1999. Mixing Income Groups in Public Housing. *Wharton Real Estate Review* 3 (Fall): 7–15.

Barnett, Jonathan. 1986. *The Elusive City: Five Centuries of Design, Ambition, and Miscalculation*. New York: Harper and Row.

———. 1995. *The Fractured Metropolis: Improving the New City, Restoring the Old City, Reshaping the Region*. New York: HarperCollins.

———. 2003. *Redesigning Cities: Principles, Practice, Implementation*. Chicago: Planners Press.

Birch, Eugenie L. 2006. Who Lives Downtown Today? *Wharton Real Estate Review* 10 (Spring): 68–91.

Brenner, Elsa. 2006. A Piazza for a Maryland Suburb. *New York Times*, November 22, C7.

Bruegmann, Robert. 2005. *Sprawl: A Compact History*. Chicago: University of Chicago Press.

Burchard, John. 1968. Design and Urban Beauty in the Central City. In *The Metropolitan Enigma: Inquiries into the Nature and Dimensions of America's "Urban Crisis,"* ed. James Q. Wilson, 205–43. Cambridge, MA: Harvard University Press.

Dewan, Shaila. 2006. Cities Compete in Hipness Battle to Attract Young. *New York Times*, November 25, A1.

Dillon, David. 2006. Dallas Experiments with Instant Urbanism at Victory. *Architectural Record* (October): 82.

Duany Plater-Zyberk and Company. 1999. *The Lexicon of the New Urbanism*. Unpublished manuscript, version 2.0, F 1.1-F 1.2, Miami.

Florida, Richard. 2004. *The Rise of the Creative Class: And How It's Transforming Work, Leisure, Community, and Everyday Life*. New York: Basic Books.

Frieden, Bernard J., and Lynne B. Sagalyn. 1992. *Downtown, Inc.: How America Rebuilds Cities*. Cambridge, MA: MIT Press.

Garreau, Joel. 1991. *Edge City: Life on the New Frontier*. New York: Doubleday.

Garvin, Alexander. 1996. *The American City: What Works, What Doesn't*. New York: McGraw-Hill.

Greenberg, Allan. 2006. *The Architecture of Democracy: American Architecture and the Legacy of the Revolution*. New York: Rizzoli International Publications.

Gruen, Victor. 1964. *The Heart of Our Cities: The Urban Crisis: Diagnosis and Cure*. New York: Simon and Schuster.

Gyourko, Joseph, and Witold Rybczynski. 2000. Financing New Urbanism Projects: Obstacles and Solutions. *Housing Policy Debate* 11:733–50.

Jacobs, Allan B. 1993. *Great Streets*. Cambridge, MA: MIT Press.

Jacobs, Jane. 1961. *The Death and Life of Great American Cities*. New York: Vintage Books.

Kotkin, Joel. 2005a. *The City: A Global History*. New York: Modern Library.

———. 2005b. The Playground City. *Wharton Real Estate Review* 10 (Fall): 59–63.

Meyerson, Martin, et al. 1968. *The Face of the Metropolis*. New York: Random House.

Newman, Oscar. 1980. *Community of Interest*. Garden City, NY: Anchor Press/Doubleday.

Rabin, Yale. 1989. Expulsive Zoning: The Inequitable Legacy of *Euclid*. In *Zoning and the American Dream: Promises Still to Keep*, ed. Charles M. Haar and Jerold S. Kayden, 103–7. Chicago: Planners Press.

Reps, John W. 1965. *The Making of Urban America: A History of City Planning in the United States*. Princeton, NJ: Princeton University Press.

Rosenzweig, Roy. et al. 1992. *The Park and the People: A History of Central Park*. Ithaca, NY: Cornell University Press.

Russo, Karl. 2007. Neighborhoods and Local Public Finance. PhD diss., Wharton School, University of Pennsylvania.

Rybczynski, Witold. 1990. *A Clearing in the Distance: Frederick Law Olmsted and America in the Nineteenth Century*. New York: Scribner.

———. 1993a. The New Downtowns. *Atlantic Monthly* (May): 98–106.

———. 1993b. Bauhaus Blunders. *Public Interest* 113 (Fall): 82–90.

———. 1996. Tomorrowland. *New Yorker*, July 22, 36–39.

———. 1999. Hope VI: Pleasant View Gardens. *Wharton Real Estate Review* 3 (Fall): 16–21.

———. 2000. Living Downtown. *Wharton Real Estate Review* 4 (Spring): 5–12.

———. 2002. The Bilbao Effect. *Atlantic Monthly* (September): 138–42.

———. 2003. The Changing Design of Shopping Places. *Wharton Real Estate Review* 7 (Spring): 34–41.

Skaburskis, Andrejs. 2006. New Urbanism and Sprawl: A Toronto Case Study. *Journal of Planning Education and Research* 25:233–48.

Stern, Robert A. M. 2007. Garden City Suburbs. *Wharton Real Estate Review* 11 (Fall): 84–93.

Wachter, Susan M., and Michael H. Schill. 1998. The Future of Public Housing. *Wharton Real Estate Review* 2 (Spring): 39–47.

Ward, Alan ed., 2006. *Reston Town Center: A Downtown for the 21st Century.* Washington, DC: Academy Press.

Weiss, Marc A. 1987. *The Rise of the Community Builders: The American Real Estate Industry and Urban Land Planning.* New York: Columbia University Press.

Wolf, Peter. 1999. *Hot Towns: The Future of the Fastest Growing Communities in America.* New Brunswick, NJ: Rutgers University Press.

5

Housing

URBAN HOUSING MARKETS

JOSEPH GYOURKO

FORTY YEARS AGO when policymakers and scholars thought about urban housing, they invariably focused their attention on the large fraction of substandard housing units in America's cities, and the inevitable implication of this for the nation's poorer households, many but by no means all of whom were members of a minority group.[1] Fourteen percent of whites and 46 percent of nonwhites occupying housing units in urban areas in 1960 were living in substandard housing, where substandard implied the housing was unsafe or inadequate in some fundamental way. When measured along income rather than racial lines, 36 percent of those in the bottom third of the income distribution in 1960 lived in substandard units, compared to only 4 percent among those in the top third of the income distribution (Frieden 1968).

By the turn of the twenty-first century, substandard housing had become extremely rare in central cities. Data from the *American Housing Survey* show that complete plumbing facilities now are absent in only about 1 percent of owner-occupied units and just over 2 percent of rental units in the nation's primary central cities. Other indicators of very low housing quality confirm that such housing has been dramatically reduced in urban housing stocks, and space consumption by those in the bottom quartile of the income distribution has been rising.

This certainly is one of the great urban successes of the past half century. Yet it does not mean that housing issues no longer are relevant to urban policy affecting America's cities. Poverty has not been eliminated, so there still are poor households that cannot afford to purchase the decent-quality housing that now is widely available. It is important, however, to distinguish between affordability problems caused by low incomes versus those caused by house prices being above the level that would prevail in a truly free market. Affordability problems due to poverty are best resolved with income transfers to the poor. If that is not feasible, housing vouchers clearly are cheaper than public housing construction programs or subsidies to private development.

The near elimination of very low-quality housing units from the privately supplied urban stock especially and the recognition that housing consumption by the extremely poor is a problem of low income, not of low housing quality, suggests a change in focus for housing policy thinking. What heretofore has been driven by a redistributionist impetus needs to become much more cognizant of how the functioning of housing markets can affect the fortunes of cities and the welfare of their residents, for better or worse. Housing markets act as a mediator of city growth and decline, and understanding this process is important for policy in a variety of ways.

This is illustrated below by analyzing three ways in which housing markets affect the fate of cities. The first focuses on how the long-lived nature of houses helps ensure that urban decline is a lengthy process. Particularly relevant for policy purposes is the fact that durable housing in declining cities is relatively more attractive to the less skilled. Thus, it is the physical nature of cities that helps explain why low human capital and poorer workers tend to concentrate in declining markets. To the extent there are negative spillovers from such concentrations of the poor and less skilled, a policy response is almost certainly appropriate.

The second case examines local regulation pertaining to land use and residential construction. This example illustrates that housing markets mediate urban growth, not just decline. The rise of regulations restricting the ability of developers to supply new units to the market is one of the most significant developments in recent decades. First, they change the way in which strong demand trends manifest themselves. In relatively unregulated markets such as Las Vegas or Charlotte, increased demand is reflected more in terms of population and housing unit growth, and less in terms of rising house prices. The converse is true in highly regulated markets such as San Francisco, New York City, and Boston.

Recent research also suggests that sorting across cities along income lines is becoming more intense because it is the relatively rich who can best tolerate the high prices in high-demand markets with inelastic supplies of housing. More broadly, there are potentially large economic welfare losses from the misallocation of households that results from local building regulation that is too restrictive. Essentially, attractive and highly productive labor-market areas such as the Bay Area, New York City, and Boston are underpopulated. Research has only begun on this topic and more is needed, but policymakers should be considering plans to deal with the inefficient allocation of people across markets.

A third and final example focuses on how construction costs can affect the fortunes of cities by influencing the amount of reinvestment in local housing stocks. An extensive finance literature informs us that asset owners do not reinvest in an asset when its market value is less than the cost of replacing it. Homeowners have to make reinvestment decisions regularly, and the same principal applies to them. Recent research shows that if house prices are below construction costs, much less reinvestment in the existing stock occurs. Price can be below construction costs for various reasons. For instance, negative demand shocks driven by the loss of market share for U.S. car companies may lead to low house prices in Detroit. Construction costs themselves also can be high, though, and the data show meaningfully large variation in these costs across markets. And there is evidence that local conditions influence the level of those costs. Some of these conditions are at least partially under local control in a way that the fortunes of General Motors clearly are not. The policy implication is that declining cities in particular cannot afford to be high construction cost cities, and that whether they are is somewhat under their control.

Before getting to these policy matters, I first document the rise in housing unit quality that has occurred in U.S. cities over the past few decades. That is followed by a more detailed discussion and analysis of how the functioning of housing markets mediates urban growth and decline. Then there is a brief conclusion.

The Quality and Consumption of Housing in America's Cities

A natural starting point for this analysis is Bernard Frieden's chapter on housing and urban policy in *The Metropolitan Enigma*. Frieden's focus was on the housing problems faced by the poor in general and minorities in particular. The literature of the day noted that low-quality housing was associated with a variety of negative outcomes, ranging from the spread of disease to psychological problems for the occupants.[2] While the standards for ascertaining causality in such matters have changed considerably since then, there is no doubt that much substandard housing existed in our major cities, and the presence of urban slums were intimately linked with the burgeoning racial problems of the day.

The two primary measures that Frieden and other researchers employed were whether the unit was crowded and whether it was dilapidated. The traditional definition of overcrowding is more than one person per room, with severe crowding defined as more than 1.5 persons per room. What determines whether a unit is dilapidated is more complex, but it has become the definition of what it means for housing to be substandard. The U.S. Census definition in 1960 was that the unit did not provide "safe or adequate shelter." A variety of traits could lead to a unit not providing safe or adequate shelter. Among these were significant holes in the unit (over the foundation, or in the walls or roof), other damage that meant the occupants were not secure from the elements, the absence of a private toilet or bath (or shower), or a lack of hot running water.[3]

By 1960, 14 percent of whites in occupied housing units in urban areas were rated as living in "unsound" conditions or lacking in basic plumbing facilities. The fraction of nonwhites living in similar conditions was over three times greater at 46 percent. Crowding was somewhat less widespread. Eight percent of whites lived in units with more than one person per room, versus 25 percent for nonwhites.[4] Not unexpectedly, the poor were disproportionately represented in such housing. Frieden (1968, 173) divided the income distribution into thirds and showed that 36 percent of families in the bottom third lived in substandard housing, versus only 4 percent of families from the top third.

Frieden also showed that these figures for 1960 represented a fairly substantial improvement over conditions in 1950—for all races. He also noted some predictions, including one by William Grigsby (1963), that substandard housing largely would disappear over the next couple of decades. Both demand- and supply-side factors were cited as potential causes of improvement. On the demand side, rising incomes were seen as key, while more production was seen as essential on the supply side.

More recent data find that the optimists largely were correct.[5] The *American Housing Survey* (*AHS*) serves as the primary data source for my analysis over the past two decades, but the information in table 5.1 provides a broader historical overview using decennial censuses dating back to 1940. These data, which are for the entire nation (not just the central cities), document the extent to which substandard housing has virtually disappeared from the housing stock. As late as 1950, over a third of the nation's housing units did not have complete plumbing facilities, and a quarter did not have a septic system or a connection to a public sewer system. Moderate crowding existed in nearly 16 percent of the units. The improvement in quality over the 1950s that was described by Frieden (1968) is evident in these data, too, with the improving trend continuing in the ensuing decades. By the year 2000, only one in two hundred housing units did not have complete plumbing facilities. About 1 percent did not have a septic system or sewerage connection in 1990.[6] Severe crowding has not occurred in more than 2.7 percent of housing units since 1960 (column 4). Moderate crowding is more prevalent and has been present in about one in twenty units over the past two decades (column 3).

The *AHS*, which provides more detail at higher frequencies than the Census, paints a similar picture of declining fractions of substandard housing. I use data from the national files of this survey dating back to

TABLE 5.1
The Decline of Substandard Housing in the Stock

Census year	% units without complete plumbing facilities%	% units without sewer connection or septic tank	Crowding	
			%> 1 person per room	% > 1.5 person per room
1940	45.3	35.3	20.2	9
1950	35.5	24.5	15.7	6.2
1960	16.8	10.3	11.5	3.6
1970	6.9	4.3	8.2	2.2
1980	2.7	1.8	4.5	1.4
1990	1.1	1.1	4.9	2.1
2000	0.6	NA	5.7	2.7

Note: The 2000 Census stopped tabulating housing units without a sewer or septic tank.
Source: U.S. Census Bureau. The sample includes all housing units in the nation.

1985, when the new panel of housing units was begun. In many cases, disaggregated information for renters versus owners is available only beginning in 1987, but I report information from 1985 whenever possible.[7] Table 5.2 reports results on housing units only in the central cities of metropolitan areas, and disaggregates the data across owners and renters. In addition to the measure involving the presence of complete plumbing facilities, four other quality measures are reported: the fraction of units with less than one full bathroom, the fraction of units with one or fewer bathrooms, the fraction of units without full kitchen facilities, and the fraction of units without a central heating system, radiators, or a fireplace.

Each measure tells a similar story. The share of units with traits consistent with very low quality is quite small, but there generally are more substandard rental units relative to owner-occupied ones. The number of owner-occupied units in central cities without complete plumbing facilities has fallen from about one in fifty in the late 1980s to one in a hundred in the most recent data. The data for rental units show a slight decline in the fraction without complete plumbing since 1987, but there is volatility across the survey years. This should be interpreted as a relatively flat trend, with the 2005 data indicating that about one in forty apartments in primary central cities were without complete plumbing.

The fraction without a complete bathroom is even lower (column 2). Among owner-occupied units, the fraction has not been above 0.5 percent

TABLE 5.2
Substandard Housing in U.S. Cities

	AHS data on primary central cities, owner-occupied units				
Year	1 % units without complete plumbing facilities	2 % units with less than one complete bathroom	3 % units without heating facilities	4 % units without complete kitchen facilities	5 % units with one complete bathroom or less
1985	na	na	na	na	na
1987	2.17	0.10	0.84	0.64	40.14
1989	2.11	0.19	0.60	0.57	37.59
1991	1.67	0.13	0.94	0.47	36.99
1993	1.32	0.13	0.83	0.63	35.58
1995	1.40	0.17	0.97	0.65	33.35
1997	0.74	0.43	0.62	1.00	35.63
1999	1.01	0.28	0.51	0.58	31.67
2001	0.94	0.44	0.07	1.33	30.52
2003	1.27	0.35	0.18	0.65	28.97
2005	1.08	0.29	0.19	0.34	27.86

(cont.)

over the past two decades. Among rental units, barely more than one in a hundred apartments do not have a full bathroom according to the most recent surveys.

Other evidence confirming the small amount of clearly substandard housing units is provided in the next two columns. For example, almost all housing units in cities, whether owned or rented, have some type of heating system (column 3). The data in the fourth column on the fraction without a full kitchen indicate that only one in three hundred owner-occupied units now are without this feature. The fraction of rental units without full kitchens has ranged from about one in thirty-seven in the mid-1980s to one in twenty in the most recent data from 2005 (column 4). This is the only measure suggesting that quality might have decreased over time among the urban rental stock. Even so, the absolute share remains low.

The fifth column of table 5.2, which documents the fraction of units with one or fewer full bathrooms, illustrates how the average quality of

TABLE 5.2 *(cont.)*

	Renter-occupied units				
	1	2		4	5
Year	% units without complete plumbing facilities	% units with less than one complete bathroom	3 % units without heating facilities	% units without complete kitchen facilities	% units with one complete bathroom or less
1985	na	na	na	na	na
1987	2.94	1.92	1.62	2.72	81.41
1989	2.91	1.74	1.56	2.62	79.50
1991	2.30	1.56	1.89	2.38	79.04
1993	1.15	1.45	1.82	2.44	78.64
1995	1.07	1.00	1.78	1.95	78.23
1997	2.42	1.75	1.47	5.85	78.29
1999	1.95	1.53	1.28	4.80	78.32
2001	2.24	1.56	0.64	4.61	76.87
2003	2.27	1.27	0.60	4.19	76.38
2005	2.38	1.27	0.62	4.98	74.69

Notes: Data are not available for 1985 due to the fact that the *AHS* did not provide data for renters and owners separately.

Source: Table A-4 of the *AHS* report from 1987–2005. Units without heating facilities are classified AHS as those homes without central heating, fireplaces, or radiators.

the city housing stock has increased over time, especially among owner-occupied units. In 1987, about 60 percent of owner-occupied units had more than one bathroom. Well over two-thirds of owner-occupied units in cities had more than one bathroom in 2005, according to the *AHS*. More than one full bathroom is not yet the norm for apartments, but one-quarter of city rental units had more than one full bathroom in 2005, up from 19 percent in 1987. Given that much of the rental stock is targeted toward unmarried singles, one would not expect as high a share for apartments.

Table 5.3 reports data on crowding. The *AHS* does not break down these data separately for owners and renters, so figures for the combination of both groups are reported. Severe crowding as reflected in having more than 1.5 persons per room has been extremely rare (1 percent or

TABLE 5.3
Crowding in City Housing Stocks: Owners
and Renters

| | AHS *data on primary central cities* | |
Year	1 *Owners and renters, persons per room* % >1 per room	2 % >1.5 per room
1985	3.70	0.91
1987	3.82	0.80
1989	4.18	0.98
1991	4.06	0.97
1993	3.91	0.85
1995	3.94	0.87
1997	4.29	1.06
1999	3.84	0.72
2001	3.67	0.85
2003	3.48	0.66
2005	3.52	0.74

Note: Data from table 2-3 of the *AHS* from 1985–
2005.

less) over the last twenty years. Moderate crowding with more than one
person per room has existed in under 4 percent of all city housing units
since 1997. These data are slightly lower than those reported in the 2000
Census, and if accurate, indicate that city housing is slightly less
crowded than the national average. Taken together, these figures and
those in table 5.1 suggest that between one in twenty-five and one in
twenty housing units currently is crowded, as traditionally defined.

The information in table 5.4 documents changes in tenure patterns
and types of units. The first column shows that the share of the stock
that is owner-occupied has increased by about 10 percent since 1987, so
that city housing stocks nationally no longer are accurately characterized as being primarily rental in nature. Of those units that are owner
occupied, the vast majority always have been single-unit dwellings,
with that share rising marginally over time. Among rental units, the
share in traditional multifamily settings (defined as in structures with

TABLE 5.4
Tenure and Unit Type

		AHS *data on primary central cities*	
Year	*1* *% Owner-occupied*	*2* *% Owner* *Occupied units* *in one-unit buildings*	*3* *% Rental units* *in five-plus-unit* *buildings*
1985	na	na	na
1987	48.60	86.77	51.65
1989	48.73	86.00	48.99
1991	48.66	86.65	48.73
1993	49.08	86.94	50.68
1995	48.96	97.16	50.36
1997	48.92	86.81	51.34
1999	49.83	88.88	50.20
2001	53.17	88.52	48.85
2003	53.36	88.49	50.43
2005	54.30	87.73	52.64

Notes: Data for 1985 are not available due to the fact that the *AHS* did not provide unit type data for central cities separately.

Source: Data from table 1B-1 of the *AHS* from 1987–2005

five or more apartments) also has increased modestly over the past three decades.

Another important quality metric is the physical amount of housing being consumed by city residents. Since 1985, the *AHS* has asked occupants how large their units are in square feet. Figure 5.1 plots the average size of owner-occupied and rental units in central cities over the past two decades.[8] There is a slight positive trend in the size of owner-occupied units, with the average square footage increasing by about 140 feet, from 1,500 in 1985 to 1,640 in 2005. The change is less in absolute and percentage terms for rental units, but there has been no decline in square footage for this part of the stock. The typical city apartment unit contains over 800 square feet of space, which is consistent with there being two bedrooms. While one would expect stability in these series given how large the existing stock is compared to the amount of new construction in a typical year, these data still indicate that the size of new units is increasing modestly over time.

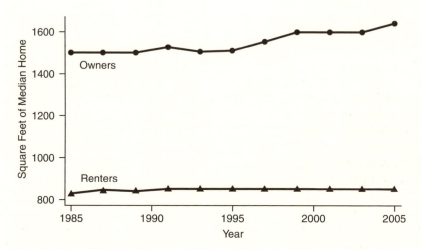

Fig. 5.1 Size of Existing Renter and Owner-Occupied Homes: Central Cities, AHS National Files

Figure 5.2 then plots unit size data scaled by the number of occupants. Living space per person has gone up slightly for both the owner-occupied and rental stock in U.S. cities. While this is useful for gauging quality at the center of the distribution, any potential problem in this regard probably lies with those at the bottom of the income distribution. To gain insight into what is happening to the housing consumption of the poor, figure 5.3 plots the unit size per person for those in the top and bottom quartiles of the income distribution.[9] Not surprisingly, housing consumption per person has increased over time among the relatively

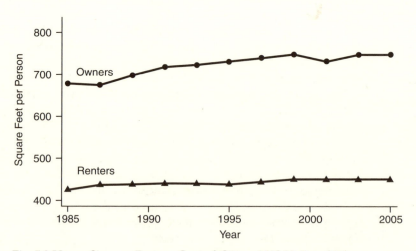

Fig. 5.2 House Size per Person: Central Cities, AHS National Files

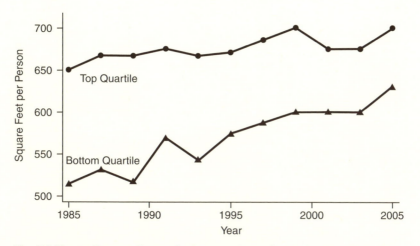

Fig. 5.3 House Size per Person by Income Quartile: Under Age 55 in Central Cities, AHS National Files

rich. Yet it has risen more so for those in the bottom quartile of the income distribution, too. Thus, the gap in space consumption between the richest and poorest city residents has narrowed considerably over the past two decades.

One final illustration of the increase in the quality of city housing stocks is in the fraction of units reporting some type of air-conditioning present.[10] The 2005 data from the *AHS* indicate that 86 percent of occupied housing units in central cities had at least one room air-conditioning unit. This is nearly double the fraction reported in the 1974 survey. While Frieden (1968) reported that 14 percent of white families living in urban areas in 1960 were in dilapidated housing, the most recent data suggest that only 14 percent of urban housing units do not have some type of air-conditioning.

Of course, rising quality does not mean housing always is affordable, although the increasing size of units suggests that space is not being sacrificed even at the low end of the income distribution. Figure 5.4 plots the median gross rent for a sample of large U.S. cities and shows that real rental costs have risen across the quality spectrum, with the increase at the top end of the distribution being relatively greater. Figure 5.5 then documents that even with rising real rents, gross rental costs as a share of real GDP per capita were much lower in 2000 than they were in 1960. City rental housing therefore is not rising in cost relative to the growth of the broader economy.[11]

While this is so for relatively cheap and expensive apartments on average, it still does not deny that there are poor people who cannot afford the plentiful decent-quality housing that is available. Nevertheless, the

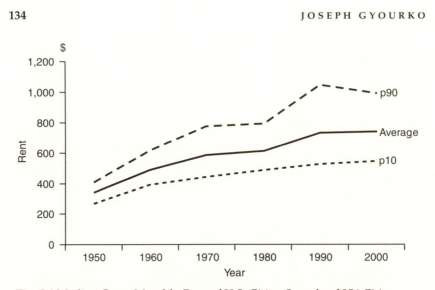

Fig. 5.4 Median Gross Monthly Rent of U.S. Cities: Sample of 254 Cities with 100,000+ People in 2000 (2005 Dollars)

data presented above indicate this is not a housing problem per se but instead a poverty problem. Decent-quality housing now is widespread, so it no longer is so critical a policy issue for urban housing stocks to be upgraded in quality in order for our poorest citizens to have a good place to live. The real issue with respect to the nation's urban poor is to provide them with enough resources so that they can afford to live in the decent housing that is available.

This basic fact should remind us that amid all the good news about the improved quality of the privately supplied urban housing stock, we should not lose sight of the ongoing poverty problem that renders even the most efficiently provided housing unaffordable for the truly poor. Not only has poverty not gone away, it remains highly concentrated in our central cities. Moreover, increased resource transfers will be needed to the extent that regulation raises the minimum quality level for residences.

This highlights the point that what constitutes a proper housing unit has changed over time. This is perhaps best illustrated by the virtual elimination via regulation of single-room occupancy hotels. Many poor and sometimes mentally ill individuals lived in such units, which con- stituted perhaps the cheapest housing in our cities, and there is a debate in the urban policy literature about the role this policy played in the rise of homelessness (Jencks 1994; O'Flaherty 1996). One does not have to take a stand on any causal relationship in that particular issue to recog- nize that there is no free lunch to raising minimum quality standards, as doing so clearly requires more resources to house poor people in the available higher-quality stock.[12]

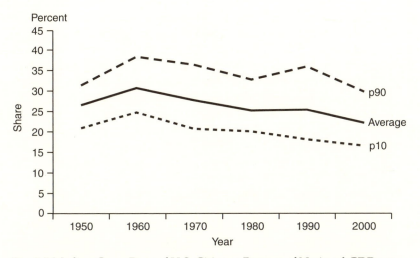

Fig. 5.5 Median Gross Rent of U.S. Cities as Percent of National GDP per Capita: Sample of 254 Cities with 100,000+ People in 2000 (2005 Dollars)

Economists prefer lump-sum transfers on efficiency grounds to achieve such redistribution. Absent that, vouchers clearly are more efficient than government building programs (e.g., public housing) or subsidies to private developers of affordable housing (U.S. Government Accounting Office 2002).[13] This is not to imply that there is no role for supply-side policies in general, only that the real issue for the poor is low income. Building more housing will not solve what fundamentally is a problem of deficient resources for them.[14]

Housing Markets as a Mediator of Urban Growth and Decline

While it clearly is a good thing for the nation that we no longer have to worry about large fractions of our urban residents living in dilapidated housing, it remains critical for urban policymakers to understand that how housing markets function can have important implications for how cities function—for better or worse. This section highlights this point by examining three facets of how housing markets influence the growth and decline of cities.

The Durability of Housing and the Nature of Urban Decline

One of the most defining traits of housing is its durability, with recent research arguing that urban decline is not the mirror image of urban growth largely because housing is so long-lived once it is produced

(Glaeser and Gyourko 2005). In the absence of constraints on the ability of home builders to supply new housing units to the market, population can expand quickly in the face of positive demand shocks to a city. Still, population loss and urban decline play out slowly over decades, because the presence of cheap housing slows the decline of population even in the presence of negative demand shocks to the city.

For this perspective on how housing markets affect city growth and decline to be true, it must be the case that the distribution of city population growth is skewed, population loss is a long-term and not a one-time event, and housing in declining cities really is cheap. Each requirement is readily confirmed in the data.

First, the distribution of city population growth is extremely skewed. In the 1990s among larger cities with at least one hundred thousand residents at the beginning of the decade, Las Vegas experienced the greatest population growth, at almost 62 percent. No large city declined nearly so much, with Hartford, Connecticut, experiencing the greatest population loss of about -14 percent in the 1990s. This pattern is similar in other decades.

Second, it is the case that urban decline generally is not a fleeting process. All but four of the fifteen-largest cities in the United States in 1950 lost population between 1950 and 2000, and eight of them (Baltimore, Buffalo, Cleveland, Detroit, Philadelphia, Pittsburgh, Saint Louis, and Washington, DC) lost population in each decade.

Third, housing costs in declining cities tend to be quite low in declining cities. Table 5.5 compares the median home price from the 2000 Census for the twenty-five-largest cities in the country as of 1990, with an estimate of the physical construction costs for a modest-quality, two-thousand-square-foot single-family home in each market.[15] The final column indicates whether the city lost population in the 1990s. A striking feature of these data is that the typical home in a declining city tends to be valued well below its construction costs. For example, even though construction costs in Detroit are lower than they are in New York City, Detroit's median house value of $63,600 according to the 2000 Census was only 59 percent of the construction costs of a modest-quality single-family home in that market. A large negative gap, typically 20 percent or more, between house prices and their construction costs is evident for other cities that lost population during the 1990s.

Figure 5.6 illustrates why this is so. Essentially, the housing market is characterized by a kinked supply schedule that tends to be elastic when house prices are above their construction costs, but is very inelastic otherwise. Because housing is so durable, the supply schedule is inelastic when the price is below the cost of construction, so a negative demand shock like that depicted by the shift in demand from D_0 to D_1 is

TABLE 5.5
Price and Construction Costs in Large Cities

				3 2000 construction cost for home	4 Population growth,
		1 1990 population	2 2000 median house value	2,000-sq-ft. home	1990–2000 (%)
Year	City				
1	New York City	7,322,564	$211,900	$136,937	9.4
2	Los Angeles	3,485,398	$221,600	$112,543	6.0
3	Chicago	2,783,726	$132,400	$113,927	4.0
4	Houston	1,630,553	$79,300	$91,782	19.8
5	Philadelphia	1,585,577	$59,700	$114,792	−4.3
6	San Diego	1,110,549	$233,100	$109,256	10.2
7	Detroit	1,027,974	$63,600	$107,872	−7.5
8	Dallas	1,006,877	$89,800	$89,100	18.1
9	Phoenix	983,403	$112,600	$91,695	34.4
10	San Antonio	935,933	$68,800	$86,246	22.3
11	San Jose	782,248	$394,000	$126,903	14.4
12	Baltimore	736,014	$69,100	$93,512	−11.5
13	Indianapolis	731,327	$98,200	$97,405	8.3
14	San Francisco	723,959	$396,400	$126,903	7.3
15	Jacksonville	635,230	$87,800	$87,803	15.8
16	Columbus	632,910	$101,400	$96,799	12.4
17	Milwaukee	628,088	$80,400	$103,547	−5.0
18	Memphis	610,337	$72,800	$87,284	6.5
19	Washington	606,900	$157,200	$98,702	−5.7
20	Boston	574,283	$190,600	$119,463	2.6
21	Seattle	516,259	$259,600	$108,304	9.1
22	El Paso	515,342	$71,300	$79,585	9.4
23	Cleveland	505,616	$72,100	$105,104	−5.4
24	New Orleans	496,938	$87,300	$87,803	−2.5
25	Nashville	488,374	$113,300	$86,765	16.7

25-largest cities according to the 1990 Census

Sources: Columns 1, 2, and 4 from the U.S. Census Bureau; Column 3 from R.S. Means construction cost data, 2000.

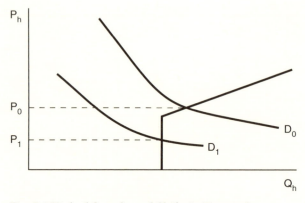

Fig. 5.6 Kinked Supply and Shifts in Demand

associated with a large drop in prices to a level well below construction costs.

Perhaps more important for policy purposes is the implication that the functioning of housing markets in declining cities has for the concentration of poverty. Declining cities tend to be both poor and have relatively low human capital levels. Regression results from Glaeser and Gyourko (2005) confirm that among cities losing residents, a greater rate of loss is associated with a significant decline in the population share of college graduates (who presumably have high skills and are not poor), while there is no statistically significant correlation between the rate of population growth and the share of college graduates in growing cities. The effects themselves are statistically different across the two sets of cities. Moreover, they are economically meaningful. A 10 percent greater rate of population loss can account for between one-quarter and one-third of the gap between the average share of college graduates in growing versus declining cities in this sample.[16]

For cheap housing to be responsible for this pattern, it must be the case that it is relatively more attractive to those with lower wages (and presumably lower skills) to remain in or move to declining cities. For that to be true, the wage premium associated with being in a growing labor market needs to be small for the unskilled compared to the difference in their housing costs across growing versus declining markets. Table 5.6 reports on the differences in wages and housing costs in the fastest- and slowest-growing cities in the United States during the 1990s. Note that there are only modest wage differences across these markets for those with no more than a high school degree, while the differences in housing costs are large. Given that strong labor markets do not pay much of a premium for less skilled labor and that weak labor markets

TABLE 5.6
Labor and Land Market Fundamentals across Growing and Declining Cities, 2000

	Growing cities	Declining cities	Percentage difference
Mean hourly wages	$14.75	$14.49	1.8
Mean contract rent for two-bedroom apartments	$585	$383	34.4
Mean house price for owned homes with three bedrooms	$112,540	$71,560	37.1

Notes: Figures computed from samples of male workers between the ages of 25 and 55 in the 10 fastest- and 10 slowest-growing central cities in the 1990s with populations in excess of 100,000 as of 1990. All monetary figures are in 2000 dollars. The 10 highest-growth central cities with populations in excess of 100,000 in 1990 are: Las Vegas, NV; Plano, TX; Boise, ID; Laredo, TX; Bakersfield, CA; Austin, TX; Salinas, CA; Durham, NC; Charlotte, NC; and Santa Clarita, CA. The 10 lowest-growth (i.e. most negative) central cities with populations in excess of 100,000 in 1990 are: Hartford, CT; Saint Louis, MO; Baltimore, MD; Flint, MI; Buffalo, NY; Norfolk, VA; Syracuse, NY; Pittsburgh, PA; Cincinnati, OH; and Macon, GA.
Source: U.S. Census Bureau, IPUMS Public Use Microdata, 5% sample.

offer much cheaper housing, a low-skill person easily can be better off by staying in, say, Detroit and economizing on housing costs that are well below the home's replacement value.[17]

The tendency of declining cities to disproportionately attract the poor because of their abundance of cheap housing is especially important if concentrations of poverty then further deter growth. If low levels of human capital foster negative externalities or result in lower levels of innovation, this can become a self-reinforcing process in which an initial decline leads to higher poverty rates, which then create further negative pressure on the city (e.g., as in Berry Cullen and Levitt 1999). In addition, as Inman's chapter in this volume documents, the poor are costly to the city in fiscal terms. Deteriorating fiscal conditions provide another pathway for negative spillovers to amplify themselves over time.

While there still is debate about these dynamic considerations, they have important implications for urban policy. They suggest that mayors of declining cities should not be in the business of supplying additional cheap housing, even when it is subsidized by higher levels of government. Public housing construction programs and policies to subsidize private development of nonmarket housing are not needed in these places, and in fact, only exacerbate the effects described above. Simply put, the problem is too much, not too little, cheap housing in these places.[18]

Nevertheless, an effective policy is needed to address any negative externalities that arise from high concentrations of poverty. It is the potential for harmful negative spillovers from concentrated poverty that make this an issue of national significance. One sensible policy would be to create a program that encouraged the mobility of the less skilled out of declining cities. The analysis here suggests that aid would need to be enough to compensate for the difference in housing expenses across growing versus declining cities, so it would cost more than a traditional voucher. At least some of the additional resources needed should come from transferring funds presently allocated for subsidized construction programs in these declining markets.

This should apply even in the case of New Orleans following the terrible tragedy from Hurricane Katrina. That city has been in long-term decline, and the private market has not supported the rebuilding of housing units with prices below their replacement costs. At least some of the monies used to subsidize the construction of these units should be allocated to a person-based voucher program that recipients could use anywhere in the country. No family should be forced to relocate, but sound policy should offer that option. This simply reflects the principle that the primary goal of policy should be to help individuals, not specific places or their developers.

Local Land-Use and Construction Regulations, and Their Impacts on Housing Markets

The rise of local land-use and residential building controls constitutes a second crucial way in which the functioning of housing markets can affect the fortunes of cities. Residential land-use regulations in the United States are widespread, largely under local community control, and are thought to be a major factor in accounting for why housing appears to be in inelastic supply in many of our larger coastal markets in particular. Their primary impact is on the nature of urban growth, not decline, because they can be binding only when the demand is growing. If the supply is very inelastic as indicated by the schedule S_0, in figure 5.7, then standard price theory indicates that increases in the demand for an area, as reflected by the shift from D_0 to D_1, will generate higher house prices with little increase in the number of homes. This is shown by the change from (P^*, Q^*) to (P_1, Q_1) in figure 5.7. If the supply is elastic as reflected in the schedule S_0, the same increased demand manifests itself in much higher quantities than in higher prices (i.e., the move to (P_2, Q_2).[19]

The nature of local land-use regulation can be described using newly available data that I gathered with my colleagues Albert Saiz and Anita

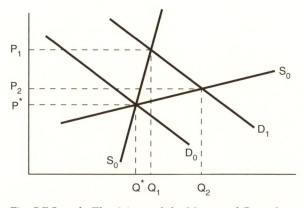

Fig. 5.7 Supply Elasticity and the Nature of Growth

A. Summers (2008).[20] We calculated a measure of regulatory stringency called the Wharton Residential Land Use Regulatory Index (WRLURI) for over twenty-six hundred communities based on a national survey conducted in 2005. We asked a broad set of questions to elicit information about the general characteristics of the local regulatory process, the formal rules of local residential land-use regulation, and certain outcomes of the regulatory process. Factor analysis was then used to create an index of regulatory stringency based on the survey responses. This measure is standardized so that the mean index value is zero with a standard deviation of one.

These data show that the average place is far from unregulated. The typical land-use regulatory environment in the nation has the following traits: two entities, be they a zoning commission, city council, or environmental review board, are required to approve any project necessitating a zoning change; more than one entity also is required to approve any project, even if it does not involve a zoning change; it is highly unlikely that any form of direct democracy is practiced in which land-use issues or projects must be put to a popular vote; there probably is no onerous density restriction such as a one-acre lot size minimum anywhere in the community, although some less stringent minimum constraint generally is in place; some type of exactions and open-space requirements exist, even though they are not as omnipresent as is the case in the more highly regulated places; and there is about a six-month lag on average between the submission of an application for a permit and the permit issuance for a standard project.

While residential land-use and building restrictions are thought to be more of an issue in the suburbs, the data show that at least some major cities have stringent regulatory environments too. The mean index value

TABLE 5.7
Residential Land-Use Stringency for Select
Major Cities

Wharton Residential Land Use Regulation Survey

	City	WRLURI value
1	Atlanta	0.70
2	Austin	2.08
3	Charlotte	−0.08
4	Chicago	−1.15
5	Dallas	−0.14
6	Denver	0.49
7	Honolulu	2.32
8	Las Vegas	−2.00
9	Los Angeles	2.00
10	Miami	0.36
11	Phoenix	1.24
12	Raleigh	1.02
13	San Diego	1.59
14	San Francisco	1.96
15	Seattle	2.39

Notes: The WRLURI is computed so that the average community has an index value of zero. The standard deviation of the distribution is one. Hence, the 0.70 index value for the city of Atlanta indicates that city's regulation climate is 0.7 standard deviations above the national average. For more detail, see discussion in the text; Gyourko, Saiz, and Summers (2008).

for the seventy-three cities in the Wharton sample with populations of at least two hundred thousand in the year 2000 is 0.27, indicating that the regulatory regime in these places is almost 0.3 standard deviations greater than the national average.[21] Yet there is great heterogeneity in conditions across cities, as indicated by the data for fifteen individual cities reported in table 5.7. Charlotte, Dallas, and Las Vegas are high-growth Sun Belt markets with local regulatory climates less stringent than average, as indicated by their negative index values. Other warm weather markets such as Phoenix and Raleigh appear more restrictive according to this measure, and virtually all the major cities on the West Coast (plus Hawaii) have index values that are more than 1.5 standard deviations above the national average.

Because housing in one community is at least somewhat substitutable for housing in another jurisdiction within a given labor-market area, the impact of binding building regulations on market prices generally will depend on the behavior of a central city's suburbs, not just its own choices (presuming it does not comprise a dominant share of the metropolitan-area housing market). One way to gauge the restrictiveness of a metropolitan area is to average the WRLURI values across communities in the area. Presuming that averaging across ten or more jurisdictions within a metropolitan area is necessary to reasonably accurately characterize the regulatory climate of the overall market, metropolitan area–wide index values can be matched with median house prices for forty-three areas.[22]

Figure 5.8's plot of 2005 house prices against the WRLURI values for these markets illustrates that the variables are strongly positively correlated. The simple correlation coefficient is 0.58, and the bivariate regression of prices on index values implies that a one-unit increase in the WRLURI value (which equals a standard deviation change by construction) is associated with a $128,008 higher median house price in the metropolitan area.[23] The magnitude roughly equals the physical construction costs of a decent-quality, single-family unit of seventeen hundred square feet. While correlation is not causality, this pattern is consistent with the implications of figure 5.7, in which the highly regulated places have relatively inelastic supplies and high prices in the face of strong demand.[24] Moreover, it is among the first direct evidence that a strict regulatory regime is associated with substantially higher house prices.[25]

Even more important for the purposes of policy analysis is whether current local land-use and building controls are efficient. It is possible that they are, as the optimal zoning tax or regulatory burden clearly is not zero because development typically generates some negative externalities. Glaeser, myself, and Saks (2005b) consider this issue in our study on the effects of local regulation on Manhattan condominium prices. We find a large regulatory burden that roughly doubles the price of condos on the island. Then, we consider three added social costs of bringing a new housing unit to market and ask whether they might justify such high prices. Those three costs are: the value associated with blocked views from the new apartment buildings; the costs created by extra crowding; and any net fiscal burden created by the new residents. Our analysis concludes that the optimal zoning tax cannot be more than half the existing regulatory burden in Manhattan.

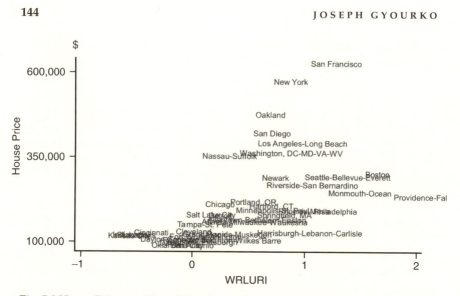

Fig. 5.8 House Prices and Local Regulatory Stringency: Forty-Three Metro Areas.
Source: Gyourko, Saiz, and Summers (2008).

This suggests that local land-use regulation in highly restrictive markets is inefficient in the sense that far less housing is being built than
would be optimal even considering the potential negative externalities
associated with such units. Essentially, markets such as New York, Washington, DC, Boston, and most of coastal California are underpopulated.
A social loss arises from the misallocation of consumers to less productive, less attractive places. To the extent that the value of productive
agglomerations in highly productivity labor-market areas is lowered,
the full social costs could be significant, but good estimates of the true
size is not available.

That said, it must be acknowledged that this type of analysis is most
straightforward in a place like Manhattan, because the increased density associated with a bigger population living in the added housing
units will not change the underlying nature of the community. Put more
starkly, it is not credible to argue that more housing and people will destroy the bucolic atmosphere of Manhattan, but the same cannot always
be said for a low-density suburb. The utility loss from having more density can be high if residents believe the fundamental nature of their
community is altered, and economics does not weight the utility of an
existing resident less than that of the marginal entrant.

However one thinks about the (in)efficiency of such regulations at
the jurisdictional level, there is little doubt that they are at least partly
responsible for why growth pressures show up in high prices in San
Francisco and increasing population in Las Vegas. Not only does high

demand manifest itself differently in these cities, but some researchers have contended that this is leading to more intense sorting by income across metropolitan areas (Gyourko, Mayer, and Sinai 2006). The rich can more readily afford higher house prices, so it makes sense that they would tend to sort into these areas over time.

In a very real sense, the rise of local residential building restrictions has created a new affordability problem—this time for the middle class in highly regulated cities and markets. Affordability is not defined here in terms of the ability to pay but rather in terms of housing being expensive relative to its fundamental costs of construction (i.e., the costs that would obtain in a truly free market).[26] This is a better benchmark for gauging affordability problems, because if one believes that there is such a crisis in a market, presumably the proper policy response is to see to it that more units are delivered to the market so that prices are bid down nearer to the cost of production. After all, the social cost of housing cannot be lower than the cost of constructing a new unit, and for new construction to offer a social benefit, the price of housing must be above that level.

By this metric, housing is far too expensive in many major cities and metropolitan areas, and policy should function to reduce barriers to new construction in these places. Table 5.8 reports data on house

TABLE 5.8
Price-to-Construction Cost Ratios (P/CC) over Time

	102 metropolitan areas		
	1 1980	2 1990	3 2000
Mean	1.15	1.35	1.46
standard deviation, 90th percentile	0.30	0.59	0.55
maximum	1.49	2.17	1.85
	2.17	3.49	4.06
	Implied Land Share (~ 1- CC/P)		
90th percentile	0.33	0.54	0.46
maximum	0.24	0.71	0.75

Notes: These data are taken from Glaeser, Gyourko, and Saks (2005 a, b, table 2). The mean house prices are constructed for each metropolitan area using county-level data from the relevant decennial census. The construction cost data are from the R.S. Means Company. See their article for more detail on various adjustments that were made to the price and cost data.

price-to-construction cost ratios and implied land shares in housing costs across major metropolitan areas since 1980. These figures show that land was not particularly expensive in most markets as recently as 1980. In that year, the average price-to-construction cost ratio of 1.15 implies a land share of only 13 percent. By 2000, the mean price-to-construction cost ratio had risen to 1.46, which implies a 32 percent land share. And for the top 10 percent of the distribution, implied land shares now are near 50 percent or more.

Because the market failure generating the high land costs probably arises from the fact that the costs of new development are borne primarily by existing residents, while the benefits are captured mostly by new entrants, any successful policy will have to compensate the existing residents to counterbalance their incentives to restrict entry. The federal government seems the appropriate level for policy initiation, as this properly is a national issue because the social losses are from a misallocation of people away from productive and attractive areas across the nation.[27]

Local Conditions, Construction Costs, and Reinvestment in the Housing Stock

A third example of how housing markets mediate the nature of growth or decline in a city focuses on the role of construction costs and reinvestment by homeowners. Investment theory suggests that owners of assets generally will not redevelop if the values of their assets are below replacement costs. Research has shown that homeowners, who have both investment and consumption motives, behave similarly. Using information on prices and construction costs, this work finds that owners of homes with market values below replacement costs spend much less (50 percent) on renovation than do owners of similar homes with market values above replacement costs (Gyourko and Saiz 2004).[28]

The relevance of this for urban policy depends on whether the reason for lower reinvestment is purely driven by (negative) demand factors or whether the supply side of the housing market plays a meaningful role. The traditional explanation for the decay of housing stocks in declining areas relies on some strong negative demand shock (e.g., the deurbanization of manufacturing in older cities in the Northeast, or the decline of U.S. automobile companies in Detroit and other parts of the Midwest) that drives prices well below the replacement value. Yet it is possible that price is below construction cost, at least in part, because those costs are high. Because the values of the marginal investment in the house (e.g., renovation, remodeling, etc.) and the marginal costs are both relevant, a potentially important question is whether construction costs themselves play a role in mediating urban decline.

The large effects on reinvestment by existing owners found in recent empirical studies indicate that declining cities in particular cannot afford to be expensive cities in terms of replacement costs. The data reported in table 5.9, however, show that there is substantial variation in construction costs across metropolitan areas and that a number of declining areas are relatively costly. Among large markets with populations of at least one million, there is a $34 per square foot difference in costs. And there are many declining areas in the upper half of this distribution, and some high-growth markets in North Carolina, Texas, and Florida that have the lowest construction costs.

Other research indicates that differences in construction levels across markets of varying size do not explain this variation, as home building appears to be a constant returns-to-scale business. Rather, a set of supply shifters seems to be responsible for the spatial variation in construction costs across markets. These include the extent of unionization in the construction trades, local wages (which reflect the opportunity cost of labor in the market), local topography as reflected by the presence of steep hills or mountains that could make it difficult to build, and the local land-use regulatory environment (Saiz and Gyourko 2006).

That some of these factors are, at least to a degree, under local control, suggests it is important that local officials in flat-to-declining markets, not encourage policies or practices that increase those costs. The topography of an area that might lead to increased construction costs is determined by long-run geologic forces, but land-use regulation and the political support for higher-cost union construction labor can be influenced by city officials. The real lesson is that declining markets cannot afford to be costly ones. Cities such Detroit or Philadelphia that have been losing population over many decades cannot control the trend that pushed manufacturers out of big U.S. cities. Still, they do have some control over the level of replacement costs, and they should work to keep them as low as possible.

Conclusions

The dramatic decline in the fraction of very low-quality units in city housing stocks is a significant urban success story, but it should not make us lose sight of the fact that there has been no similarly large drop in urban poverty. Hence, we need to recognize that sound policy requires both sufficient and efficient policies to ensure that the poor are able to consume the decent-quality housing that now is provided by the private market. Recent evaluations suggest that vouchers should play an increasingly important role in this area for efficiency reasons.

TABLE 5.9
2005 Construction Costs in Markets with 1,000,000+ People

		Cost per sq ft. ($2,000)
		Economy unit: cost per sq.ft.
1	New York	$78.92
2	San Francisco	$73.10
3	Boston–Worcester–Lawrence–Lowell–Brockton	$69.00
4	Philadelphia	$67.69
5	Minneapolis–Saint Paul	$66.96
6	Chicago	$66.88
7	Newark	$66.68
8	Bergen–Passaic	$66.31
9	Sacramento	$65.54
10	New Haven–Bridgeport–Stamford–Danbury–Waterbury	$65.42
11	Hartford	$64.93
12	Los Angeles–Long Beach	$63.91
13	Orange County	$63.67
14	Detroit	$63.54
15	Riverside–San Bernardino	$63.22
16	Seattle–Bellevue–Everett	$62.61
17	San Diego	$62.57
18	Portland–Vancouver	$61.92
19	Kansas City	$61.55
20	Las Vegas	$60.82
21	Saint Louis	$60.78
22	Buffalo–Niagara Falls	$60.78
23	Milwaukee–Waukesha	$60.37
24	Cleveland–Lorain–Elyria	$60.17
25	Rochester	$59.92
26	Pittsburgh	$59.64
27	Denver	$57.40

(cont.)

TABLE 5.9 *(cont.)*

		Cost per sq ft. ($2,000)
		Economy unit: cost per sq.ft.
28	Columbus	$56.14
29	Indianapolis	$55.90
30	Cincinnati	$55.65
31	Baltimore	$55.25
32	Louisville	$54.96
33	Atlanta	$53.58
34	Salt Lake City–Ogden	$52.64
35	Houston	$52.48
36	Memphis	$52.32
37	Phoenix–Mesa	$52.28
38	Nashville	$52.03
39	Tampa–Saint Petersburg–Clearwater	$51.95
40	Miami	$51.71
41	New Orleans	$51.34
42	Fort Lauderdale	$51.26
43	Orlando	$51.26
44	Richmond–Petersburg	$51.01
45	Dallas	$50.32
46	Norfolk–Virginia Beach–Newport News	$50.24
47	Grand Rapids–Muskegon–Holland	$50.08
48	Oklahoma City	$49.47
49	San Antonio	$49.35
50	Fort Worth–Arlington	$48.57
51	Jacksonville	$48.49
52	Austin–San Marcos	$47.96
53	Raleigh–Durham–Chapel Hill	$45.60
54	Greensboro–Winston–Salem–High Point	$45.60
55	Charlotte–Gastonia–Rock Hill	$44.95

Note: The data correspond to an average 2,000-square-foot housing unit of low-quality (economy cost) MSA with a population over 1,000,000 in 2003.

Source: Data from R. S. Means Company construction cost series, 2005.

Perhaps even more important, the significant reduction in the amount of truly dilapidated urban housing affords us the opportunity to rethink housing policy more generally. First and perhaps foremost, we need to recognize that housing does not hold the key to urban growth or decline per se. Human capital, as Glaeser's chapter in this volume explains, is more crucial than physical capital in that regard. Housing policy thus will not provide some type of magic bullet with which declining cities can revitalize themselves.

Nevertheless, it is vital that both policymakers and scholars recognize how the workings of housing markets mediate urban growth and decline. The most important lesson in this regard surrounds the need for public officials to better comprehend how land-use regulation increasingly is determining how growth manifests itself. Where regulation does not raise costs much, increased demand results in a growing population with only modest increases in house prices. Where land-use and building controls are much stricter, strong demand results in higher prices with little population growth for the city. While city residents may well favor this outcome in some cases, the available evidence indicates that it is not justified on economic grounds, resulting in these markets being inefficiently small. Given the role of cities in providing productive agglomeration economies, this makes land-use policy an issue of national, not just local, significance. State and federal policymakers, not only city mayors, need to work to ensure that growth is allowed to occur where it will be most productive for the nation.

Not all cities grow, and leaders in declining places also need to understand how the workings of housing markets impact them. Recognizing that cheap housing is disproportionately attractive to the relatively poor, who tend to be among the less skilled, is particularly important. Mayors in cities experiencing weak demand should not exacerbate the situation by providing additional low-cost housing, even though it is subsidized by various existing federal programs. That being said, there is a good case for policy to address the negative externalities that arise from concentrated poverty in such places. Individual cities should not be held responsible for the financial burden of these policies, so there is a key role for higher levels of government here, too. For example, housing voucher programs should be made national in scope so that poor recipients can use them anywhere in the country. This encourages mobility of the less skilled to places with stronger labor markets by counterbalancing the incentives to stay in depressed markets with cheap housing that is priced well below construction costs.

Finally, city leaders always should work to see that they are not high construction cost markets. Homeowners are like all asset owners in that they will not reinvest if the benefits do not outweigh the costs of doing so. More specifically, they will not reinvest if their asset value is below its replacement cost. This can happen because of a secular decline in demand or because costs themselves are artificially high. Research shows that local construction costs can be high for a variety of reasons, including union power in the building trades and land-use regulations. Mayors who want their homeowners to rehabilitate their homes through reinvestment should encourage policies that make the cost of doing so as cheap as possible, consistent with the workings of an efficient market. This means supporting market-rate labor costs and sound land-use regulations that are not unduly burdensome.

Notes

This chapter was prepared for the conference Unraveling the Urban Enigma: City Prospects, City Policies, in honor of the late Kathy Engebretson. Writing it has been a bittersweet experience. At different points in our careers, Kathy was a doctoral student, and then a friend and adviser from her post as president of the William Penn Foundation. She was a lover of cities, but never forgot to approach them or urban public policy with a scholar's skeptical eye. That is a wonderful combination, and it is one reason why she is so missed. Finally, I thank Andrew Moore for providing excellent research assistance.

1. The words "urban" and "city" are used interchangeably in this chapter. Unless specifically noted, all data reported refer to conditions in the central cities of metropolitan areas, not the broader labor-market area.

2. For a leading example that was extensively discussed by Frieden (1968), see Schorr (1963).

3. For more detail, see Siegelman (1963).

4. See table 2 in Frieden (1968, 172). His figures are based on decennial census data analyzed by the U.S. Housing and Home Finance Agency.

5. Real disposable income per capita in the United States has more than tripled since 1960, implying a compound annual growth rate of about 2.5 percent (table B31 of the *Economic Report of the President*, which can be accessed at http://www.gpoaccess.gov/eop/tables07.html). With housing being a normal good, one would expect the market to deliver higher-quality units to satisfy the demand for them. The regulation of housing quality also has tightened over this time period. For example, single-room occupancy hotels in cities largely have been regulated out of existence, and the Department of Housing and Urban Development imposes minimum habitability standards for all units covered by its subsidy programs. In addition, housing quality controls at the local level in particular have become more stringent, as I discuss below. Thus, income growth and regulation are both relevant in accounting for the rise in city housing quality documented immediately below, but research has not convincingly identified which is the more important factor.

6. No question about sewerage connections was asked in the 2000 U.S. Census.

7. Prior to 1985, the survey was conducted annually. Many questions were changed when the house panel was changed in 1985, making it problematic to compare answers before and after that year. I do not use weights in calculating the figures, as they are relevant for scaling to the national level, and this sample is for housing units in the primary central cities of metropolitan areas. Sample sizes are large in every year, which suggests these data are likely to be representative of city housing stocks, although there is a significant change in the number of observations in 1997 that is discussed below.

8. The data for 1997 in figures 5.1–5.3 are smoothed via interpolation between the results for 1995 and 1999. These figures are created from the microdata provided by the *AHS*. The national sample was significantly smaller in 1997 compared to all other surveys, and there is a spike in central city dwelling size for that year. The weights provided by the *AHS* do not correct for this. Hence, I interpolate using data from adjacent survey years.

9. The data used in this plot are restricted to units occupied by households with heads under fifty-five years old. This is necessary to avoid the confusion caused by retirees, who report little or no income, living in large housing units. If the elderly are included in the sample, the bottom quartile of the income distribution lives in the largest units on average.

10. This includes a room unit, not only central air-conditioning.

11. I thank Ed Glaeser for providing these data.

12. Moreover, the costs of the necessary transfers to facilitate the consumption of decent residences would be greater were we not "housing" over 1.5 million more individuals in jail or prison in 2006 than in 1980 (for the precise numbers, see the Bureau of Justice Statistics, available at http://www.ojp.usdog.gov/bjs/glance/tables/corr2tab.htm). This certainly is not to argue that it would not be socially and fiscally beneficial to develop policies to reduce our prison populations (see Cook's chapter in this book for more on that), only to note that we still need good policy and sufficient resources to house our least fortunate residents. The same assertion applies to the elderly and others residing in nursing homes, which also tend to be outside the traditionally defined housing stock.

13. Recent work by Kling, Liebman, and Katz (2007) suggests there are limited economic and social spillovers associated with the mobility provided by vouchers, so their benefits should not be overstated.

14. As is discussed later in this chapter, however, an inefficiently low supply is a growing problem in many markets. In those places, more construction is needed to help bring down the prices, but that construction should not be targeted only at one income group.

15. The construction cost data are for the year 2000 and are taken from *Residential Cost Data*, published by the R. S. Means Company, a consultant and data provider to the building industry, located in Kingston, Massachusetts. These particular figures reflect the physical costs of constructing a modest-quality home, which the R. S. Means Company terms an economy-quality house. This is the lowest-quality unit they cost out, but it meets all local building code requirements.

16. For the underlying specification and coefficient estimate details, see table

5 in Glaeser and Gyourko (2005). The underlying data include observations on 321 cities over the three most recent decades: 1970s, 1980s, and 1990s.

17. More formally, if a favorable trade-off between wages and housing costs does account for why the relatively less skilled tend to stay in declining cities, then controlling for the ex post facto distribution of housing costs should eliminate (or substantially weaken) the correlation pattern discussed just above in which a greater rate of population decline was associated with an increasing concentration of the less skilled. Glaeser and Gyourko (2005, table 5) show that controlling for the (log) median house price completely eliminates the relationship between city decline and the share of college graduates in the population.

18. If dispersed, low-density public housing were being brought to market to replace high-density, high-rises, the benefits well could outweigh the costs. Yet it is difficult to imagine that a voucher program for the poor would not be far more efficient from an economic perspective.

19. The literature on this issue is expanding rapidly. Just the empirical studies on the linkage between the stringency of the local regulatory environment and home prices or the intensity of new construction include Noam (1983); Katz and Rosen (1987); Pollakowski and Wachter (1990); Malpezzi (1996); Levine (1996); Mayer and Somerville (2000); Glaeser and Gyourko (2003); Glaeser, Gyourko, and Saks (2005a, 2005b); Quigley and Raphael (2005); Quigley and Rosenthal (2005); Saks (2005); Glaeser and Ward (2006); Ihlanfeldt (forthcoming).

20. This source is used for the obvious reason that it is readily available to the author. Two other important databases have been released within the last year. Pendall, Puentes, and Martin (2006) provide another recent cross-section of communities based on a national survey, while Glaeser, Scheutz, and Ward (2006) offer a detailed look at the local regulatory environment for the Boston metropolitan area. Saks (2005) supplies a useful summary of earlier data sets for the interested reader.

21. The sample includes communities not in metropolitan areas. The mean index value for the 1,904 places located within well-defined metropolitan areas is 0.17, so the typical large city still is slightly more regulated than the average suburb according to these data.

22. The house price data, which are taken from Glaeser and Gyourko (2006), are for 2005 to match the time period of the land-use regulation survey. They represent the real value (in 2000 dollars) of a house with the traits of the median-priced home for each metropolitan area, as reported in the 2000 Census.

23. The actual regression is HousePrice$i$ = 184,174(17,535) + 128,008(28,367)* WRLURIi, where i indexes the metropolitan areas, R^2 = 0.33, n = 43, and standard errors are in parentheses.

24. Caution is in order about attributing all of the house price differential to stricter regulation, because one can imagine higher house prices leading to more regulations. For example, communities in coastal areas might want to use regulations to protect valuable amenities such as access to a beautiful coastline.

25. For more evidence, see Quigley and Raphael (2005). Most other evidence on the impacts on prices is indirect. Glaeser and Gyourko (2003) and Glaeser,

Gyourko, and Saks (2005b) are typical examples in that they infer the influence of regulation by comparing the price of land on its intensive and extensive margins. More specifically, standard hedonic techniques are employed to estimate the value that consumers place on larger lots (the intensive margin). The value of land on the extensive margin equals the worth of a lot with a home on it, which is imputed by subtracting estimates of physical construction costs from home prices. One minus the ratio of the value on the intensive to extensive margins provides an estimate of the impact of regulation on land values. These estimates find that local regulation, which the authors refer to as a "zoning tax," amounts to from one-third to one-half of land value in the big coastal California markets. In markets such as Boston and Washington, DC, the zoning tax represents about 20 percent of the total property value. The impact of regulation is negligible in many markets ranging from Philadelphia and Pittsburgh to Minneapolis, presumably because local regulations are not binding in those places.

26. This is an important distinction because using ability-to-pay metrics such as the share of income spent on housing often confuses the issue and mistakenly leads to concluding that there is an affordability problem in high-cost markets. This can be seen more clearly with the following simple example comparing two metropolitan areas that contain the same quality homes, but have different levels of productivity. In the first market, the average household earns $50,000 per year and housing costs $100,000. Moreover, assume that interest, maintenance, and taxes are such that the household must pay 10 percent of the cost of the home each year to live in it. This implies the annual costs of housing are $10,000 (0.1*$100,000). Abstracting from any complications associated with changing housing prices or incomes, the household has $40,000 left over to spend on other goods ($50,000 – $10,000 = $40,000). In the second metropolitan area, productivity is higher so the households earn $75,000. This $25,000 difference in household incomes requires that house prices be $250,000 greater if people are not to continue to move into this more productive area. Note that with house prices of $350,000 and the same assumption that the annual costs equal 10 percent of house value (or $35,000), after-housing income is $40,000, which is identical to that in the first market ($75,000 – $35,000 = $40,000).

Thus, modest differences in income levels across metropolitan areas require fairly wide gaps in house prices for spatial equilibrium to occur. In the less productive, low-cost region, households are spending 20 percent of their incomes on housing each year ($10,000/$50,000 = 0.2). In the high-cost region, households are spending almost 50 percent of their income on housing annually ($35,000/$75,000 = 0.47). The traditional price-to-income affordability index would suggest that the low-cost region is highly affordable, while the high-cost region is unaffordable. But this is not true, as the example shows. Households are equally well-off in either market, so that there is no meaningful sense in which there is a housing affordability crisis in the second market. Nobody in that market has any incentive to leave for the cheaper market because they will have the same amount left over to spend on other goods in either place (presuming you earn the assumed average income in each market, of course).

And mean income differences of $25,000 across labor markets are not extreme. According to 2000 Census data, family income averaged just over $107,000 in the San Francisco primary metropolitan area, about $75,000 in the Dallas and Atlanta metros, and about $66,000 in the Phoenix market. In addition, the assumption that the annual user costs of living in a home are 10 percent of the house value is not extreme. This number varies by income because of mortgage interest deductibility, but it is well within the range of annual user costs estimated by Poterba (1992) and others who have studied this issue.

27. Aura and Davidoff (2006) have pointed out that new supply need not result in dramatic falls in house values if there is a long queue of people waiting to enter a market at slightly lower prices. Their argument suggests that the biggest impacts on prices are likely to be had from a national effort, not one that focuses on a single market. Yet even for a single market with little fall in price from added supply, welfare still is improved from the superior allocation of people across space.

28. There are a variety of reasons that the fraction is not 100 percent. One is the consumption motive that consumers also have. Another is that these decisions may be relevant to particular attributes of the house (as opposed to the entire structure) that have market values above the replacement costs. In addition, some maintenance and repair may be optimal for durable goods such as housing even if their value has fallen below the replacement cost. If the asset's remaining life is sufficiently long relative to the current maintenance costs, some reinvestment can be rational even if one would not rebuild the entire asset. For a more extensive discussion of these issues and the underlying estimation strategy, see Gyourko and Saiz (2004).

References

Aura, Saku, and Thomas Davidoff. 2006. Supply Constraints and Housing Prices. Working paper, University of California, Berkeley, December.

Berry Cullen, Julie, and Steven Levitt. 1999. Crime, Urban Flight, and the Consequences for Cities. *Review of Economics and Statistics* 81, no. 2 (May): 159–69.

Frieden, Bernard. 1968. Housing and National Urban Goals: Old Policies and New Realities. In *The Metropolitan Enigma: Inquiries into the Nature and Dimensions of America's Urban Crisis*, ed. James Q. Wilson. Cambridge, MA: Harvard University Press.

Glaeser, Edward, and Joseph Gyourko. 2003. The Impact of Building Restrictions on Housing Affordability. *FRBNY Economic Policy Review* (June): 21–39.

———. 2005. Urban Decline and Durable Housing. *Journal of Political Economy* 113 (2): 345–75.

———. 2006. Housing Dynamics. NBER working paper no. 12787, December. Cambridge, MA: National Bureau of Economic Research.

Glaeser, Edward, Joseph Gyourko, and Raven Saks. 2005a. Why Have Housing Prices Gone Up? *American Economic Review* 95 (2): 329–33.

———. 2005b. Why Is Manhattan So Expensive? Regulation and Rise in Housing Prices. *Journal of Law and Economics* 48 (2): 331–70.

Glaeser, Edward, Jenny Schuetz, and Bryce Ward. 2006. Regulation and the Rise of Housing Prices in Greater Boston. Cambridge, MA: Rappaport Institute for Greater Boston, Harvard University.

Glaeser, Edward, and Bryce Ward. 2006. The Causes and Consequences of Land Use Regulation: Evidence from Greater Boston. Harvard University Economics Department working paper, September.

Grigsby, William. 1963. *Housing Markets and Public Policy*. Philadelphia: University of Pennsylvania Press.

Gyourko, Joseph, Christopher Mayer, and Todd Sinai. 2006. Superstar Cities. NBER working paper no. 12355, June. Cambridge, MA: National Bureau of Economic Research.

Gyourko, Joseph, and Albert Saiz. 2004. Reinvestment in the Housing Stock: The Role of Construction Costs and the Supply Side. *Journal of Urban Economics* 55 (2): 238–56.

Gyourko, Joseph, and Albert Saiz. 2006. Construction Costs and the Supply of Housing Structure. *Journal of Regional Science* 46 (4): 661–80.

Gyourko, Joseph, Albert Saiz, and Anita A. Summers. 2008. A New Measure of the Local Regulatory Environment for Housing Markets. *Urban Studies*, 45 (3): 693–729.

Ihlanfeldt, Keith. Forthcoming. The Effect of Land Use Regulation on Housing and Land Prices. *Journal of Urban Economics*.

Jencks, Christopher. 1994. *The Homeless*. Cambridge, MA: Harvard University Press.

Katz, Lawrence, and Kenneth T. Rosen. 1987. The Interjurisdictional Effects of Growth Controls on Housing Prices. *Journal of Law and Economics* 30 (April): 149–60.

Kling, Jeffrey, Jeffrey Liebman, and Lawrence Katz. 2007. Experimental Analysis of Neighborhood Effects. *Econometrica* 75 (1): 83–119.

Levine, Ned. 1996. The Effects of Local Growth Controls on Regional Housing Production and Population Redistribution in California. *Urban Studies* 36 (12): 2047–68.

Malpezzi, Stephen. 1996. Housing Prices, Externalities, and Regulation in U.S. Metropolitan Areas. *Journal of Housing Research* 7 (2): 209–41.

Mayer, Christopher, and Tsur Sommerville. 2000. Residential Construction: Using the Urban Growth Model to Estimate Housing Supply. *Journal of Urban Economics* 48 (1): 85–109.

Noam, Eli. 1983. The Interaction of Building Codes and Housing Prices. *Journal of the American Real Estate and Urban Economics Association* 10 (4): 394–403.

O'Flaherty, Brendan. 1996. *Making Room: The Economics of Homelessness*. Cambridge, MA: Harvard University Press.

Pendall, Rolf, Robert Puentes, and Jonathan Martin. 2006. From Traditional to Reformed: A Review of the Land Use Regulations in the Nation's 50 Largest Metropolitan Areas. Metropolitan Policy Program, Brookings Institution.

Pollakowski, Henry O., and Susan M. Wachter. 1990. The Effects of Land-Use Constraints on Housing Prices. *Land Economics* 66 (3): 315–24.

Poterba, James. 1992. Taxation and Housing: Old Questions, New Answers. *American Economic Review* 82 (2): 237–42.

Quigley, John M., and Steven Raphael. 2005. Regulation and the High Cost of Housing in California. *American Economic Review* 94 (2): 323–28.

Quigley, John M., and Larry Rosenthal. 2005. The Effects of Land Regulation on the Price of Housing: What Do We Know? What Can We Learn? *Cityscape* 8 (1): 69–137.

R. S. Means. 2000. *Residential Cost Data*. Kingston, MA: R. S. Means Company.

Saks, Raven. 2005. Job Creation and Housing Construction: Constraints on Metropolitan Area Employment Growth. Federal Reserve Board of Governors working paper 2005-49.

Schorr, Alvin. 1963. *Slums and Social Insecurity*. Washington, DC: Division of Research and Statistics, Social Security Administration, U.S. Department of Health, Education, and Welfare.

Siegelman, Leonore. 1963. A Technical Note on Housing Census Comparability, 1950–1960. *Journal of the American Institute of Planners* 29 (February): 48–54.

U.S. Government Accounting Office. 2002. Federal Housing Assistance: Comparing the Characteristics and Costs of Housing Programs. GAO-02-76.

6

Immigration

HOW IMMIGRATION AFFECTS U.S. CITIES

DAVID CARD

THE UNITED STATES is once again becoming a country of immigrants. Immigrant arrivals—currently running about 1.25 million people per year—account for 40 percent of the population growth nationally, and a much larger share in some regions (see U.S. Department of Commerce 2006). The effects of these inflows are controversial, in part because of their sheer size and in part because of their composition. Something like 35 to 40 percent of new arrivals are undocumented immigrants from Mexico and Central America with low education and limited English skills (Passel 2005). Although another quarter of immigrants—from countries like India and China—are highly skilled, critics of current immigration policy often emphasize the presumed negative effects of lower-skilled people in the overall economy (e.g., Rector, Kim, and Watkins 2007). Moreover, even the most highly skilled immigrants are predominantly nonwhite, contributing to a growing presence of visible minorities in the U.S. population.

The size and composition of immigrant inflows is a special concern in the nation's largest metropolitan areas, where most immigrants live. To illustrate this point, table 6.1 presents data from the most recent Current Population Surveys (CPS) on the seventeen-largest metropolitan areas (with populations of two million or more).[1] The average share of immigrants in these cities is nearly 27 percent—two times the level in the nation as a whole—although the fraction varies from a low of 8 percent in Philadelphia and Detroit to a high of 35 percent in Los Angeles and Miami. Large cities also have a disproportionate share of second-generation Americans: people born in the United States with at least one foreign-born parent. This group represents about 20 percent of the population in the seventeen-largest cities (versus 11 percent in the nation as a whole), with a range between 8 percent (in Atlanta, Minneapolis, and Philadelphia) and 25 percent (in Los Angeles).

The final column of table 6.1 shows the overall share of minorities (i.e., people who are either nonwhite or Hispanic) in each major city.[2] As

TABLE 6.1
Immigrant and Minority Presence in Top U.S. Cities

	Population (in thousands)	Share of U.S. population (percent)	Immigrant presence		Overall minority share (percent)
			Immigrants (percent)	Second generation (percent)	
All United States	299,398	100.0	12.1	10.6	33.1
Outside top cities	194,311	64.9	6.8	7.5	26.1
Top cities	105,087	35.1	26.9	19.8	45.9
By city (CBSA):					
New York	18,819	6.3	26.9	18.8	47.2
Los Angeles	12,950	4.3	35.0	24.7	63.7
Chicago	9,506	3.2	15.0	14.4	40.1
Dallas	6,004	2.0	17.4	12.0	45.9
Philadelphia	5,827	1.9	7.9	8.2	31.0
Houston	5,540	1.9	19.8	13.3	57.2
Miami	5,464	1.8	36.0	21.3	59.5
Washington, DC	5,290	1.8	21.3	12.2	46.6
Atlanta	5,138	1.7	13.5	8.0	44.1
Detroit	4,469	1.5	8.5	9.3	30.6
Boston	4,455	1.5	15.3	15.7	20.9
San Francisco	4,180	1.4	29.9	22.6	55.4
Phoenix	4,039	1.3	16.1	14.0	40.4
Riverside	4,026	1.3	20.7	21.5	59.6
Seattle	3,263	1.1	12.4	10.9	26.5
Minneapolis	3,175	1.1	9.7	8.0	19.0
San Diego	2,941	1.0	23.8	20.4	48.8

Notes: Population counts are U.S. Census Bureau estimates for July 1, 2006. Immigrant, second-generation, and minority fractions are based on tabulations of 2005 and 2006 March CPS. Second generation are native-born individuals with at least one immigrant parent. Minorities include non-whites and Hispanics of any race.

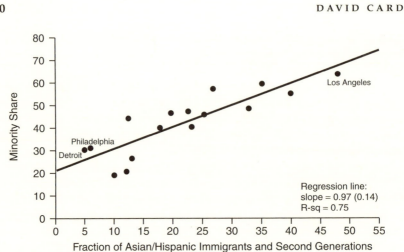

Fig. 6.1 Immigrant/Second-Generation Contribution to Minority Share

illustrated in figure 6.1, the fraction of minorities rises one for one with the share of Asian and Hispanic first- and second-generation immigrants. Thus, the "diversity" of a city's population is directly affected by the immigrant presence in that city, linking the issue of immigration to underlying issues of race and ethnicity.

This chapter tries to summarize what we know about the economic effects of immigration on major U.S. cities. I begin with the basic question of how immigration impacts the total size of a city. Immigrants, like natives, are drawn to cities with expanding opportunities, making it hard to separate the "demand pull" effect (people go where the local economy is expanding) from the "supply push" effect (the arrival of immigrants *causes* a city to grow). Unlike natives, however, immigrants are particularly attracted to cities with historical enclaves of earlier immigrants. Exploiting this *immigrant-specific* "pull factor," I infer that immigrant arrivals actually increase the local population, rather than simply displacing natives who already live there, or would have moved there if the immigrants had not arrived.

I then consider the effects of immigration on the composition of a city's workforce. Immigrants as a whole are less skilled than natives, so in the absence of selective outflows more immigrants tend to *reduce* the average skills of the local population. Although the native populations of certain high-immigrant cities—like San Francisco and Boston—are relatively skilled, I show that offsetting native population flows tend to be small, so on average cities with more immigration have a larger share of lower-skilled workers.

I then turn to the implications of this unbalanced population growth for local incomes and the structure of the local economy. Despite the impact of immigration on the skill composition of the local labor market, there is only a small effect on the structure of relative wages.[3] The wage gap between the lowest-skilled natives (who are in the most direct competition with immigrants) and natives at the middle of the skill distribution is 3 to 5 percent wider in high-immigrant cities like New York and Los Angeles than in low-immigrant ones. The gap between the wages of the highly skilled natives and those in the middle is also somewhat wider in high-immigrant cities.

An equally important issue is the effect of immigration on the *average* wages of native workers. Even after controlling for city size effects, human capital spillovers, and the possibility that immigrants are drawn to cities with stronger local economies, the evidence suggests a positive effect. Taken together with the rather small magnitude of the relative wage effects, it appears that immigration exerts a modestly positive effect on the labor-market outcomes of most natives. This parallels the conclusion reached in simulations of the *national* impacts of immigration by Gianmarco Ottavanio and Giovanni Peri (2006), and in a recent empirical study for California by Peri (2007).[4]

Immigrants also affect the well-being of urban residents through a variety of other non-labor-market channels. One important channel is the housing market; research by Albert Saiz (2003, 2006), Scott Susin (2001), and Erica Greulich, John M. Quigley, and Steven Raphael (2004) suggests that rents are higher in cities with increased immigration, although Greulich, Quigley, and Raphael (2004) find that the mean ratio of rent to income (the "rent burden") among natives is unaffected by immigrant inflows. In fact, the estimated impacts of immigration on average rents in the studies by Saiz (2006) and Greulich, Quigley, and Raphael (2004) are about the same magnitude as the estimated impacts on average native earnings. This parallel shift explains the absence of an effect on the average rent burden and indicates that the net housing market effects on natives are small.

Another channel is through government revenues and expenditures. Simple comparisons suggest that immigrants pay about $100 per capita less than natives in state, federal, and Social Security taxes, and receive about $600 per capita less in cash transfers. As has been pointed out in a number of recent studies, however, the fiscal impact of immigrants depends critically on the fiscal impacts of immigrant children (most of whom are counted as natives). These comparisons also ignore the effects of immigrants on *local* taxes (mainly property and sales taxes) and *local* expenditures (mainly on schools and other services). And perhaps most important, they ignore the general equilibrium effects of immigration on the earnings and program participation of the local native population.

To provide a broader perspective, I consider the relationship between the fraction of immigrants in a city and various indicators of local fiscal conditions, including average earnings per capita (a simple measure of the tax base) and school enrollment rates. This analysis suggests that cities with more or less immigrants have similar (or slightly higher) earnings per capita as well as similar "demographic burdens."

Even apart from housing prices or fiscal concerns, immigrant families pose a potential externality on other urban residents through their impacts on school and neighborhood "peer groups." While the monetary value is hard to quantify, existing research indicates that people value neighborhoods and schools with better-educated, higher-income, and nonminority neighbors and schoolmates. Indeed, my reading is that peer-group externalities are a first-order concern for many urban residents, though research on the magnitude of these effects is still in its infancy.

Immigration and Population Growth

A critical first question is how immigrant inflows affect population growth. Since the U.S. born have low emigration rates, at the national level each additional immigrant adds one person to the total population. At the level of an individual city, though, there are substantial movements of population that can potentially offset immigrant inflows.

To begin, note that the total population in a city at a point in time t, P_t, is the sum of the number of native-born people in the city at that time N_t, and the number of foreign-born people, M_t: $P_t = N_t + M_t$. The proportional change in the population from period s to period t can then be written as:

$$(P_t - P_s)/P_s = (N_t - N_s)/P_s + (M_t - M_s)/P_s$$
$$= [N_s/P_s] (N_t - N_s)/N_s + [M_s/P_s] (M_t - M_s)/M_s. \quad (6.1)$$

The first line decomposes the overall growth rate into the sum of the changes in the native and immigrant populations, each divided by the initial total population stock. The second line writes the overall growth rate as a weighted average of the group-specific growth rates, with weights equal to their initial (period s) population shares.

Table 6.2 shows the relative magnitudes of the terms in equation (6.1) for the seventeen-largest cities in the United States and a broader sample of the hundred-largest cities, using Decennial Census data for people age sixteen to sixty-five from 1980, 1990, and 2000.[5] The average growth in the adult population of the nation's largest cities was about 9 percent in the 1980s (i.e., 0.9 percent per year) and 21 percent in the 1990s. In the United States as a whole, the adult population rose by 9.1 percent over the 1980s and 12.8 percent over the 1990s. The largest cities therefore kept pace with population growth elsewhere in the country during the 1980s, but grew faster than the rest of the country in the 1990s.

TABLE 6.2
Contributions of Immigrants to Overall Population Growth

	Overall	Natives/ population	Immigrants/ population	Growth rates: natives	immigrants
Top (17-largest) Cities					
1980–2000	30.1	10.1	20.0	9.7	209.5
1980–1990	9.0	1.2	7.8	0.5	62.9
1990–2000	21.1	8.8	12.2	9.2	146.7
Largest 100 MSAs					
1980–2000	36.9	20.5	16.3	21.6	203.5
1980–1990	15.3	9.3	6.0	9.8	56.0
1990–2000	21.5	11.2	10.3	11.7	147.5

Notes: Based on tabulations of 1980, 1990, and 2000 censuses. Population refers to people age 16–65 only. Top cities include only the primary PMSA included in the set of counties in a CBSA. Changes from 1990 to 2000 use a 1980 base to facilitate adding up.

The average values for the two terms in the first line of equation (6.1) are displayed in the second and third columns of the table. During the 1980s, the native population of larger U.S. cities was essentially stagnant. Most urban population growth was attributable to immigrants, who experienced an average growth rate of 63 percent.[6] The growth of the native population in the country's larger cities resumed in the 1990s, but contributed only 40 percent of total population increase in the face of a nearly 150 percent average growth rate in the immigrant populations of these cities. As shown in the lower panel of able 6.2, the trends were broadly similar in the hundred-largest cities.

While informative, the simple decompositions in table 6.2 do not address the key question of whether immigrant population growth *causes* overall population growth. To make some headway on this issue, consider a simple causal model for population growth between a base period s and some later period t:

$$(P_t - P_s)/P_s = \alpha + \beta (M_t - M_s)/P_s + \gamma X + \varepsilon, \text{ (6.2)}$$

where X represents a set of city characteristics and ε is an unexplained component. In this model, the coefficient β summarizes the *causal effect* of immigrant inflows on the overall population growth. A value of $\beta = 1$ means that each additional immigrant adds 1 to the total city population. A value of $\beta < 1$ means that for each additional 100 immigrants, a total of $100(1 - \beta)$ native-born residents leave. In the extreme case, $\beta = 0$ and immigrant inflows are completely offset by native outflows.

The obvious problem with this model is that the unobserved determinants of population growth (the factors represented in ε) are likely to be correlated with immigrant inflows, leading to an upward-biased estimate of β. The conventional econometric solution is to find some characteristic or attribute of a city that induces more immigrants to move there, but that is not directly related to the city's growth, and then use this as an instrumental variable for the immigrant inflow rate. As noted in earlier work (Altonji and Card 1991; Card 2001), the tendency of immigrants to move to preexisting enclaves provides an appealing instrument. Specifically, suppose that in the absence of particularly good or bad economic conditions in a given city, the fraction of all arriving immigrants who would choose to move to that city is equal to the share of earlier immigrants who resided there in the initial period s ($\lambda_s = M_s/M^{US}$). Then, if the total number of new immigrants to the country is ΔM^{US}, the expected number of immigrants who would go to the city is $\lambda_s \Delta M^{US}$, and a plausible instrument for the immigrant inflow rate is $\lambda_s \Delta M^{US}/P_s = (M_s/P_s) \times \Delta M^{US}/M^{US}$, which is just a fixed multiple of the fraction of immigrants in the city in year s.[7]

The predictive power of this instrument is illustrated in figure 6.2, which plots the immigrant inflow rate for each of the top seventeen cities between 1980 and 2000 against the fraction of immigrants in the city in 1980. Although there is a lot of "noise," there is a clearly discernible correlation between the initial fraction of immigrants and the subsequent inflow rate, confirming the enclave effect.[8]

Table 6.3 presents estimation results for a simple specification of equation (6.2) that includes only one X variable: the log of the city's population in 1980.[9] I present OLS estimates for the sample of top cities in column 1, OLS estimates for the broader sample of the hundred-largest cities in column 2, and instrumental variables (IV) estimates for the latter sample in column 3.[10] The OLS results yield large estimates of β, on the order of 2. Taken literally, an estimate of this magnitude implies that each newly arriving immigrant *attracts* one additional native-born worker to the same city. A more likely interpretation is that booming cities (like Riverside, California) attracted *both* immigrants and natives from elsewhere in the country over the 1980–2000 period. The instrumental variables estimates, though imprecise, are consistent with this interpretation, and point to an estimate of β close to 1.[11]

The results in table 6.3 are consistent with earlier analyses of immigration inflows and native outflows between 1985 and 1990 (Card 2001), which used a more sophisticated enclave instrument, and with models in a study by myself and John E. DiNardo (2000) that explored move-

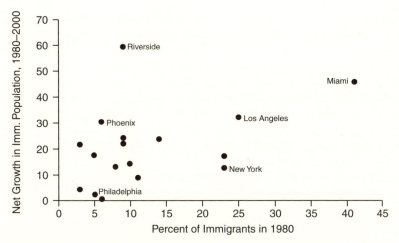

Fig. 6.2 Immigrant Presence in 1980 and Growth of Immigrant Population

TABLE 6.3
Models for Contribution of Immigrants to Overall Population Growth

Period of analysis	Top cities only (OLS)	Largest 100 MSAs	
		OLS	IV
1980–2000	2.0	2.0	1.0
	(0.5)	(0.2)	(0.3)
1980–1990	2.0	2.3	1.5
	(0.6)	(0.3)	(0.4)
1990–2000	2.4	1.8	0.2
	(0.5)	(0.2)	(0.6)
1990–2000*	—	—	0.9
			(0.3)

Notes: Standard errors in parentheses. Entry is coefficient of the growth in the number of immigrants in the city over the period of analysis (relative to the initial population of the city) in a model for the overall growth rate of the population of the city. All models also include a log of the city population in 1980 as a control. See table 6.2 for city definitions. IV models use the fraction of immigrants in the city in 1980 as an instrument, except as noted. Models weighted by population in 1980.

* IV estimate uses fractions of immigrants in the city in 1980 and 1990 as instruments.

ments between 1980 and 1990, allowing for dynamic feedback between city-specific growth rates across decades.[12] While further work would be useful to refine these estimates, my interpretation of the available evidence is that immigrant inflows to specific cities lead to relatively modest offsetting responses, so that on average immigrant inflows drive up population nearly one for one.

Immigration and the Skill Composition of the Local Population

I turn now to a second crucial question: How do immigrant arrivals affect the skill composition of the adult population in different cities? A necessary first step is to define skill groups. I use a simple approach, motivated by previous studies of the wage structure (e.g., Fortin and Lemieux 1998). Specifically, I classify workers into four skill groups based on their predicted probabilities of having hourly wages in the different quartiles of the national wage distribution.[13] I begin by fitting ordered probit models for the probability that a given adult worker in the public-use file of the 2000 Census would earn an hourly wage in each of four quartiles, using separate models for immigrants and native-born wage earners.[14] I then use the coefficients of these models to assign the *probabilities* that a given adult is classified in skill quartiles one, two, three, or four. (Note that the ordered probit models are fit to workers, but the probabilities are assigned to all working-age adults, including nonworkers.) This procedure explicitly models the uncertainty in assigning a person to a unique skill group, and uses a probabilistic rather than deterministic assignment.[15]

Using these "skill weights," it is straightforward to construct estimates of the labor-market outcomes for different skill groups by taking an appropriately weighted average across the entire adult population. To calculate the mean wage of quartile one workers from a given city, for example, I form a weighted average of the observed wages for workers in that city, using as weights the probability each worker is assigned to quartile one.

The characteristics of people assigned to the four quartiles are summarized in table 6.A.2. Briefly, the lowest-quartile group includes more women (59 percent), Hispanics (19.4 percent), and high school dropouts (40 percent) than the overall population, while the highest-quartile group includes more men (62 percent) and college graduates (46 percent). The geometric mean wage earned in 1999 for workers in quartile one is $9.50 per hour, while the corresponding averages for quartiles two, three, and four are $11.75, $13.71, and $17.00, respectively.

Although natives are (approximately) evenly distributed across the four quartiles, immigrants are overrepresented in the lowest quartile and underrepresented in the top two.[16] The top row of table 6.4 shows the skill distribution for *all* working-age immigrants, while the remaining rows show the distributions for immigrants from the twenty most important source countries (ranked by the number of immigrants from each country). The skill distributions vary widely by the country of origin, with relatively skilled immigrants coming from India, Canada, and western Europe, and relatively unskilled immigrants from Mexico, El Salvador, and Guatemala.

The uneven distribution of immigrants across the quartiles has a crucial implication: all other things being equal, high-immigration cities will tend to have relatively more low-skilled (i.e., low-wage) people in their local populations. To formalize this insight, let π_j represent the fraction of residents in a given city in skill group j (for j = 1, 2, 3, 4), let p_j represent the fraction of *native* residents in the city in skill group j, and let q_j represent the fraction of *foreign-born* residents in the skill group. Letting f denote the fraction of immigrants in the local population, the local share of the overall population in skill group j is $\pi_j = f q_j + (1 - f) p_j$. In the absence of immigration, or any differential sorting of the native population across cities, the local fraction of skill group j in each city would be $p_j^{US} \approx 0.25$. The deviation from this counterfactual can be written as the sum of three terms:

$$\pi_j - p_j^{US} = f(q_j^{US} - p_j^{US}) + f(q_j - q_j^{US}) + (1 - f)(p_j - p_j^{US}). \quad (6.3)$$

The first term is the "pure compositional" effect of higher immigration: since the national fraction of immigrants in skill group j (q_j^{US}) differs from the national fraction of natives (p_j^{US}), a city with more immigrants will tend to have a bigger deviation from the counterfactual share p_j^{US}. The second term represents the local selectivity of the immigrant population. To the extent that the immigrants in a given city are more or less skilled than the national immigrant pool, this term will be larger or smaller.[17] The third component of equation (6.3) is a parallel term representing the local selectivity of the native population.

The distortionary effect of an immigrant inflow depends on the *selective* responses of natives (and earlier immigrants) to the immigrant arrivals. If, for example, inflows of immigrants in the bottom skill group cause natives in that skill group to leave (or induce natives in other skill groups to move in), some of the distortionary effect will be mitigated. The magnitude of the net mitigation effect is captured by the native selectivity term.

Tables 6.5a and 6.5b present city-specific estimates of the three terms in equation (6.3) for the lowest- and highest-skill quartiles, respectively. Focusing first on the lowest-skill quartile, there are clearly big differences across major cities in the relative share of low-skilled people. Los Angeles and Miami, for instance, have a much higher fraction of

TABLE 6.4
Immigrant Characteristics by Country of Birth

	Number of adults (16–65)	Mean years of education	Mean wage (geometric)
All	23,400,000	11.4	12.00
Country of Birth			
Mexico	7,478,180	8.4	9.09
Philippines	1,077,560	13.9	14.63
Vietnam	806,100	11.5	12.24
India	801,260	15.4	18.30
El Salvador	695,180	8.8	9.66
China	687,140	13.3	13.32
Cuba	583,400	12.1	12.43
Korea	542,120	13.8	13.69
Canada	524,880	14.1	17.03
Dominican Republic	511,020	10.6	10.40
Germany	462,800	13.7	15.10
Jamaica	407,300	12.5	13.41
Guatemala	395,060	8.7	9.37
Columbia	391,300	12.4	11.44
Haiti	319,920	11.6	11.07
Poland	297,080	13.2	13.85
England	291,900	14.2	17.53
Taiwan	279,360	15.3	17.67
Italy	267,900	11.7	16.28
Japan	251,140	14.3	17.55

Notes: Based on tabulations from 2000 Census. Sample includes individuals 16–65 only.

low-skilled people than other cities (or the nation as a whole), whereas Seattle and Boston have a lower-than-average fraction. Most of the variation across cities in the presence of low-skilled people is driven by the compositional effect associated with the presence of more immigrants in the city, although there is also some variation in the selectivity of the native population across cities. San Francisco, Seattle, Boston, and Washington, DC, for example, all have relatively few natives in skill quartile one, while Los Angeles, Miami, and Riverside have relatively more.

Table 6.4 (cont.)

Distribution across skill quartiles			
Quartile 1	Quartile 2	Quartile 3	Quartile 4
38.4	25.9	18.8	16.9
53.1	26.2	13.8	6.9
24.9	25.8	23.8	25.4
36.9	27.4	19.9	15.8
18.5	22.7	24.3	34.5
51.7	26.5	14.4	7.4
33.5	26.2	20.8	19.5
37.4	26.8	19.5	16.2
31.1	26.7	21.8	20.4
16.2	22.1	24.8	36.9
46.2	27.1	16.5	10.2
20.0	24.1	24.4	31.5
28.0	27.1	23.0	21.9
53.5	25.8	13.7	7.0
40.8	27.0	18.5	13.7
40.9	27.3	18.4	13.3
28.2	26.5	22.5	22.8
14.8	21.5	24.8	39.0
21.7	23.6	23.8	30.9
18.4	24.5	25.3	31.9
21.2	24.8	24.5	29.5

The patterns in table 6.5b are for the most part mirror images of those in table 6.5a New York, Los Angeles, and Miami all have a relative shortage of top quartile residents, whereas Boston, Seattle, and San Francisco have a relative surplus. Again, most of the cross-city variation is associated with the compositional effect, though there is some positive selectivity in the native populations of San Francisco, Seattle, Boston, and Washington, DC—the cities most closely associated with the high-tech boom.

The decomposition in equation (6.3) shows that in the absence of selectivity effects, the fractions of local residents in different skill categories

TABLE 6.5A
Contribution of Immigrants to Fraction of Bottom Skill Quartile in Local Population

	Population share in quartile 1	Gap relative to U.S. natives	Decomposition of gap		
			Excess immigrants	Immigrant selectivity	Native selectivity
All United States	27.0	1.7	1.7	0.0	0.0
Outside top cities	26.7	1.3	1.1	0.0	0.2
By city (primary PMSA)					
New York	30.2	4.9	5.4	−1.0	0.5
Los Angeles	34.2	8.8	6.1	1.6	1.1
Chicago	27.0	1.6	2.7	0.0	−1.1
Dallas	28.6	3.2	2.5	1.5	−0.8
Philadelphia	24.8	−0.6	1.1	−0.7	−0.9
Houston	30.9	5.5	3.3	1.5	0.7
Miami	36.4	11.0	7.9	1.0	2.1
Washington, DC	24.1	−1.3	2.6	−1.0	−3.0
Atlanta	25.9	0.5	1.6	0.1	−1.1
Detroit	25.2	−0.1	1.1	−0.7	−0.5
Boston	22.6	−2.8	2.3	−1.2	−3.9
San Francisco	23.5	−1.9	4.7	−2.1	−4.5
Phoenix	28.4	3.0	2.3	1.4	−0.7
Riverside	32.2	6.9	3.3	1.3	2.3
Seattle	22.5	−2.8	2.1	−1.1	−3.8
Minneapolis	23.0	−2.4	1.0	−0.1	−3.3
San Diego	28.3	3.0	3.5	0.0	−0.5

Notes: See text. Share in top quartile is fraction of all adults in local area predicted to earn in bottom quartile of wages.

will vary linearly with the fraction of immigrants. The strength of this connection across the top cities in the country is illustrated in figures 6.3a and 6.3b. The former shows a clear positive correlation between $\pi_{\pi 1}$ (the fraction of city residents in skill quartile one) and f (the fraction of immigrants in the city), while the latter shows a negative correlation between π_4 (the fraction in the top skill quartile) and f. In contrast to these

TABLE 6.5B
Contribution of Immigrants to Fraction of Top Skill Quartile in Local Population

	Population share in quartile 4	Gap relative to U.S. natives	Decomposition of gap		
			Excess immigrants	Immigrant selectivity	Native selectivity
All United States	22.7	–0.9	–0.9	0.0	0.0
Outside top cities	22.6	–1.0	–0.6	0.0	–0.4
By city (primary PMSA)					
New York	21.4	–2.2	–2.7	0.3	0.3
Los Angeles	19.1	–4.4	–3.1	–1.3	0.0
Chicago	23.8	0.3	–1.4	0.0	1.6
Dallas	22.5	–1.0	–1.3	–0.9	1.2
Philadelphia	24.6	1.1	–0.5	0.6	1.0
Houston	21.0	–2.5	–1.7	–0.9	0.1
Miami	17.0	–6.6	–4.0	–1.5	–1.1
Washington, DC	27.3	3.8	–1.3	0.8	4.3
Atlanta	24.0	0.4	–0.8	0.0	1.2
Detroit	23.4	–0.1	–0.6	0.6	–0.1
Boston	28.2	4.7	–1.2	0.9	5.0
San Francisco	28.3	4.8	–2.4	1.5	5.7
Phoenix	22.4	–1.1	–1.2	–0.8	0.9
Riverside	18.9	–4.6	–1.7	–1.0	–1.9
Seattle	27.7	4.2	–1.1	0.8	4.4
Minneapolis	26.8	3.2	–0.5	0.1	3.7
San Diego	23.1	–0.5	–1.8	–0.1	1.4

Notes: See text. Share in top quartile is fraction of all adults in local area predicted to earn in top quartile of wages.

graphs, figures 6.4a and 6.4b suggest that the selectivity of the local *native* population is not strongly related to the local immigrant fraction. If anything, it appears that the native population tends to be relatively unskilled in cities with more immigrants. There is certainly no indication that unskilled natives move out of the large cities with more immigrants.

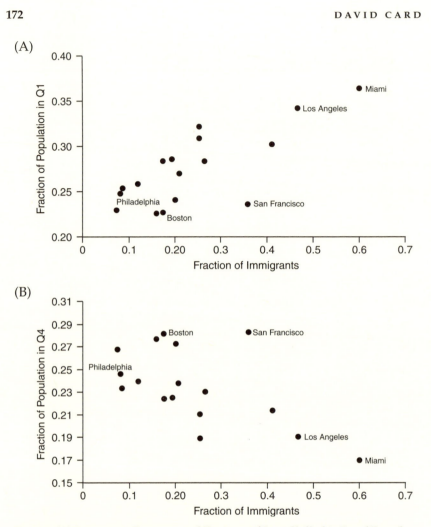

Fig. 6.3 (A) Immigrant Presence and Fraction of Low Skilled in Local Population. (B) Immigrant Presence and Fraction of High Skilled in Local Population.

To examine the data more systematically, table 6.6 presents estimates from models in which the various components of equation (6.3) for each of the four skill groups are regressed against the fraction of immigrants in the corresponding city (as measured in the 2000 Census). The models in the upper panel are fit to the small sample of only seventeen top cities, while the models in the lower panel are fit to the broader sample of one hundred larger cities. Note that since equation (6.3) holds identically, the coefficients in the three right-hand columns (representing regressions of the compositional effect, the immigrant selectivity term, and the native selectivity term on the fraction of immigrants in the city)

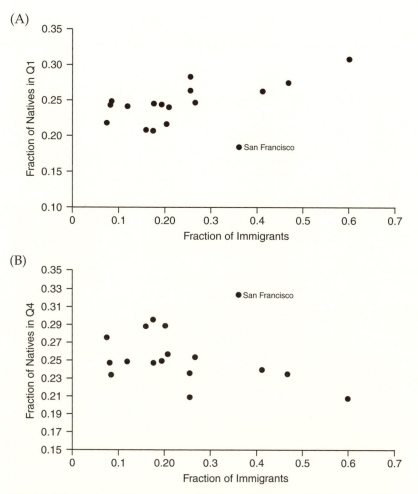

Fig. 6.4 (A) Immigrant Presence and Relative Fraction of Natives in Skill Quartile 1. (B) Immigrant Presence and Relative Fraction of Natives in Skill Quartile 4.

sum up to the coefficient in the first column (representing regressions of the city-specific excess fraction of residents in the skill group on the fraction of immigrants in the city). Also note that the models for the compositional effect "fit perfectly," since by construction this term is a linear function of the fraction of immigrants in the city.

The results from these models are quite similar for the smaller top-city sample and the larger hundred-city sample, though the top-city models show slightly stronger native selectivity effects that tend to *reinforce* the compositional effect. Overall, there is a strong positive relationship between the fraction of immigrants in a city and the fraction of

TABLE 6.6
Models Relating Skill Shares (and Components) to Local Fraction of Immigrants

	Excess fraction of skill group in city	Composition effect due to excess immigrants	Selectivity effects	
			Immigrants	Natives
Top cities				
Share in quintile 1	0.217 (0.049)	0.131	0.019 (0.020)	0.068 (0.032)
Share in quintile 2	0.026 (0.014)	0.010	0.01 (0.010)	0.006 (0.013)
Share in quintile 3	−0.104 (0.013)	−0.074	−0.003 (0.007)	−0.027 (0.008)
Share in quintile 4	−0.139 (0.049)	−0.067	−0.026 (0.014)	−0.046 (0.037)
100 larger cities				
Share in quintile 1	0.173 (0.017)	0.131	0.016 (0.007)	0.026 (0.011)
Share in quintile 2	0.004 (0.004)	0.010	0.006 (0.001)	−0.012 (0.004)
Share in quintile 3	−0.095 (0.005)	−0.074	−0.003 (0.003)	−0.018 (0.003)
Share in quintile 4	−0.082 (0.017)	−0.067	−0.019 (0.005)	0.003 (0.013)

Notes: Standard errors in parentheses. Entries are regression coefficients from a regression of variable denoted by column heading for specific skill quartile on the local fraction of immigrants.

residents in the lowest-skill quartile, attributable mainly to the compositional effect. Specifically, the model for the larger hundred-city sample implies that each 10 percent increase in the local fraction of immigrants is associated with a 1.73 percent increase in the fraction of the adult population in skill quartile one, of which 1.31 percent is attributable to the pure compositional effect, 0.16 percent is attributable to the fact that the immigrant population tends to be less skilled in high-immigrant cities, and 0.26 percent is attributable to the fact that the native population is less skilled in high-immigrant cities. Likewise, for the top skill quartile there is a strong negative relationship with the fraction of immigrants, attributable mainly to the compositional effect.

A potential concern with the OLS models in table 6.6 is that the strong positive correlation between the fraction of immigrants in a city and the local fraction of low-skilled natives is driven by city-specific demand shocks that attract both immigrants and low-skilled natives (such as a boom in residential construction). One way to address this is to fit the models in table 6.6 by IV, using as an instrument the fraction of immigrants in the city some years earlier (e.g., in 1980). In principle, this instrument isolates the immigrant-specific enclave effect and purges the estimates of demand conditions in the mid- to late 1990s. IV estimates of the models in the lower panel of table 6.6 using the immigrant fraction in 1980 are similar to the simple OLS models. For example, the IV estimate of the coefficient for the overall effect on skill quartile one is 0.175 (versus the OLS estimate of 0.173), with a standard error of 0.018, while the IV estimate of the coefficient for the native selectivity effect for quartile one is 0.031 (versus the OLS estimate of 0.026), with a standard error of 0.012. These estimates do not point to an obvious endogeneity problem in interpreting the relationship between the *relative* skill composition of a city and the fraction of immigrants there.

The estimates in table 6.6 confirm an important conclusion that has emerged in previous studies of city-specific labor markets (e.g., Card and DiNardo 2000; Card 2001; Card and Lewis 2007). Inflows of immigrants *are not* associated with offsetting outflows of lower-skilled natives. On average, immigration inflows substantially raise the fraction of local residents in lower skill groups and lower the fraction in higher skill groups.

The Effects of Immigration on Relative Wages

If immigration shifts the fractions of local residents in different skill groups, how do local labor market adjust to absorb the imbalances? One obvious mechanism is via relative wage changes. In particular, standard economic models of a closed local economy (with elastically supplied capital) suggest that increases in the relative supply of a particular skill group will lower the relative wages of that group, while raising the average wages for workers as a whole. A useful framework for investigating the relative wage effect is a model of the form:

$$\log [w_j/w_k] = a + b \log [\pi_j/\pi_k] + cX + e, \text{(6.4)}$$

where $\log w_j$ represents the mean log wage for workers in skill group j in a given local labor market, $\log w_k$ is the corresponding mean for skill group k, π_j and π_k are the shares of the groups in the local population, X represents a set of control variables, and e is an error component.[18] Since the workers in different skill groups are slightly different in different cities, I estimate this model using mean *residual* wages for people in each skill group, obtained from a linear regression model that includes the same covariates used in the skill quartile assignment model.

The correlation across the top U.S. cities between the relative supplies and relative wages for different skill groups is illustrated in figures 6.5a and 6.5b.[19] Figure 6.5a shows that there is a lot of variation across large cities in the relative size of skill quartiles one and two, but not much connection to the relative wage differential between workers in the two groups. There is an even larger range in the relative size of skill quartiles four and two (figure 6.5b), but again the correlation with relative wages is weak.

Table 6.7 presents estimates from a series of models based on equation (6.4). The upper panel of the table shows estimated models for the wages of quartile one relative to quartile two (roughly comparable to the gap between high school dropouts and high school graduates), while the lower panel shows models for the wages of quartile four relative to quartile two (roughly comparable to the gap between college graduates and high school graduates). Each panel presents two rows: one containing estimates of the effect of relative supply on the relative wages of natives, and the other reporting parallel estimates for the relative wages of immigrants. The various columns present OLS and IV models, with and without a control for population size.

Looking first at the estimates for quartile one relative to two, the OLS models show small effects of relative supply on relative wages of both natives and immigrants. The IV models show more systematic evidence of negative wage impacts, with an estimated value for the coefficient b of about -0.10. To interpret this magnitude, note from figure 6.5a that the log relative supply of quartile one relative to quartile two ranges from approximately 0.0 in low-immigration cities like Philadelphia to 0.35 in Los Angeles and Miami. Assuming a -0.10 coefficient, the implied effect of the increased relative supply of lowest-quartile workers in Miami relative to Philadelphia is a 3.5 percent reduction in relative wages.[20]

The estimates of the effect of relative supply on the wages of quartile four relative to quartile two are comparable, though slightly less precise, with the IV estimates again centering around -0.10. As shown in figure 6.5b, the log relative supply of quartile four relative to quartile two ranges from approximately -0.4 in a high-immigration city like Miami to 0.0 in a low-immigration city like Philadelphia. Assuming a -0.10 coefficient, the implied effect of the relative shortage of top-quartile workers in Miami relative to Philadelphia is a 4.0 percent increase in relative wages.[21]

The results from this analysis closely parallel the findings from earlier studies of the relative wage effects of immigration on local labor

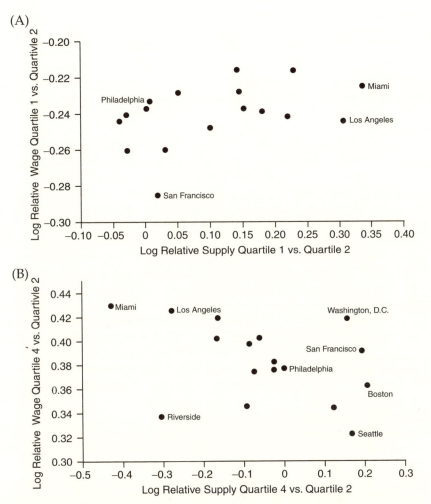

Fig. 6.5 (A) Relative Supply and Relative Wages of Lowest-Skill Quartile. (B) Relative Supply and Relative Wages of Highest-Skill Quartile.

markets (Card 2001; Orrenius and Zavodny 2006; Card and Lewis 2007). The presence of immigrants exerts a powerful and systematic effect on the relative supplies of different skill groups in different cities. These differences appear to shift the local wage structure in the expected direction, though the impacts are modest. Comparing high-immigration cities like Miami and Los Angeles to low-immigration cities like Philadelphia or Detroit, the relative wages of workers in the lowest skill group are about 3 to 4 percent lower, while relative wages for those in the highest skill group are 3 to 4 percent higher.

TABLE 6.7
Estimated Models for Effect of Relative Supply on Relative Wages

	OLS models		IV Models	
	(1)	(2)	(3)	(4)
Models for wage of quartile 1 relative to wage for quartile 2				
Natives	−0.03	0.00	−0.10	−0.07
	(0.02)	(0.02)	(0.02)	(0.03)
Immigrants	−0.06	−0.04	−0.11	−0.10
	(0.02)	(0.02)	(0.02)	(0.03)
Models for wage of quartile 4 relative to wage for quartile 2				
Natives	−0.02	−0.02	−0.09	−0.03
	(0.01)	(0.01)	(0.04)	(0.03)
Immigrants	0.01	0.01	−0.13	−0.09
	(0.02)	(0.02)	(0.06)	(0.06)
Controls for log city size	no	yes	no	yes

Notes: Standard errors in parentheses. Entries are estimated coefficients from a regression of the city-specific gap in mean log wages between the skill groups indicated on the log of the ratio of the relative fraction of the skill groups in the local population. Mean log wages are adjusted for observable characteristics of samples in each quartile in each city.

The Effects of Immigration on Average Wages

A final issue in the analysis of labor markets is how immigration affects the average wages of native workers. This is potentially a more difficult question to answer than the effect on *relative* wages, in part because economic models give a clearer prediction for the effect of relative supply on relative wages, and in part because of the difficulty of controlling for city-specific factors that may lead to higher or lower wages for all the workers in a given city, but are "differenced out" of a relative wage comparison.[22]

Figure 6.6 shows the relationship between the mean of (regression-adjusted) log wages for all native workers in each of the seventeen top cities and the fraction of immigrants in the city. Overall, the correlation appears to be positive but rather noisy. This is confirmed by the models in columns 1 and 2 of table 6.8, which relate the adjusted wage measure for workers in the seventeen top cities to the log of the fraction of immigrants in each city and two control variables: the log of the city size, and the fraction of college-educated workers in the city.[23] The addition of the latter covariate is suggested by Enrico Moretti's (2004) study of human

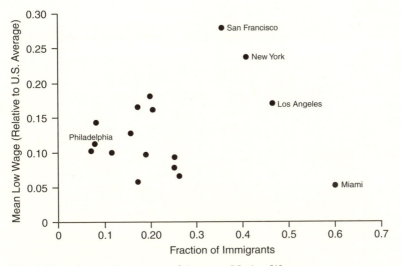

Fig. 6.6 Immigrant Presence and Average Native Wages

capital spillovers, which finds a strong positive correlation between average wages and the fraction of college graduates in a city that could bias the observed relation between wages and the fraction of immigrants.[24] On the other hand, population size and the fraction of college workers are obviously affected by immigrant inflows, so one might prefer the models without the added controls.

Regardless of whether the controls are added or not, the relationship between the fraction of immigrants and mean wages is positive as well as highly significant in the broader sample of one hundred large cities (columns 3 to 6 of table 6.8). The implied effects in this sample are also economically important. The 0.06 coefficient from the IV model in column 6, for example, implies that the increase in the fraction of immigrants from Philadelphia (immigrant share = 8 percent) to Los Angeles (immigrant share = 47 percent) raises the average wages of natives about 10 percent. This effect is large enough to more than offset the 4 to 5 percent reduction in the *relative* wages of low-skilled workers in moving between a typical low-immigrant city (like Philadelphia) and a typical high-immigrant city (like Los Angeles), and suggests that the wages of native workers in the bottom skill quartile are about 5 percent higher in the latter than the former.

The inference that the wages of low-skilled natives are actually *higher* in high-immigrant cities is confirmed by models that relate the mean of adjusted log wages for natives in skill quartile one to the fraction of immigrants in a city. OLS and IV versions of these models (available from the author) show a significant positive effect of the fraction of immigrants

TABLE 6.8
Models for Average Native Wages Across MSAs, 2000 Census

	Top cities (OLS)		100 larger MSAs			
			OLS		IV	
	(1)	(2)	(3)	(4)	(5)	(6)
Log fraction immigrants	0.02	0.02	0.08	0.06	0.08	0.06
	(0.03)	(0.02)	(0.01)	(0.01)	(0.01)	(0.01)
Fraction college graduates		0.61		0.74		0.73
		(0.15)		(0.09)		(0.09)
Log population		0.05		0.03		0.02
		(0.02)		(0.01)		(0.01)
R-squared	0.04	0.65	0.50	0.73	0.37	0.72

Notes: Standard errors in parentheses. Dependent variable is mean of regression-adjusted log wage for each city. Models in columns 1–2 fit to 17 larger cities by OLS. Models in columns 3–6 fit to sample of larger MSAs by weighted OLS (columns 3–4) or weighted IV (columns 5–6). Instrument for log fraction of immigrants is fraction of immigrants in city in 1980.

on the levels of wages for the lowest-skill quartile, with a coefficient on the log fraction of immigrants in the range of 0.05 to 0.07. Thus, even though the *relative* wages of low-skilled natives are depressed in high-immigrant cities, the absolute *level* of their wages appears to be higher.

Immigration Effects outside the Labor Market

Housing Market Effects

Although most of the existing research on the economic impacts of immigration has focused on the labor market, immigrant inflows can have other effects on the quality of urban life. An important example is the housing market: immigrant arrivals might be expected to have some effect on rents and housing prices, leading to changes in the welfare of preexisting residents. Saiz (2006), for instance, presents a simple theoretical model in which an inflow of immigrants causes an initial increase in rents as families compete for a fixed stock of housing units. In the longer run, new housing units are built and some residents move to other cities, offsetting the initial rent increase. Consistent with this model, studies of the effect of the Mariel Boatlift by Saiz (2003) and Susin (2001) find a positive impact on rents in Miami following the arrival of the Marielitos. The evidence on longer-run impacts is less clear. Saiz (2006) argues that rents are substantially increased by immigrant inflows, while

Greulich, Quigley, and Raphael (2004) find no effect of immigrant inflows on the ratio of rent to income among natives in a city.

These findings can be reconciled by noting that the magnitude of the immigrant impact on average rents estimated by Saiz (2006) is comparable to the magnitude of the impacts on average wages estimated in table 6.8. For example, using Census data for 1970–2000, Saiz (2006, table 5) estimates that a 10 percent immigrant inflow over a decade (expressed as a fraction of the initial population of an MSA) raises log median rents by 6.2 percent. Similarly, using 1980–2000 data, Greulich, Quigley, and Raphael (2004, table 4) find that a 10 percent increase in the fraction of immigrants in a city raises the mean rents for natives by 6.5 percent, although the effect is concentrated in the 1980s (19.4 percent impact) and statistically insignificant in the 1990s (2.7 percent impact). The models in table 6.8, by comparison, suggest that a 10 percent increase in the fraction of immigrants was associated with 4 percent higher native wages in 2000. The comparable reactions of both wages and rents provide a simple explanation for the absence of any effect on the rent-to-income ratio among natives.

Greulich, Quigley, and Raphael (2004, table 6) also find that the effects of increased immigration on rental prices are similar for housing units with higher and lower probabilities of being rented by immigrants. As noted by Joseph Tracy (2004), this uniform effect across different ends of the rental market is hard to reconcile with the housing competition model described by Saiz (2006), and points instead to a model in which immigrants raise the average productivity of natives, and rents respond to restore equilibrium across cities. While additional work is clearly warranted, my assessment of the existing evidence is that the increase in housing prices caused by immigration is small enough to be offset by the impacts on average earnings, at least in most cities with some elasticity in the local supply of housing.[25]

Fiscal Effects

Another link between immigration and native well-being arises through the local tax and transfer system. If both the quantity and quality of public services remain constant, the fiscal impact of increased immigration on the existing population can be assessed by measuring the "fiscal surplus" generated by the new immigrants (i.e., the gap between the taxes they pay and the cost of the services they receive).[26] More generally, the effect has to be adjusted for changes in the quality or quantity of public services attributable to immigrant inflows (say, congestion effects in local schools).

A number of early studies focused on the question of whether immigrants are more or less likely to receive welfare benefits or certain types of government transfers than natives (e.g., Blau 1984; Jensen 1989; Borjas and Hilton 1996). A few have extended this framework to look at the sum of the benefits received *and* the taxes paid by current immigrants versus natives (e.g., Borjas 1994; Garvey and Espenshade 1998; Clune 1998). Table 6.9 presents a simplified version of these analyses using information from the March 2005 and 2006 CPS. I show the average per capita transfers and estimated taxes for the overall population (column 1), and then separately for immigrants and natives (columns 2 and 3). I also present data in the fourth column of the table for the native-born children of immigrants, and a pooled sample of immigrants and second-generation natives in column 5.

The CPS collects information on most of the major cash transfer programs as well as rates of receipt of subsidized housing benefits and public health insurance (Medicare and Medicaid), and school enrollment data for individuals between the ages of sixteen and twenty-four.[27] On the tax side, the Census Bureau provides estimates of the federal and state taxes paid by individuals in the survey (net of tax credits like the Earned Income Tax Credit). I have supplemented these with my own estimates of the Social Security (FICA and Medicare) payroll taxes paid by individuals and their employers.

It is worth emphasizing that the tax and transfer information in table 6.9 is incomplete. The CPS does not collect information on sales or property taxes, local payroll taxes, or the taxes used to finance Unemployment Insurance and Workers' Compensation. Nor does it include information on the use of certain public services (like emergency rooms in county hospitals). Moreover, CPS respondents are believed to underreport government transfers by 10 to 25 percent (Ruser, Pilot, and Nelson 2004). Finally, the estimated tax calculations in table 6.9 ignore noncompliance—a particular concern for undocumented immigrants.

With these caveats in mind, a simple comparison of the transfer and tax amounts for immigrants and natives suggests that immigrants pay about $80 per person less than natives in annual state, federal, and Social Security taxes, but receive about $600 less in cash transfers.[28] Immigrants are also less likely to participate in Medicare or Medicaid, or be enrolled in school. A key factor in these comparisons is the age distribution of immigrants (row 1). Only 6 percent of immigrants are under the age of sixteen, versus 23 percent of natives.[29] Since children are eligible for transfers and government benefits, but do not work or pay taxes, the smaller fraction of immigrant children helps create a favorable fiscal balance for immigrants relative to natives.

This comparison, however, ignores the fact that many immigrants have nonimmigrant (i.e., U.S.-born) children. Arguably the fiscal costs of these children should be allocated to immigrants (see, e.g., Edmon-

TABLE 6.9
Average per Capita Transfers and Taxes, 2004–2005

	All	Immigrants	Natives	Second generation	Immigrants and second generation
Percent age 16–65	66.5	83.0	64.2	43.5	64.2
Percent working	52.8	63.1	51.4	33.6	48.9
Mean annual hours	979	1,211	947	595	915
Mean annual earnings	20,390	22,486	20,101	13,161	17,757
Value of					
Food Stamps	53	38	55	51	47
Unemployment insurance	82	83	82	51	67
Workers' Compensation	44	43	44	22	33
Social Security	1,512	970	1,586	1,820	1,266
Supplemental Security	107	132	104	58	97
Welfare	21	30	20	12	22
Total transfers	**1,820**	**1,295**	**1,892**	**2,014**	**1,532**
Federal taxes	2,617	2,275	2,664	1,885	2,007
State taxes	708	688	711	471	564
FICA Taxes	2,203	2,434	2,171	1,408	1,920
Medicare Taxes	588	650	580	380	514
Total Taxes	**6,117**	**6,047**	**6,127**	**4,145**	**5,005**
In-kind benefits					
Public Housing[1] (%)	3.7	3.5	3.7	3.6	3.6
Medicare (%)	13.6	10.9	14.0	16.7	12.8
Medicaid (%)	11.3	10.3	11.5	16.0	13.7
Enrolled in K–12[2] (%)	17.7	8.0	19.0	27.9	18.0
Enrolled in college[2] (%)	3.4	2.5	3.5	4.0	3.2

Notes: Based on tabulations of March 2005 and 2006 CPS. Federal and state taxes are imputed by the U.S. Census Bureau. FICA and Medicare taxes are imputed using total reported earnings. Dollar amounts in 2005 dollars. Sample of immigrants and second generation (column 5) reweights second generation to be 48% Hispanic.

[1] Includes residents of public housing units and residents of households that receive subsidized rent.

[2] Enrollment is assumed to be 0 for those over 24 or under 6. Children age 6–15 are assumed to be enrolled in K–12.

ston and Lee 1996; Auerbach and Oreopoulos 1999; Lee and Miller 2000; Storesletten 2000). While a complete analysis is beyond the scope of this chapter, I formed a simple "steady state" approximation by taking an average of immigrants and second-generation natives, and then re-weighting the second generation to have the same fraction of Hispanics as the immigrant population.[30] The characteristics of this artificial popu-lation are summarized in the final column of the table. Note that 64.2 per-cent of the pooled sample is between sixteen and sixty-five, close to the average for natives as a whole. The average per capita transfers of the combined immigrant/second-generation sample are $1,532 ($360 less than natives as a whole), while the average per capita taxes are $5,005 ($1,122 less than natives as a whole). Thus, once their children are taken into account, immigrants appear to impose a fiscal burden on natives.

The simple comparisons in table 6.9 have two key limitations. First, since the CPS lacks information on local payroll, sales, or property taxes, the comparisons do not shed much light on *local* fiscal impacts. Second, they fail to account for the effects of immigrants on the incomes and program participation of preexisting residents—that is, the "gen-eral equilibrium" effects suggested by the analyses in tables 6.7 and 6.8.

A potentially more informative way of assessing the local fiscal im-pacts of immigration is to compare measures of local spending and local tax revenue in cities with higher and lower fractions of immigrants.[31] In lieu of results from such an analysis, table 6.10 presents a cross-city analy-sis of the relationship between the fraction of immigrants in a metro area and a set of "indicators" of local fiscal pressure. The first three indicators are the fraction of the population under sixteen, the fraction either under sixteen or over sixty-five (i.e., the "dependency ratio"), and the fraction enrolled in elementary or secondary schools. Higher values for any of these indicators would be expected to lead to a higher local tax burden on the working-age population. The fourth indicator is earnings per capita (i.e., the total wages, salaries, and self-employment income per person, including children and retirees in the denominator). Cities with higher earnings per capita can set lower local tax *rates* and still achieve the same level of government services per capita.[32]

The table presents models relating these indicators to the fraction of immigrants in a metro area (or the log of the fraction of immigrants).[33] Two specifications are presented: simple univariate models, and mod-els with a control for the skill characteristics of the native workforce in different cities.[34] Although native skill levels are potentially endoge-nous, the analysis earlier shows little evidence of selective native mobil-ity responses to immigrant inflows, and the addition of this control greatly improves the predictive power of the models. OLS models fit to the seventeen-largest metro areas are reported in columns 1–2, OLS models fit to the hundred-largest cities are shown in columns 3–4, and

TABLE 6.10
Models for Effect of Immigration on Fiscal Indicators, 2000 Census

| | Top cities (OLS) | | 100 larger MSAs | | | |
| | | | OLS | | IV | |
	(1)	(2)	(3)	(4)	(5)	(6)
Models for fraction of population under 16						
Fraction of immigrants	0.00	−0.06	0.03	0.02	0.01	0.00
	(0.04)	(0.03)	(0.01)	(0.01)	(0.02)	(0.01)
Skill index of natives		−0.35		−0.23		−0.24
		(0.08)		(0.04)		(0.04)
Models for fraction of population under 16 or over 65						
Fraction of immigrants	0.00	−0.04	−0.01	−0.02	0.00	−0.01
	(0.03)	(0.03)	(0.01)	(0.01)	(0.02)	(0.01)
Skill index of natives		−0.31		−0.18		−0.17
		(0.07)		(0.04)		(0.04)
Models for fraction of population enrolled in grades K–12						
Fraction of immigrants	0.03	−0.02	0.03	0.02	0.03	0.01
	(0.03)	(0.02)	(0.01)	(0.01)	(0.01)	(0.01)
Skill index of natives		−0.29		−0.22		−0.22
		(0.06)		(0.03)		(0.03)
Models for log of per capita earnings						
Log fraction of immigrants	−0.11	0.00	0.05	0.04	0.00	0.04
	(0.06)	(0.03)	(0.02)	(0.01)	(0.03)	(0.01)
Skill index of natives		2.93		3.21		3.21
		(0.33)		(0.19)		(0.19)

Notes: Standard errors in parentheses. Models in columns 1–2 fit to sample of 17-largest cities. Models in columns 3–6 fit to sample of 100 larger MSAs, by weighted OLS in columns 3–4 and by weighted IV, using fraction of immigrants in city in 1980 as an instrument, in columns 5–6. Skill index of natives is mean log predicted wage for natives age 16–65 in city.

IV models using the fraction of immigrants in 1980 as an instrument for the immigrant presence in 2000 are presented in columns 5–6.

The univariate models give no indication that the relative size of the dependent population is larger in cities with higher immigration, but suggest a small positive effect of immigration on local school enrollment rates. In the models that control for the average earnings potential of the native population, however, the school enrollment effect is smaller, and in the IV specification in column 6 is close to zero. Overall, there is not much evidence that cities with more immigrants face a higher local tax burden due to the presence of more dependents, or more children in school.

The models for the log of earnings per capita, in the bottom rows of table 6.10, likewise suggest little reason for concern that a greater fraction of immigrants in a city reduces the potential tax base of the city. Indeed, controlling for the skills of the local native population, the models fit to the sample of hundred larger metro areas show a small yet significantly positive effect on per capita earnings. The 0.04 coefficient from the IV model in column 6, for example, implies that moving from a low-immigrant city like Philadelphia to a high-immigrant one like Los Angeles raises per capita earnings by about 7 percent. These results, which closely mirror the findings for average native wages in table 6.8, indicate that immigration is, if anything, a positive stimulus to the local tax base.

Peer Effects

A third channel through which immigrant inflows may affect natives and earlier immigrants is "peer group" or "neighborhood" effects. There is overwhelming evidence that homeowners and renters value the characteristics of other residents in a neighborhood (e.g., Duncan and Duncan 1957; Taeuber and Taeuber 1965; Farley et al. 1978), and that parents value the characteristics of the other students in a school (e.g., Black 1999). Such preferences are thought to be a primary cause of the high levels of segregation (by race, ethnicity, and income) that characterize neighborhoods and schools throughout the United States (e.g., Schelling 1971; Clark 1991; Cutler, Glaeser, and Vigdor 1999; Card, Mas, and Rothstein 2008).

New immigrants may be perceived as an undesirable peer group for at least two reasons. First, a majority of immigrants are either nonwhite or Hispanic. Existing research on the attitudes and mobility patterns of white non-Hispanics in the United States suggests that neighborhoods and schools with a higher fraction of either group are perceived as less attractive.[35] For example, Lincoln Quillian (2002), Scott South and Kyle Crowder (1998), and Elizabeth Bruch and Robert Mare (2006) show that whites are more likely to leave neighborhoods with a higher fraction of nonwhite residents, while William Easterly (2005) and myself, Alexandre Mas, and Jesse Rothstein (2008) show that Census tracts with a higher fraction of minority (nonwhite or Hispanic) residents tend to lose white residents. Charles Clotfelter (1979, 2001), Finis Welch and Audrey Light (1986), and Sarah Reber (2005) present similar findings for school districts. Estimates presented by Patrick Bayer and Robert McMillan (2005) suggest that whites in the San Francisco–Oakland–San Jose consolidated metro area are willing to pay a premium for houses in neighborhoods with lower fractions of Asians, blacks, and Hispanics.

Second, immigrants tend to have less education and lower incomes than natives, making them potentially less desirable as neighbors and as parents of the children in local schools. Patrick Bajari and Matthew Kahn (2003) and Bayer and McMillan (2005) report significant estimates of the willingness to pay for homes in neighborhoods with more college-educated householders. Bayer and McMillan (2005) also find a premium for areas with higher-income neighbors (controlling for education). A number of studies have demonstrated that parents will pay more for houses with access to public schools with higher test scores (e.g., Black 1999; Kane, Staiger, and Samms 2003). Since parental income and education are powerful predictors of student test performance (Rothstein 2004; Card and Rothstein 2007), these preferences mean that native families view many immigrant children as "bad" peers.

Despite these findings, it is difficult to place an overall valuation on the cost of the peer group effects posed by immigrants, since the magnitude depends on the degree of segregation between recent immigrants and natives across the neighborhoods and schools in a city. In fact, white non-Hispanics in most large U.S. cities are relatively isolated from Hispanics—the largest group of low-income and poorly educated immigrants. The dissimilarity index of segregation between white non-Hispanics and Hispanics in public elementary schools in 2002–2003, for example, has a value of 72 percent in New York and Los Angeles, 70 percent in Chicago and Philadelphia, and between 50 and 70 percent for most of the other top cities listed in table 6.1.[36]

One piece of evidence that points toward a significant perceived cost of increased Hispanic immigration is the existence of "tipping points" in white out-migration rates. I found with my colleagues Mas and Rothstein (2008) that neighborhoods in most of the larger U.S. cities have a critical minority threshold—typically around 5 to 15 percent—beyond which white families quickly leave the neighborhood. Importantly, the tipping point is based on the *sum* of the number of Hispanics and nonwhites in the neighborhood. This behavior suggests that the arrival of substantial numbers of nonwhite or Hispanic immigrants into previously low-minority neighborhoods induces substantial moving costs for the white non-Hispanic residents of those neighborhoods.

Diversity and Political Economy

A final reason why natives may prefer fewer immigrants in their local area arises through the political process. A number of recent studies have argued that ethnic, linguistic, and cultural diversity pose obstacles to effective governance and growth.[37] At least three mechanisms have been hypothesized for this effect. First, people from different ethnic groups may have different preferences over public goods, leading to difficulty in reaching political consensus and a lack of support for spending on public goods (Alesina, Baquir, and Easterly 1999). Second, homogeneous societies may be able to enforce "good" behaviors (such as compliance with tax laws) through social sanctions that lose their effectiveness in more diverse settings (Miguel and Gugerty 2005). Third, for whatever reason, people from different ethnic, linguistic, or cultural groups may have trouble interacting or getting along, leading to social tensions and weak/ineffective institutions.[38] All of these mechanisms raise a potential concern about the impact of increased immigration, particularly if it is expected to lead to a rise in ethnic, linguistic, or cultural diversity that diminishes the smooth functioning of local political systems (Alesina, Glaeser, and Sacerdote 2001).

This line of reasoning indicates that higher levels of immigration lead to lower output per capita, lower native wages, and lower property values. If anything, however, the evidence suggests the opposite: cities with more immigrants tend to have higher native wages, higher rents, and higher income per capita. Indeed, many of the most vibrant cities in the United States—including New York, Los Angeles, and Chicago—have high rates of ethnic and racial diversity, attributable in large part to immigration. Thus, my reading of the cross-city evidence is that the political-economy costs of diversity in the U.S. context are not large enough to offset the more conventional economic benefits of immigration.

Summary and Conclusions

Immigration is changing the size and composition of major cities in the United States. Cities with larger immigrant inflows have experienced faster population growth, increased racial and ethnic diversity, and a rise in the share of lower-skilled workers. In many respects, these changes parallel the experiences of high-immigrant cities in the late nineteenth and early twentieth centuries (Perlmann 2005). And as in the earlier wave of immigration, they have led to extensive debates about the impacts on native labor-market opportunities, housing prices, local government finances, and the overall quality of urban life.

This chapter presents an overview of the evidence on the magnitudes of these effects. Building on the past two decades of labor economists' research on immigration, most of this evidence is based on cross-city comparisons. The variation in the fraction of immigrants across different U.S. cities is enormous, providing a powerful research design. A key limitation is that immigrants are drawn to cities with better job prospects, potentially obscuring the negative impacts of their presence. The main solution that has been devised is to use the pull of city-specific enclaves to isolate a component of immigrant inflows that is unaffected by local demand conditions. This approach has been supplemented in the literature by case studies of events like the Mariel Boatlift that provided large and arguably exogenous inflows to specific cities based on external political events.

More than two decades of research on the local labor-market impacts of immigration has reached a near consensus that increased immigration has a small yet discernible negative effect on the *relative* wages of low-skilled native workers (i.e., the ratio of low-skilled wages to wages in the middle of the skill distribution). Less is known about the impact on the average level of native wages, but theoretical reasoning as well as the evidence presented here (and in a few other studies, mainly at the national level) suggests a small positive effect. Overall, I conclude that native wages are a little higher, on average, but a little more unequally distributed in a high- immigrant city like Los Angeles than in a low-immigrant city such as Philadelphia.

Moving beyond the labor market, economists have recently investigated the impacts of immigration on housing markets as well as government expenditures and revenues. My reading of the existing housing market studies is that increased immigration leads to somewhat higher rents, with an effect that is widely diffused across the market (i.e., across units that are more or less likely to be rented by new immigrants), and about the same size as the effect on average wages. So far, studies of the fiscal impacts of immigration have not used a cross-city research design. Simple comparisons of some key indicators of local fiscal impact—including the local share of the population that is of working age and per capita earnings—suggest that local fiscal impacts are small, although these conclusions may be refined in subsequent work. Taken together with the labor-market evidence, it seems that the direct economic impacts of immigration on existing native residents of major U.S. cities are relatively small and may well be positive.

Nevertheless, there is strong evidence that many U.S. natives prefer to live in neighborhoods and school districts with fewer minorities and more high-income/highly educated residents. Newly arriving immigrants pose a peer group effect that may partially offset or even completely reverse any positive labor-market impacts. One clear indicator of a reaction to this effect is the rise in measures of school segregation between white non-Hispanics and Hispanics in many large cities over the 1990s. My view is that such peer effects—whether driven by genuine concern about spillovers from neighbors or schoolmates, or perceived threats to social or group identity—may well be the most important cost of increased immigration in many natives' minds.

Appendix

TABLE 6.A.1
Immigrant Presence and Minority Shares—Detailed Composition

	Composition of overall population			
	Minority	Black	Asian	Hispanic
All United States	33.1	13.1	4.6	14.5
Outside top cities	26.1	11.5	2.7	10.3
All top cities	45.9	16.1	7.9	22.3
By city (CBSA)				
New York	47.2	20.3	8.9	20.7
Los Angeles	63.7	8.2	12.9	42.4
Chicago	40.1	18.0	5.8	16.1
Dallas	45.9	15.2	5.0	25.1
Philadelphia	31.0	21.9	3.5	5.9
Houston	57.2	19.9	4.5	32.9
Miami	59.5	21.1	2.2	37.0
Washington, DC	46.6	25.7	8.3	12.8
Atlanta	44.1	30.2	3.8	10.0
Detroit	30.6	23.5	3.5	3.2
Boston	20.9	7.3	7.1	7.8
San Francisco	55.4	8.3	24.2	22.2
Phoenix	40.4	4.9	3.2	30.8
Riverside	59.6	9.9	4.6	44.2
Seattle	26.5	6.3	12.0	5.1
Minneapolis	19.0	7.2	6.9	4.6
San Diego	48.8	8.1	12.3	27.4

Notes: Minorities include nonwhites and Hispanics of any race. Black population include mixed race individuals with some black heritage. See notes to table 6.1. Data derived from 2005 and 2006 March CPS. Entry in right-hand column represents sum of population shares of Asian and Hispanic immigrants and second-generation individuals, deviated from corresponding total for United States as a whole.

TABLE 6.A.1 *(cont.)*

Asian Imm.	Hispanic Imm.	Asian 2nd Gen.	Hispanic 2nd Gen.	Excess minority share attributable to Imm. & 2nd Gen.
2.7	5.8	1.4	4.1	—
1.5	3.3	0.9	2.7	−5.8
5.0	10.4	2.4	6.8	10.5
5.8	9.4	2.7	4.8	8.6
8.2	20.1	3.7	16.0	33.9
3.4	6.8	2.1	5.6	3.8
3.4	12.4	1.4	8.0	11.2
2.6	1.6	0.7	1.0	−8.1
3.1	13.4	1.3	9.1	12.8
1.6	23.6	0.5	9.4	21.0
5.5	8.6	2.5	3.1	5.6
2.6	6.0	1.0	2.8	−1.6
2.4	0.9	0.8	0.9	−9.0
4.3	3.4	2.6	1.8	−2.0
13.7	10.9	8.4	6.9	25.9
1.9	11.8	1.0	8.6	9.2
2.9	15.2	1.4	15.7	21.1
6.9	1.6	3.3	1.3	−1.0
4.1	2.4	2.5	1.1	−4.1
6.6	12.1	4.1	10.0	18.7

TABLE 6.A.2
Characteristics of Workers in Four Skill Quartiles

	Quartile 1	Quartile 2	Quartile 3	Quartile 4
Percent immigrants	18.3	13.3	9.6	9.6
Percent female	58.7	54.4	48.5	38.3
Years completed schooling	11.3	12.3	13.2	14.5
Percent Hispanic	19.4	12.5	8.4	5.4
Percent living in top 17 cities	32.6	31.2	30.8	32.9
Percent worked last year	71.1	78.0	81.6	85.4
Mean hours last year (unconditional)	1109	1397	1559	1734
Mean hours last year (conditional on working)	1560	1791	1911	2030
Mean hourly wage last year	12.73	15.54	18.16	22.95
Mean log hourly wage last year	2.26	2.46	2.62	2.83

Notes: Based on tabulations of 2000 Census. Means for each quartile are weighted means, using as a weight the estimated probability a given person would earn a wage in the respective quartile (if they worked).

Notes

1. I use the term "cities" in this chapter to refer to wider metropolitan areas rather than to specific political entities. As of 2003, the federal government has defined a new set of metro areas—so-called Core Based Statistical Areas (CBSAs)—that are similar to the Metropolitan Statistical Areas (MSAs) and Consolidated Metropolitan Statistical Areas (CMSAs) used in the past two decades. For the largest metro areas—like New York—the CBSA is comparable to the older CMSA, though typically smaller.

2. Table 6.A.1 presents a more detailed comparison between the racial/ethnic breakdown of the first- and second-generation immigrants in each city.

3. For a survey of the literature up to the mid-1990s, see Friedberg and Hunt (1995). More recent studies of local labor impacts include Card (2001); Orrenius and Zavodny (2006); Card and Lewis (2007); Dustmann et al. (2003); Glitz (2006).

4. Ottavanio and Peri (2006) extend the model developed by Borjas (2003) to allow for imperfect substitution between immigrants and natives with similar age and education. In their simulations that allow for capital growth, the wages of most natives are increased by immigration.

5. In table 6.2, I am redefining the top cities to include only the primary city

in the metro area (i.e., the main Primary Metropolitan Statistical Area (PMSA), in pre-2005 terminology). This is necessary to allow comparisons over time.

6. This pattern of growth in the immigrant population, with little or no growth in the native population, is sometimes interpreted as evidence that immigrant arrivals squeezed out the native born from the top cities in the 1980s (Frey 1995).

7. This formula can be refined by dividing immigrants into origin groups, and then constructing a group-specific inflow rate for each city. See, for example, Card (2001); Lewis (2004); Saiz (2006).

8. The correlation across the seventeen top cities is 0.41. Across the hundred-largest cities it is 0.50.

9. As noted by Wright, Ellis, and Reibel (1997), city growth rates are strongly correlated with city size, and failure to control for city size effects can lead to misleading inferences about the relation between immigrant inflows and population growth. In the simple models presented in table 6.3, the log of city size has a t-ratio of five or higher in models for overall city growth rates.

10. To facilitate "adding up," the growth rates between 1990 and 2000 are expressed as a ratio of the 1980 population in a city. I use the total population in 1980 as a weight in estimating the models over the broader hundred-city sample.

11. The IV estimate in the bottom row of the table for the period 1990–2000 uses immigrant shares of the city in 1980 and 1990 as instruments. The use of the two shares leads to a substantial gain in precision.

12. Borjas, Freeman, and Katz (1997) argue that immigrant arrivals almost fully displace natives. Their preferred model of population growth (for states, rather than cities) expresses the *change* in the decadal growth rate of the native population as a function of the *change* in the decadal growth rate of the immigrant population (expressing growth rates relative to the total population, as in equation [6.2]). Fitting their specification to the changes in city-specific native population growth rates (from 1980 to 1990 and 1990 to 2000) yields a coefficient of 1.56 (std. error = 0.39) on the change in the immigrant growth rate, implying an estimate of $\beta = 2.56$, which is obviously too large. I conclude that their specification does not adequately control for demand effects in a city model.

13. Thus, skill is measured by the predicted wage that a person would earn.

14. The model for natives includes a total of twenty-five covariates, formed from interactions between the individual's age, gender, education, and race/ethnicity. The model for immigrants is richer (a total of eighty-two covariates), and includes country-of-origin effects for each of the forty-largest sending countries as well as region-of-origin interactions with age, gender, and years in the United States.

15. Workers and nonworkers are assigned probabilities from the same model. In principle the procedure could be modified to account for the unobserved skill characteristics that partially determine a person's skill quartile and their likelihood of working.

16. The fractions of the native population in groups one to four are 25.4, 24.9, 26.2, and 23.5 percent, respectively. These differ from exactly 25 percent each because the quartile cutoffs were designed to divide *workers* in the seventeen top cities into four groups.

17. In view of the results in table 6.4, it is clear that immigrant selectivity is closely related to the source country composition of the immigrants in a given city. It would be interesting and useful to examine the role of historical enclaves in specific cities in determining the source country flows to each city. Card (2001) presents some data along these lines for the 1990s.

18. For a derivation of this reduced form equation from a supply-demand model, see Card (2001). The underlying assumptions are that natives and immigrants in the same skill group are perfect substitutes, the local production function is separable in labor and capital, and local labor input is a CES aggregate of the inputs of different skill groups with equal elasticities of substitution across all skill groups. It is also assumed that the per capita labor supply functions for the different skill groups have the same (constant) elasticity. If the elasticity of substitution across skill groups is σ, and the elasticity of the per capita labor supply is η, then $b = -1/(\sigma + \eta)$.

19. For simplicity, the relative wages plotted in figures 6.5.A and 6.5.B are *not* adjusted for differences in the observable characteristics of workers in each skill group in different cities.

20. The same coefficient would imply that the Mariel Boatlift, which increased the share of low-skilled workers in Miami by about 7 percent, would have lowered wages for the lowest-skill quartile by about 2.5 percent. Card (1990, table 5) presents mean wages for workers in four skill groups in Miami over the 1979 to 1985 period. The wage gap between the lowest group and the middle two shows no trend, but varies too much from year to year to make any precise inference.

21. I also estimated parallel models for the wage of quartile four relative to quartile one. These models yield OLS and IV estimates that are similar to those in table 6.7. For example, the IV estimates of the effect of relative supply on the relative wages of native and immigrant workers, with no other controls, are -0.10 (standard error = 0.03) and -0.12 (standard error = 0.04), respectively.

22. Assuming a single output is produced in each city and sold at a fixed price, the impact of immigrant arrivals on the mean wages of natives depends on how closely substitutable immigrants are for natives in the same skill group, the elasticities of substitution between skill groups, the relative skill distributions of immigrants and natives, and whether capital is supplied elastically or inelastically to a given city. For discussions of this, see Ottavanio and Peri (2006); Manacorda, Manning, and Wadsworth (2006). If capital is elastically supplied and immigrants are perfect substitutes for natives, then the average wages of natives will increase whenever the skill distribution of new immigrants differs from the distribution of the existing workforce. If immigrants are imperfect substitutes for natives, the positive effects on the average wages of natives will be larger. More general (trade-theoretic) models allow for firms in different cities to produce different products, some of which are exported (with a potentially downward-sloping export demand function) and others of which are consumed locally. In these models, the effect of immigrant inflows on the average wages will tend to be less positive and may be zero.

23. I also tried specifications that included a more flexible control for the city size (a third-order polynomial in log population), but found little change from

the models in table 6.8. Specifications that control for a polynomial in the average predicted wages of adults in a city also lead to similar estimates of the coefficient on the fraction of immigrants.

24. Ciccone and Peri (2006) have argued that one should test for human capital spillovers by relating the mean of log wages, holding skill composition constant, to the share of highly educated workers. I constructed a fixed composition index by using a simple average of mean log residual wages for native workers in each of the four skill quartiles. The use of this variable leads to estimates that are close to those in table 6.8.

25. Gyourko, Mayer, and Sinai (2006) discuss the wide heterogeneity across cities in the extent to which the housing supply and housing prices have risen in recent decades.

26. For a concise derivation of this result, see Inman (1997). If incomes and the local services available to natives are held constant, the utility of a representative native varies with the net local tax bill of natives, which will fall or rise depending on whether immigrants contribute more or less to local tax revenues than to local expenditures. MaCurdy, Nechyba, and Bhattacharya (1998) develop a richer intertemporal framework, which recognizes that although immigrants are typically young adults when they arrive, they eventually age and have children who also contribute to the fiscal surplus.

27. Medicare is available to people over age sixty-five with at least ten years of covered earnings, and is received by about 98 percent of the elderly population. It is also available to nonelderly recipients of federal Disability Insurance and people with end-stage renal disease. Medicaid is a means-tested program available to children, some adults, and low-income elderly people (including many nursing home residents).

28. Federal welfare reform legislation passed in 1996 made immigrants ineligible for many forms of government aid (including cash assistance and Medicaid) for their first five years in the country, although some states, including California, offer limited benefits to all immigrants. Undocumented immigrants are ineligible for most transfers and services, but are allowed to enroll in public elementary and secondary school in most states.

29. There are also relatively fewer immigrants than natives who are age sixty-five and older (10.9 versus 12.2 percent).

30. The fraction of Hispanics among second-generation natives is 39 percent, whereas 48 percent of immigrants are Hispanic. Up-weighting the fraction of Hispanics in the second-generation population makes the population more representative of the children who are or will be born to the current immigrant population, as suggested by Lee and Miller (2000).

31. This method is suggested in Edmonston and Lee (1996), but to the best of my knowledge has not been used in the literature.

32. If local taxes are proportional to earnings, the effect of immigration on the tax side of the fiscal burden equation can be summarized by examining the impact on per capita earnings.

33. To retain comparability with earlier tables, I measure the fraction of immigrants among sixteen to sixty-five year olds. Results using the fraction of immigrants in the entire population are similar.

34. The prediction model was used earlier to develop "adjusted" wages for natives in each skill group. I use the predicted log wage for all working-age adults.

35. Research on "social identity" suggests that immigrant groups with a different language, or different religious and cultural practices, will be perceived as particularly threatening. See Brown (1995, 2000); Monroe, Hankin, and Van Hecken (2000); Stets and Burke (2000).

36. These data are taken from the diversitydata.org site maintained by the Harvard School of Public Health (http://diversitydata.sph.harvard.edu), and based on data collected by the National Center for Education Statistics. The dissimilarity index (for Hispanics relative to white non-Hispanics) is the fraction of Hispanic students who would have to be relocated to other schools to achieve a uniform ratio of Hispanics to white non-Hispanics across all area schools.

37. These include Mauro (1995), Easterly and Levine (1997), La Porta et al. (1998), and Alesina, Baquir, and Easterly (1999). Although these studies are all at the cross-country level, the results may apply at the local level.

38. Lazear (1999) has developed a possible model along these lines, which hypothesizes that linguistic diversity presents a barrier to "trade" between people.

References

Alesina, Alberto F., Reza Baqir, and William Easterly. 1999. Public Goods and Ethnic Divisions. *Quarterly Journal of Economics* 114:1243–84.

Alesina, Alberto F., Edward L. Glaeser, and Bruce Sacerdote. 2001. Why Doesn't the United States Have a European-Style Welfare State? *Brookings Papers on Economic Activity* 2001:187–248.

Altonji, Joseph G., and David Card. 1991. The Effects of Immigration on the Labor Market Outcomes of Less-Skilled Natives. In *Immigration, Trade, and the Labor Market*, ed. John M. Abowd and Richard B. Freeman, 201–34. Chicago: University of Chicago Press.

Auerbach, Alan J., and Philip Oreopoulos. 1999. Analyzing the Fiscal Impacts of U.S. Immigration. *American Economic Review* 89:1276–80.

Bajari, Patrick, and Matthew E. Kahn. 2003. Estimating Housing Demand with an Application to Explaining Racial Segregation in Cities. NBER working paper no. 9891, August. Cambridge, MA: National Bureau of Economic Research.

Bayer, Patrick, and Robert McMillan. 2005. Racial Sorting and Neighborhood Quality. NBER working paper no. 11813, November. Cambridge, MA: National Bureau of Economic Research.

Black, Sandra E. 1999. Do Better Schools Matter? Parental Valuation of Elementary Education. *Quarterly Journal of Economics* 114:577–99.

Blau, Francine D. 1984. The Use of Transfer Payments by Immigrants. *Industrial and Labor Relations Review* 37:222–39.

Borjas, George. 1994. The Economics of Immigration. *Journal of Economic Literature* 32:1667–1717.

———. 2003. The Labor Demand Curve Is Downward Sloping: Re-examining the Impact of Immigration on the Labor Market. *Quarterly Journal of Economics* 118:1335–74.

Borjas, George, and Lynnette Hilton. 1996. Immigration and the Welfare State: Immigrant Participation in Means-Tested Entitlement Programs. NBER working paper no. 5372. Cambridge, MA: National Bureau of Economic Research.

Borjas, George, Richard B. Freeman, and Lawrence F. Katz. 1997. How Much Do Immigration and Trade Affect Labor Market Outcomes? *Brookings Papers on Economic Activity* 1997:1–90.

Brown, Rupert. 1995. *Prejudice: Its Social Psychology*. Cambridge, MA: Oxford University Press.

———. 2000. Social Identity Theory: Past Achievements, Current Problems, and Future Challenges. *European Journal of Social Psychology* 30:745–78.

Bruch, Elizabeth E., and Robert D. Mare. 2006. Neighborhood Choice and Neighborhood Change. *American Journal of Sociology* 112:667–709.

Card, David. 1990. The Impact of the Mariel Boatlift on the Miami Labor Market. *Industrial and Labor Relations Review* 43:245–57.

———. 2001. Immigrant Inflows, Native Outflows, and the Local Labor Market Impacts of Higher Immigration. *Journal of Labor Economics* 19:22–64.

Card, David, and John E. DiNardo. 2000. Do Immigrant Inflows Lead to Native Outflows? *American Economic Review* 90:360–67.

Card, David, and Ethan Lewis. 2007. The Diffusion of Mexican Immigrants during the 1990s: Explanations and Impacts." In *Mexican Immigration*, ed. George Borjas, 193–228. Chicago: University of Chicago Press.

Card, David, Alexandre Mas, and Jesse Rothstein. 2008. Tipping and the Dynamics of Segregation. *Quarterly Journal of Economics* 123:177–218.

Card, David, and Jesse Rothstein. 2007. Racial Segregation and the Black-White Test Score Gap. *Journal of Public Economics* 91: 2158–84

Ciccone, Antonio, and Giovanni Peri. 2006. Identifying Human-Capital Externalities: Theory with Applications. *Review of Economic Studies* 73:381–412.

Clark, William A. V. 1991. Residential Preferences and Neighborhood Racial Segregation: A Test of the Schelling Segregation Model. *Demography* 28:1–19.

Clotfelter, Charles T. 1979. Urban School Desegregation and Declines in White Enrollment: A Reexamination. *Journal of Urban Economics* 6 (July): 352–70.

———. 2001. Are Whites Still Fleeing? Racial Patterns and Enrollment Shifts in Urban Public Schools, 1987–1996. *Journal of Policy Analysis and Management* 20 (Spring): 199–221.

Clune, Michael S. 1998. The Fiscal Impacts of Immigration: A California Case Study. In *The Immigration Debate: Studies on the Economic, Demographic, and Fiscal Effects of Immigration*, ed. James P. Smith and Barry Edmonston, 120–82. Washington, DC: National Academy Press.

Cutler, David M., Edward L. Glaeser, and Jacob L. Vigdor. 1999. The Rise and Decline of the American Ghetto. *Journal of Political Economy* 107:455–506.

Duncan, Otis Dudley, and Beverly Duncan. 1957. *The Negro Population of Chicago: A Study of Residential Succession*. Chicago: University of Chicago Press.

Dustmann, Christian, Francesca Fabbri, Ian Preston, and Jonathan Wadsworth. 2003. The Local Labor Market Effects of Immigration in the U.K. Home Office online report 06/03. London: Home Office.

Easterly, William. 2005. Empirics of Strategic Interdependence: The Case of the Racial Tipping Point. New York University DRI working paper no. 5, October.

Easterly, William, and Ross Levine. 1997. Africa's Growth Tragedy: Policies and Ethnic Divisions. *Quarterly Journal of Economics* 112:1203–50.

Edmonston, Barry, and Ronald Lee, eds. 1996. *Local Fiscal Impacts of Illegal Immigration*. Washington, DC: National Academy Press.

Farley, Reynolds, Howard Schuman, Suzanne Bianchi, Diane Colasant, and Shirley Hatchett. 1978. Chocolate City, Vanilla Suburbs: Will the Trend toward Racially Separate Communities Continue? *Social Science Research* 7: 319–44.

Fortin, Nicole M., and Thomas Lemieux. 1998. Rank Regressions, Wage Distributions, and the Gender Gap. *Journal of Human Resources* 33:610–43.

Friedberg, Rachel M., and Jennifer Hunt. 1995. The Impact of Immigration on Host Country Wages, Employment, and Growth. *Journal of Economic Perspectives* 9 (Spring): 23–44.

Frey, William H. 1995. Immigration and Internal Migration "Flight" from US Metropolitan Areas: Toward a New Demographic Balkanisation. *Urban Studies* 32:733–57.

Garvey, Deborah L., and Thomas J. Espenshade. 1998. Fiscal Impacts of Immigrant and Native Households: A New Jersey Case Study. In *The Immigration Debate: Studies on the Economic, Demographic, and Fiscal Effects of Immigration*, ed. James P. Smith and Barry Edmonston, 66–119. Washington, DC: National Academy Press.

Glitz, Albrecht. 2006. The Labour Market Impact of Immigration: Quasi Experimental Evidence. CREAM discussion paper no. 12/06. London: Department of Economics, University College London.

Greulich, Erica, John M. Quigley, and Steven Raphael. 2004. The Anatomy of Rent Burdens: Immigration, Growth, and Rental Housing. *Brookings Papers on Urban Affairs* 2004:149–87.

Gyourko, Joseph, Christopher Mayer, and Todd Sinai. 2006. Superstar Cities. NBER working paper no. 12355. Cambridge, MA: National Bureau of Economic Research.

Inman, Robert P. 1997. Do Immigrants Pose a Net Fiscal Burden? Annual Estimates." In *The New Americans: Economic, Demographic, and Fiscal Effects of Immigration*, ed. James P. Smith and Barry Edmonston, 254–96. Washington, DC: National Academy Press.

Jensen, Lief. 1989. *The New Immigration: Implications for Poverty and Public Assistance Utilization*. New York: Greenwood Press.

Kane, Thomas J., Douglas O. Staiger, and Gavin Samms. 2003. School Accountability Ratings and Housing Values. *Brookings Papers on Urban Affairs* 2003:83–137.

La Porta, Rafael, Florencio Lopez de Silanes, Andrei Schleifer, and Robert Vishny. 1998. The Quality of Government. *Journal of Law, Economics, and Organization* 15:222–79.

Lazear, Edward P. 1999. Culture and Language. *Journal of Political Economy* 107:S95–S126.

Lee, Ronald, and Timothy Miller. 2000. Immigration, Social Security, and Broader Fiscal Impacts. *American Economic Review* 90 (May): 350–54.

Lewis, Ethan G. 2004. Local Open Economies within the U.S. How Do Industries Respond to Immigration? Federal Reserve Bank of Philadelphia working paper, December.

MaCurdy, Thomas, Thomas Nechyba, and Jay Bhattacharya. 1998. An Economic Framework for Assessing the Fiscal Impacts of Immigration. In *The Immigration Debate: Studies on the Economic, Demographic, and Fiscal Effects of Immigration*, ed. James P. Smith and Barry Edmonston, 13–65. Washington, DC: National Academy Press.

Manacorda, Marco, Alan Manning, and Jonathan Wadsworth. 2006. The Impact of Immigration on the Structure of Wages: Theory and Evidence from Britain. CREAM discussion paper no. 08/06. London: Department of Economics, University College London.

Mauro, Paulo. 1995. Corruption and Growth. *Quarterly Journal of Economics* 110:681–712.

Miguel, Edward, and Mary Kay Gugerty. 2005. Ethnic Diversity, Social Sanctions, and Public Goods in Kenya. *Journal of Public Economics* 89:2325–68.

Monroe, Kristen Renwick, James Hankin, and Renée Bukovchik Van Vechten. 2000. The Psychological Foundations of Identity Politics. *Annual Review of Political Science* 3:419–47.

Moretti, Enrico. 2004. Estimating the Social Return to Higher Education: Evidence from Longitudinal and Repeated Cross-Sectional Data. *Journal of Econometrics* 112:175–212.

Orrenius, Pia M., and Madeline Zavodny. 2006. Does Immigration Affect Wages? A Look at Occupation-Level Evidence. IZA discussion paper no. 2481. Bonn: Institute for the Study of Labor.

Ottavanio, Gianmarco, and Giovanni Peri. 2006. Rethinking the Effects of Immigration on Wages. NBER working paper no. 12497, August. Cambridge, MA: National Bureau of Economic Research.

Passel, Jeffrey S. 2005. Estimates of the Size and Characteristics of the Undocumented Population. Research Report of the Pew Hispanic Center, March. Washington DC: Pew Hispanic Center.

Peri, Giovanni. 2007. Immigrants Complementarities and Native Wages: Evidence from California. NBER working paper no. 12956, March. Cambridge, MA: National Bureau of Economic Research.

Perlmann, Joel. 2005. *Italians Then, Mexicans Now: Immigrant Origins and Second-Generation Progress, 1890–2000*. Annandale on Hudson, NY: Levy Economics Institute.

Quillian, Lincoln. 2002. Why Is Black-White Residential Segregation So Persistent? Evidence on Three Theories from Migration Data. *Social Science Research* 31:197–229.

Reber, Sarah J. 2005. Court-Ordered Desegregation: Successes and Failures Integrating American Schools since *Brown versus Board of Education*. *Journal of Human Resources* 40:559–90.

Rector, Robert E., Christine Kim, and Shanea Watkins. 2007. The Fiscal Cost of Low-Skill Households to the U.S. Taxpayer. Special report no. 12. Washington DC: Heritage Foundation.Rothstein, Jesse. 2004. College Performance Predictions and the SAT. *Journal of Econometrics* 121:297–317.

Ruser, John, Adrienne Pilot, and Charles Nelson. 2004. Alternative Measures of Household Income: BEA Personal Income, CPS Money Income, and Beyond. Paper prepared for the Federal Economic Statistics Advisory Board, November.

Saiz, Albert. 2003. Room in the Kitchen for the Melting Pot: Immigration and Rental Prices. *Review of Economics and Statistics* 85:502–21.

———. 2006. Immigration and Housing Rents in American Cities. IZA discussion paper no. 2189. Bonn: Institute for the Study of Labor.

Schelling, Thomas C. 1971. Dynamic Models of Segregation. *Journal of Mathematical Sociology* 1:143–86.

South, Scott J., and Kyle D. Crowder. 1998. Leaving the 'Hood: Residential Mobility between Black, White, and Integrated Neighborhoods. *American Sociological Review* 63:17–26.

Stets, Jan E., and Peter J. Burke. 2000. Identity Theory and Social Identity Theory. *Social Psychology Quarterly* 63:224–37.

Storesletten, Karl. 2000. Sustaining Fiscal Policy through Immigration. *Journal of Political Economy* 108:300–323.

Susin, Scott. 2001. The Impact of the Mariel Boatlift on the Miami Housing Market. Unpublished working paper. Washington, DC: U.S. Bureau of the Census.

Taeuber, Karl E., and Alma R. Taeuber. 1965. *Negroes in Cities*. Chicago: Aldine Press.

Tracy Joseph. 2004. Comment on "The Anatomy of Rent Burdens: Immigration, Growth, and Rental Housing." *Brookings Papers on Urban Affairs* 2004:188–92.

U.S. Department of Commerce, Bureau of the Census. 2006. Table 4: Cumulative Estimates of the Components of Population Change for the United States, Regions and States, April 1, 2000 to July 1, 2006. NST-EST2006-04. December 22.

Welch, Finis, and Audrey Light. 1987. *New Evidence on School Desegregation*. Washington, DC: U.S. Civil Rights Commission.

Wright, Richard, Mark Ellis, and Michael Reibel. 1997. The Linkage between Immigration and Internal Migration in Large Metropolitan Areas in the United States. *Economic Geography* 73:234–53.

7

Race

THE PERPLEXING PERSISTENCE OF RACE

JACOB L. VIGDOR

FORTY YEARS AGO, the problems of African Americans in cities were at the forefront of public consciousness. In 1966, Dr. Martin Luther King Jr., emboldened by success in forwarding the civil rights agenda in the U.S. South, took up residence on the west side of Chicago, one of two mono-lithic ghetto neighborhoods in that city. Chicago, along with other large industrial cities across the country, had witnessed a half century's worth of unprecedented migration, as blacks abandoned the rural South in search of higher living standards. Escaping the legal segregation of the South, black families encountered a different form of segregation in many of these destination cities: residential separation on a scale much greater than that witnessed in southern communities, enforced by a system of discriminatory actions; restrictive covenants prohibiting the sale of property to blacks; redlining, which restricted the availability of mortgage finance to black families in certain neighborhoods; and outright violence. Because of these actions, urban blacks found themselves confined to crowded, relatively expensive neighborhoods. When black families escaped these neighborhoods, usually to nearby areas, a process of "tipping" often ensued, as white families—often encouraged by profiteering real estate agents—fled in anticipation of racial change, creating a self-fulfilling prophecy in the process.

As King took up residence in Chicago, and as Daniel Patrick Moynihan, Charles Tilly, and other academics wrote treatises on the plight of the urban black in *The Metropolitan Enigma* and other sources, immense changes in the economic fortunes of central cities were already under way.[1] The manufacturing jobs that drove many African Americans to migrate were beginning to relocate overseas; the absolute peak of manufacturing employment in the United States occurred in 1967. The most egregious legalized forms of housing market discrimination were under assault. Twenty years earlier, the U.S. Supreme Court had ruled that restrictive covenants were unenforceable, and the Fair Housing Act of 1968 would strike another blow. Rapid suburbanization was eroding the population and employment base of many central cities: Baltimore, Boston, Chicago, Cleveland, Detroit, Philadelphia, Saint Louis, San Francisco, and Washington, DC, among others, all reached their maximum population around 1950 and declined thereafter.

What has happened in the forty years since this turning point? As this chapter will discuss, the trajectory of urban African Americans in the post–civil rights era has been a perplexing mix of success and failure. The profound residential segregation of the early postwar period has dissipated, largely because a number of black families have managed to break through the color line and establish themselves in formerly all-white neighborhoods. At the same time, however, most ghetto neighborhoods established by 1970 continue to be almost entirely black, and economic conditions in those neighborhoods worsened over much of the past few decades. While racial segregation declined, economic segregation—the separation of rich and poor—worsened for most of the period. The plight of economically marginalized, declining, predominantly black neighborhoods was especially evident in the aftermath of Hurricane Katrina in 2005. On the whole, progress toward racial equality has been notably absent since the civil rights movement, even as a number of African Americans have ascended to the highest rungs of the economic ladder.

Throughout this time period, social scientists in academia and government continually expressed concern that the lack of economic progress among African Americans could be attributed, at least in part, to their concentration in segregated neighborhoods. After reviewing changes in the urban landscape, this chapter then considers the evolution of thought regarding the impact of segregation on African Americans. This impact could, in theory, operate through several channels, including the importance of proximity to employment opportunities, racial disparities in public school quality, or via social networks. In practice, the most recent, reliable evidence on these channels suggests that they are at best minor determinants of educational and economic success. Perhaps the most compelling evidence to this effect derives from studies of randomized mobility experiments, or quasi-experimental analyses of events and policies that redistributed poor, predominantly minority families to more prosperous neighborhoods. These studies uniformly find no significant impact of segregation or neighborhood characteristics more generally on economic outcomes. Segregation persists, and black-white inequality persists, but it is inappropriate to conclude that the former is the cause of the latter. Racial inequality is a stubborn societal problem, yet it is not inherently an urban one. The belief that inequality can be significantly reduced by integrating America's urban neighborhoods is simply not consistent with modern evidence.

Segregation in the Post–Civil Rights Era

The word "segregation" means different things to different people. To many, it signifies the legally enforced system of racial separation utilized in the U.S. South between Reconstruction and the last decades of the twentieth century. To social scientists, though, the term also refers to a pattern of separation that need not be imposed by any authority but rather could occur as the result of freely made individual choices. Abstracting from the issue of whether segregation results from legal restrictions, illegal patterns of discrimination, or free choice, social scientists have devoted considerable effort to quantifying the amount of segregation that exists in a number of settings. When analyzing whether individuals of different races tend to reside in separate neighborhoods, sociologists and economists tend to use one of several segregation indexes. The typical segregation index ranges from 0 to 100 percent. A value of 0 indicates that there is no racial separation across neighborhoods; each neighborhood is a microcosm of the entire society. A value of 100 indicates that individuals of different races occupy entirely separate neighborhoods. Segregation indexes differ in their manner of judging intermediate situations, when there is some degree of mixing in neighborhoods but not everyone is representative of society as a whole.[2]

To compute a segregation index, it is necessary to have detailed information on the racial composition of individual neighborhoods within a metropolitan area. In the United States, the only consistent source of such data is the decennial Census of Population and Housing. Over time, the Census has collected and released increasingly detailed data on the population of small geographic areas. Between 1890 and 1940, published Census reports provided information on the racial composition of each ward in large cities. Starting in 1940, these reports added information on the composition of Census tracts, geographically compact areas with an average of four thousand residents each. Most efforts to measure segregation in U.S. cities have defined neighborhoods as Census tracts. In recent decades, public reports have detailed the racial composition of individual city blocks, enabling even more elaborate measures of segregation. The most cutting-edge measures of segregation take into account not only the racial composition of individual blocks but also the composition of nearby blocks (see, for example, Echenique and Fryer 2007). These measures are generally difficult to compute with older Census data.

The dissimilarity index, proposed by sociologists Julius Jahn, Calvin Schmid, and Clarence Schrag (1947), is one of the most commonly re-

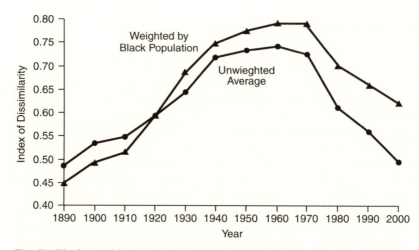

Fig. 7.1 Black-Nonblack Dissimilarity, 1890–2000. *Source*: Glaeser and Vig-dor (2003).

ported segregation measures. While it has been criticized in some circles for having little scientific justification, the index can be computed with relatively primitive data and has a straightforward interpretation: the proportion of a racial group that would have to move across neighbor-hoods in order to achieve an even distribution throughout the city or metropolitan area. In a city with black-nonblack dissimilarity equal to 80 percent, for example, four of every five black (or nonblack) residents would have to change neighborhoods to make each one representative of the area as a whole.

Figure 7.1 presents the average degree of segregation, as measured by the dissimilarity index, for each Census enumeration between 1890 and 2000.[3] The average is computed by aggregating dissimilarity index val-ues for individual cities (before 1960) or metropolitan areas (in 1960 and thereafter), attaching greater weight to those cities with a higher black population in a given year. The average thus represents the experience of the typical black city resident in the United States in each year.

Over the eighty-year period between 1890 and 1970, segregation in-creased dramatically, as the population of most major cities in the United States transformed from almost exclusively white to racially mixed. At the time of the civil rights movement, U.S. cities had reached the apex of racial segregation. The typical African American lived in a metro-politan area where more than three-quarters of the black population would have to be moved in order to achieve an even distribution across neighborhoods.

In the post–civil rights era, segregation—whether measured using dissimilarity or other indexes—declined substantially. By 2000, the typical African American resided in a metropolitan area where just over 60 percent of the black population would have to switch neighborhoods in order to achieve perfect integration. The thirty years after 1970 witnessed a decline in segregation that offset the increase of the prior half century.

Why has segregation declined over the past generation? Some observers are inclined to believe that the diversification of the U.S. population is responsible—that blacks are now more likely to live with other minority groups, particularly Hispanics, but still have limited exposure to non-Hispanic whites. This is a misleading point of view, however. Overwhelmingly black neighborhoods—those where less than 20 percent of the population belongs to any other race—actually increased in number over this time period. While the number of such neighborhoods increased, the population of these neighborhoods declined substantially. In 1960, about 50 percent of the urban African American population lived in neighborhoods where at least 80 percent of their neighbors were black. By 2000, less than 30 percent of African Americans lived in such neighborhoods. Ghetto neighborhoods, especially in the older manufacturing-dependent cities of the Northeast and Midwest, have lost a substantial proportion of their residents over the past forty years.

If ghetto neighborhoods remain overwhelmingly black, how can we explain the decline in segregation since 1970? The answer has much to do with the families that left the ghetto. Many of them took up residence in formerly all-white neighborhoods. In 1960, more than three-fifths of metropolitan neighborhoods canvased by the Census Bureau had less than one black resident in every hundred. One Census tract in every six had exactly zero black residents—out of an average of four thousand. By 2000, the proportion of neighborhoods with less than one black resident for every hundred declined to less than one-quarter. Between 1960 and 2000, the proportion of neighborhoods with between one and ten black residents in every hundred increased from 18 to 45 percent. The decline of segregation since 1970 can be attributed almost entirely to the movement of African American families from overwhelmingly black neighborhoods to more racially integrated settings. This movement, in turn, can be attributed largely, if not entirely, to the Fair Housing Act of 1968 and other official actions that criminalized the practice of racial discrimination in the housing market. Such discrimination may well persist into the twenty-first century, but the loss of official sanctions from the Federal Housing Administration, among other organizations, has undoubtedly done much to reduce it.

Implications of the Exodus from Ghetto Neighborhoods

What has become of U.S. ghetto neighborhoods in the wake of integration driven by black suburbanization? In many cases, these areas have
undergone a profound economic decline. This decline has been most
pronounced in the cities most affected by the decline of manufacturing
employment in the United States in the postwar era: Detroit and Saint
Louis, for example, have lost more than half their population since 1950.
In these economically obsolete cities, ghetto neighborhoods are marked
by high rates of vacancy and abandonment, unless cities have been proactive in removing dilapidated structures. The excess supply of housing
in these neighborhoods, coupled with weak demand, has depressed
prices dramatically. In June 2007, for instance, there were over six thousand properties listed for sale in Detroit at a price of $50,000 or below—at
a time when the national median was more than four times that level.
Among the largest of these was a twenty-two-hundred-square-foot,
four-bedroom brick colonial listed at $44,900, or just over $20 per square
foot. The most conservative estimates suggest that a house of this size
would cost nearly four times this price to build from the ground up.[4]
The owners of this house have cut the price far below the construction
cost because it is in a part of the country where few people wish to
move—a neighborhood that is 94 percent black, and where one home in
every twelve stands vacant.[5]

The devaluation of predominantly black neighborhoods has many
implications, some positive but many negative. The availability of abundant and inexpensive housing has led to a remarkable increase in black
homeownership rates, and the amount of housing consumed by the
typical black family. Relative to the immediate postwar era, when African Americans were crowded into geographically constrained neighborhoods, the average black family lives in a much larger house. The
low valuation of such houses, however, implies that one of the most reliable methods of building wealth in the United States—owning one's
home—has been substantially less lucrative for African Americans
(Collins and Margo 2001). The abandonment of traditionally black
neighborhoods, by depressing housing values, has prevented many
black families from accumulating assets at the same rate as equivalent
white families. Low valuation also creates difficulties for local governments, which rely on property taxes as a primary source of revenue.
When property values decline, governments must increase the tax rate
on those properties in order to maintain a steady budget.

African American families choosing to relocate away from traditionally black neighborhoods are in many cases more affluent than those

families that remain behind. There are many potential explanations for this pattern. Suburbanization, in the United States at least, has histori-cally been a trend driven by the moves of the affluent.[6] Suburban resi-dence is more likely to be automobile dependent, and not every family can afford to purchase and maintain its own vehicle. More generally, the amenities associated with the suburban lifestyle—more open space, better schools, and larger houses—are not strictly necessary for sur-vival. As a result, the post–civil rights era depopulation of ghettos has been associated with a rise in the concentration of poverty in those areas.

Indeed, while racial segregation was declining in the 1970s and 1980s, economic segregation, the separation of poor and rich households by neighborhood, increased (Jargowsky 1997). Over this twenty-year pe-riod, the number of census tracts with poverty rates above 40 percent—that is, where at least two of every five families had incomes below the federal poverty line—doubled, as did the number of individuals living in such neighborhoods. This concentration of poor households eased during the 1990s, as the numbers of both high-poverty neighborhoods and individuals living in those neighborhoods declined (Jargowsky 2003). Even so, nearly eight million individuals lived in a neighborhood with a poverty rate above 40 percent in 2000, substantially more than in 1970. Three million of these individuals were black; nearly one in five poor African Americans resides in a neighborhood where 40 percent of all households have an income below the poverty line.

Explaining What Remains of Racial Segregation: Income or Preferences?

Based on these patterns, it is tempting to conclude that racial segrega-tion has given way to economic segregation: that the predominant pat-tern of separation in U.S. cities is between rich and poor, and that racial segregation persists primarily because of the strong association be-tween race and income. Such a conclusion would be erroneous, though. Several studies have documented a tendency for African American families at all income levels to have a higher proportion of black neigh-bors than their white counterparts (see, for example, Sethi and So-manathan 2004; Bayer, Fang, and McMillan 2005). Although it is true that higher-income black families have experienced the highest degree of integration in the post–civil rights era—between 1970 and 1990, the decline in racial segregation experienced by college-educated blacks was nearly three times greater than that of high school dropouts—even these families continue to witness substantial residential segregation (Cutler, Glaeser, and Vigdor 1999).

Fig. 7.2 Card Presented to MCSUI Respondents to Elicit Neighborhood Racial Composition Preferences. *Source*: Vigdor (2003).

If the racial gap in income can't explain the persistence of segregation since 1968, what can? Illegal discrimination in the housing and mortgage markets undoubtedly plays some role. The continued existence of discrimination, sometimes subtle yet often blatant, is supported by the results of housing audit studies. In housing audits, paired testers, one black and one white, but with identical fabricated backgrounds and preferences, approach real estate agents, landlords, or mortgage brokers in search of assistance with finding, renting, or purchasing a home. Study investigators analyze the results of these interactions to determine whether there is any systematic steering of black testers toward homes in certain neighborhoods, away from certain properties, or toward loans with higher interest rates or otherwise inferior terms. These studies quite commonly find evidence of disparate treatment.

Even if housing market discrimination were to be completely eradicated, however, it would still be reasonable to expect racial segregation to persist. This is a clear prediction of Nobel laureate economist Thomas Schelling's (1978) tipping model. The model pertains to situations where individuals of different races have varying preferences for the racial composition of their neighbors. Even slight differences in preferences across groups can lead to stark degrees of segregation in equilibrium.

Do families of different races have different ideas of the neighborhood racial composition they would most prefer? In 1996, a team of researchers presented white, black, Asian, and Hispanic householders residing in the Boston and Los Angeles metropolitan areas with cards similar to the one illustrated in figure 7.2.[7] The card depicts fifteen houses, one with an X in the middle. The researchers asked each individual to put a letter in each of the other houses, to illustrate the level of diversity they would consider "ideal." The researchers encouraged the respondents to imagine that varying the racial composition of this ideal neighborhood would not change anything else about it. Yet in practice, it is possible that individuals imagining neighborhoods of differing racial composition imagine differences along other dimensions as well. If diverse neighborhoods are generally perceived as having lower-quality schools or higher crime rates, for example, these perceptions

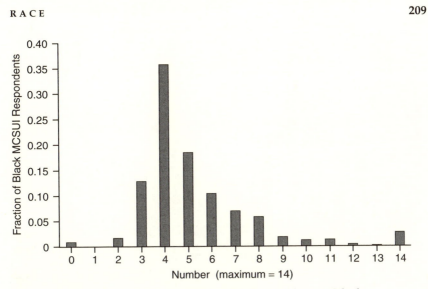

Fig. 7.3 Black Preferences for Number of Black Neighbors in Ideal Neighborhood. *Source*: MCSUI, Vigdor (2003).

may have influenced the respondents' answers. With this caveat in mind, the pattern of responses provides fascinating evidence on the prospects for stable integration in U.S. neighborhoods.

Figure 7.3 shows how black respondents filled out the card. More than a third indicated that their ideal number of black neighbors was four out of fourteen. More than three-quarters of them indicated that their ideal neighborhood would be somewhere between 25 and 50 percent African American. Figure 7.4 shows the responses given by white householders. While most indicated that they would most prefer to live in a neighborhood with at least one black neighbor, about 80 percent reported that their ideal neighborhood would be no more than 20 percent African American. Whereas 35 percent of black households would most prefer a neighborhood where one of every three households was African American, less than 5 percent of white households indicated the same preference.

Consider the implications of this discrepancy in the housing market. Begin with a neighborhood of fifteen houses, three black and twelve white. A white household moves out and is replaced by a black one. From the perspective of the other black residents, this is likely to be perceived as a good thing: few wish to live in a neighborhood where they are one of only three black households, and most would prefer to have at least four black neighbors. From the vantage point of the white residents, however, the move from three to four black neighbors is likely to

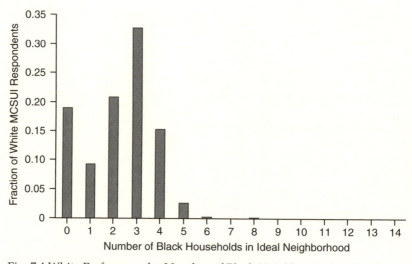

Fig. 7.4 White Preferences for Number of Black Neighbors in Ideal Neighborhood. *Source*: MCSUI, Vigdor (2003).

be viewed negatively. While most whites prefer to have some diversity in their neighborhoods, the move above 20 percent black makes the neighborhood a bit more diverse than their ideal.

Now suppose another white household moves out. Who will win the bidding war for the vacant house? The typical white family looks at the neighborhood as slightly too diverse for its tastes. The typical black family, though, faces the prospect of moving into a neighborhood that is one-third black—for a large number of such families, this is the ideal scenario. It is not unreasonable to think that a black family will outbid a white one and move into the newly vacant house.

The process repeats itself. As the neighborhood's racial composition tilts more heavily African American, a larger number of white households will consider the area too far from their ideal. Beyond a certain point, the black families will also consider the neighborhood far from their ideal. Few individuals of any race indicate that they would most prefer to live in a neighborhood that is more than two-thirds black. Still, when a house comes up for sale in such a neighborhood, who is likely to bid the most for it? While no group considers the racial composition ideal, it appears probable from the two preference distributions that African Americans are likely to outbid other groups for housing in these types of neighborhoods.

Tipping is more than just a theoretical notion. A recent study of neighborhood dynamics between 1970 and 2000 by economists David Card,

Alexandre Mas, and Jesse Rothstein (2007) documents that neighbor-hoods reaching a threshold percent black, usually around 15 percent, tend to transition rapidly in subsequent decades.

Segregation can thus occur without any discrimination whatsoever, as long as preferences for neighborhood racial composition vary by race and housing is consistently sold to the highest bidder (which seems to be the rule in most housing markets these days).[8] A lingering question is whether these preference disparities should be interpreted as "racism." Whites would rather not be in a majority-black neighborhood; blacks appear more tolerant of residential neighborhoods where their group forms the minority. Consider the following, though: only 7 percent of the population of the Boston metro area and 10 percent of the popula-tion of Los Angeles County are African American. If perfectly inte-grated, each neighborhood of fifteen houses in either area would have only one or two black households. As figure 7.4 shows, the vast major-ity of white survey respondents would be quite willing to accept one or two black neighbors—and that is all that integration requires. The over-whelming majority of black survey respondents, by contrast, would rather be in a neighborhood with a higher concentration of African Americans. Even if white householders were completely color-blind, this distribution of preferences would ensure continued segregation in Boston and Los Angeles. In fact, the dissimilarity index would actually increase in both cities.

All in all, it is probably not productive to spend a lot of time worry-ing about which group, if either, has stronger racial preferences in their location choice—particularly given the concerns raised above that the preferences elicited in surveys may be tainted by the respondents' asso-ciations of racial composition with other neighborhood characteristics. The most straightforward thing to say is that black and white prefer-ences are misaligned—incompatible with one another, and hence prone to cause tipping problems of the sort that Schelling predicted. It is also clear that one need not take continued segregation as evidence of con-tinued discrimination in housing markets. In at least some areas, segre-gation may actually be *below* the level one would predict under a truly free choice of neighborhood racial composition.[9]

When Black Neighborhoods Integrate

As discussed above, predominantly black neighborhoods, on the whole, declined in population but not number following the civil rights move-ment. While this is true in the aggregate, it is not universally so for all neighborhoods. Indeed, there are prominent examples of urban neighborhoods that underwent a process of integration over the past several decades. When it occurs, this process is likely to be labeled gentrification. Washington, DC's Columbia Heights and Boston's South End, among other neighborhoods, are instances of this phenomenon.

Gentrification occurs in growing cities that are unable (or unwilling) to produce new housing fast enough to accommodate newcomers. As demand outpaces supply, prices increase, and some households respond by seeking out housing in formerly unfashionable neighborhoods. The stereotypical pattern is for artists, possessing notoriously fickle incomes yet strong tastes for urbanity and the aesthetic appeal of older neighborhoods, to enter such areas first. Young professional singles and couples, who worry little about the quality of local schools but value urbanity and proximity to work, soon follow. Individuals who lament the alteration in the neighborhood's character often use the term gentrification pejoratively. Few observers, however, connect the phenomenon of gentrification with its root cause. It is rare to find gentrifying neighborhoods in declining cities. Housing prices fall rather than rise in these areas, and the pressure to find temporarily cheap neighborhoods is not present. Rather, it is the nearly exclusive domain of growing areas, particularly those where housing is not built rapidly enough to keep up with demand.[10]

Can Segregation Explain Persistent Black-White Inequality?

Since the late 1960s, there has been notable progress toward residential integration in the United States: black and white families are now more likely to reside in proximity to one another in almost every region of the country. Progress toward racial equality along dimensions other than residence is a different story. In the labor market, black-white income disparities closed rapidly during the 1960s, and showed some additional narrowing in the first half of the 1970s. Since that time, though, inequality has stagnated by some measures and widened by others (see Bound and Freeman 1992). The black-white differences in hourly wages have narrowed slightly over time. Yet the black-white differences in the number of hours worked per year have widened considerably.[11] The likelihood of being employed in any particular week declined for blacks relative to whites, as did the average number of hours worked per week. Thus, while blacks have shown some improvement in their return to an hour of labor, the number of hours spent laboring has declined precipitously.

The disappearance of manufacturing jobs from northeastern and midwestern cities over the latter part of the twentieth century has been blamed for much of this trend. Manufacturing drew many unskilled

and semiskilled black workers to cities during World War II and immediately afterward. As these jobs began to disappear from cities, unskilled
workers found themselves with few strong prospects, even in regions
that successfully transitioned to a knowledge-based economy. The erosion of manufacturing employment has also been blamed for a host of
other social ills befalling predominantly black neighborhoods during
this time period. For example, the black-white gap in academic performance, as measured by standardized tests, stopped narrowing some-
time in the mid-1980s, roughly ten years after the opening of the labor
force participation gap.[12]

Trends in the manufacturing industry are not the only broad ones im-
plicated by observers of black-white inequality. Indeed, residential segregation itself has been quite frequently mentioned as a cause of continued
or worsened inequality between blacks and whites. Can segregation be
exerting a negative and growing impact even as it declines? What does
the available evidence tell us about this possibility?

Social scientists have proposed a number of pathways through which
residential segregation might perpetuate racial inequality.[13] At least one
of these pathways involves factors already mentioned above. The failure of housing values in predominantly black neighborhoods to appreciate at the same rate as in white neighborhoods has contributed to the
wealth gap. Ironically, this effect can be traced most specifically to the
Fair Housing Act, which paved the way for many black families to exit
ghetto neighborhoods. Wealthier households, in turn, can invest more
in the well-being and academic success of their children. Wealthier
families can afford more books and educational toys for their young
children, and frequently have more available time to read and interact
with them. At the other end of the education spectrum, the children of
wealthy families are disproportionately represented at the nation's elite
colleges, and are more likely to successfully complete degree programs
wherever they enroll.

Beyond those effects operating directly through the housing market,
segregation has been proposed as a cause of black-white inequality
through three main mechanisms:

- *Differential access to jobs.* Since the 1960s, employment growth in
  the United States has been concentrated on the suburban fringe of
  cities—where the population growth has also been concentrated.
  Economist John Kain (1968) is widely credited with proposing the
  "spatial mismatch" hypothesis, which argues that black employment outcomes are harmed by the sheer physical distance between predominantly black neighborhoods and places of rapid
  employment growth within metropolitan areas.

- *Disparities in school quality and other local government services.* Segregated neighborhoods often lead to segregated schools, except in those districts that bus students across neighborhoods to achieve balance. The use of busing has been on the wane in recent decades (Clotfelter 2004). Separate schools may be inherently unequal. Similar contentions apply to other goods and services that local governments provide, including police and fire protection, parks and recreation, or sanitation (see Inman and Rubinfeld 1979).
- *Differences in social networks.* One individual's likelihood of finding a job may depend on the number of neighbors who already have jobs. This sort of social network effect could occur because individuals strive to emulate their neighbors ("keeping up with the Joneses," one might say), because employees inform their neighbors about job openings at their workplace, or because neighbors put in a good word with their own employers. In any case, one would expect individuals to be less likely to find work, either because they are less motivated or able to get their foot in the door in an environment where few of their neighbors work (see Bayer, Ross, and Topa 2005).

Are there any strong reasons to think that segregation *shouldn't* have an impact on black-white inequality? The strongest argument leans on the economic concept of revealed preference. If residing in a segregated neighborhood has such a negative impact on one's well-being, why would anybody choose to live in one? The instinctive response to this assertion is that African Americans move to segregated neighborhoods not by choice but rather because they face discrimination in the housing market. Recall, though, that the broad declines in segregation since 1970 show that a large number of black families have moved to predominantly white neighborhoods. Recall also that the level of segregation currently observed in many U.S. cities could be mostly, if not entirely, explained by tipping models that make no mention of discrimination.

A second response to the revealed preference argument is that modern segregated neighborhoods are in many cases inexpensive relative to other parts of the same metropolitan area. Housing is a durable good; the abandonment of segregated neighborhoods in the wake of fair housing legislation in the 1960s left many of those neighborhoods with a substantial surplus of housing units, which naturally led to declines in price. Black families may choose to live with the negative consequences of residence in segregated neighborhoods largely because they cannot afford a better alternative.

Outside the revealed preference contention, which is admittedly rhetorical, there are some reasons to think that residence in a ghetto could

be beneficial for certain types of people. Segregated central-city neighborhoods are frequently better served by public transportation than
sprawling suburban areas. For families without a car, or with fewer cars
than workers, living far from the transit grid could be a difficult proposition. Public schools that serve disadvantaged children could, in theory, specialize in more appropriate learning techniques—indeed, there
are charter schools in many cities that emphasize a distinctly African
American curriculum. Finally, an individual may benefit little from
having employed neighbors if those neighbors work in occupations for
which the individual is not qualified. If all your neighbors work for a
pharmaceutical research firm, but you are a high school dropout, the
odds that your neighbors will land you a job are slim.

Which arguments are the most plausible? Readers of different per-
suasions will think differently. Free market economists are most likely
to be swayed by the revealed preference arguments. Many social scientists and civil rights lawyers are likely to take the opposite set of claims
as an article of faith. In situations like this, the social scientist's usual re-
course is to consider the available empirical evidence. For several reasons, however, the evidence is controversial and more subject to interpretation than one might hope.

To determine whether a new medical treatment benefits or harms patients, researchers conduct a controlled experiment. After recruiting a
number of willing subjects, the researchers randomly—that is, by the flip
of a coin—choose half of them to receive the new treatment. The other
half continue with regular medical care. Researchers then track the outcomes of the two groups; any systematic differences between them, for
better or worse, are inferred to be the result of the new treatment.

Inferences about the impact of neighborhoods on the people who live
in them are almost never able to use this research method, with one notable exception discussed below. The simplest inferences are taken just
by directly comparing, say, African Americans who reside in ghetto
neighborhoods with those who live in more integrated settings. The
difficulty with interpreting these types of comparisons is that families
choose their own neighborhoods. Widespread differences between
groups who live in different settings might tell us something about the
impact of settings, but it might also tell us something about the kinds of
people who choose to live in such settings. A discovery that families living in gated communities have higher incomes than those who do not
does not imply that other families' incomes would increase if we moved
them into such communities. Rather, it simply shows that gated communities tend to attract families with higher incomes to start with.

Most modern research on neighborhood effects eschews such primitive comparisons, using a variety of statistical techniques to attempt to

restrict analysis to individuals who were similar to one another, but opted for idiosyncratic reasons to live in different neighborhoods. Still, most of these statistical techniques can be criticized for failing to match the ideal of a controlled experiment, where the only factor differentiating the individuals to be compared is a coin flip.

For example, some researchers attempt to make comparisons among individuals who appear close to identical along all the dimensions they can measure. Using large databases on individuals, researchers pick pairs of people who match up on a set of background characteristics, such as age, gender, and educational attainment, but who live in different neighborhoods. When the two individuals are close to identical in background, the logic goes, any differences in outcomes such as employment or income must be attributable to neighborhood.[14]

This method, known as "propensity score matching," sounds good in theory. In practice, matching individuals along a small set of characteristics could simply guarantee that there are huge differences along dimensions that researchers can't observe. Few databases used for research record information on past substance abuse problems, criminal records, or inheritances. When comparing two forty-year-old black male college dropouts, one living on Chicago's South Side and the other in a leafy suburb, it might easily be the case that one of these unseen factors explains more about their differences in employment than their neighborhood does.

A second major strategy exploits the fact that in certain cities, it is difficult for families to choose neighborhoods with certain environments. In Detroit, there are few integrated neighborhoods, so even the most integration-minded household, black or white, will have a hard time choosing one. In Charlotte, by contrast, such neighborhoods can be found. Rather than match individuals living in the same city, then, this strategy matches people who live in cities where integrated neighborhoods can be found with similar individuals living in cities where there are no integrated neighborhoods.

This strategy breaks down if we introduce the possibility that individuals might move between cities to take advantage of, among other things, the availability of integrated neighborhoods. This sort of cross-city mobility has occurred quite frequently over the past few decades: the broad movement of the U.S. population from the Rust Belt to the Sun Belt has taken it away from some of the nation's most segregated cities to some of its least segregated ones. Researchers will occasionally fight this sort of trend by focusing on young adults, such as those under the age of thirty, on the theory that these individuals are more likely to have inherited their choice of city from their parents. But even this strategy is an imperfect control for unmeasured personal attributes if young adults inherit more than just a location from their parents.

While a thorough review of studies examining the link between neighborhood and outcomes would require a book-length manuscript, a few deserve mention as exemplars of the group. Several thorough reviews of the literature on neighborhoods and outcomes have been written through the years (see Jencks and Mayer 1990; Ellen and Turner 1997; Gephart 1997; Vigdor 2006).[15]

In one prominent study, economists David Cutler and Edward Glaeser (1997) looked at the impact of residential segregation on black-white disparities in employment, educational, and fertility outcomes, using data on young adults age twenty to thirty from the 1990 Census. Segregation was associated with wider outcome disparities between whites and blacks, controlling for a number of additional characteristics. The primary issue with this finding is one of interpretation: Should we conclude that segregation worsens the relative outcomes of African Americans, or that segregated cities happen to attract black residents predisposed to poor outcomes? Cutler and Glaeser addressed this question in several respects. Their analysis focused on young adults, who generally live in a metropolitan area because they were born there, not because they chose to live there. They controlled statistically for a number of correlates, both at the individual and metropolitan level. Finally, the authors conducted a comparison of individuals in cities with differing numbers of municipal and township governments in 1962, under the hypothesis that governmental fragmentation encouraged segregation in that earlier era, but should not otherwise have had any impact on individual outcomes. Cutler and Glaeser concluded that the correlation between segregation and outcomes was indeed causal, and that segregation had a negative impact on blacks relative to whites.

Subsequent analysis has provided additional insight into this question of interpretation. Two economic historians attempted to replicate the analysis using earlier Census data, and found no association between segregation and black-white disparities, utilizing similar methods, as recently as 1980 (Collins and Margo 2000). The negative impact of segregation on economic outcomes may have been muted in this earlier era, when job opportunities for unskilled workers were in greater supply. The networking advantage of living in a neighborhood with other unskilled workers may be minimal if there are few jobs to go around. Other studies have emphasized the changing nature of migration to and away from segregated cities over time (Vigdor 2002b; Ananat 2007). In the heyday of U.S. manufacturing, the highly segregated large cities of the Northeast and Midwest attracted a disproportionate share of the most educated black migrants. In later years, however, this pattern shifted—black abandonment of the Rust Belt has been selective, with the "best and brightest" being most likely to move to more rapidly growing areas of the country, including the South. The evidence on migration points away from a causal interpretation of the link between segregation and outcomes, and toward the view that ghettos were selectively abandoned as fair housing laws took effect and manufacturing employment eroded, creating a noncausal correlation between segregation and poor black outcomes.

Cutler, Glaeser, and I (2008) released a follow-up study examining the relationship between segregation and outcomes among immigrants to the United States.[16] This study found a negative association between residence in a segregated neighborhood and labor-market outcomes in certain circumstances, but not in others. Members of immigrant groups with lower average levels of education tend to suffer when concentrated in ghetto neighborhoods. Members of more educated groups, by contrast, actually fare better when residentially concentrated. Brought to bear on the experience of African Americans, this evidence suggests that the selective abandonment of ghetto neighborhoods by upwardly mobile blacks in the post–civil rights era may have introduced a more negative causal impact on the outcomes of individuals left behind.

Spurred in part by questions of whether correlations between neighborhood segregation and outcomes could be treated as causal, the Department of Housing and Urban Development in the mid-1990s initiated a controlled experiment known as the Moving to Opportunity (MTO) demonstration program.[17] The experiment divided research subjects, poor single-parent families residing in housing projects in one of five cities, into three groups. Two of these groups received housing vouchers, which enabled them to move to a housing unit outside the projects while applying a government subsidy toward the rent. Of the two groups, one received a restricted voucher, which could only be redeemed for housing in a neighborhood where the poverty rate was less than 10 percent. A third group received no voucher. If living in an environment of concentrated poverty is detrimental to a family's well-being, then one would expect families receiving a voucher, particularly those steered toward lower-poverty neighborhoods, to end up faring much better than those who did not.

Before reviewing the results of this experiment, and other noteworthy studies of neighborhoods and outcomes, think about the MTO program from the free market economists' perspective. A central tenet of free market economics is that one cannot make an individual better-off by taking a choice away from them. At best, the removed choice will be irrelevant. At worst, the removed choice will force the individual to pick something else that they find less satisfying. From this vantage point, it seems unlikely to expect the MTO participants who received restricted vouchers to be better-off than those who received unrestricted vouchers. Those who received unrestricted vouchers could, after all, always use them to move into low-poverty neighborhoods if they really wanted to. Plus, they had the option of choosing a higher-poverty neighborhood if that is what they preferred. The MTO program thus serves as a sort of litmus test for whether standard free market arguments can be applied to the decisions of poor, predominantly African American households to live in high-poverty neighborhoods.

To the surprise of many, the MTO program has in general failed to show any significant impact of neighborhood location on an array of child and adult outcomes. Adult employment and earnings show no impact (Kling, Liebman, and Katz 2005). Child standardized test scores show no difference (Kling and Liebman 2004). Child behavior, in aggregate, shows no difference, although researchers have shown that this aggregate effect masks significantly different impacts on boys and girls: girls behave better in low-poverty environments, but boys behave worse (Clampet-Lundquist et al. 2006). Adults who relocated to lower-poverty neighborhoods report improved mental health, but this has not translated into improvements along any other dimensions (Kling et al. 2004).

Surprising though these results may seem, they have been corroborated by other recent studies that exploit near experiments, where families have been randomly assigned to locations not for scientific purposes but administratively. Philip Oreopoulos (2003), for example, studied families on the waiting list for public housing units in Toronto. Toronto's public housing complexes occupy a wide range of neighborhoods, from high to moderate poverty. Families at the top of the waiting list are required to occupy the first unit that becomes available or return to the bottom of the list. From the family's perspective, the assignment to a neighborhood is effectively random. Oreopoulos's results mirror those of the MTO: no impact of neighborhood characteristics on the outcomes.

A final near experiment in mobility resulted from the mass evacuation of New Orleans in the wake of Hurricane Katrina in 2005. I (2007) tracked the labor market outcomes of Katrina evacuees, many of whom moved to metropolitan areas with much more robust labor markets than New Orleans. Even fifteen months after the initial evacuation, long-term evacuees were faring much worse, not better, in their destination labor markets. Even relocation to a booming metropolis, such as Atlanta or Las Vegas, appears to have had little positive impact on the evacuees' prospects.

Recent near-experimental literature does offer a few hints that segregation matters in certain contexts. For instance, two recent studies show that court-mandated changes in school desegregation policy, which are clearly beyond any individual student's control, lead to significant changes in high school completion rates for African American youth. These studies compare the experiences of cohorts reaching the legal dropout age just before and after the court order; one examines the late 1960s, when courts commonly mandated the use of busing programs to desegregate, and another focuses on the past decade, when courts commonly rescinded those orders (see Guryan 2004; Lutz 2005). Given the well-established link between high school completion and later success in life, these are key findings. Note, however, that these findings speak to the importance of school segregation, not neighborhood segregation per se.

Overall, the most reliable evidence clearly supports the view that segregated neighborhoods aggregate individuals predisposed to poor labor-market outcomes. Whether neighborhoods themselves have effects on these individuals over and above this predisposition is a matter of some controversy. Experimental evidence suggests that the answer is no, although no experiment to date has manipulated the racial composition of neighborhoods, rather than the socioeconomic composition. There is stronger quasi-experimental evidence to support a role for school segregation, but school segregation is largely a function of governmental decisions rather than residential patterns. Perhaps the least controversial way to summarize the existing state of knowledge is to assert that the collapse of labor force participation among black males over the past four decades is primarily a problem of people, not places. Unskilled workers were bound to fare poorly in the transition to a postindustrial, knowledge-based economy, regardless of where they lived. Any influence of place must be small relative to the influence of skill itself.

Conclusion

Racial segregation has declined substantially in the forty years since the civil rights movement. Racial inequality has not. In hindsight, the opposing nature of these two trends was our first clue that there is no enduring causal link between the two of them. As more affluent African American families departed from ghetto neighborhoods, for the suburbs or more integrated parts of the country, those neighborhoods became increasingly marked by concentrated poverty, vacancy, and a number of social ills that go along with those two phenomena.

Over time, government strategies toward ending racial inequality have shifted. Beginning with the *Brown v. Board of Education* decision of

1954, the federal government mandated an end to legal segregation, followed later by affirmative mandates to counteract its effects through busing and other remedies. Yet there has always been a limit to these remedies: courts have never mandated that schools be integrated by busing across district lines. White parents have thus always had the option of moving to the suburbs or enrolling in private school, rather than face integration.

Integration efforts began to erode in the 1980s, increasingly replaced by an emphasis on accountability. Government acknowledged the reality of persistent school segregation and shifted its attention to the effective delivery of services to disadvantaged populations, either by direct mandate or by introducing competition. The No Child Left Behind Act of 2002 intended to reduce black-white test score disparities not by integrating schools but rather by sanctioning schools that failed to produce results. The initial reports on the impact of these post–civil rights era policies on black-white disparities are mixed; the debate will probably continue for many years to come.

The shift from integration to incentives is in some sense rational given recent findings in the academic literature. Integration, whether realized through families' own choices or government intervention, has had at best a small impact on black-white disparities. Incentives have little track record of their own, but are backed by strong economic arguments. Only time will tell whether this grand shift in policy will lead to a historic change in racial inequality.

In summer 2005, the problems of urban African Americans were once again brought to the forefront of public consciousness when the aftermath of Hurricane Katrina highlighted the existence of a poor, almost exclusively black underclass in the city of New Orleans. Forty years from now, the lessons of experiments recently undertaken may have provided us with more information about the nature of racial inequality in the United States and the policy remedies most likely to reduce it. For the time being, however, we continue to live in a society where race matters, but almost certainly not because of segregation.

Notes

1. See Wilson (1968), especially Daniel P. Moynihan's chapter on poverty, Charles Tilly's chapter on migration, and Edward C. Banfield's chapter on riots.

2. For a discussion of various types of segregation index, see Massey and Denton (1988).

3. This figure and much of the discussion of trends in segregation that follows is drawn from Cutler, Glaeser, and Vigdor (1999); Glaeser and Vigdor (2003).

4. Estimates of construction costs are typically derived from sources such as RS Means.

5. The property in question is 5082 Buckingham Avenue, Detroit, Michigan 48224. Neighborhood data are taken from the 2000 Census, Wayne County, Michigan, tract 5013.

6. For a comprehensive history of suburbanization in the United States, see Jackson (1985).

7. The referenced study is the Multi-City Study on Urban Inequality (MCSUI). The figures and much of the discussion accompanying them are derived from Vigdor (2004).

8. For more formal econometric evidence indicating that individuals prefer to reside in neighborhoods with members of their own race, see Bayer, Ferreira, and McMillan (2007).

9. Bayer, Fang, and McMillan (2005) go so far as to argue that progress toward racial economic equality will actually produce higher levels of residential segregation. These authors contend that high-income black households would prefer to locate in neighborhoods that are both affluent and predominantly black. When residing in a metropolitan area without such neighborhoods, these households choose to live in predominantly white affluent neighborhoods. Bayer, Fang, and McMillan conjecture that an increase in the number of affluent black households will lead to the establishment of more affluent black neighborhoods, and the relocation of existing affluent black households to those neighborhoods.

10. For a further discussion of gentrification, see Vigdor (2002a).

11. For a discussion of trends in wage and earning disparities over time, see Chandra (2003).

12. For more information on the black-white test score gap and recent trends therein, see Magnuson and Waldfogel (forthcoming).

13. For a further discussion of potential mechanisms linking neighborhood to individual outcomes, see Ellen and Turner (1997).

14. For a prominent example of the use of propensity score matching in the context of neighborhood effects, see Harding (2003).

15. An additional literature, not directly reviewed in this chapter, has analyzed the role of school segregation in the perpetuation of black-white inequality in educational outcomes. For a review of the relationship between school segregation and educational outcomes, see Vigdor and Ludwig (2007).

16. For a thorough description of the MTO program, see Orr, Feins, and Popkin (2003).

References

Ananat, Elizabeth O. 2007. The Wrong Side(s) of the Tracks: Estimating the Causal Effects of Racial Segregation on City Outcomes. NBER working paper no. 13343. Cambridge, MA: National Bureau of Economic Research.

Bayer, Patrick, Hanming Fang, and Robert McMillan. 2005. Separate When

Equal? Racial Inequality and Residential Segregation. NBER working paper no. 11507. Cambridge, MA: National Bureau of Economic Research.

Bayer, Patrick, Fernando Ferreira, and Robert McMillan. 2007. A Unified Framework for Measuring Preferences for Schools and Neighborhoods. *Journal of Political Economy* 115:588-638.

Bayer, Patrick, Stephen Ross, and Giorgio Topa. 2005. Place of Work and Place of Residence: Informal Hiring Networks and Labor Market Outcomes. NBER working paper no. 11019. Cambridge, MA: National Bureau of Economic Research.

Bound, John, and Richard B. Freeman. 1992. What Went Wrong? The Erosion of Relative Earnings and Employment among Young Black Men in the 1980s. *Quarterly Journal of Economics* 107:201–32.

Card, David E., Alexandre Mas, and Jesse Rothstein. 2008. Tipping and the Dynamics of Segregation. *Quarterly Journal of Economics* 123:177-218.

Chandra, Amitabh. 2003. Is the Convergence of the Racial Wage Gap Illusory? NBER working paper no. 9476. Cambridge, MA: National Bureau of Economic Research.

Clampet-Lundquist, Susan, Kathryn Edin, Jeffrey R. Kling, and Greg J. Duncan. 2006. Moving At-Risk Teenagers Out of High-Risk Neighborhoods: Why Girls Fare Better Than Boys. Princeton University, Department of Economics, working paper no. 509.

Clotfelter, Charles T. 2004. *After Brown: The Rise and Retreat of School Desegregation*. Princeton, NJ: Princeton University Press.

Collins, William J., and Robert A. Margo. 2000. Residential Segregation and Socioeconomic Outcomes: When Did Ghettos Go Bad? *Economics Letters* 69:239–43.

———. 2001. Race and Home Ownership: A Century-Long View. *Explorations in Economic History* 38, no. 1 (January): 68–92.

Cutler, David M., and Edward L. Glaeser. 1997. Are Ghettos Good or Bad? *Quarterly Journal of Economics* 112:827–72.

Cutler, David M., Edward L. Glaeser, and Jacob L. Vigdor. 1999. The Rise and Decline of the American Ghetto. *Journal of Political Economy* 107:455–506.

———. 2008. When Are Ghettos Bad? Lessons from Immigrant Segregation in the United States. *Journal of Urban Economics* 63:759–74.

Echenique, Federico, and Roland G. Fryer Jr. 2007. A Measure of Segregation Based on Social Interactions. *Quarterly Journal of Economics* 122:441–85.

Ellen, Ingrid Gould, and Margery Austin Turner. 1997. Does Neighborhood Matter? Assessing Recent Evidence. *Housing Policy Debate* 8:833–66.

Gephart, Martha A. 1997. Neighborhoods and Communities as Contexts for Development. In *Neighborhood Poverty, Vol. 1: Context and Consequences for Children*, ed. Jeanne Brooks-Gunn, Greg J. Duncan, and J. Lawrence Aber, 1–43. New York: Russell Sage Foundation.

Glaeser, Edward L., and Jacob L. Vigdor. 2003. Racial Segregation: Promising News. In *Redefining Urban and Suburban America: Evidence from Census 2000, Volume I*, ed. Bruce Katz and Robert E. Lang, 211–34.Washington, DC: Brookings Institution Press.

Guryan, Jonathan. 2004. Desegregation and Black Dropout Rates. *American Economic Review* 94 (4): 919–43.

Harding, David J. 2003. Counterfactual Models of Neighborhood Effects: The Effect of Neighborhood Poverty on Dropping Out and Teenage Pregnancy. *American Journal of Sociology* 109:676–719.

Inman, Robert P., and Daniel L. Rubinfeld. 1979. Judicial Pursuit of Local Fiscal Equity. *Harvard Law Review* 92:1662–1750.

Jackson, Kenneth T. 1985. *Crabgrass Frontier: The Suburbanization of the United States*. Oxford: Oxford University Press.

Jahn, Julius, Calvin F. Schmid, and Clarence Schrag. 1947. The Measurement of Ecological Segregation. *American Sociological Review* 12:293–303.

Jargowsky, Paul A. 1997. *Poverty and Place: Ghettos, Barrios, and the American City*. New York: Russell Sage Foundation.

———. 2003. Stunning Progress, Hidden Problems: The Dramatic Decline of Concentrated Poverty in the 1990s. Brookings Institution Center on Urban and Metropolitan Policy, Living Cities Census Series.

Jencks, Christopher, and Susan Mayer. 1990. The Social Consequences of Growing Up in a Poor Neighborhood. In *Inner-City Poverty in the United States*, ed. Laurence E. Lynn Jr. and Michael G. H. McGreary, 111–86. Washington, DC: National Academy Press.

Kain, John F. 1968. Housing Segregation, Negro Employment, and Metropolitan Decentralization. *Quarterly Journal of Economics* 82:175–97.

Kling, Jeffrey R., and Jeffrey B. Liebman. 2004. Experimental Analysis of Neighborhood Effects on Youth. Princeton University, Department of Economics, working paper 483.

Kling, Jeffrey R., Jeffrey B. Liebman, and Lawrence F. Katz. 2005. Experimental Analysis of Neighborhood Effects. *Econometrica* 75:82–119.

Kling, Jeffrey R., Jeffrey B. Liebman, Lawrence F. Katz, and Lisa Sanbonmatsu. 2004. Moving to Opportunity and Tranquility: Neighborhood Effects on Adult Economic Self-Sufficiency and Health from a Randomized Housing Voucher Experiment. Princeton University, Department of Economics, working paper 481.

Lutz, Byron F. 2005. Post *Brown vs. the Board of Education*: The Effects of the End of Court-Ordered Desegregation. Federal Reserve Board, Finance and Economics Discussion Series working paper no. 2005–64.

Magnuson, Katherine A., and Jane Waldfogel, eds. Forthcoming. *Steady Gains and Stalled Progress: Inequality and the Black-White Test Score Gap*. New York: Russell Sage Foundation.

Massey, Douglas S., and Nancy A. Denton. 1988. The Dimensions of Segregation. *Social Forces* 67:281–315.

Oreopoulos, Philip. 2003. The Long-Run Consequences of Living in a Poor Neighborhood. *Quarterly Journal of Economics* 118:1533–75.

Orr, Larry L., Judie D. Feins, and Susan Popkin. 2003. *Moving to Opportunity for Fair Housing Demonstration Interim Impacts Evaluation*. Washington, DC: U.S. Department of Housing and Urban Development.

Schelling, Thomas. 1978. *Micromotives and Macrobehavior*. New York: W. W. Norton.

Sethi, Rajiv, and Rohini Somanathan. 2004. Inequality and Segregation. *Journal of Political Economy* 112:1296–1321.

Vigdor, Jacob L. 2002a. Does Gentrification Harm the Poor? *Brookings-Wharton Papers on Urban Affairs*, 133–73.

———. 2002b. Locations, Outcomes, and Selective Migration. *Review of Economics and Statistics* 84, no. 4 (November): 751–55.

———. 2004. Residential Segregation and Preference Misalignment. *Journal of Urban Economics* 54:587–609.

———. 2006. Peer Effects in Neighborhoods and Housing. In *Deviant Peer Influences in Programs for Youth: Problems and Solutions*, ed. Kenneth A. Dodge, Thomas J. Dishion, and Jennifer E. Lansford, 185–202. New York: Guilford Press.

———. 2007. The Katrina Effect: Was There a Bright Side to the Evacuation of Greater New Orleans? *Berkeley Electronic Journal in Economic Analysis and Policy (Advances)* 7, article 64.

Vigdor, Jacob L., and Jens Ludwig. 2007. Segregation and the Black-White Test Score Gap. Forthcoming in Magnuson, Katherine A., and Jane Waldfogel, eds. *Steady Gains and Stalled Progress: Inequality and the Black-White Test Score Gap*. New York: Russell Sage Foundation.

Wilson, James Q., ed. 1968. *The Metropolitan Enigma: Inquiries into the Nature and Dimensions of America's Urban Crisis*. Cambridge, MA: Harvard University Press.

8

Poverty

POVERTY AMONG INNER-CITY CHILDREN

JANET CURRIE

THE CONCENTRATION of poverty in decaying inner-city neighborhoods has proven to be among the most intractable of social problems. In fact, poverty has increasingly become an urban problem: in 1979, rural poverty exceeded urban poverty, but by 1999, the situation had been reversed. In 2003, 17.5 percent of central-city urban residents were poor compared to 9.1 percent in other urban areas, and 14.2 percent outside metro areas (Weinberg 2005).

The negative effects of poverty on children can be especially pernicious, blighting lives before they really start. Jeanne Brooks-Gunn and Greg Duncan (1997) document that children who grow up in poverty suffer worse outcomes than other children. This is especially true of those who live in extreme poverty or who live below the poverty line for many years (and about 15 percent of children who ever become poor will live in poverty for at least ten years). My research with Wanchuan Lin (2007) shows that low-income children are more likely than other children to suffer from virtually every type of health insult, and perhaps as a result, are in worse overall health. Poor children are more likely than other children to suffer mental health problems, including learning disabilities and developmental delays, in addition to their physical health problems. These problems in turn may be linked to higher rates of school failure, teen parenthood, and risky behaviors among poor children.

Poverty may affect child outcomes through any number of pathways, including reduced access to medical care, poor nutrition, poor home environments (including exposure to violence and crime), and negative parenting behaviors. For example, poor children are more likely to be subject to maltreatment than other children (Currie and Tekin 2006). The theme of this chapter is that cash-benefit programs are unlikely to ever do enough to remediate the effects of child poverty. Instead, we need programs targeted to the specific problems facing poor children. City governments have a huge role to play in administering these programs, even though higher levels of government largely fund (and should continue to do so) such programs. City governments are close to neighborhoods and community needs, and thus perhaps in the best position to actually administer the services. City governments can also be leading advocates for federal- and state-level funding for programs that work. This chapter discusses what we have learned about programs that work to reduce the effects of poverty among inner-city children.

Changes in Poverty and Its Meaning

The earliest official measurement of U.S. poverty is from 1959. From 1959 to 1973, the rate of poverty fell dramatically from 22.4 to 11.1 percent. Since that time, it has fluctuated between 11 and 15 percent, and was roughly the same in 1970 as it was in 2000 (Weinberg 2005). The failure to make further progress in reducing poverty over the past thirty years has led many to argue that the War on Poverty has failed—for example, on January 22, 1988, Ronald Reagan famously quipped in his State of the Union address, "The government declared war on poverty, and poverty won."

Yet this assessment ignores the real progress that has been made. Many new "great society" programs such as Medicaid, Food Stamps, school nutrition programs, and Head Start were introduced in the 1960s, while others such as public housing were greatly expanded. These programs had a substantial impact on the nature of poverty in the United States that is not reflected in official statistics. Indeed, since official statistics do not include "in-kind" transfers or tax credits (which have become an increasingly important way of supporting low-income families), such programs cannot have an impact on official measures of poverty no matter how good they are for families.

Improvements in medical care for poor children, for instance, have dramatically decreased infant mortality rates. In 1960, over twenty-five children out of every one thousand born died before their first birthday. By 2004, this rate had dropped to fewer than seven per thousand. Douglas Almond, Kenneth Chay, and Michael Greenstone (2004) show that in the 1960s, much of this improvement was driven by improved access to hospitals for southern African Americans. And this increase in access occurred because hospitals that wanted reimbursements from the new federal Medicare and Medicaid programs were forced to end segregationist policies. In the late 1980s and early 1990s, expansions of the federal Medicaid program led to additional declines in infant mortality (Currie and Gruber 1996b).

More generally, I show, with my colleague V. Joseph Hotz (2004), that deaths among children from birth to age nineteen fell more than a third between 1980 and 1998, from about 120 per 100,000 to just over 70 per 100,000. Child deaths due to medical causes, auto accidents, and other accidents all fell dramatically over this period. Since child deaths have always been concentrated among the poor, this represents a real improvement in the lives of poor children.

There are now few cases of outright starvation among poor children. Indeed, obesity is now more of a threat. This was not always the case. In 1968, a group of physicians issued *Hunger in America*, a landmark report documenting appalling levels of malnutrition among poor children. They wrote that "wherever we went and wherever we looked, whether it was the rural south, Appalachia, or an urban ghetto, we saw children in significant numbers who were hungry and sick, children for whom hunger was a daily fact of life and sickness in many forms, an inevitability." Their report to the U.S. Congress (1968) exposed shocking levels of nutritional deficiencies in areas of the United States that were comparable to those in developing countries.

The food safety net put in place has resulted in the virtual disappearance of frank starvation and childhood diseases caused by insufficient nutrient intakes, and has caused us to redefine hunger. Rather than looking for children with skeletal deformities as a result of chronic malnutrition (such as rickets), we now look for households in which members miss meals or worry about having enough food to eat. Official statistics on hunger now reflect this later concept (also called food insecurity).

As a third example, the Housing Act of 1949 called for the "elimination of substandard and other inadequate housing." Inadequate housing is still a concern for many people. Among extremely low-income renter households with children (defined as households with incomes less than 30 percent of the area median income), 16 percent have housing with "severe or moderate physical problems." That is, their homes may be lacking complete plumbing, have unvented room heaters as primary heating equipment, or have multiple upkeep problems such as water leaks, open cracks, or rats. But even among these households, over 80 percent are now in housing that is physically adequate (U.S. Department of Housing and Urban Development 1998).

Advocates for the poor often seem reluctant to acknowledge the progress that has been made, perhaps for fear of encouraging complacency. Yet failure to acknowledge the gains that have been made results in the common view that urban poverty is a completely intractable problem. Still, while we have come a long way, there is also a long way to go. For example, the one cause of death that has shown little downward trend among children is deaths due to intentional injuries. While the number of violent child deaths has stayed relatively constant over time, the fraction of all deaths accounted for by violence has grown, which may account for the public perception that there is increasing violence against children.

Programs to Address Child Poverty and Its Effects

The most obvious approach to alleviating child poverty is to give poor households with children money. This is in fact what most other Western countries do and what was done in the United States under the Aid to Families with Dependent Children (AFDC) program. The shortcomings of AFDC have been extensively documented. On the one hand, the benefits were set by the states, and most states did not provide enough money to raise families above the poverty line. On the other hand, AFDC created many perverse incentives: given that a mother's benefits were reduced with every dollar that she earned, and that she was likely to be cut off altogether if she married, the program discouraged mothers from working and marrying. In 1996, these shortcomings led to the demise and replacement of the program with the Temporary Assistance for Needy Families (TANF) program, which emphasizes work incentives and has resulted in a sharp decline in the welfare rolls.

From 1996 to 2002, the welfare caseload declined from 12,645,000 to 5,146,000 recipients. The fraction of all U.S. children on TANF plummeted from 12.5 to 5.3 percent in only six years. Studies find that between 30 and 60 percent of the decline in welfare participation was due to welfare reform (see Grogger, Karoly, and Klerman 2002). The caseload decline was accompanied by a dramatic increase in employment among single mothers. The employment rate for single mothers with children under age six went from 52.5 percent in 1995 to 67.5 percent in 2001. At the same time, poverty rates for female-headed households fell, from 36.5 to 28.6 percent. For black and Hispanic families, the declines were even steeper: from 48.2 to 37.4 percent and from 52.8 to 37.8 percent, respectively (Smolensky and Appleton 2003).

Children who are or have been on welfare often remain worse off than other children. This does not necessarily mean, however, that welfare has failed them. Without welfare, their situation might have been even worse. Phillip Levine and David Zimmerman (2000) showed that children who spent time on AFDC scored lower than other children on a range of tests, but that this difference disappeared when the test scores of their mothers were controlled for, suggesting that welfare had little effect either positive or negative. Similarly, Zimmerman and Levine (1996) argue that children of welfare mothers were more likely to grow up to be welfare mothers, mainly because of other characteristics of the household they grew up in.

Given that research has shown little evidence of positive effects of cash welfare on children, it is not surprising that the literature evaluating welfare reform has produced similarly null findings. The National Research Council (Smolensky and Appleton 2003) concluded that "no strong trends have emerged, either negative or positive, in indicators of parent well-being or child development across the years just preceding and following the implementation of [welfare reform]."

Conditional tax credits represent an alternative approach to providing income to poor families. The early years of the Clinton administration saw a huge expansion of the Earned Income Tax Credit (EITC). The number of recipients grew from 12.5 million families in 1990 to 19.8 million in 2003, and the maximum credit grew from $953 to $4,204. The rapid expansion of this formerly obscure program run through the tax system has resulted in cash transfers to low-income families that are larger than those that were available under welfare. Craig Gunderson and James Ziliak (2004) estimate that the EITC accounted for half of the reduction in after-tax poverty that occurred over the 1990s (the other half being mainly accounted for by strong economic growth).

The EITC is a tax credit available to poor working families. Its essential feature is that it is "refundable"—in other words, a family whose credit exceeds its taxes receives the difference in cash. The size of this refundable part of the credit relative to other transfers is shown in table 8.1. The EITC is like welfare in that it gives cash payments to poor families. But EITC recipients need to work and file tax returns in order to be eligible. The size of the payment increases with earnings up to a maximum level before being phased out, so that it creates an incentive to work among the poorest households (though it also creates work disincentives for households in the phase-out range).

The credit is set at a level high enough that a family with one earner working full time is raised above the poverty line. In 2003, 19.8 million families received an average credit of around $1,784. Eighty-nine percent of this money went to tax payers with incomes less than $30,000. The EITC raises many families above the poverty line, as it was intended to do. The EITC has resulted in dramatic increases in the employment of single mothers (Eissa and Liebman 1996; Meyer and Rosenbaum 2001). Jeffrey Grogger (2003) demonstrates that the expansion of the EITC raised the incomes of many women enough to make them ineligible for welfare.

There are, however, several downsides to the EITC. Because it is part of the tax code, the EITC is complicated, and many poor families do not fully understand the provisions that apply to them (Romich and Weisner 2000). These families often end up paying some of the credit to commercial tax preparers. Wojciech Kopczuk and Cristian Pop-Eleches (2007) show that participation in the EITC rose dramatically with the introduction of electronic filing, because it gave commercial tax preparers an incentive to aggressively court this market. On the positive side, perhaps because help from paid preparers is available, the take up of the EITC by eligible families has been high, especially relative to that of other antipoverty programs (Scholz 1994).

Lawrence Berger, Christina Paxson, and Jane Waldfogel (2007) explore the relationship between family income, home environments, and child mental health outcomes (and cognitive test scores) at age three in the "Fragile Families and Child Well-being Study." This study is following a cohort of five thousand children born in several large U.S. cities between 1998 and 2000, and oversamples births to unmarried couples. Presumably we think income matters because it affects something about the home environment. Berger, Paxon, and Waldfogel show that all of the measures they examine (which include measures of parenting skills as well as physical aspects of the home) are highly related to income. Moreover, controlling for these measures reduces the effects of income on outcomes considerably.[1] The effects of income are small enough though that they imply that even cash subsidies that brought every family up to the poverty line would not eliminate gaps in child outcomes. If we want to help disadvantaged children realize their potential, it will be necessary to have other strategies.

Gordon Dahl and Lance Lochner (2005) provide the most recent and compelling evidence that cash may matter; they use expansions of the EITC as instruments for household income and find that each $1,000 of income improves childrens' test scores by 2 to 4 percent of a standard deviation. An attractive feature of the changes in the EITC is that households may well have regarded them as permanent, so this experiment may approximate the effects of changes in permanent rather than transitory income. Their result implies, though, that it would take on the order of a $10,000 transfer to having an educationally meaningful effect on test scores, so that the result is not inconsistent with that of Berger, Paxson, and Waldfogel.

In-Kind Programs

By 2002, only $31.5 billion, or 15.9 percent of the approximately $198 billion that was spent on assistance for families with children, was spent on cash welfare payments (TANF payments plus Old Age, Survivors,

TABLE 8.1
Expenditures and Caseloads for Safety Net Programs, 1980 and 2002

	1980			2002	
	Expenditure (1980 billions)	Expenditure (2002 billions)	Caseload (millions)	Expenditure (billions)	Caseload (millions)
Cash					
TANF payments	**12.0**	**26.2**	10.6	**11.1**	5.1
Other TANF services	NA	NA		**13.4**	
Earned Income Tax Credit	**2.0**	**4.4**	7.0	**35.8**	19.8
Old age and disability benefits	120.5	263.1	30.9	453.8	46.5
OASDI for children	**10.3**	**22.5**	3.3	**20.4**	3.9
Health Care					
Total Medicare	35.0	76.4	28.5	256.8	40.0
Total Medicaid	23.3	50.9	21.6	213.5	49.8
Medicaid (dependent children and their adults)	**6.4**	**14.0**	14.2	**54.7**	37.8
SCHIP				**3.0**	5.4
Nutrition					
Total Food Stamps	9.2	20.1	21.1	21.7	20.2
Food Stamps—families with children	**5.5**	**12.1**	12.7	**11.7**	10.9
School lunch and breakfast	**3.3**	**7.2**	14.9	**8.4**	22.7
WIC	**0.7**	**1.5**	1.9	**4.4**	7.5

Housing

Low-rent public housing	2.2	4.8	NA	8.9	NA
Section 8 and other assisted rental housing	3.1	6.8	NA	20.0	NA
Homeless programs				1.4	NA
Housing block grants				1.8	NA
USDA rural programs	NA	NA		9.3	NA
Total Assuming half of spending is for children	**2.7**	**5.8**		**20.7**	

Child Care

Child care and development block grant	NA	NA	NA	7.9	1.8
Head Start	**0.7**	**1.5**	0.4	**6.5**	0.9
Total spent on children (bolded entries only)	43.6	93.7		198.0	
Cash welfare as percent of total	52.0	52.0		15.9	

Notes: OASDI for children figures are for 1985. Medicare enrollment figures are for 2001. Number of Food Stamp recipients under families with children is estimate based on table 15–10 that 60% of 1980 recipients had children and 54% of 2002 recipients had children. Figures for school nutrition programs include only free and reduced-price meals. The school lunch and breakfast figures may double count the number of children (also note that the Green Book's lunch table is wrong, replicating breakfast table). Caseload for CCDBG includes individuals affected by state-only programs. Public postsecondary figures are for 2001. EITC caseloads and housing caseloads are number of families, and all others are number of individuals.

Sources:

Green Book

2004: Tables 1–9, 1–11, 2–1, 2–2, 3–1, 3–11, 4–1, 7–6, 9–16, 9–26, 13–14, 15–11, 15–21, 15–22, 15–24, 15–25, 15–26, 15–27, 15–28, 15–31, 15–33, K–10, and chart 7–3.

1996: Table 16–34.

1986: Tables 7–1 and 8–15.

Statistical Abstract of the United States

2006: Tables 232, 243, 265, and 277.

1998: Table 310.

Annual Statistical Supplement

2005: Table 8.E2.

and Disability Insurance), while only twenty years earlier the comparable figure had been 52 percent. Table 8.1 shows how federal in-kind aid grew over time, program by program.

Ziliak (2004) looks at the fraction of the "poverty gap" that is filled by safety net programs. The poverty gap is defined as the difference between the poverty line and the average income of poor families. He finds that on average, antipoverty programs filled a little more than 55 percent of the gap in 2001. This fraction is little changed since 1991, suggesting that transfers from other programs have filled in the declines in cash welfare.

These figures show the importance of programs other than traditional cash welfare in supporting low-income families. A brief description of each of the major in-kind programs shown in table 8.1 follows.[2]

Medicaid

Medicaid is the main public health insurance program that covers poor women and children, along with those who are disabled and some elderly. Slightly less than half of Medicaid recipients are children, while another fifth are low-income women. Yet although they account for three-quarters of the recipients, women and children account for only about a quarter of Medicaid expenditures. The lion's share of the spending is on the elderly and disabled. For example, in 2000 the government spent $1,237 per child on Medicaid compared to $11,928 per elderly adult. By 2003 the cost of Medicaid had grown to $280 billion, which means that even the fraction of those dollars devoted to women and children (about $44.6 billion) dwarfed the approximately $16 billion per year spent on traditional cash welfare under the TANF program. We can also compare spending for mothers and children to the huge expenditures made under the Medicare program. Medicare, the main public health insurance program for people over sixty five, cost $239 billion in 2003 (U.S. Committee on Ways and Means 2005).

Medicaid costs are shared by states and the federal government. To receive their federal "match," states are required to run the programs within certain guidelines, which used to require that families be on welfare. Beginning in the mid-1980s, the federal government progressively increased the income cutoffs for the program, first giving states the option to cover additional groups and then requiring it. By 2001 all poor children were eligible for Medicaid, a remarkable legislative accomplishment. In addition, the State Child Health Insurance Program funded in 1997 had extended eligibility to an additional 1.2 million children by April 1998 (Associated Press 1998).

Legislators also targeted pregnant women. By April 1990, new guidelines required that all states wishing to participate in the Medicaid program cover pregnant women (and children under six) with incomes up
to 133 percent of the poverty line. States also had the option of receiving matching funds to cover women with incomes up to 185 percent of
the poverty line.

Through this combination of carrots and sticks, states were all gradually brought up to the same, more generous standard. But given that
they started at different levels and took up the expansion options at different rates, income thresholds for Medicaid eligibility varied wildly
across states in the intervening years. For example, in Texas, only 3 percent of pregnant women would have been eligible for Medicaid coverage
in 1979, while half were eligible by 1992. In contrast, in more generous
states like New York, a quarter of women were eligible in 1979, while
again, half were eligible by 1992.

With my colleague Jonathan Gruber (1996a, 1996b), I construct an
index of Medicaid generosity that depends only on state rules and use
it as an instrument for Medicaid eligibility. We show that the 30 percent
increase in the eligibility of pregnant women that took place during the
1980s and early 1990s was associated with an 8.5 percent decline in the
infant mortality rate. The roughly 15 percent increase in Medicaid eligibility for children that occurred over the same period reduced the probability that a child went without any doctor visits during the year by 9.6
percent. Roughly 20 percent of children receive no doctor visits at all in
a given year, although it is recommended that children receive at least
an annual checkup. Our results suggest that this number would have
been closer to 30 percent in the absence of the Medicaid expansions, so
that as many as six million children gained a doctor's visit. We also
found a significant increase in the fraction of those visits that took place
in doctors' offices. Similarly, Anna Aizer (2003) and Leemore Dafny and
Gruber (2000) find that increases in eligibility for Medicaid and Medicaid enrollments reduced preventable hospitalizations, indicating that
children gained access to necessary preventive care.

These studies demonstrate that extending Medicaid has had important positive effects on child health. Medicaid also has a major impact
on poor children who are not covered, by sustaining providers who
offer indigent care and allowing providers to bill Medicaid for the care
of children who are eligible but uncovered at the time of service.

Nevertheless, many problems remain. Twenty percent of U.S. pedia-
tricians refuse to see Medicaid patients at all, and 40 percent limit the
number of Medicaid patients in their practices, largely because Medicaid pays less than private insurance companies (Yudkowsky, Cartland,
and Flint 1990). Children on Medicaid are more likely than uninsured

children to have a usual source of care and receive routine care on an appropriate time frame, but they are less likely than privately insured children to be seen in doctors' offices rather than clinics or emergency rooms. Children on Medicaid are less likely to see specialists than other children—54 percent see a general practitioner compared to 34 percent of non-Medicaid children, and may have visits that are up to 40 percent shorter (relative to the average visit time of thirteen minutes) than non-Medicaid children (St. Peter, Newacheck, and Halfon 1992; Decker 1992). An additional problem is that it is often difficult for parents to maintain continuous coverage for their children, given the need to reapply at frequent intervals combined with fluctuations in family income. And although the rates of private health insurance coverage have been declining for most nonelderly groups, Medicaid expansions may have hastened the decline among families with children (Cutler and Gruber 1996; Gruber and Simon 2007).

Medicaid's largest problem, however, is rising costs. Thomas Macurdy et al. (2005) show, for example, that in California, costs are likely to rise from $30 billion in 2003 to $80 billion in 2015. But these costs are extremely unevenly distributed: 60 percent of the Medicaid expenditures are on 5 percent of the population, and these people are overwhelmingly elderly and disabled. Seventy-five percent of the Medicaid population, including most child enrollees, incurs less than 6 percent of the costs. These facts about Medicaid show that cutting children from the rolls, as many states have done in response to budget crises, is likely to have little impact on Medicaid costs.

Food and Nutrition Programs

One in five Americans uses a federal food program every day (Currie 2003). The creation of the food safety net began in earnest in 1946 with the creation of the National School Lunch Program. The *Hunger in America* report was followed by an expansion of the food safety net. The Food Stamp Program (FSP), which had begun as a small pilot in 1961, was greatly expanded over the next sixteen years. By 1974, states were required to extend the program statewide rather than offering it only in selected counties. The Special Supplemental Nutrition Program for Women, Infants, and Children (WIC) was established in 1972 to provide nutritious food to pregnant women, infants, and preschool children. The National School Lunch Program was expanded, as was the School Breakfast Program, which had begun in 1966 as another pilot program. Ten years after their initial report rocked the nation, the authors of *Hunger in America* went back to inner-city areas and found that while poverty was still there, widespread malnutrition was gone (U.S. Congress 1979).

Now, we are bombarded with stories about an epidemic of obesity in the United States. The 2001 Surgeon General's report (U.S. Department of Health and Human Services 2001) reveals that obesity has been rising more quickly among children than among adults, and that poor children are at greater risk than others. In the future, more children are projected to die from complications of obesity than from smoking. Jayanta Bhattacharya, myself, and Steven Haider (2004) show that in a national sample, poor, food-insecure teens are almost twice as likely to be obese as teens who are neither poor nor food insecure (18.1 percent compared to 10.8 percent). One study of homeless people in a New York City shelter found that 39 percent were obese (Luder et al. 1990). The relationship between poverty, food insecurity, and obesity means that it is more important than ever to ensure that safety net programs deliver nutritious foods rather than simply adding calories to the diet.

The FSP is by far the largest federal food program with 19.1 million recipients in 2002 and expenditures of $24.1 billion. The program is also the most similar to a cash welfare program because there are few restrictions on the types of food that can be purchased, and because the amount that most households receive in FSP benefits is less than the amount of their food budgets. This means that the bulk of the FSP benefits are likely to be used to buy food that the household would have purchased in any case, and that the money saved by using the Food Stamps can then be spent on other things (such as housing).

Several Food Stamp "cash out" demonstrations have asked whether people actually treat Food Stamps the same as cash. In these experiments, households were issued checks instead of Food Stamps. Diane Whitmore (2002) reexamined data from an experiment in San Diego, and found that the majority of households received Food Stamps worth less than their food budgets and treated them like cash. Only households that initially received more in Food Stamps than they wanted to spend on food increased their food consumption, and much of this increase was spent on items such as soda with little nutritional value.

It is clear that the FSP has not eliminated nutritional problems. The National FSP Survey of 1996 found that 50 percent of FSP participants experienced food insecurity and substantial numbers of FSP recipients fell short of the recommended daily allowances for essential nutrients— 31 percent of FSP households were short of iron, while 21 percent were short of folate (Cohen et al. 1999). At the same time, FSP participants are more likely to be obese (Bhattacharya and Currie 2000). The problem may be that, as discussed above, FSP participants are free to use their benefits to buy foods of little nutritional value.

Still, Bhattacharya and I (2000) find that controlling for characteristics such as age of household head, education, race, and household structure, teenage FSP participants are less likely to be food insecure. Similarly, P. Peter Basiotis, Carol S. Kramer-LeBlanc, and Eileen T. Kennedy (1998) and other colleagues have found that the incidence of food insecurity decreases with the size of the FSP benefit that a household is eligible to receive. These findings suggest that the FSP may not improve the quality of the diet but does perhaps smooth consumption.

Finally, it is important to note that the FSP is the closest thing that the United States has to a universal safety net program because anyone who meets the income requirements is eligible. Most other programs have some sort of "categorical" restriction—that is, rules such that only certain categories of people are eligible. Even programs such as unemployment insurance serve only a minority of the unemployed because of requirements that people work a certain amount before they can qualify. Thus, the FSP has a significance beyond any direct impact on nutrition as a program that serves families that somehow "fall through the cracks" of other programs.

The WIC Program

If the FSP is similar to cash, then the WIC program is at the opposite end of the spectrum. WIC offers coupons that can be redeemed only for specific types of food by eligible women and children who are certified to be at nutritional risk. These foods are chosen to meet the nutritional needs of the caseload of pregnant and nursing women, infants, and children under five, and are good sources of protein, iron, calcium, and vitamins A and C. The monthly value of WIC benefits is small compared to Food Stamps; in 2005, the average was about $37 per month. WIC agencies are also required to help participants obtain preventive health care either by providing services on-site or through referrals. WIC is widely available both because the income cutoffs are higher than for Food Stamps (at 185 percent of the poverty line) and also because Medicaid recipients are automatically eligible for WIC, and many states have raised Medicaid cutoffs for pregnant women, infants, and children above the WIC cutoff. Marianne Bitler along with me and our colleague John Karl Scholz (2003) find that in any given month of 1998, 58 percent of infants and children under five were eligible for WIC.

WIC is the most studied federal food program, and the evidence shows that "WIC Works." In 1992, the U.S. General Accounting Office (1992) reviewed seventeen studies of the effects of prenatal WIC participation on newborns. All seventeen found that WIC participation reduced the incidence of low birth weight (birth weight less than twenty-five hundred grams) by between 10 and 43 percent, and that it reduced the incidence of very low birth weight (birth weight less than fifteen hundred grams) between 21 and 53 percent. According to the General Accounting Office, providing WIC services to mothers of babies born in 1990 saved federal taxpayers more than $337 million in medical costs so that $1 invested in WIC saves at least $3.50 in other costs. Since the General Accounting Office evaluation, many other studies have reported similar positive findings (compare Ahluwalia et al. 1992; Brown, Watkins, and Hiett 1996; Gordon and Nelson 1995; Devaney 1992).

Concerns have been raised, however, that positive results are driven by the way that mothers are selected into the program. If mothers who signed up for WIC had better characteristics than those who did not, then perhaps they would have had healthier babies in any case. Direct investigation of how WIC mothers differ from other eligible mothers should allay these concerns. Bitler and I (2004) examine detailed information about women whose deliveries were paid for by Medicaid, and find that those on WIC were worse off in every observable dimension than those who were not. Nancy Burstein and her colleagues (2000) found that WIC mothers scored lower on a test of coping skills than other low-income mothers. If anything, then, selection would cause WIC mothers to have less healthy babies on average than other mothers, which makes the finding of positive WIC effects all the more remarkable. One especially notable study by Duncan and Lori Kowaleski-Jones (2002) compares siblings in pairs in which one participated in WIC prenatally and one did not, and finds that participation in WIC increases birth weight by seven ounces. Comparing siblings offers a powerful way to control for common aspects of family background.

While the provision of WIC to pregnant women is a great success story, the effects of WIC on infants and children are less well studied. One downside to WIC is that it discourages breast-feeding by subsudizing formula. Although WIC centers are required to teach pregnant women that "breast is best," the net effect of WIC on breast-feeding has been negative.

A simple solution to this problem would be to make it more difficult for women to receive formula. But such a policy could backfire because if women are not going to nurse their babies, then WIC ensures that the babies get proper formula and infant cereal. Instead of making it difficult for women to get formula, WIC agencies have intensified their efforts to encourage breast-feeding by increasing the value of packages given to nursing mothers (among other measures). Pinka Chatterji and

Brooks-Gunn (2004) suggest that these efforts may be paying off, since they do not find any negative effect of WIC on breast-feeding in recent years.

WIC increases the consumption of the target nutrients that are included in the foods WIC participants are allowed to purchase (Rose, Habicht, and Devaney 1998), and WIC has been credited with a dramatic decline in the incidence of anemia among young children from 7.8 to 2.9 percent in the ten years following the introduction of the program (Yip et al. 1987). Some studies indicate that these improvements in nutrition affect children's behavior and ability to learn. Children on WIC prenatally have been found to have higher scores on the Peabody Picture Vocabulary Test, which is a good predictor of future scholastic achievement (Kowaleski-Jones and Duncan 2000).

School Nutrition Programs

School nutrition programs fall between WIC and the FSP in terms of expenditures, the extent to which they target particular groups, and the emphasis on supplying only nutritious foods. School nutrition programs provide free or reduced price meals to low-income children in schools. Like the FSP, both the National School Lunch Program and the School Breakfast Program are entitlement programs, which means that every eligible person must be served. Almost all public schools participate in the lunch program, and about four out of five schools that offer lunch also offer a school breakfast. Every day, 6.7 million children receive a free or reduced price school breakfast, while 16 million receive a free or reduced price school lunch.

School meals programs work by reimbursing schools a small amount for the meals that are served. Children with incomes less than 130 percent of poverty (the same cutoff as the FSP) are eligible to receive free meals, and the school gets reimbursed $2.19 for each lunch and $1.17 for each breakfast; children with incomes between 130 and 185 percent of poverty (the cutoffs for the FSP and WIC) can be charged no more than $.40 for lunch and $.30 for breakfast. Schools get reimbursed $1.79 for each reduced price lunch and $.87 for each reduced price breakfast. Schools can be reimbursed a small amount ($.22 per meal) for serving students with incomes higher than these cutoffs.

Unlike the FSP, which can be used to purchase even junk food, in principle, school meals must follow government-approved meal plans. Since 1995, meals have been required to follow the *Dietary Guidelines for Americans*. Critics from the Left and the Right have roundly condemned school meals for failing to live up to this standard. The government's own studies paint a rosier picture. School meals provide the vitamins and minerals that children need for a healthy diet, and while many schools fail to meet the targets for fat and saturated fat, they are much closer now than they were before the new standards were implemented. Many U.S. children at all income levels have diets that fall far short of the *Dietary Guidelines for Americans,* so that the food in school meals may be significantly better than the food children would eat otherwise.

Barbara Devaney, Anne R. Gordon, and John A. Burghardt (1993) examine data from 1991 to 1992, before the new dietary guidelines went into effect, and find that the average child who ate school lunch on the day they were surveyed ate the same number of calories as the average child who did not, and was more likely to consume many target nutrients. Bhattacharya and I (2000) compared children eligible for school lunch to those who were not, when schools were in and out of session, and found that school lunch was associated with reductions in blood cholesterol and improvements in diet quality. Sandra Hofferth and Sally Curtin (2004) use data from the 1997 *Panel Study of Income Dynamics* (collected after the new guidelines went into effect), and see no evidence that school nutrition programs contribute to being overweight when differences between families and children are accounted for.

Nevertheless, Whitmore (2005) examines data on kindergarten and first graders from 1995 to 1996, right around the time that the new meal guidelines came in, and observes that students who start out at the same weight as other students but ate lunch at school in kindergarten were about 2 percent more likely to be overweight in first grade. Part of the discrepancy between these studies may lie in the definition of school lunch. Many schools now have à la carte and vending machine items that do not comply with school nutrition program regulations.

The School Breakfast Program is less controversial. It improves children's nutrition by increasing the consumption of vitamins and minerals while reducing the percentage of calories from fat (Bhattacharya, Currie, and Haider 2006). Studies have examined the impact of school breakfast on children's academic achievement by measuring the same children before and after school breakfast became available at their schools. These studies find that school breakfast improves both attendance and test scores (Myers et al. 1989; Murphy et al. 1998).

Housing Programs

The Housing Act of 1937, which began federal housing programs, was enacted in order to "remedy the acute shortage of decent, safe, and sanitary dwellings." The Housing Act of 1949 called for the "elimination of substandard and other inadequate housing." Clearly, the primary focus of early legislation was on the quality of the individual housing units. Housing policy has been successful in greatly reducing the number of substandard units so that even among very low-income households with incomes less than 30 percent of the area median income, over 80 percent are in housing that is physically adequate. Yet over 70 percent of these households pay more than 30 percent of their income in rent and utilities, and 40 percent pay more than 50 percent of their income for these basics (U.S. Department of Housing and Urban Development 1992). Hence, in recent years the focus of policy has been on reducing this rent burden.

Public housing programs are among the costliest and least popular government interventions in urban areas. For many, the phrase public housing has become identified with crime and decay. But public housing is incredibly heterogeneous: approximately 3,300 public housing authorities own and operate 13,200 developments with a total of 1.4 million units. Large "projects" represent the most visible "face" of public housing, but they account for less than a quarter of the almost $50 billion that the federal government spends on housing programs for low-income people, and no new projects have been built for over twenty-five years.

Two other types of programs assist renters. (For overviews of project-based aid and other programs to assist renters, see Olsen 2003a; Millennial Housing Commission 2002.) The first subsidizes the construction or rehabilitation of low-income housing. The most rapidly growing federal housing program is the Low Income Housing Tax Credit (LIHTC), which offers tax credits to builders who set aside a fraction of their units to be rent restricted and occupied by low-income households. Since 1987, about 1.1 million units have been built under the LIHTC, and the annual $5 billion in funding for this program produces about 100,000 new units yearly.

The third type of assistance available to renters is a Section 8 voucher. Whether families live in projects or receive vouchers, their rent is capped at 30 percent of their income. Families with vouchers find housing on their own that meets certain conditions (the rent must be less than a specified "fair market rent" and minimum housing standards must be met). The government pays the landlord the difference between the market rent and 30 percent of the family's income.

In 2002, about 1.3 million families lived in public housing projects, almost 2 million received Section 8 vouchers, about 800,000 lived in units subsidized under mostly discontinued builder-subsidy programs, and a further million lived in housing funded under the LIHTC.

Despite the bad reputation of public housing, huge waiting lists show that the demand far outstrips the supply. In New York City, as of

March 31, 2004, there were 142,514 families on the waiting list for conventional public housing, 129,551 families on the waiting list for
vouchers, and 28,582 families on both waiting lists (New York City
Housing Authority 2004). When the waiting list for Section 8 recently
opened in February 2007 after being closed for twelve years, the housing authority received almost a half million applications within three
months. In Los Angeles, the average wait for family housing is three
years (Los Angeles County Community Development Commission
n.d.). In Boston, Chicago, and Philadelphia, families can't even get on
the waiting list for Section 8 because the lists have been closed—too
many families are already waiting (Boston Housing Authority n.d.; Chicago Housing Authority 2003; Philadelphia Housing Authority 2004).

Waiting lists and closures of waiting lists illustrate the main problem
with federal low-income housing programs: lucky families win the
waiting list lottery and receive a big subsidy; unlucky families can't
even get on a waiting list. In contrast, Medicaid and most nutrition programs are entitlement programs available to all eligible families. Despite the fact that we spend almost as much on housing programs as on
medical care for poor women and children, most poor people get no
housing assistance. Only 30 percent of poor renters are served (U.S. Department of Housing and Urban Development 1992).

More families could be served with existing resources. Estimates suggest that it costs at least 35 percent and perhaps as much as 91 percent
more to house a family through the construction or rehabilitation of
housing rather than through Section 8 vouchers. Public housing project
residents could be given vouchers that they could use either to stay in
their current locations (though some of the worst housing projects
would not even meet Section 8 standards) or move elsewhere.

Edgar Olsen (2003b) calculates that switching all project-based aid to
vouchers would allow nine hundred thousand more families to be
served. In fact, by switching to an all-voucher policy and lowering the
subsidy level, we could create an entitlement program that served all of
the poorest families at the same cost as current housing policies. Amy
Cutts and Olsen (2002) calculate that the payment standard exceeded
the minimum subsidy necessary to rent an apartment by a median of 68
percent in 2001. So payment standards could be lowered by a considerable amount and the poorest families would still be able to find units
meeting Section 8 standards. A possible problem with vouchers in tight
housing markets is that having more dollars chasing a fixed number of
units could drive up rents. Vouchers, however, may also increase the
supply of low-income housing if landlords are enticed to bring units up
to Section 8 standards in order to participate in the program.

Current public housing construction programs such as the LIHTC and HOPE VI are also more expensive than vouchers (Wallace et al. 1981; Olsen and Baron 1983; Schnare et al. 1982; U.S. General Accounting Office 2001). And many households with incomes less than 30 percent of the area median income cannot afford to live in the LIHTC-sponsored units unless they also receive vouchers (Center on Budget and Policy Priorities 2000). Moreover, new construction under the LIHTC program may crowd out the private provision of affordable housing. Michael Murray (1999) finds that while conventional public housing adds to the stock of affordable housing, subsidizing the construction of moderate-income housing has less impact on the stock.

One of the main rationales for subsidizing mixed-income housing through programs such as the LIHTC is the idea that such programs improve neighborhoods. The importance of neighborhoods may seem self-evident, but there is actually intense debate among social scientists about whether neighborhoods have an effect on children over and above the influence of their own families. William Julius Wilson (1987) argues that the increasing concentration of poor black children in neighborhoods with few positive role models has had devastating consequences. Jobs have moved away from poor neighborhoods so that "spatial mismatch" makes it difficult for the poor to find work. On the other hand, people who move into a given neighborhood differ from those in other neighborhoods before they arrive, and those who leave differ from those who stay. So even if it appears that children from bad neighborhoods do worse than other children, one cannot assume that it is the neighborhood rather than the family that matters.

The most careful studies have found surprisingly little negative effect of living in projects (or alternatively, surprisingly small positive effects of moving out of them). I and my colleague Aaron Yelowitz (2000) note that families that had a boy and a girl are more likely to live in public housing than those with two same-sex children, because they are entitled to larger apartments. Using this observation as a way to separate the effect of living in public housing from that of being in a poor family, we find that children in projects were 11 percent less likely to have repeated grades than other similar children, and that they lived in housing that was less crowded. Surprisingly, given the stereotype of large public housing projects, the children in public housing were also less likely to live in buildings with fifty or more units than other similar children.

Brian A. Jacobs (2004) studies students displaced by demolitions of the most notorious Chicago high-rise projects. Congress passed a law in 1996 that required local housing authorities to destroy units if the cost of renovating and maintaining them was greater than the cost of providing a voucher for twenty years. Jacobs contends that the order in which doomed buildings were destroyed was approximately random. For example, in January 1999, the pipes froze in some buildings in the Robert Taylor Homes, which meant that those buildings were demolished before others in the same complex. By comparing children who stayed in buildings that were scheduled to be demolished, to other children who had already been displaced by demolitions, Jacobs obtains a measure of the effect of living in high-rise public housing. Despite the fact that the high-rises in Jacob's study were among the most notorious public housing projects in the country, he sees little effect of relocation on children's educational outcomes.

The most exhaustive examination of the effects of giving vouchers to project residents is the ongoing Moving to Opportunities (MTO) experiment. MTO was inspired by the Gautreaux program in Chicago, which resulted from a consent decree designed to desegregate Chicago's public housing by relocating some black inner-city residents to white suburbs. A series of studies by James Rosenbaum (compare Rosenbaum, Rubinowitz, and Kulieke 1986; Rosenbaum 1992, 1995) found large positive effects of relocation on children and their mothers. Still, limitations such as high attrition from the study cast some doubt on these findings.

MTO is a large-scale social experiment that is being conducted in Chicago, New York, Los Angeles, Boston, and Baltimore (see Orr et al. 2003). Between 1994 and 1998, volunteers from public housing projects were assigned by lottery to one of three groups. The first group received a voucher that could only be used to rent housing in a low-poverty area (a Census tract with a poverty rate of less than 10 percent). This group also received help locating a suitable apartment. I will call this the MTO group. The second group of volunteers received a normal Section 8 voucher, which they could use to rent an apartment in any neighborhood. The third group of volunteers was the control, and received no vouchers or assistance, although they were eligible to remain in their project apartment.

Families in the first group did move to lower-poverty neighborhoods, and the new neighborhoods of the MTO group were also considerably safer. Contrary to expectations, though, the move to new neighborhoods had positive effects on girls, but had either no effect or negative effects on boys. Girls in the MTO group were more likely than the controls to graduate from high school and were much less likely to suffer from anxiety. Girls in the regular Section 8 group also experienced improvements in mental health relative to the controls. Finally, girls in the MTO and Section 8 groups were much less likely to have ever been arrested than the controls.

In contrast, boys in the experimental group were 13 percent more likely than the controls to have ever been arrested. This increase was due largely to increases in property crimes. These boys also report more risky behaviors such as drug and alcohol use. And boys in the MTO and voucher groups were more likely to suffer injuries. These differences between boys and girls are apparent even within families (Orr et al. 2003). These results indicate that moving boys from housing projects to wealthier neighborhoods is not a panacea.

It remains to be seen how the long-term outcomes of the MTO children will differ from the controls. Philip Oreopoulos (2003) uses data from Canadian income tax records to examine the earnings of adults who lived in public housing projects in Toronto as children. There are large differences between projects in Toronto, both in terms of the density of the projects and the poverty of the neighborhoods. As in the Gautraux project, the type of project a family lives in is approximately randomly assigned because the family is offered whatever happens to be available when they get to the top of the waiting list. Oreopoulos discovers that once the characteristics of the family are controlled, the neighborhood has no effect on future earnings or the likelihood that someone works.

Overall these results suggest that despite the popularity of the idea among urban planners, moving poor children to mixed-income neighborhoods may have relatively little impact on their prospects. Hence, one of the major rationales for favoring programs such as the LIHTC over vouchers that could serve more families with the same budget may be invalid.

A number of other arguments are often advanced against voucher programs. First, some families have difficulty using vouchers and return them unused. But the fact that some vouchers are returned does not mean that any are wasted because the number of families that are allowed to search at any point in time is greater than the number of vouchers. For example, if only 50 percent of the searchers were expected to be successful in a given search period, a housing authority could make sure that all of the vouchers were used by authorizing twice as many people to search as it had vouchers for. Most housing authorities also have a reserve fund to ensure that everyone who successfully finds an apartment is able to rent it. This system works well enough that at any point in time, most available vouchers are being used (Kennedy and Finkel 1994).

Similarly, low vacancy rates in a particular housing market don't mean that voucher recipients won't be able to find housing. Many voucher recipients are able to use their vouchers to stay in their existing apartments. Stephen Kennedy and Meryl Finkel (1994) look at data from thirty-three housing authorities, and find that 30 percent of the voucher recipients stayed in the apartments they were in. Forty-one percent of these apartments already met Section 8 standards, and the rest were repaired to meet the standards. Of the 70 percent of the recipients who moved to new apartments, about half moved into apartments that were upgraded to meet Section 8 standards. In New York City, which has a tight housing market, only 31 percent of the apartments that Section 8 recipients lived in had to be repaired to meet the program standards.

In fact, greater availability of Section 8 vouchers would encourage landlords to repair existing housing. This conclusion is supported by evidence from the Experimental Housing Allowance Program (EHAP). Part of this experiment involved running a voucher program for ten years in South Bend, Indiana, and Green Bay, Wisconsin. Unlike Section 8 vouchers, the EHAP vouchers were available to all low-income households in the counties. Landlords were motivated to fix their apartments to qualify for EHAP vouchers because given that all the low-income households now had vouchers, EHAP was the only game in town. Over the first five years of the experiment, eleven thousand homes were repaired to meet the program standards (Cutts and Olsen 2002).

A potential drawback to a large voucher program like EHAP is that it might drive up rents at the bottom of the market. But if the supply of low-rent apartments also increases in response to the voucher program, then the effects on rents will be mitigated. The EHAP voucher program had little effect on market rents (Rydell, Neels, and Barnett 1982).

Voucher programs cannot be expected to solve the problem of homelessness, which has multiple causes. Christopher Jencks's (1994) pathbreaking study of homelessness found that the majority of the three hundred thousand to six hundred thousand homeless were single men with substance abuse or mental illness, not families with excessive rent burdens. Jencks argues that even this population could benefit from housing voucher programs, but that other policies such as changing zoning to allow single-room occupancy dwellings and restoring psychiatric hospital beds for the hard-core mentally ill are necessary to make a real dent in homelessness. Martha Burt and Laudan Aron (2001) distinguish between people experiencing short-term crises (which might be solved by preventive measures such as emergency financial aid) and the chronically homeless. For the latter, they advocate transitional housing with supportive services. For both groups, they maintain that programs (including rental assistance through vouchers) that make housing more affordable are necessary.

Finally, while the preceding discussion emphasizes more efficient use of existing resources targeted to low-income housing, it is worth asking whether society should pay more overall for these kind of programs? An obvious comparison is to the amounts we pay to subsidize the housing of those who are better off. Tax deductions for mortgage interest, property taxes, capital gains, and investments in housing totaled roughly $120 billion per year between 2002 and 2007, with most of this money going to higher-income individuals. Given the large tax expenditures on homeowners, expenditures on housing for the poor are comparatively modest (National Low Income Housing Coalition 2001).

Still, the research summarized above has made a strong case that vouchers may be preferable to project-based aid on efficiency grounds. But it has not shown that children in households with vouchers generally do any better than children living in housing projects. And the evidence that public housing of any kind (project or voucher) improves child outcomes is extremely limited, consisting of the single study that I did with Yelowitz (2000). Thus, support for public housing rests primarily on beliefs about the importance of affordable housing to low-income families.

Early Intervention

A good deal of evidence suggests that it is possible to intervene early in the lives of poor children in order to improve their outcomes. The two interventions that have been shown to be most effective are high-quality child care settings and nurse home-visiting programs, though of course programs such as WIC and Medicaid coverage beginning in pregnancy should also be thought of as forms of early intervention.

The most convincing evidence of the positive potential role of quality child care comes from experiments in which disadvantaged children were randomly assigned to a treatment group that got high-quality care and a control group that did not. These studies generally find that early intervention has long-lasting effects on schooling attainment and other outcomes, such as teen pregnancy and crime, even though it often results in no lasting increase in cognitive test scores. These results point to the tremendous importance of "noncognitive skills" (compare Heckman and Rubinstein 2001), or alternatively, the significance of mental as well as physical health in the production of good child outcomes (Currie and Stabile 2006).

Three studies of "model" early intervention child care programs stand out because they randomly assigned children to treatment and a control group, had low dropout rates, and followed children at least into middle school. The three studies are the Carolina Abecedarian Project, the Perry Preschool Project, and the Milwaukee Project. (A fourth, the Infant Health and Development Project, also used a randomized design and had few dropouts, but followed children only to age eight. A long-term follow-up is currently in the field.) Of these, only the Milwaukee Project found any long-term effect on IQ. But the Carolina Abecedarian and Perry Preschool projects both found positive effects on schooling. A recent cost-benefit analysis of the Abecedarian data through age twenty-one found that each dollar spent on Abecedarian saved taxpayers four dollars. And by focusing only on cost savings, this calculation does not even include the value of higher achievement to the individual children and society (Masse and Barnett 2002). Each dollar spent on the Perry Preschool has been estimated to save up to seven dollars in social costs (Karoly et al. 1998).

These interventions prove, then, that it is possible to have an impact on the lives of poor children. Yet each intervention involved a package of high-quality services that was delivered to small numbers of children. Moreover, a recent reanalysis by Michael L. Anderson (2005) suggests that like the MTO, the significant effects of these interventions were largely concentrated among girls. The fact that particular interventions of this type had an effect on at least some children does not prove that the types of programs typically available to poor inner-city children will do so.

Head Start is a preschool program for disadvantaged three, four, and five year olds that currently serves about eight hundred thousand children each year. It is funded as a federal-local matching grant program, and over time, the federal funding has increased from $96 million when the program began in 1965 to $6.2 billion in 2001. Head Start is not of the same quality as the model interventions, and the quality varies from center to center. But Head Start centers have historically been of higher average quality than other preschool programs available to low-income people. This is because in contrast to the private child care market, there are few low-quality Head Start programs (for an overview, see Blau and Currie 2004).

An experimental evaluation of Head Start is currently being conducted (U.S. Department of Health and Human Services 2005). The evaluation compares Head Start children to peers who may or may not be in some other form of preschool (including state-funded preschools modeled on Head Start). Even relative to this baseline, the initial results show that Head Start children make some gains, particularly in terms of language ability. But the experiment follows children only into the first grade, and so will not address the crucial issue of whether Head Start has longer-term effects.

In a series of studies with Duncan Thomas and other colleagues (Currie and Thomas 1995, 1999, 2000; Garces, Thomas, and Currie 2002), I have used national survey data to try to measure the effect of Head Start. In most of these studies, we compare the outcomes of children who attended Head Start to their own siblings who did not attend. The idea is that siblings share many common background characteristics. By choosing the child's own sibling as a control for the Head Start child, we effectively eliminate the effect of shared family background on child outcomes. We have found significant positive effects of Head Start on educational attainments among white youths, and reductions in the probabilities of being booked or charged with a crime among black youths. Test score gains for blacks and whites were initially the same, but these gains tended to fade out more quickly for black than white students, perhaps because black former Head Start students typically attend worse schools than other students.

It should also be noted that since its inception, Head Start has aimed to improve a broad range of child outcomes (not just test scores). When the program was launched in 1965, the Office of Economic Opportunity assisted the three hundred poorest counties in applying for Head Start funds, and these counties were far more likely than others to receive funds. Using a regression discontinuity design, Jens Ludwig and Douglas Miller (2007) show that mortality from causes likely to be affected by Head Start fell among children age five to nine in the assisted counties relative to the others. Mortality did not fall in slightly older cohorts who would not have been affected by the introduction of the program.

Head Start has served as a model for state preschools targeted to low-income children in states such as California, and also for new (voluntary) universal preschool programs in Georgia and Oklahoma. The best available evaluations of universal preschool programs highlight the importance of providing a high-quality program that is utilized by the neediest children. Michael Baker, Gruber, and Kevin Milligan (2005) examine the introduction of a universal, five dollars per day (later seven dollars) preschool program in the Canadian province of Quebec. The authors find a strong response to the subsidy in terms of maternal labor supply and the likelihood of using care, but they observe negative effects of children on a range of outcomes.

Several caveats to the Baker, Gruber, and Milligan study are in order. First, the sample children cannot be followed for long, so it is not known, for example, whether the program had negative effects on schooling attainment. More substantively, because poor children were already eligible for subsidies, the marginal child affected by this program was a child who probably would have stayed home with a middle-class, married mother and instead was put into child care. Moreover, the marginal child care slot made available by the program was low quality—the province placed much more emphasis on making slots available than on regulating their quality. It is not possible, therefore, to draw any conclusion from this study about the effect of drawing poor children into care of good quality.

William Gormley and his colleagues (2005) examine the effects of Oklahoma's universal pre-K program, which is run through the public schools and is thought to be of high quality. They take advantage of strict age cutoffs for the program and compare children who had just attended for a year to similar children who were ineligible to attend because they were slightly younger. They find a 52 percent gain in prereading skills, a 27 percent gain in prewriting skills, and a 21 percent gain in premath skills. These results suggest that a high-quality universal pre-K program might well have positive effects, though one would have to track children longer to determine whether these initial gains translate into longer-term gains in schooling attainment. Universal programs are often popular, but can be an expensive way of benefiting low-income children, since most of the children who are subsidized are likely to be of higher income.

New Jersey has taken an innovative approach to the issue of providing high-quality care for low-income children as a result of a long-running lawsuit, *Abbott v. Burke*. In 1998, the New Jersey Supreme Court ordered the state to establish preschool programs in thirty needy, mostly urban school districts. In 2000, the state Department of Education mandated that the districts provide full-day preschool. The "Abbott program" now enrolls forty-three thousand students in high-quality child care centers. In fact, the court took the unprecedented step of defining quality by mandating pupil-teacher ratios, staff qualifications, and access to special services, if needed. In terms of these measurable aspects of quality, the Abbott program centers now look better than many Head Start centers in New Jersey. But this judicial solution has not been without controversy—several school districts have filed a lawsuit against the state because the state did not fully finance the cost of running these centers (Schwanebert 2004). Still, the Abbott program represents a promising model for state initiatives because it targets scarce child care dollars to the children who need them most and provides high-quality programming.

One reason for focusing on early intervention through the provision of quality child care is that the majority of young children are likely to be placed in some form of care. In 2000, 65.3 percent of single women with children under six were in the workforce. The majority of infants are placed in some sort of nonmaternal care by four months of age. Even mothers who do not work use child care. A third of their newborn to four-year-old children are in nonparental care for an average of more than twenty hours per week (compare Blau and Currie 2004). Moreover, the government is already a major player in the market for child care, covering a third of the costs of child care for children less than six. The government intervenes in the market for child care through tax credits, subsidies, and regulations as well as by directly providing care.

Given these other available mechanisms, an important question is why the government should be in the business of directly providing care through, for example, Head Start centers? The simple answer is that the other mechanisms (at least as currently formulated) do not do the job of providing quality child care to low-income children. Tax credits such as the Dependent Care Tax Credit generally do not benefit low-income families. State subsidy programs such as those funded by the federal Child Care and Development Fund typically place more emphasis on supporting maternal employment than on ensuring that the subsidized care is of good quality, and many families eligible for these subsidies are not served.

Finally, regulation (which is done at the state level) generally sets bare minimum standards, which are weakly enforced and do not even aspire to ensure that the quality of care provided will be sufficient to offer benefits to children. It is interesting to compare the federal approach to child care subsidies to housing subsidies under the Section 8 voucher programs. Section 8 standards potentially provide incentives to landlords to upgrade their housing. The federal government also gives money to local housing authorities that is used to pay for the inspections necessary to ensure that subsidized housing meets these standards. If the federal government adopted similar policies with respect to child care, it would make child care subsidies contingent on the quality of care provided, and impose much higher standards than many states have adopted. Failing this, the direct provision of care through a proven program may be a better alternative.

Nurse home-visiting programs are a second form of early intervention that has proven to be effective. David Olds (compare Olds et al. 1999) has conducted experimental evaluations of such programs in several settings (Elmira, New York; Memphis, Tennessee; and Denver). Olds's programs focus on families that are at risk because the mother is young, poor, uneducated, and/or unmarried, and involve nurse visits from the prenatal period up to two years postpartum. Evaluations have shown many positive effects on maternal behavior and child outcomes. As of two years of age, children in Elmira were much less likely to have been seen in a hospital emergency room for unintentional injuries or ingestion of poisonous substances, although this finding was not replicated at other study sites. As of age fifteen, children of visited mothers were less likely to have been arrested or to have run away from home, had fewer sexual partners, and smoked and drank less.

The children were also less likely to have been involved in verified incidents of child maltreatment. This finding is important given the high incidence of maltreatment among U.S. children (and especially among poor children) and the negative outcomes of maltreated children (Currie and Tekin 2006).

There was little evidence of the effects on cognition at four years of age (except among children of initially heavy smokers), although one might expect the documented reduction in delinquent behavior among the teens to be associated with improvements in schooling attainment.

Olds's results should not be interpreted to mean that all home-visiting programs are likely to be effective. The evaluations suggest that using nurses as home visitors is key to the acceptability of the visitors (families want medical services, but may be suspicious of social workers or community workers). Also, Olds's programs are strongly targeted at families considered to be at risk and so they do not shed light on the cost-effectiveness of universal home-visiting programs.

Home-visiting programs can be viewed as a type of parenting program—presumably the reason why Olds's home visitors improved outcomes is because they taught mothers to be better parents. Since parents are so crucial to children, programs that seek to improve parenting practices are perennially popular. Yet studies of these programs indicate that it is remarkably difficult to change parents' behavior and that many attempted interventions are unsuccessful. The most successful parenting programs are those that combine parent education with some other intervention that parents want, such as visits by nurses (as in Olds's case) or child care (Brooks-Gunn and Markham 2005).

After-School Care

Older children also frequently need nonparental care. In 1999, 10.5 percent of five- to fourteen-year-old children of employed mothers were unsupervised for part of the day. The fraction of children who are unsupervised rises sharply with age. Only 8.1 percent of nine year olds are left unsupervised, compared to 44.9 percent of fourteen year olds. Children left to their own devices are at increased risk of truancy, poor grades, and risky behaviors of all sorts. Juvenile crime rates triple between 3:00 and 6:00 p.m., when children are most likely to be left unattended. Children are also most likely to be victims of violent crimes committed by people outside their families in these after-school hours. Clearly, lack of supervision is a serious problem, at least for some children (compare Blau and Currie 2004; Aizer 2004; U.S. Office of Juvenile Justice and Delinquency Prevention 1996).

After-school care has been widely endorsed as a way to improve child outcomes and reduce crime. Between 1997 and 2002, the U.S. Department of Education increased funding for 21st Century Community Learning Centers, which are school-based after-school programs, from $40 million to $1 billion. In 2001, 1.2 million elementary and middle school students participated in this program in 3,600 schools. State governments have also increased their spending through, for example, California's Proposition 49.

Patricia Seppanen and her colleagues (1993) point out that there is a large gap between the rhetoric of after-school programs and what is actually provided. In a national survey, they found that 83 percent of enrollees in after-school programs were children in pre-K through grade three, so that the programs were not used much for the older children who are most at risk of being left on their own. Fewer than half of all programs offer creative writing, sports, field trips, or science activities at least once a week. Measures of quality are uneven, with some programs employing high school dropouts as child minders, and ratios of twenty-five children to one teacher.

Most evaluations of after-school programs focus on model programs that offer tutoring. For example, the Howard Street Tutoring Program randomly assigned second- and third-grade students with poor reading scores to a treatment group, which received tutoring, or a control group. The treatment group showed improvements in basal word recognition and spelling. The LA's Best program has also received a great deal of attention. This program offered comprehensive after-school tutoring, cultural enrichment, recreation, computer, and nutrition services to kindergarten and elementary school children in nineteen of the poorest schools in Los Angeles. Three studies have compared the LA's Best children to control children drawn from the same schools. There is some evidence that the LA's Best children did better in certain respects than the controls. But many of the analyses are flawed. For instance, Denise Huang and various colleagues (Huang et al. 2000; Huang, Lin, and Henderson 2001) report increases in the Stanford 9 test scores of LA's Best children, but do not compare them to Stanford 9 test scores of other children. This is a potentially important omission as test scores in the Los Angeles Unified School District have shown overall increases in recent years—between 1998–1999 and 2000–2001, the mean percentile on the Stanford 9 reading increased from 27 to 38 for grade two students.

There have been few evaluations of programs aimed at keeping older children in school and out of trouble. The Quantum Opportunities program randomly assigned ninth-grade students who were on public assistance either to a control group or a treatment group, which got after-school educational activities and community service activities each year for four years. Treatment students received monetary rewards for completing each portion of the program. Participants in this program were more likely to graduate from high school or obtain a GED than the controls, and they were more likely to go on to postsecondary education. They also had significantly fewer children and reported being more hopeful about the future than other teens. But there was no significant difference in the probability that the participants would be "in trouble with police" the following year (Hahn, Leavitt, and Aaron 1994).

Big Brothers/Big Sisters has been shown to be effective in improving a range of outcomes. For example, it reduces the probability that a little brother or sister hits someone or starts taking drugs, and improves schooling attendance (Tiernay, Grossman, and Resch 1995). The "I Have a Dream" program, which pays college tuition if children graduate from high school, has had large impacts on high school graduation (Kahne and Bailey 1999).

These model programs show that it is possible to make a difference in the lives of school-age children. But these intensive, expensive, privately funded programs bear little resemblance to the after-school programs available to most children, and cannot even be regarded primarily as child care programs. At this point, there is simply no evidence that the publicly funded after-school programs that have been adopted in most jurisdictions have any effect on child outcomes or that they reduce crime (Bodilly and Beckett 2005).

A recent evaluation of the 21st Century Community Learning Centers Program reinforces this conclusion (Dynarski et al. 2004). This evaluation included a large number of both elementary and middle school children. Twenty-six programs serving elementary students were assessed using random assignment. By creating a matched sample of control children to compare to the program children, a national sample of programs for middle school children was assessed. One of the more startling conclusions of the evaluation is that the program had no impact on the number of latchkey children or on children's academic achievement. The elementary school children did report feeling safer, though the middle school children did not.

Most of these programs offered homework assistance and enriching activities, so given the rhetoric surrounding the importance of after-school programs, it is surprising that they did not have more impact. One possible explanation is that on average, most students attended only two days a week. Another possibility is that some types of programs were more effective than others, and that these programs have not yet been identified. But the most reasonable conclusion is that the quality of typical after-school programs will have to be upgraded significantly before they can be expected to have impacts similar to those of model programs. In particular, if the aim of the program is to reduce crime, then it needs to be geared toward youths, and it needs to ensure that they participate regularly (perhaps through incentives). If it is aimed at improving scholastic achievement, then a successful program will offer intensive tutoring rather than "homework help."

Take Up

"Take up" refers to the rate at which people who are eligible for programs make use of them. Poor children in the United States would be much better off if there was full take up of the benefits that they and their families are already entitled to receive. For example, take up of the State Children's Health Insurance Program has been low (8 to 14 percent), with the result that the number of uninsured children has changed relatively little since the introduction of the program. Take up of Medicaid coverage among children is also low; in my exploration with Gruber (1996a), we estimated that even though the fraction of children eligible for Medicaid increased by 15.1 percent between 1984 and 1992, the fraction covered increased only 7.4 percent, while David Card and Lara Shore-Sheppard (2004) find that expansions of eligibility to all poor children born after September 30, 1983, led to about a 10 percent rise in Medicaid coverage for children born just after the cutoff date. On the other hand, the Medicaid program now pays for 35 to 40 percent of all U.S. births, suggesting extremely high take up of Medicaid by pregnant women.

There is considerable evidence that transactions costs are important determinants of take up rates. For example, my (2000) finding that enrollments in Medicaid among immigrant children increase with family size strongly indicates that it is benefits relative to transactions costs (or stigma) that matter. Rebecca Blank and Patricia Ruggles's (1996) study of participation in AFDC and the FSP showed that participation increased with the size of the benefits people were eligible for, suggesting a key role for transactions costs/stigma. Beth Daponte, Seth Sanders, and Lowell Taylor (1999) conducted an experiment, and found that informing people about their eligibility for the FSP increased the probability of participation. Still, people eligible for larger benefits were more likely to take them up, once again suggesting a nontrivial role for transactions costs/stigma.

I and my colleague and Grogger (2002) show that reducing recertification intervals had a negative effect on participation in the FSP, particularly among single heads of households and people in rural areas—both groups that could be expected to have relatively high transactions costs. Michael Brien and Christopher Swann (1999) show in cross-sectional data that requiring income documentation of WIC applicants reduced the participation rates. Bitler, myself, and Scholz (2003) observe that requiring more frequent visits to the WIC office also reduces participation, while Chatterji and her colleagues (2002) find that restricting the types of foods that can be purchased (i.e., reducing the value of the benefit) discourages take up. Hence, transactions costs relative to benefits appear to be important determinants of take up.

The climate in local welfare offices can have a large effect on take up by altering these transactions costs. For example, a September 2003 undercover investigation in New York City discovered that 11 percent of the sites listed by the city's Human Resource Administration as Food Stamp offices did not exist; that investigators were not able to obtain an application for the FSP from the existing sites a quarter of the time; that 27 percent of these sites did not have any written information about the program available on-site; and that 52 percent of the time applicants were illegally asked personal information while attempting to get an application. Since the FSP is federal, it is not in the interest of city or state welfare agencies to make it difficult for people to enroll, which is why New York City conducted this investigation. The hostility and misinformation found by the New York investigators are just one case of the barriers to accessing safety net programs faced by the poor (Sender et al. 2003).

What can be done to increase take up among eligibles? Evidentally, barriers such as those discussed above should be removed. Giving business as well as individuals a stake in promoting take up can be effective. In the case of the EITC, many preparers advertise instant cash back, which is essentially the person's EITC credit less the preparer's fee. Kopczuk and Pop-Eleches (2007) show that the introduction of state electronic filing programs significantly increased participation in the EITC, by giving commercial tax preparers an incentive to serve the low-income market.

In the case of Medicaid, hospitals have a stake in getting pregnant women who are eligible signed up, because they are required to serve women in active labor whether or not the women can pay (as long as the hospital accepts any payments from Medicare). There is evidence that pregnant women were responsible for much of the uncompensated care provided by hospitals prior to the Medicaid expansions (Saywell 1989). Many hospitals have subsequently established Medicaid enrollment offices on-site. These offices assist people in completing applications and tell them how to obtain the necessary documentation.

Conversely, Medicaid enrollment rates may have remained low for other groups despite increases in income cutoffs because of the lack of support for the program among vendors of medical services. Laurence Baker and Anne Royalty (1996) use data from a longitudinal survey of

California physicians observed in 1987 and 1991, and find that expansions of Medicaid eligibility to previously uninsured women and children increased the utilization of care provided by public clinics and hospitals, but had little effect on visits to office-based physicians.

California recently conducted an experiment in which community organizations were paid fifty dollars per successfully completed Medicaid application. Aizer (2003) notes that this program had a large impact on Medicaid enrollments, particularly in the Hispanic and Asian communities, and that the increase in Medicaid coverage resulted in fewer preventable hospitalizations among eligible children. In contrast, statewide advertising of Medicaid and the Healthy Families program seemed to have effects only on the enrollment of infants. It appears that people with older children already knew about these services, but needed more specific assistance enrolling.

Yelowitz (2000) provides evidence that altering enrollment requirements for one program can have spillover effects on to the enrollments in other programs. He estimates that for every ten newly eligible families who took up Medicaid benefits, four also took up the FSP. It is possible that families learned about their eligibility for the FSP when they went to the welfare office to apply for Medicaid. Alternatively, it may be more worthwhile to bear the application costs in the case of Medicaid and the FSP together than in the case of the FSP alone. Thus, making it easier to apply for multiple programs might also increase take up among eligibles.

In summary, we could increase the take up of effective antipoverty programs by reducing the barriers to participation and giving institutions incentives to assist individuals in taking up their benefits. As the entities charged with overseeing many antipoverty programs, cities have a large role to play in this effort.

Conclusions

Many of the programs developed to help poor children have had a huge positive impact on inner-city children. The challenge going forward is to improve the services available and prevent the gains from being lost. For example, the increasing cost of providing Medicaid services to the elderly and disabled threatens to undermine the viability of the program. Ironically, it is often mothers and children who are cut from the rolls because of funding problems, although they tend to cost relatively little. Nutrition programs have been successful in all but eliminating diseases related to nutrient deficiencies. Now these programs must be refined so that they do not encourage diseases linked to the overconsumption of empty calories.

Public housing continues to have many problems, although an over-haul has been under way now for many years with the demolition of some large projects, the rehabbing of others, and a move toward voucher-based programs. At the same time, the increasing funds being funneled to construction-based programs may not be the best use of scarce public housing funds. Surprisingly, there is little evidence that poor children benefit from living in a mixed-income development per se, and many of these developments displace considerable numbers of traditional public housing residents.

Early intervention programs show a lot of promise and are the most effective proven way to improve the outcomes of poor children. But we should beware of calls to dismantle programs like Head Start in order to, for example, give block grants to states for child care. While some states have developed excellent public preschool programs, most have not, and most offer little oversight of private child care. Successful federal policy in this area would involve continuing to improve Head Start and attaching strict quality standards to transfers to states for child care. The government should also consider the feasibility of a home-visiting program along the lines that Olds has tested.

The continuing enthusiasm for after-school and parenting programs needs to be tempered by a hard look at the data. While some after-school programs are effective, these tend to be highly specialized model programs with clear goals for the children. There is little evidence that the average program has any positive effect. And while it stands to reason that changing parents' behavior could be one of the most effective ways to benefit children, it appears to be remarkably difficult to accomplish this. Parenting programs that take place in conjunction with quality preschools have the best track record.

So what can cities do? They can make sure that their agencies help needy people to participate in federally funded programs such as Food Stamps, WIC, and school meals. They can take lessons from successful federal programs when deciding on what sort of local programs to support; the evidence suggests that narrowly targeted programs that provide benefits specifically to children are likely to have the largest effects on children's outcomes. They can support rigorous evaluations of programs to ensure that they use scarce resources to fund interventions that are effective. In many cases, this might take the form of being open to collaborations with academics who are interested in working with city data, rather than putting out expensive requests for proposals.

Finally, whatever programs are adopted, we need to pay more attention to their design and implementation, so that they actually serve those who are intended to benefit. Programs that have a broad base of political support (e.g., housing programs that are popular with both developers and advocacy groups) may not yield the most value for the money.

Cities should work with state governments to crack down on fraud in programs such as Medicaid, since this undermines support for the program and diverts monies from the needy. Cities bear much of the cost of failed human development in the form of poverty, crime, and other social problems. Hence, cities must be on the front lines of the effort to reduce child poverty, advocating for funding for programs that work, and ensuring that eligible children receive the benefits.

Notes

1. Even so, the estimates are likely to overstate the effect of income, because there may be other factors such as ambition or enterprise that are correlated with income. If we could control for these unobserved factors, one would expect the estimated effect of income to fall even further.

2. For further details about these programs, see Currie (2006).

References

Ahluwalia, I. B., V. K. Hogan, L. Grummer-Strawn, W. R. Colville, and A. Peterson. 1992. The Effect of WIC Participation on Small-for-Gestational-Age Births. *American Journal of Public Health* 88 (9): 1374–77.

Aizer, Anna. 2003. Low Take-Up in Medicaid: Does Outreach Matter and for Whom? *American Economic Review* (May): 238–46.

———. 2004. Home Alone: Child Care and the Behavior of School-Age Children. *Journal of Public Economics* 88, nos. 9–10 (August): 1835–48.

Almond, Douglas, Kenneth Chay, and Michael Greenstone. 2004. Civil Rights, the War on Poverty, and Black-White Convergence in Infant Mortality in Mississippi. NBER working paper no. 10552, June. Cambridge, MA: National Bureau of Economic Research.

Anderson, Michael L. 2005. Uncovering Gender Differences in the Effects of Early Intervention: A Reevaluation of the Abecedarian, Perry Preschool, and Early Training Projects. Department of Economics, Massachusetts Institute of Technology, September 25.

Associated Press. 1998. CHIP Extends to 1.2 Million Kids, 8 States. April 1.

Baker, Laurence C., and Anne Beeson Royalty. 1996. Medicaid Policy, Physician Behavior, and Health Care for the Low-Income Population. December. Department of Economics, Stanford University.

Baker, Michael, Jonathan Gruber, and Kevin Milligan. 2005. Universal Childcare, Maternal Labor Supply, and Family Well-being. NBER working paper no. 11832, December. Cambridge, MA: National Bureau of Economic Research.

Basiotis, P. Peter, Carol S. Kramer-LeBlanc, and Eileen T. Kennedy. 1998. Maintaining Nutrition Security and Diet Quality: The Role of the Food Stamp Program and WIC. *Family Economics and Nutrition Review* 11 (1–2): 4–16.

Berger, Lawrence, Christina Paxson, and Jane Waldfogel. 2007. Income and Child Development. Paper presented at the American Economic Association meetings, Chicago.

Bhattacharya, Jayanta, and Janet Currie. 2000. Youths at Nutritional Risk: Malnourished or Misnourished? In *Youths at Risk*, ed. Jonathan Gruber. 483–522. Chicago: University of Chicago Press.

Bhattacharya, Jayanta, Janet Currie, and Steven Haider. 2004. Poverty, Food Insecurity, and Nutritional Outcomes in Children and Adults. *Journal of Health Economics* 23, no. 2 (July): 839–62.

———. 2006. Breakfast of Champions? The Effects of the School Breakfast Program on the Nutrition of Children and Their Families. *Journal of Human Resources* 41, no. 3 (Summer): 445–66.

Bitler, Marianne, and Janet Currie. 2004. Does WIC Work? The Effect of WIC on Pregnancy and Birth Outcomes. *Journal of Policy Analysis and Management* 23, no. 4 (Fall): 73–91.

Bitler, Marianne, Janet Currie, and John Karl Scholz. 2003. WIC Eligibility and Participation. *Journal of Human Resources* 38:1139–79.

Blank, Rebecca M., and Patricia Ruggles. 1996. When Do Women Use Aid to Families with Dependent Children and Food Stamps? The Dynamics of Eligibility versus Participation. *Journal of Human Resources* 31 (1): 57–89.

Blau, David, and Janet Currie. 2004. Preschool, Day Care, and Afterschool Care: Who's Minding the Kids. NBER working paper no. 10670. Cambridge, MA: National Bureau of Economic Research.

Bodilly, Susan, and Megan Beckett. 2005. Making Out-of-School Time Matter. Santa Monica, CA: RAND.

Boston Housing Authority. N.d. Housing Services. Available at http://www .bostonhousing.org/housgin_services.html.

Brien, Michael J., and Christopher A. Swann. 1999. Government Intervention and Health: The Impact of WIC Participation on Children. Unpublished manuscript.

Brooks-Gunn, Jeanne, and Greg Duncan, eds. 1997. *Consequences of Growing Up Poor*. New York: Russell Sage.

Brooks-Gunn, Jeanne, and Lisa Markham. 2005. The Contribution of Parenting to Racial and Ethnic Gaps in School Readiness. *Future of Children: School Readiness: Closing Racial and Ethnic Gaps* 15, no. 1 (Spring): 139–68.

Brown, Haywood L., Kevin Watkins, and A. Kinney Hiett. 1996. The Impact of the Women, Infants, and Children Food Supplemental Program on Birth Outcome. *American Journal of Obstetrics and Gynecology* (174): 1279–83.

Burstein, Nancy, Mary Kay Fox, Jordan B. Hiller, Robert Kornfeld, Ken Lam, Cristofer Price, and David T. Rodda. 2000. *WIC General Analysis Project, Profile of WIC Children*. March. Cambridge, MA: ABT Associates.

Burt, Martha, and Laudan Aron. 2001. Helping America's Homeless. Washington DC: Urban Institute Press.

Card, David, and Lara Shore-Sheppard. 2004. Using Discontinuous Eligibility Rules to Identify the Effects of the Federal Medicaid Expansions on Low Income Children. *Review of Economics and Statistics* 86, no. 3 (November): 752–66.

Center on Budget and Policy Priorities. 2000. Section 8 Utilization and the Proposed Housing Voucher Success Fund. March 22. Washington, DC: Center on Budget and Policy Priorities.

Chatterji, Pinka, Karen Bonuck, Simi Dhawan, and Nandini Deb. 2002. WIC Participation and the Initiation and Duration of Breastfeeding. Discussion paper 1246-02. Institute for Research on Poverty, University of Wisconsin at Madison.

Chatterji, Pinka, and Jeanne Brooks-Gunn. 2004. WIC Participation, Breast-feeding Practices, and Well-Baby Care among Unmarried, Low-Income Mothers. *American Journal of Public Health* 94, no. 8 (August): 1324–27.

Chicago Housing Authority. 2003. A Voice for Change. Available at http://www.thecha.org/.

Cohen, Barbara, James Ohls, Margaret Andrews, Michael Ponza, Lorenzo Moreno, Amy Zambrowski, and Rhoda Cohen. 1999. *Food Stamp Participants' Food Security and Nutrient Availability, Final Report*. Contract no. 53-3198-4-025, July. Washington, DC: Food and Nutrition Service, U.S. Department of Agriculture.

Currie, Janet. 2000. Do Children of Immigrants Make Differential Use of Public Health Insurance? In *Issues in the Economics of Immigration*, ed. George Borjas, 271–308. Chicago: University of Chicago Press.

———. 2003. U.S. Food and Nutrition Programs. In *Means-Tested Transfer Programs in the United States*, ed. Robert Moffitt, 199–290. Chicago: University of Chicago Press.

Currie, Janet. "The Invisible Safety Net: Protecting the Nation's Poor Children and Families," Princeton, NJ: Princeton University Press, 2006.

Currie, Janet, and Jeffrey Grogger. 2002. Medicaid Expansions and Welfare Contractions: Offsetting Effects on Maternal Behavior and Infant Health. *Journal of Health Economics* 21:313–35.

Currie, Janet, and Jonathan Gruber. 1996a. Health Insurance Eligibility, Utilization of Medical Care, and Child Health. *Quarterly Journal of Economics* 111, no. 2 (May): 431–66.

———. 1996b. Saving Babies: The Efficacy and Cost of Recent Expansions of Medicaid Eligibility for Pregnant Women. *Journal of Political Economy* 104, no. 6 (December): 1263–96.

Currie, Janet, and V. Joseph Hotz. 2004. Inequality in Life and Death: What Drives Racial Trends in U.S. Child Death Rates? In *Social Inequality*, ed. Kathryn M. Neckerman, 569–632. New York: Russell Sage.

Currie, Janet, and Wanchuan Lin. 2007. Chipping Away at Health: More on the Origins of the SES-Health Gradient. *Health Affairs* 26, no. 2 (March–April): 331–44.

Currie, Janet, and Mark Stabile. 2006. Child Mental Health and Human Capital Accumulation: The Case of ADHD. *Journal of Health Economics* 25, no. 6 (November): 1094–1118.

Currie, Janet, and Erdal Tekin. 2006. Does Child Abuse Cause Crime? NBER working paper no. 12171, April. Cambridge, MA: National Bureau of Economic Research.

Currie, Janet, and Duncan Thomas. 1995. Does Head Start Make a Difference? *American Economic Review* 85 (3): 341–64.

———. 1999. Does Head Start Help Hispanic Children?" *Journal of Public Economics* 74 (2): 235–62.

———. 2000. School Quality and the Longer-Term Effects of Head Start. *Journal of Human Resources* 35 (4): 755–74.

Currie, Janet, and Aaron Yelowitz. 2000. Are Public Housing Projects Good for Kids? *Journal of Public Economics* 75, no. 1 (January): 99–124.

Cutler, David, and Jonathan Gruber. 1996. Does Public Insurance Crowd Out Public Insurance? *Quarterly Journal of Economics* 111, no. 2 (May): 391–430.

Cutts, Amy, and Edgar Olsen. 2002. Are Section 8 Housing Subsidies Too High? *Journal of Housing Economics* 11:214–43.

Dafny, Leemore, and Jonathan Gruber. 2000. Does Public Insurance Improve the Efficiency of Medical Care? Medicaid Expansions and Child Hospitalizations. NBER working paper no. 7555, February. Cambridge, MA: National Bureau of Economic Research.

Dahl, Gordon, and Lance Lochner. 2005. The Impact of Family Income on Child Achievement. NBER working paper no.11279, April. Cambridge, MA: National Bureau of Economic Research.

Daponte, Beth, Seth Sanders, and Lowell Taylor. 1999. Why Do Low-Income Households Not Use Food Stamps? Evidence from an Experiment. *Journal of Human Resources* 34, no. 3 (Summer): 612–28.

Decker, Sandra. 1992. The Effect of Physician Reimbursement Levels on the Primary Care of Medicaid Patients. November. New York: New York University Graduate School of Public Service.

Devaney, Barbara. 1992. *Very Low Birthweight among Medicaid Newborns in Five States: The Effects of Prenatal WIC Participation.* Alexandria, VA: Food and Nutrition Service, U.S. Department of Agriculture.

Devaney, Barbara, Anne R. Gordon, and John A. Burghardt. 1993. *The School Nutrition Dietary Assessment Study: Dietary Intakes of Program Participants and Nonparticipants.* Alexandria, VA: Food and Nutrition Service, U.S. Department of Agriculture.

Dynarski, Mark, Susanne James-Burdumy, Mary Moore, Linda Rosenberg, John Deke, and Wendy Mansfield. 2004. When Schools Stay Open Late: The National Evaluation of the 21st Century Community Learning Centers Program. October. Washington, DC: U.S. Department of Education, National Center for Education Evaluation and Regional Assistance.

Eissa, Nada, and Jeffrey Liebman. 1996. Labor Supply Response to the Earned Income Tax Credit. *Quarterly Journal of Economics* 112, no. 2 (May): 605–37.

Garces, Eliana, Duncan Thomas, and Janet Currie. 2002. Longer-Term Effects of Head Start. *American Economic Review* 92 (4): 999–1012.

Gordon, Anne R., and Lyle Nelson. 1995. *Characteristics and Outcomes of WIC Participants and Nonparticipants: Analysis of the 1988 National Maternal and Infant Health Survey.* Alexandria, VA: Food and Nutrition Service, U.S. Department of Agriculture.

Gormley, William, Ted Gayer, Deborah Phillips, and Brittany Dawson. 2005. The Effects of Universal Pre-K on Cognitive Development. *Developmental Psychology* 41 (6): 872–84.

Grogger, Jeffrey. 2003. Welfare Transitions in the 1990s: The Economy, Welfare Policy, and the EITC. NBER working paper no. 9472, February. Cambridge, MA: National Bureau of Economic Research.

Grogger, Jeffrey, Lynn Karoly, and Jacob Klerman. 2002. *Consequences of Welfare Reform: A Research Synthesis*. Santa Monica, CA: RAND.

Gruber, Jonathan, and Kosali Simon. 2007. Crowd-Out Ten Years Later: Have Recent Public Insurance Expansions Crowded Out Private Health Insurance? NBER working paper no.12858, January. Cambridge, MA: National Bureau of Economic Research.

Gunderson, Craig, and James Ziliak. 2004. Poverty and Macroeconomic Performance across Space, Race, and Family Structure. *Demography* 41, no. (February): 61–86.

Hahn, Andrew, Tom Leavitt, and Paul Aaron. 1994. *Evaluation of the Quantum Opportunities Program: Did the Program Work? A Report on the Postsecondary Outcomes and Cost-Effectiveness of the QOP, 1989–1993*. Waltham, MA: Brandeis University, Heller Graduate School Center for Human Resources.

Heckman, James, and Yona Rubinstein. 2001. The Benefits of Skill: The Importance of Noncognitive Skills: Lessons from the GED. *American Economic Review* 91 (2): 145–49.

Hofferth, Sandra, and Sally Curtin. 2004. Do Food Programs Make Children Overweight? Department of Family Studies, University of Maryland, College Park, September 30.

Huang, Denise, Barry Gribbons, Kyung Sung Kim, Charlotte Lee, and Eva L. Baker. 2000. A Decade of Results: The Impact of LA's BEST After School Enrichment Program on Subsequent Student Achievement and Performance. University of California at Los Angeles, Center for the Study of Evaluation, Graduate School of Education and Information Studies, mimeo.

Huang, Denise, Shu-jiao Lin, and Tina Henderson. 2001. Evaluating the Impact of LA's BEST on Students' Social and Academic Development: Study of 74 LA's BEST Sites, 2001–2002, Phase I Preliminary Report. Los Angeles: University of California at Los Angeles, Center for the Study of Evaluation, Graduate School of Education and Information Studies, mimeo.

Jacob, Brian A. 2004. Public Housing, Housing Vouchers, and Student Achievement: Evidence from Public Housing Demolitions in Chicago. *American Economics Review* 94, no. 1 (March): 233–58.

Jencks, Christopher. *The Homeless*. Cambridge, MA: Harvard University Press.

Kahne, Joseph, and Kim Bailey. 1999. The Role of Social Capital in Youth Development: The Case of "I Have a Dream" Programs. *Educational Evaluation and Policy Analysis* 21 (3): 321–43.

Karoly, Lynn A., Peter W. Greenwood, Susan S. Everingham, Jill Houbé, M. Rebecca Kilburn, C. Peter Rydell, Matthew Sanders, and James Chiesa. 1998. *Investing in Our Children: What We Know and Don't Know about the Costs and Benefits of Early Childhood Interventions*. Santa Monica, CA: RAND.

Kennedy, Stephen, and Meryl Finkel. 1994. Section 8 Rental Voucher and Rental Certificate Utilization Study. Cambridge, MA: Abt Associates.

Kopczuk, Wojciech, and Cristian Pop-Eleches. 2007. Electronic Filing, Tax

Preparers, and Participation in the Earned Income Tax Credit. *Journal of Public Economics* 91, nos. 7–8 (August): 1351–67.

Kowaleski-Jones, Lori, and Greg Duncan. 2000. Effects of Participation in the WIC Food Assistance Program on Children's Health and Development: Evidence from NLSY Children. Discussion paper no. 1207-00. Madison, WI: Institute for Research on Poverty.

Levine, Phillip, and David Zimmerman. 2000. Children's Welfare Exposure and Subsequent Development. NBER working paper no. 7522, February. Cambridge, MA: National Bureau of Economic Research.

Los Angeles County Community Development Commission. N.d. How to Apply for Public Housing. Available at http://www.lacdc.org/housing/apply_public/apply.shtm.

Luder, Elizabeth, E. Ceysens-Okada, A. Koren-Roth, and C. Martinez-Weber. 1990. Health and Nutrition Surveys in a Group of Urban Homeless Adults. *Journal of the American Dietetic Association* 90:1387–92.

Ludwig, Jens, and Douglas Miller. 2007. Does Head Start Improve Children's Life Chances? Evidence from a Regression Discontinuity Design. *Quarterly Journal of Economics* 122, no. 1 (January): 159–208.

Macurdy, Thomas, Raymond Chan, Rodney Chun, Hans Johnson, and Margaret O'Brien-Strain. 2005. Medi-Cal Expenditures: Historical Growth and Long Term Forecasts. June. San Francisco: Public Policy Institute of California.

Masse, Leonard, and W. Steven Barnett. 2002. A Benefit Cost Analysis of the Abecedarian Early Childhood Intervention. New Brunswick, NJ: National Institute for Early Education Research, Rutgers University.

Meyer, Bruce, and Daniel Rosenbaum. 2001. Welfare, the Earned Income Tax Credit, and the Labor Supply of Single Mothers. *Quarterly Journal of Economics* 116, no. 3 (August): 1063–1115.

Millennial Housing Commission. 2002. Meeting Our Nation's Housing Challenges: Report of the Bipartisan Millennial Housing Commission Appointed by the Congress of the United States. Appendix 3. Washington, DC: U.S. Government Printing Office.

Murphy, J. Michael, Maria E. Pagano, Joan Nachmani, Peter Sperling, Shirley Kane, and Ronald E. Kleinman. 1998. The Relationship of School Breakfast to Psychosocial and Academic Functioning: Cross-Sectional and Longitudinal Observations in an Inner-City School Sample. *Archives of Pediatric and Adolescent Medicine* 152, no. 9 (September): 899–907.

Murray, Michael. 1999. Subsidized and Unsubsidized Housing Stocks, 1935 to 1987: Crowding Out and Cointegration. *Journal of Real Estate Economics and Finance* 19:107–204.

Myers, Alan, Amy E. Sampson, Michael Weitzman, Beatrice Rogers, and Herb Kayne. 1989. School Breakfast Program and School Performance. *American Journal of Diseases of Children* 143 (October): 1234–39.

National Low Income Housing Coalition. 2001. Changing Priorities: The Federal Budget and Housing Assistance, 1996–2006. Washington, DC: National Low Income Housing Coalition.

New York City Housing Authority. 2004. About NYCHA: Factsheet. April 19. Available at http://www.nyc.gov/html/nycha/html/about/factsheet.shtml.

Olds, David L., Charles R. Henderson, Harriet J. Kitzman, John J. Eckenrode, Robert E. Cole, and Robert C. Tatelbaum. 1999. Prenatal and Infancy Home Visitation by Nurses: Recent Findings. *Future of Children* 9, no. 1 (Spring–Summer): 44–65.

Olsen, Edgar. 2003a. Housing Programs for Low-Income Households. In *Means Tested Transfer Programs in the United States*, ed. Robert Moffitt, 365–442. Chicago: University of Chicago Press.

———. 2003b. The Millennial Housing Commission Report: An Assessment. Paper presented at the American Real Estate and Urban Economics Association midyear meeting, May 28.

Olsen, Edgar, and David Baron. 1983. The Benefits and Costs of Public Housing in New York City. *Journal of Public Economics* 20 (April): 299–332.

Oreopoulos, Philip. 2003. The Long-Run Consequences of Living in a Poor Neighborhood. *Quarterly Journal of Economics* 118, no. 4 (November): 1533–75.

Orr, Larry, Judith Feins, Robin Jacob, Eric Beecroft, Lisa Sanbonmatsu, Lawrence Katz, Jeffrey Liebman, and Jeffrey Kling. 2003. Moving to Opportunity: Interim Impacts Evaluation. Washington, DC: U.S. Department of Housing and Urban Development.

Philadelphia Housing Authority. 2004. How to Apply for Public Housing. Available at http://www.pha.phila.gov/housing/admis-default.aspx.

Romich, Jennifer L., and Thomas Weisner. 2000. How Families View and Use the EITC: Advance Payment versus Lump Sum Delivery. *National Tax Journal* 53:1245–64.

Rose, Donald, Jean-Pierre Habicht, and Barbara Devaney. 1998. Household Participation in the Food Stamp and WIC Programs Increases the Nutrient Intakes of Preschool Children. *Journal of Nutrition* 128:548–55.

Rosenbaum, James. 1992. Black Pioneers: Do Their Moves to the Suburbs Increase Economic Opportunity for Mothers and Children. *Housing Policy Debate* 2 (4): 1179–1213.

———. 1995. Changing the Geography of Opportunity by Expanding Residential Choice: Lessons from the Gautreaux Program. *Housing Policy Debate* 6 (1): 231–69.

Rosenbaum, James, Leonard S. Rubinowitz, and Marilynn J. Kulieke. 1986. Low Income African-American Children in White Suburban Schools. Evanston IL: Center for Urban Affairs and Policy Research, Northwestern University.

Rydell, Peter, Kevin Neels, and Lance Barnett. 1982. Price Effects of a Housing Allowance Program. RAND report no. R-2720-HUD, September. Santa Monica, CA: RAND Corporation.

Saywell, Robert M., Jr., Terrell W. Zollinger, David K. W. Chu, Charlotte A. Macbeth, and Mark E. Sechrist. 1989. Hospital and Patient Characteristics of Uncompensated Hospital Care: Policy Implications. *Journal of Health Politics, Policy, and Law* 14:287–307.

Schnare, Ann, Carla Pendone, William Moss, and Kathleen Heintz. 1982. The Costs of HUD Multifamily Housing Programs: A Comparison of the Development, Financing, and Life Cycle Costs of Section 8, Public Housing, and Other Major HUD Programs. Vols. 1 and 2. May. Cambridge MA: Urban Systems Research and Engineering, Inc.

Scholz, John Karl. 1994. The Earned Income Tax Credit: Participation, Compliance, and Anti-Poverty Effectiveness. *National Tax Journal* (March): 59–81.

Schwanebert, Robert. 2004. Preschool Program's Cost Lands in Court. *Star-Ledger*, October 25.

Sender, Keri, Jackie Sherman, Lenny Adams, Torrence Allen, Patrick Boggs, Alex Fu, Vilma Perusina, Evonna Sistruck, and Triada Stampas. 2003. Stamping Out Hunger: Access to Food Stamp Applications in New York City. Report to the New York City Council, September.

Seppanen, Patricia S., John M. Love, Dianne Kaplan deVries, Lawrence Bernstein, Michelle Seligson, Fern Marx, and Ellen E. Kisker. 1993. *National Study of Before- and After-School Programs.* Washington, DC: U.S. Department of Education.

Smolensky, Eugene, and Jennifer Appleton, eds. 2003. *Working Families and Growing Kids: Caring for Children and Adolescents.* Washington, DC: National Academies Press.

St. Peter, Robert F., Paul Newacheck, and Neal Halfon. 1992. Access to Care for Poor Children: Separate and Unequal? *Journal of the American Medical Association* 267, no. 20 (May 27): 2760–64.

Tiernay, Joseph P., Jean Baldwin Grossman, and Nancy Resch. 1995. Making a Difference: An Impact Study of Big Brothers/Big Sisters. Philadelphia: Public/Private Ventures.

U.S. Committee on Ways and Means. 2005. *2004 Green Book.* Ways and Means of Committee Print: 108-6. Washington, DC: U.S. Government Printing Office.

U.S. Congress. Senate Committee on Agriculture, Nutrition, and Forestry. Subcommittee on Nutrition. 1979. *Hunger in America, Ten Years Later: Hearing before the Subcommittee on Nutrition of the Committee on Agriculture, Nutrition, and Forestry.* April 30. Washington, DC: U.S. Government Printing Office.

U.S. Congress. Senate Committee on Labor and Public Welfare. Subcommittee on Employment, Manpower, and Poverty. 1968. *Hunger in America; Chronology and Selected Background Materials.* Washington, DC: U.S. Government Printing Office.

U.S. Department of Health and Human Services. 2001. *The Surgeon General's Call to Action to Prevent and Decrease Overweight and Obesity.* Rockville MD: Office of the Surgeon General.

———. 2005. Head Start Impact Study: First Year Findings. May. Washington, DC: Administration for Children, Youth, and Families.

U.S. Department of Housing and Urban Development. 1992. Characteristics of HUD-Assisted Renters and Their Units in 1989. Table 1.1. Washington, DC: U.S. Government Printing Office.

———. 1998. Rental Housing Assistance. The Crisis Continues: The 1997 Report to Congress on Worst Case Housing Needs. Washington, DC: U.S. Department of Housing and Urban Development.

U.S. General Accounting Office. 1992. *Federal Investments Like WIC Can Produce Savings.* GAO/HRD9218. Washington DC: U.S. Government Printing Office.

———. 2001. Federal Housing Programs: What They Cost and What They Provide. GAO-01-901R, July 18. Washington, DC: U.S. Government Printing Office.

U.S. Office of Juvenile Justice and Delinquency Prevention. 1996. Juvenile Offenders and Victims: A National Report. Washington, DC: Office of Juvenile Justice and Delinquency Prevention.

Wallace, James, Susan Bloom, William Holshouser, Shirley Mansfield, and Daniel Weinberg. 1981. Participation and Benefits in the Urban Section 8 Program: New Construction and Existing Housing. Vols. 1 and 2. January. Cambridge MA: Abt Associates.

Weinberg, Daniel. 2005. Poverty Estimates for Places in the United States. U.S. Bureau of the Census, Center for Economic Studies, Working Paper CED05-12, September.

Whitmore, Diane. 2002. What Are Food Stamps Worth? Princeton Industrial Relations Section working paper no. 468, July.

———. 2005. Do School Lunches Contribute to Childhood Obesity? Harris School of Public Policy, University of Chicago, xerox, April.

Wilson, William Julius. 1987. The Truly Disadvantaged: The Inner City, the Underclass, and Public Policy. Chicago: University of Chicago Press.

Yelowitz, Aaron. 2000. Did Recent Medicaid Reforms Cause the Caseload Explosion in the Food Stamps Program? Department of Economics, University of California at Los Angeles, unpublished paper.

Yip, R., N. Binkin, L. Fleshood, and F. L. Trowbridge. 1987. Declining Prevalence of Anemia among Low-Income Children in the United States. Pediatrics 258 (12): 1619–23.

Yudkowsky, Beth, Jennifer Cartland, and Samuel Flint. 1990. Pediatrician Participation in Medicaid: 1978 to 1989. Pediatrics 85, no. 4 (April): 567–77.

Ziliak, James 2004. Filling the Poverty Gap, Then and Now. University of Kentucky Center for Poverty Research Online Discussion Paper. Available at http://papers.ssrn.com/sol3/papers.cfm?abstract_id=624602.

Zimmerman, David, and Phillip Levine. 1996. The Intergenerational Correlation in AFDC Participation: Welfare Trap or Poverty Trap? University of Wisconsin, Institute for Research on Poverty Discussion Paper, 1100-96, July.

9

Education

EDUCATING URBAN CHILDREN

RICHARD J. MURNANE

URBAN SCHOOLS in the United States are like mirrors, reflecting both the accomplishments and failures of our society.[1] The accomplishments are evident in graduation ceremonies at urban high schools throughout the country, when students bound for college thank their teachers for the opportunities their parents did not have. The failures are evident in the high dropout rates and low average test scores of students attending urban public schools.

Neither the accomplishments nor the failures of students in urban public schools are recent phenomena. Throughout the last century, America's urban public schools have provided the staircase to a better life for vast numbers of children. The failures are just as long-standing, as described in books written at the end of the nineteenth century by reformers such as Jacob Riis (1892) and Jacob Mayer Rice (1969).

The tendency throughout U.S. history has been to blame the public schools for the perceived shortcomings of the nation's young people. Urban schools have been particularly frequent targets. Urban public schools do need to increase their effectiveness markedly, and the primary goal of this chapter is to offer suggestions for improvement. Nevertheless, the academic performances of urban children will lag behind those of suburban children so long as the nation continues to view the problems facing urban children growing up in poverty as the sole responsibilities of urban public school systems.

What Has Not Changed

Ever since free public education became a U.S. institution in the nineteenth century, urban public schools have served large numbers of children from low-income families, many of whom did not speak English at home. Educating poor children is more difficult than educating children from more affluent families, in part because poor children often come to school hungry and in poor health, and in part because many of their parents lack the resources and knowledge to reinforce good school-based instruction or compensate for poor school-based instruction. *Equality of Educational Opportunity*, by James Coleman and his colleagues (1966), documented in enormous detail the power of the challenge facing schools serving large numbers of poor children.

A related problem is the high mobility rate of children in urban schools—a pattern that Theodore Sizer (1968) described some four decades ago, and that urban school principals today count as one of their greatest challenges. For example, the student mobility rate at Boston's English High School, the nation's oldest public high school, was 32 percent in the 2005–2006 school year. A continual flow of new students entering classes during the school year requires teachers to devote scarce instructional time to assessing the skills and knowledge of the new entrants, and socializing them to classroom norms of behavior. For this reason, it is no surprise to urban teachers that nonmobile students enrolled in classes with high mobility rates make less academic progress during the school year than comparable students enrolled in stable classes (Hanushek and Rivkin 2006).

High student poverty and student mobility rates make working conditions in urban schools difficult. A result is that a great many skilled teachers avoid urban schools serving high concentrations of poor children. If they do begin their careers in such schools, they transfer out as soon as possible. A consequence is that children who are in especially great need of the nation's best teachers are the least likely to get them. This too is an old pattern—one that the sociologist Howard Becker (1952) found in Chicago schools in the early 1950s.

What Has Changed

Until about thirty years ago, the primary goals for urban schools were to socialize waves of recent immigrants about the duties of citizenship, provide all students with quite basic cognitive skills, and prepare a minority of students for postsecondary education (Graham 2006). These goals made economic sense even as late as 1970 because the economies of most cities provided large numbers of jobs involving routine manual or routine cognitive work in manufacturing and administrative support occupations. While not exciting, these were jobs that most high school graduates could do. More important, they paid enough to allow large numbers of high school graduates and many school dropouts who were willing to follow directions and carry out repetitive tasks to earn a middle-class living.

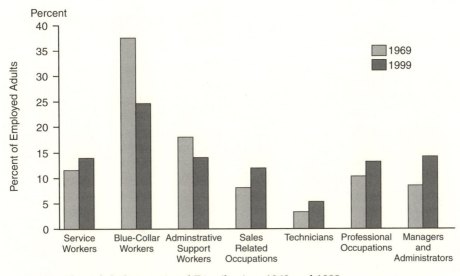

Fig. 9.1 The Adult Occupational Distribution, 1969 and 1999

Changes in the U.S. economy in recent decades have created pressures on urban schools to reach a new, unprecedented goal: to prepare all students to master a demanding set of academic standards that will prepare them for postsecondary education and training, or jobs with promising futures (Murnane and Levy 1996). The economic basis for this new demand is illustrated in figure 9.1, which displays the distribution of U.S. jobs by occupational categories arrayed from lowest paying on the left to highest paying on the right. Between 1969 and 1999, the proportion of the nation's jobs in manufacturing and administrative support occupations—the two occupations that provided work for vast numbers of urban high school graduates—fell from 55 to 39 percent.[2] In contrast, growth took place in higher-paying occupational categories that typically require postsecondary education, and lower-paying service sector jobs such as food preparation and janitorial work. A consequence of these changes in the occupational distribution is that high school graduates who leave high school with the skills to succeed in postsecondary education and training find growing opportunities. Those graduates and dropouts who lack these skills, however, are increasingly relegated to service sector jobs that are growing in number, but that do not pay enough to support children.

Figure 9.2, which provides an update of the trends in figure 9.1, shows that the same trends prevail in the most recent data. During the six-year period from May 2000–May 2006, when the number of jobs in the U.S. economy increased by 7.4 million, the number of jobs in manufacturing

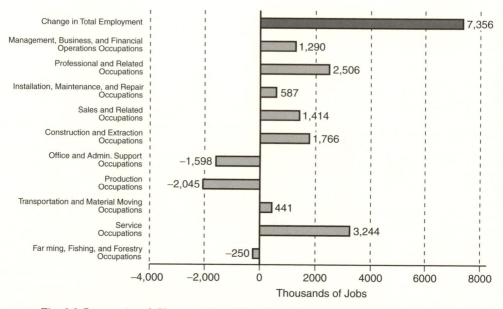

Fig. 9.2 Occupational Change, May 2000–May 2006

and administrative support occupations declined by 3.5 million. While the economic forces underlying these trends are complex, there is every reason to believe that the trends will continue.[3]

The changes in the U.S. economy have resulted in quite dramatic shifts in the distribution of tasks done by U.S. workers and in the skills needed to do these tasks. This is illustrated in figure 9.3, which shows how changes in the job mix over the last three decades of the twentieth century affected the types of tasks carried out by the U.S. workforce.[4] Especially critical are the growing importance of jobs requiring expert thinking and complex communication. I will return to these skills later in the chapter in discussing strategies for improving urban high schools.

The economic trends displayed in figures 9.1, 9.2, and 9.3 all play a large role in explaining the trends in the wages of U.S. workers with different educational attainments that are displayed in figure 9.4.[5] In 1979, four-year college graduates earned 46 percent more than high school graduates on average. In 2005 the comparable figure was 74 percent. During this same period, the average real earnings of high school dropouts fell by 16 percent.[6] It is these economic trends that have created the demand on urban high schools to prepare all students to master the skills needed for success in postsecondary education and training.

The best information on the skills of urban students relative to those of students attending suburban schools shows disturbing patterns. In

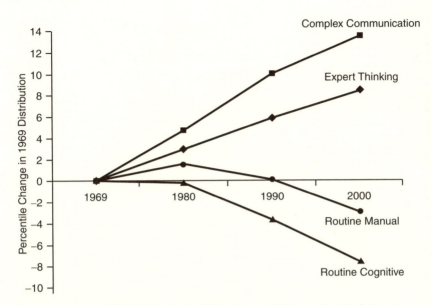

Fig. 9.3 Economy-Wide Measures of Routine and Nonroutine Task Input, 1969–1998 (1969 = 0)

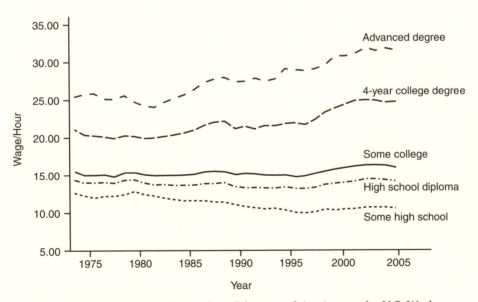

Fig. 9.4 Real Hourly Wage by Highest Educational Attainment for U.S. Workers, 1973–2005 (2005 Dollars)

2003, 50 percent of eighth graders attending schools in large cities scored below basic on the National Assessment of Educational Progress mathematics test, compared to 29 percent of eighth graders attending suburban schools. The comparable figures for reading scores are 43 and 24 percent, respectively (U.S. Department of Education 2005).

In summary, as a result of changes in the economy, the consequences of leaving school with weak skills are much greater than they were forty years ago. This is why improving the skills of urban students is the nation's most pressing educational problem.

Standards-Based Educational Reforms

In the last twenty years almost every state has adopted standards-based educational reforms, often called test-based accountability, as its primary strategy for improving public education. To a significant extent, this strategy is a response to state legislators' frustrations with the consequences of court-mandated school finance reform—the dominant approach to improving public schools during the previous two decades. Under court-mandated school finance reforms, many states assumed greater responsibility for funding public schools, thereby reducing the reliance on local property taxes. These reforms did lead to a significant equalization of per pupil spending across school districts, usually by increasing expenditures in low-spending school districts. In particular, school spending rose markedly in districts serving high percentages of children from poor families and children of color. The increased spending, though, was not accompanied either by a marked increase in or equalization of student achievement (see Evans, Murray, and Schwab 1999). This led legislators to the conclusion that simply providing public schools with more money was not an effective strategy for improving their performance. Instead, increased funding must be accompanied by increased accountability.

While details of accountability systems vary greatly from state to state, all standards-based educational reforms include three components:

- Content standards that specify what students should know and be able to do, performance standards that describe how students should demonstrate their knowledge and skills as well as what levels of performance meet the standards, and assessments that measure the extent to which students meet performance standards
- Incentives for educators to do the hard work required to prepare all students to meet the performance standards, and incentives for students to devote the time and energy needed to meet the performance standards

- Instructional materials and professional development aimed at providing teachers with the knowledge, skills, and resources needed to prepare all students to meet the performance standards[7]

The passage of the No Child Left Behind Act of 2001 marked a significant change in the federal role in public K–12 education in the United States. No Child Left Behind requires that states annually test the reading and mathematics skills of all public school students in grades three through eight. It also specifies that all schools are expected to make adequate yearly progress toward ensuring that all groups of students, including groups defined by race/ethnicity and poverty, reach proficiency by 2014. School districts and schools that fail to demonstrate adequate yearly progress for all groups of students are subject to corrective actions that can ultimately include staff replacement and school reconstitution.[8] No Child Left Behind and state accountability systems have put the spotlight on urban schools, highlighting the weak reading and math skills of urban students, and their low graduation rate. In particular, they have put great pressure on urban school systems to improve the English language arts and mathematics skills of students.

Isolation of Urban Schools

One troubling change in urban schools is that they serve many fewer middle-class children today than they did in the past. In fact, the vast majority of students served by the nation's largest urban school districts are children of color from low-income families. Among the many factors contributing to this disturbing trend is the 1974 decision by the U.S. Supreme Court in the *Milliken v. Bradley* case. In this decision, the Court ruled that communities neighboring Detroit had no obligation to participate in an interdistrict desegregation plan aimed at improving educational opportunities for Detroit's overwhelmingly low-income minority student population. The decision in effect meant that the problems facing urban school districts serving concentrations of minority group children were the responsibility of cities, not of broader communities of Americans. The flight of middle-class families from urban schools has markedly increased the challenge of improving these schools.

Competition for Teaching Talent

Forty years ago, K–12 teaching was one of the few professional work opportunities available to female college graduates. This was especially the case for female graduates of color. A consequence was that education did not need to compete intensely for academically talented female college graduates. In the intervening decades, employment opportunities in other professions have improved markedly for women and minorities. The competition for talent is thus much more intense than in the past. The public schools are not faring well in this competition, as indicated by the 50 percent decline over the last thirty-five years in the percentage of the nation's most academically strong college graduates who enter teaching (Corcoran, Evans, and Schwab 2004). The problem is acute for urban school districts, where the teaching challenges are especially difficult and the working conditions are often particularly poor.

Teachers' Unions

Forty years ago, few urban school districts engaged in collective bargaining with teacher unions. Today, teacher unions are important players in most urban school districts. Many urban teachers' contracts specify not only salary scales and fringe benefits. They also specify many things once considered management decisions, such as the maximum class size, the length of the school day and school year, the number of teaching preparations, the amount of time devoted to training (typically called professional development), and procedures for filling teaching vacancies.

There is no question that changes are needed in the contracts under which teachers in many urban school districts work. Particularly troubling are the seniority rules governing transfers that contribute to high teacher turnover rates in schools serving concentrations of poor children. At the same time, I believe it is a mistake to view teacher unions as powerful villains opposing needed reforms. Urban teacher unions became powerful because many urban teachers felt besieged by the conditions under which they worked and wanted a voice in improving these conditions. Tenure and seniority rights to transfers are not new. They became part of contracts long before urban public schools were charged with preparing all students to meet demanding academic standards. They were among the modest perquisites that came with relatively low-paying, difficult jobs with few opportunities for advancement.

Urban school districts today face unprecedented challenges and need employment contracts that are different from those negotiated in the past. In particular, contracts are needed that enable school districts to attract and retain academically talented teachers in all subject fields, that induce them to work in the schools where they are most needed, that create incentives and opportunities for teachers to work together to improve instruction, and that define strategies for identifying ineffective teachers, supporting their improvement, and dismissing those who remain inadequate. Unfortunately, it is not obvious just what contract provisions will contribute to these objectives. Mistakes, especially if not corrected in a timely fashion, are costly because the teachers that urban districts most want to attract and retain have compelling alternative employment opportunities. Unions can play a critical role in enabling urban school districts to move toward human resource policies aligned with standards-based educational goals. They can do this by articulating the concerns of effective teachers, collaborating on the design of teacher evaluation procedures, and providing timely feedback about potential reactions to proposed changes in contracts and human resource policies.[9]

Peer Assistance and Review programs provide one example of promising collaborations. Districts including Toledo, Cincinnati, and Montgomery County have negotiated Peer Assistance Review programs, under which teacher unions and school district management work together in evaluating teachers, providing assistance to those whose performance is subpar, and dismissing those teachers whose performance does not improve remarkably after receiving assistance. Bonnie Cullison, the president of the Montgomery County Teachers Union, provided the following summary of her district's program: "For the 10 years prior to PAR being instituted in Montgomery County, exactly one person had left the system because of performance. . . . In the six years since PAR has come in, 400 people have left the system because of performance. Now many of them decide to leave without going through the dismissal process" (quoted in Johnson et al. 2007, 15).

Of course, using the collective bargaining process to reach agreements that result in improved education for children requires great skill on the part of both union and school district leaders. Frequently these skills have been lacking.

In summary, improving urban education is both more important now than in the past and more difficult. It is more important because the economic consequences of leaving school without strong skills are greater than in the past. The work is more difficult because urban schools lack the human resources provided by middle-class students and their parents, and because they must compete for teaching and leadership talent to a much greater extent than they did in the past.

Two quite different bodies of research offer ideas for improving the performance of urban school districts. One group of studies, conducted primarily by scholars of organizational design, examines the effectiveness of particular district management strategies. The second group of studies, conducted primarily by economists, focuses on the need to improve incentives. Each body of research supplies crucial insights. Each is somewhat insensitive to the significance of the insights offered by the other literature. A theme of this chapter is that insights from both literatures are critical to improving urban schools.

District Improvement Strategies

A consensus is emerging on the components of urban school district reform strategies that are successful in improving elementary schools. Elements include systemwide, demanding curricula that are well aligned with state standards and assessments, a new partnership between the central office and city schools known as reciprocal accountability, the use of student assessment results to guide decision making, and a consistent strategy to support English-language learners. Since each of these elements is either relatively new or controversial, I provide an explanation of each.

There are two advantages to adopting common curricula for all elementary schools. First, it facilitates the integration into classes of the many students who move during the school year from one district elementary school to another. Second, it reduces the cost of providing professional development aimed at increasing teachers' skill in teaching core curricula. The alignment of curricula with state standards is essential so that teachers have reason to believe that helping their students to master the curriculum will result in good scores on mandatory state tests. The reason to adopt relatively demanding curricula is to assure the district's best teachers that they have the tools to prepare students to succeed in subsequent education. Since curricula that challenge students to master higher-order skills are difficult to teach effectively, however, a corollary is the importance of providing the ongoing training needed to learn to teach the curricula well. This is where the new role for the central office comes in.[10]

Reciprocal accountability is a term characterizing the relationship between the central office and individual schools (see Elmore 2002, 40). On the one hand, the district leadership requires that schools make progress in improving student achievement. If they do not, there are consequences, often beginning with a change in leadership. On the other hand, the district leadership commits itself to providing the resources that schools need to accomplish this goal. These include well-educated teachers, ongoing training that increases principals' and teachers' effectiveness, enough time in the school day for teachers to both work together at instructional improvement and offer extra help to lagging students, and the resources needed to support the learning of students with varying needs.

Making reciprocal accountability a reality requires a new role for the central office. It must recognize that schools vary in capacity and need to be treated differently. Low-performing schools need special attention and support. Schools making real progress need the freedom to use resources in new ways. To provide the resources schools need, the district leadership must reallocate resources away from the many programs and activities that absorb funds, but do not contribute in a coherent fashion to improving students' literacy and mathematics skills in the district as a whole.

Given the importance of preparing all students to master state learning standards, it is essential to track progress toward this goal and use the data to inform decision making. One use of data is to assess whether professional development is making a difference. Another is to identify schools in need of intervention. Yet a third is to provide school faculties with up-to-date, fine-grained information on the extent to which individual students are mastering critical skills. (Formative assessment is the term used to describe such information.) School faculties need to learn how to use the results of formative assessments to determine the effectiveness of their instruction, identify skills that need to be taught again or taught differently, and figure out ways to improve instruction and provide lagging students with extra learning time. Central office leadership is needed in developing or purchasing the assessments, providing school faculties with the results in an easy-to-understand format, and supplying the training school faculties need to learn to make constructive use of the assessment results (Sharkey and Murnane 2006).

A critical challenge in most urban school districts is educating students who come to school with little or no proficiency in English. For example, in 2007, 18 percent of Boston's fifty-seven thousand public school students were English-language learners. They came from forty different countries. The largest native-language groups were Spanish, Haitian Creole, and Chinese, but there also were students speaking dozens of other languages. State and federal accountability systems requiring that the scores of English-language learners on state examinations be included in calculations of schools' performance ratings have increased the pressure on schools to develop the English proficiency of English-language learners.

How best to teach English-language learners has been the subject of great controversy in the United States.[11] On the one side are advocates of bilingual education, an approach that combines some native-language instruction with instruction in English. They argue that developing students' reading abilities in their native language will help them to learn to read in English. On the other side are advocates of English-only instruction, who contend that instruction in a student's native language slows progress in mastering English. In practice, the choice of instructional method is much less clear-cut than a dichotomous choice between bilingual education or English-only instruction. Some bilingual programs, for example, begin with instruction solely in students' native language and then make a transition to English. Others employ two teachers with each group of students from the outset, one of whom teaches in the student's native language for part of the day and the other teaches in English for part of the day. Some programs aim to move children to English-only instruction within a year, while others continue with instruction in two languages for several years.

There are also many variants of English-only approaches. At one extreme, students are placed in regular classes with native-English speakers and expected to "catch-up." In another approach, called structured English immersion, students are grouped together for a specific period of time and taught content in English using special techniques accessible to English-language learners.

Of course, the quality of implementation of any particular approach, whether it be a form of bilingual education or English-only instruction, varies from classroom to classroom, depending on the skills of the teachers, the time allotted to learning to read, the availability of resource materials, and the backgrounds and skills of the students. Yet such subtleties are typically lost in the heat of debates about bilingual education. The intensity of the controversy is illustrated by the passage of laws in several states, including California and Arizona, prohibiting or severely restricting the use of bilingual education in public schools.

While many evaluations of the relative effectiveness of bilingual education and English-only instruction have been conducted, only a small percentage of studies have sufficiently rigorous designs to provide compelling evidence. A recent meta-analysis of evaluations with satisfactory designs reached two important conclusions. The first is that bilingual instruction does not hamper academic progress in either a student's native language or English. Indeed, bilingual education has a small advantage, on average, over the English-only approach. The second is that the program quality matters more than the choice of a bilingual education or an English-only approach. In other words, what is most crucial is having instructors skilled in teaching English-language learners, curriculum that is accessible to and engages English-language learners, sufficient time devoted to acquiring literacy skills, close monitoring of the progress of each child, and rapid intervention when a child is lagging. All of this is just one more aspect of reciprocal accountability between the central office and individual schools.

The four elements that are part of successful school district improvement strategies make sense. In fact, to some readers, they may seem obvious. But implementing them requires a significant reorganization of central offices, which historically have been large bureaucracies divided into departments (often derogatively labeled "silos"), each of which functioned with its own standard-operating procedures and did not coordinate its work with that of other departments. The typical district had hundreds of programs with different objectives and funding sources. The central office's role was to administer the funding of these programs, not to ask whether they contributed to a coherent instructional program. Most districts kept track of students' scores on end-of-the-year achievement tests, and some eventually sent these scores to schools. Until quite recently, though, most central offices did not think in terms of an obligation to put in place a system of formative assessments that would provide school faculties with timely, fine-grained information on students' skills. In most urban districts there was one office responsible for the education of English-language learners, with little coordination between the work of that office and the operations of other central office departments.

Improving Urban Secondary Schools

Among the most troubling indicators of the problems of urban education are the extraordinarily high dropout rates of students from urban high schools, and the large number of urban high school graduates who enroll in two- and four-year colleges but fail to pass the exams required for entry into credit-bearing courses. Fifteen years ago, when states began standards-based education reforms, many analysts thought that these problems would go away in time. The logic was that the poor reading and math skills of a great many ninth graders stemmed from low-quality elementary school education. Thus, improving elementary schools would solve crippling problems that besiege secondary schools. This logic has turned out to be faulty. Many urban school districts have markedly improved the reading and math scores of elementary school students. Yet the dropout rates of students from their urban high schools do not seem to have declined. Nor have the scores on state tests administered to urban tenth graders improved nearly as much as the scores of elementary school students. This pattern has led to the realization that improving secondary schools, including both middle schools and high schools, is the biggest challenge facing urban school districts.

Recent research has shed light on the elements of effective strategies to improve urban secondary schools. The critical dimensions include:

- Creating a personalized and orderly learning environment in which students and teachers treat each other respectfully

- Identifying students who enter middle schools and high schools with poor academic skills, and intervening intensively to improve these skills
- Improving the quality of instruction, and making a stronger case to students that particular skills and knowledge are important to acquire
- Connecting students to the world of work
- Strengthening connections between high schools and community colleges (Quint 2006)

The most visible evidence of this strategy is the creation of many small high schools—frequently by dividing large comprehensive high schools into three or four smaller schools housed in the same building. Other common actions are the creation of double-length instructional periods in English and mathematics for ninth graders with weak skills. In many districts these sensible changes have taken place quite rapidly, to a large extent because they could be done by administrative fiat, if sufficient resources are available. It has proven more difficult, however, to improve instruction and engage students.

Why Is Progress So Slow?

If urban districts such as Boston and San Diego have made progress by embracing the district improvement strategy described above, why have not all urban districts done so? Why has the rate of progress been so modest in even the most rapidly improving urban districts? There are several contributing explanations. First, attempts to implement the districtwide improvement strategies described above encounter significant political resistance. Some resistance comes from central office staff who lose their jobs as resources are reallocated from peripheral programs to school-based professional development aimed at improving English and mathematics instruction. Some comes from central office staff told that reciprocal accountability means they must serve schools rather than require that schools follow their rules. Some comes from teachers who are told that they must work with colleagues and coaches to improve instruction and make it more consistent instead of closing the classroom door. Some comes from parents angry that principals whom they personally like are replaced due to stagnant test scores. Sustaining commitment to a coherent district improvement strategy in the face of such resistance requires significant support from the school board and the business community. Often such support dwindles as the resistance to change becomes evident (see Hess 2005). The brief tenure of urban superintendents (less than three years, on average) also contributes to resistance. Why should central office staff, teachers, and parents embrace significant systemwide changes if the initiator of the changes is unlikely to see them through? Of course, the causation works the other way as well: resistance leads many superintendents to resign rather than to fight for change.

A related reason why only a relatively small minority of urban districts has successfully embraced a coherent systemwide instructional improvement strategy is that there is no recipe for doing so. Instead, superintendents must find their own way of building and sustaining support for change as well as overcoming the many sources of resistance. This is vividly illustrated by the different approaches taken by Alan Bersin and Thomas Payzant, both of whom led districts that greatly improved student achievement under their leadership (see Hess 2005; Reville 2007).

A third reason is that the incentives in place for many actors in urban education do not support an unwavering commitment to improving student achievement. These incentives are a legacy of a time when students needed fewer skills to earn a decent living and an industrial mode of production was a serviceable way to organize schooling. These incentives hinder progress today.

Improving Incentives

In analyzing the problems with U.S. public schools and urban public schools in particular, economists have emphasized that the system provides the wrong incentives for teachers, school administrators, and students. In this section, I explain these arguments.

Incentives for Teachers

Virtually all public school districts in the United States use compensation systems for teachers that reward advanced degrees and years of teaching experience, and nothing else. School districts typically adopted these uniform salary scales in the middle of the twentieth century as part of efforts to professionalize teaching. Often they replaced arrangements in which the compensation of individual teachers depended on their gender and their relationships with school board members.

While the uniform salary schedule may have made sense in the past, it creates a variety of problems today for urban school districts striving to use scarce resources wisely. One problem is the difficulty of attracting skilled teachers in fields such as chemistry and computer science that offer strong private sector employment opportunities, and in fields such as special education where the work with children may be especially draining. A second is that the pay scale creates incentives for teachers to acquire master's degrees even though most studies indicate that teachers with master's degrees are not any more effective than those without them. A third is the lack of incentives for teachers to invest in developing skills that do enhance their effectiveness. A fourth is the lack of incentives for skilled teachers to work in the schools serving high concentrations of low-achieving students. Indeed, teachers use the seniority rights that are part of most collectively bargained contracts to move away from such schools (Hanushek 1994).

Among the most common initiatives aimed at improving incentives for teachers are pay premiums for teaching in schools serving high percentages of poor children. Frequently the pay premiums are coupled with increases in the length of the school day and school year, and with training aimed at improving instructional quality. To date the evidence on the consequences of these initiatives is extremely limited. Still, one study based on data from North Carolina suggests that initiatives of this kind have promise. This study found that a $1,800 per year retention bonus for math, science, and special education teachers working in high-poverty or academically failing secondary schools reduced eligible teachers' turnover rates by 12 percent (Clotfelter et al. 2006). Unfortunately, the study did not address the critical question of whether the reduction in teacher turnover resulted in increases in student achievement.

Another type of initiative ties teachers' pay to demonstration of mastery of particular knowledge bases and skills. One well-known initiative of this type is National Board Professional Teacher Certification, a voluntary program under which teachers with at least three years of experience who successfully demonstrate a range of skills over a yearlong evaluation process are designated as Board Certified Teachers. A number of states and school districts offer significant pay premiums to teachers who have acquired this status. A recent study showed that elementary school teachers who achieved board certification were more effective in increasing students' reading and math test scores than were teachers who applied for board certification but did not succeed in obtaining it (Cantrell et al. 2007). These results suggest the value of using aspects of the board certification process in making teacher licensing and tenure decisions.

Yet another type of initiative provides pay premiums to teachers or the entire faculties of schools that are effective in improving students' scores on standardized tests. The direct link between student performance gains and teachers' pay makes this type of policy attractive to many policymakers. It troubles many teacher union leaders, however. One reason is that test scores are imperfect indicators of the skills that students should master. A second is that test scores depend not only on teachers' efforts and skills but also on many factors beyond their control. It is clear that the consequences of performance-based pay plans (sometimes called "new-style merit pay") will depend critically on the quality of the student assessments and the development of "value-added" models that provide credible estimates of teachers' contributions to test score gains (Lavy 2007). While there is little evidence on the consequences of teacher compensation plans that link pay to student test scores, a recent evaluation of a short-lived program in Israel found a positive impact on student achievement (ibid.).

Perhaps the most interesting teacher compensation plan adopted by an urban school district is Denver's ProComp. This plan includes a combination of the type of incentives described above: extra pay for teaching hard-to-staff subjects or teaching in hard-to-staff schools, extra pay for demonstrated mastery of knowledge and skills, and extra pay for students' growth in test scores. To date, there is no solid evidence on the extent to which the plan increased the district's ability to attract and retain skilled teachers as well as increase students' achievement. Yet the plan does show that it is possible for school district management and teacher union leaders to bring about significant changes in teachers' contracts through collective bargaining.

Incentives for School Leaders

School principals play key roles in determining the effectiveness of the schools that they lead. Typically they hire teachers, specify their teaching assignments, and evaluate their performances. In many school districts principals also specify the professional development activities that teachers engage in. Principals also typically assign students to classes and decide which students must repeat a grade. The value of skilled principals is frequently illustrated by profiles that appear in the media of schools with strong leaders that have been uncommonly successful in educating disadvantaged students.

Despite the central role of school principals in leading schools, many urban school districts do not provide incentives to attract and retain effective school leaders. The problems are of three kinds. First, in many urban districts school principals do not have control over many resources. Consequently they lack the tools to lead schools effectively. Second, the job has become much more difficult, with pressure to improve the test scores of all students. Many districts lack effective training for developing the skills that principals need to achieve these relatively new goals. Third, in many districts, effective principals are paid on the same scale as ineffective ones. Moreover, some state labor laws make it difficult for school district superintendents to remove ineffective principals. The net result is that many urban public schools lack effective leaders.

In recent years some states have passed legislation that makes it easier for school district superintendents to remove school principals who are not effective. Some states and urban districts have also introduced performance-based contracts for school leaders. These types of initiatives make sense as part of strategies to improve school leadership. Nevertheless, whether particular initiatives succeed in attracting talented educators to leadership positions and ultimately in improving student achievement is an empirical question. Currently, there is little evidence about the design of incentives that contribute to these goals.

Incentives for Students

Mastering difficult skills takes hard work. Students who aspire to attend highly competitive colleges know this and do the requisite work. Historically, however, the majority of urban high school students have seen little reason to do the hard work that skill mastery takes. They could obtain enough credits to graduate from high school by doing minimal work in undemanding courses. They correctly perceive that differences in math and reading skills are not rewarded when they apply for entry-level jobs as eighteen year olds. There is always some college that will accept them if they have a diploma (Bishop et al. 2001).

A number of initiatives are under way to improve incentives for students. More than twenty states currently require high school students to pass state-mandated English and mathematics examinations in order to obtain a high school diploma. The intent of these test-based graduation requirements is to create incentives for students to focus greater attention on academic work and to signal to employers that high school graduates do possess basic cognitive skills. But passing these exams does not mean that students are ready for college or the demands of jobs with promising futures. While more than 70 percent of high school graduates enter two- and four-year colleges, more than one-quarter must take remedial English and mathematics courses before registering for courses that provide college credit, and the percentage is much higher for urban students. More than 60 percent of employers rate high school graduates' skills in writing and basic math as only "fair" or "poor" (TAD Project 2004, 2).

A new initiative undertaken by a growing number of states, working together under the auspices of the American Diploma Project, seeks to align high school standards, assessments, and graduation requirements with the knowledge and skills needed for success in postsecondary education and jobs with growth potential. The hope is that this will pro-vide educators and students with clear signals about the adequacy of the work they do together in high schools.

It makes sense for states to align high school standards, assessments, and graduation requirements with the knowledge and skills needed for postsecondary education and work. Public higher educational institu-tions could create incentives for high school students to master the more demanding skills required for high school graduation by commit-ting to use students' scores on recalibrated state exams for college course placement. In other words, knowledge that scoring well on high school exit exams would guarantee acceptance into college courses that count toward degree attainment (as opposed to being funneled into "developmental courses" that do not) would increase students' incen-tives to do the hard work needed to attain mastery of important skills.[12]

There is another benefit of encouraging states to align high school graduation requirements with the skills needed to do college-level work. This would almost inevitably lead states to modify content stan-dards at the earlier grades so that students would be prepared to do more demanding high school work. The net result is likely to be a re-duction in the variation across states in standards and assessments. Moving toward a common set of national standards and assessments makes sense in a country with a mobile population and an increasingly integrated economy.

One caution is the need for care in determining just what skills are important for success after high school graduation. The tendency is to ratchet up standards in areas in which it is relatively easy to measure skills, such as mathematics, and to neglect skills that are critical to suc-cess in a variety of postsecondary educational and work settings, but that are difficult to measure. These include oral communication skills, teamwork skills, and job search and interviewing skills.[13]

A ten-year experimental study of career academies illustrates that reading and math skills are not the only skills important to success after high school. Career academies are schools within schools that embrace three design principles. First, they are generally small learning commu-nities, and are comprised of a group of students embedded within a larger high school who take classes together for at least three years and who are taught by a team of teachers drawn from different disciplines. Second, they offer a college preparatory curriculum with a career theme, which enables students to identify relationships among academic sub-jects and understand how they are applied in a broad field of work. Third, they generally include partnerships with local employers who provide work-based learning opportunities for students enrolled in the academies.

In 1993, one of the nation's leading contract research firms, MDRC, undertook an experimental study of the educational impact of career academies. Nine career academies, for which there was excess student demand, participated. All of these academies were located in urban school districts and served large percentages of students living in poverty. Lotteries were used to determine which interested students were offered places in the career academies. Both the students who were offered places (the treatment group) and those who lost out in the lottery and enrolled in other school programs (the control group) were followed through high school and for four years after graduation. A variety of indicators of success (reading and math scores, course grades, on-time graduation, college enrollment and completion, and labor-market earnings) were measured for all participants.

The results of the career academy evaluation are quite striking. Both treatment and control group members had academic skills, high school graduation rates, and college enrollment rates that were higher, on average, than the national average for students with similar demographic characteristics. (This reflects the greater than average motivation of students who wanted to enroll in career academies.) Yet students who were offered places in the career academies did not fare better on these measures of academic success than the students in the control group. Fortunately, MDRC researchers continued to follow students from the treatment and control groups into the labor market. They found that males who had been offered places in a career academy earned $10,000 (18 percent) more than males in the control group in the four-year follow-up period after high school. The labor-market benefits were especially large for males who were at risk of dropping out of high school at the beginning of the experiment. The likely explanation for this pattern is that enrollment in career academies and the associated opportunities for workplace internships and jobs enabled students to acquire skills that were key to labor-market success, even though they were not captured by scores on standardized reading and math tests (Kemple 2004).

A critical lesson from the MDRC study is the importance of supporting the development and implementation of programs like career academies that offer rich opportunities for urban students to acquire the communication and teamwork skills needed in middle-class workplaces. One way to do this might be to make demonstration of these skills a condition for high school graduation. Of course, doing this would require different and more expensive types of skill assessments than the standardized examinations that states currently use to measure mathematics and English skills. Experimenting with such alternative assess-

ments is crucial in that it might stimulate the development of high
school programs that provide urban students with key skills not captured by scores on standardized reading and mathematics tests.

Incentives and Capacity Building Are Complements

As described above, states and urban school districts have recently introduced a wide variety of policies aimed at improving the alignment
between incentives and the goal of dramatically improving students'
skills. This concern with incentives is a step forward for public education. It is necessary to keep in mind, though, that it is much more
difficult to get incentives right than it is to point out the flaws in current
incentives. Many initiatives that have seemed promising in the past,
such as basing teachers' pay on supervisors' evaluations (sometimes
called "old-style merit pay"), have not improved the performance of
urban school districts (Murnane and Cohen 1986). Moreover, some incentives have elicited dysfunctional responses. Documented examples
include changing students' answers on high stakes tests (Jacob and
Levitt 2003) and suspending students likely to score poorly on such
tests (Figlio 2005).

Stating the incentive challenge in a positive way, people like to do
what they do well (Loewenstein 1999). Consequently, a critical complement to appropriate incentives is a management system that provides
teachers and administrators with the skills to improve student achievement, and students with the consistently high-quality instruction they
need to master important skills.

Catalyzing and Monitoring Progress

As described above, research on the reform efforts of states and urban
school districts over the last twenty years offers guidelines about the
elements of successful school improvement strategies and promising
changes in incentives. These are steps forward. Still, guidelines are not
recipes. Every district will need to work out the details of its strategy for
systemic change and improved incentives.

Given the power of inertia, it is essential to catalyze change. Given
the potential for mistakes in designing and implementing systemic improvements and new incentives, it is crucial to monitor whether changes
are resulting in better education. Two types of information can be important in catalyzing change and monitoring progress. The first comes
from the choices that parents make about where to send their children

to school. The second comes from systematic evaluations of student outcomes. I consider each in turn.

A Role for School Choice

One source of information about the effectiveness of incentives and school management initiatives are parents' choices about where to send their children to school. Parents with significant financial resources who are unhappy with their child's public school can either move to a school district with better public schools or send their child to a private school. Historically, low-income parents have typically lacked these options.

In an attempt to provide parents with choices, many urban school districts have established public school choice programs. While details vary greatly among districts, choice plans typically allow parents to rank their school preferences, and then a system that gives priority to neighborhood students and their siblings (and sometimes to racial balance) is used to determine assignments to oversubscribed schools. The 2001 No Child Left Behind law takes school choice a step further by mandating that school districts provide school choices for children currently attending schools that have not made adequate yearly progress for two years in a row.

Most public school choice plans suffer from two related problems. First, the supply of effective schools does not grow over time. Many parents consequently do not get their first choices and remain frustrated with their children's schooling options. Second, schools that are not popular among parents are typically filled with students who lose out in the lottery. There are thus no strong signals to the educators staffing these schools that the schools need to change or close.

In recent years, forty states have passed legislation that supports the creation of charter schools, which are publicly funded schools that typically establish their own curricula and do not operate under many of the rules that constrain conventional public schools. There are currently almost four thousand charter schools in the United States serving approximately one million students.

Supporters of charter schools envision two types of benefits. The first is that they provide new schooling options for parents who are dissatisfied with conventional public schools and lack the resources to use private schools. Second, by competing with conventional public schools for money and students, they will catalyze improvement in public schools. One plausible improvement mechanism is that the potential loss of students to private schools will nudge urban school districts and teacher unions toward contract revisions that offer a better alignment of incentives with school district improvement goals.

A related initiative is the call to have public education funding follow students. In other words, a particular funding level would be attached to each student, with the level higher for students with documented special learning needs. Whether a conventional public school or a charter school, every public school would operate on the revenues from the students it attracted. If a student changed schools, the funding would move with the student. The aim of this proposal is to establish strong incentives for school districts and individual schools to create educational programs that appeal to parents and students.

In principle, both charter schools and funding that follows students make sense as components of a strategy to improve urban education. Nevertheless, whether they fulfill their promise depends critically on the details of the laws and rules governing their operation. To cite just one example, currently urban charter schools are less likely to serve students with special needs than are conventional urban public schools. Whether this puts conventional urban districts at a disadvantage in competing for students depends critically on whether funding formulas accurately reflect the extra costs of educating children with special needs.

Currently, charter schools laws and school funding formulas vary enormously across states. It is much easier to start a charter school in some states than in others. In some states, charter schools are significantly disadvantaged relative to conventional public schools in access to funding and physical facilities. In other states the playing field is more equal. In yet other states, legislation and rules make it difficult for public schools to compete with charter schools. Much needs to be learned about the tensions between designs of charter school laws and funding formulas that encourage the creation of educational alternatives and designs that create a level playing field on which schools can compete for students as well as funding.

Monitoring Progress

Advances in computer-based administrative record keeping and data retrieval make it increasingly possible to monitor a variety of student outcomes. For instance, most urban districts presently have, or could develop, the data-analytic capacity to monitor progress in attracting and retaining a skilled teaching force. Critical data to track would be the percentage of new teachers hired before the start of the school year, the number of teachers who apply for openings in schools targeted for improvement, and these schools' success in attracting and retaining their first choices.

A second important type of information consists of longitudinal data on students' mathematics and reading skills. Such data can support the tracking of students' achievement growth over time—something that can be especially crucial in judging the performance of schools serving extremely mobile student populations. For example, some of these schools have low average test scores, but have achieved significant success in increasing the achievement of students who had spent the entire year at the school. Identifying such schools is critical to making informed judgments about which schools are doing a good job under difficult circumstances and which schools are in need of significant intervention.

Another area in which better data are available than in the past concerns outcomes for high school students. A growing number of states, for example, have statewide student tracking systems that provide more accurate information on student dropout rates than was available in the past. It is also possible now at a relatively low cost to track the college progress of high school graduates of particular schools or districts through a service called StudentTracker, provided by the National Student Clearinghouse. As stated on its Web site, this service supplies answers to the following questions:

- Where did my program's former participants enroll in college?
- How long did their educational efforts persist?
- Did they transfer between colleges?
- Did they receive a college degree? If so, which degree?
- Where did they graduate from college?
- What was their college major?[14]

Tracking this information over time would produce important evidence of the progress that urban high schools are making in preparing students to thrive after graduation.

A National Problem Requiring a National Solution

Putting in place the type of systemwide school improvement plan and incentives described in this chapter will improve urban schools. Yet urban school districts cannot do these things on their own. Progress will also depend critically on state and federal policies.

State collective bargaining laws play an important role in either facilitating or hindering changes in incentives for teachers and school administrators. State school finance policies influence whether urban districts have the resources to serve intensely disadvantaged student populations. State educational accountability systems influence the incentives for skilled teachers to work in urban school systems, and the consequences when schools are judged to be failing or succeeding.

Federal government policies also influence urban school districts in significant ways. For example, No Child Left Behind creates strong pressures on urban districts to improve the reading and math scores of all groups of students defined by race/ethnicity, and poverty and special education status. While this is the law's strength, it also has great weaknesses that affect urban school districts. By placing schools and districts in only one of two categories (making adequate yearly progress or failing to), for example, the law does not distinguish between schools in drastic need of intervention, and those that are making progress with most groups of students. Another respect in which federal government education policies matter is in supporting research. The federal government provides a significant portion of the funding for research on the consequences of systemic reform strategies as well as new incentives for educators and students. This research is critical to increasing the knowledge base available to policymakers charged with improving urban schools.

In closing, I return to the image of urban schools as mirrors. The accomplishments and failures of children growing up in large cities reveal a great deal about the nation's success in providing high-quality education to urban students. Yet they also reflect the nation's success in providing employment, health care, and public safety to city dwellers. Finally, they provide us with an image of the future of U.S. cities. For all these reasons, improving the lives of urban children is a pressing national priority.

Notes

1. I would like to thank Patricia Albjerg Graham, Robert Inman, and Thomas Payzant for helpful comments on an earlier draft of this chapter, and Elisabeth Duursma for research assistance.

2. Figure 9.1 is taken from Levy and Murnane (2004).

3. Figure 9.2 is based on data taken from the U.S. Current Population Survey.

4. Figure 9.3 is a revised version of a figure that originally appeared in Autor, Levy, and Murnane (2003).

5. Figure 9.4 is constructed from data taken from the U.S. Current Population Survey, as reported on the Economic Policy website: http://www.epi.org/content.cfm/datazone_dznational.

6. Data are from U.S. Current Population Survey and were taken from the Economic Policy Institute Data Zone, available at http://www.epinet.org/datazone/05/wagebyed_a.xls.

7. This description of standards-based educational reforms is taken from Levy and Murnane (2004, 134–35).

8. For a discussion of the strengths and weaknesses of No Child Left Behind, see Murnane (2007).

9. For a discussion of this line of reasoning, see Freeman (1985).

10. For a discussion of the elements of urban school district reform, see Reville (2007).

11. This description of the evidence about how to teach English-language-learners effectively is taken from Francis, Lesaux, and August (2006).

12. The text in this section borrows heavily from Murnane (2007).

13. For a discussion of the reason these skills are increasingly important in workplaces full of computers, see Levy and Murnane (2004).

14. Information copied from the following Web site on April 17, 2007: http://www.nslc.org/outreach/default.htm. The Web site reports that the National Student Clearinghouse currently provides information for students attending more than twenty-nine hundred institutions. Currently, 91 percent of the nation's college and university students are enrolled in these institutions.

References

Autor, David H., Frank Levy, and Richard J. Murnane. 2003. The Skill Content of Recent Technological Change: An Empirical Exploration. *Quarterly Journal of Economics* 118 (4): 1279–1333.

Becker, Howard S. 1952. The Career of the Chicago Public School Teacher. *American Journal of Sociology* 57 (5): 470–77.

Bishop, John H., Ferran Mane, Michael Bishop, and Joan Moriarty. 2001. The Role of End-of-Course Exams and Minimal Competency Exams in Standards-Based Reforms. Brookings Papers in Education Policy. Washington, DC: Brookings.

Cantrell, Steven, Jon Fullerton, Thomas J. Kane, and Douglas O. Staiger. 2007. National Board Certification and Teacher Effectiveness: Evidence from a Random Assignment Experiment. National Bureau of Economic Research Economics of Education Workshop, Cambridge, MA.

Clotfelter, Charles T., Elizabeth Glennie, Helen F. Ladd, and Jacob Vigdor. 2006. Would Higher Salaries Keep Teachers in High-Poverty Schools? Evidence from a Policy Intervention in North Carolina. NBER working paper no. 12285. Cambridge, MA: National Bureau of Economic Research.

Corcoran, Sean P., William N. Evans, and Robert M. Schwab. 2004. Women, the Labor Market, and the Declining Relative Quality of Teachers. *Journal of Policy Analysis and Management* 23 (3): 449–70.

Coleman, James S., Ernest Q. Campbell, Carol J. Hobson, James McPartland, Alexander M. Mood, Frederic D. Weinfeld, and Robert L. York. 1966. *Equality of Educational Opportunity*. Washington, DC: Office of Education, U.S. Department of Health, Education, and Welfare.

Elmore, Richard F. 2002. Bridging the Gap between Standards and Achievement: The Imperative for Professional Development in Education. Washington, DC: Albert Shanker Institute.

Evans, William N., Sheila E. Murray, and Robert M. Schwab. 1999. The Impact of Court-Mandated School Finance Reform. In *Equity and Adequacy in Edu-*

*cation Finance: Collected Pape*rs, ed. Helen F. Ladd, 72–98. Washington, DC: National Academies Press.

Figlio, David N. 2005. Testing, Crime, and Punishment. NBER working paper no. 11194. Cambridge, MA: National Bureau of Economic Research.

Francis, David J., Nonie K. Lesaux, and Diane L. August. 2006. Language of Instruction for Language Minority Learners. In *Developing Literacy in a Second Language: Report of the National Literacy Panel*, ed. Diane L. August and Timothy Shanahan, 365–414. Mahwah, NJ: Erlbaum Associates.

Freeman, Richard Barry. 1985. *What Do Unions Do*. New York: Basic Books.

Graham, Patricia Albjerg. 2006. *Schooling America: How the Public Schools Meet the Nation's Changing Needs*. New York: Oxford University Press.

Hanushek, Eric A. 1994. *Making Schools Work: Improving Performance and Controlling Costs*. Washington, DC: Brookings.

Hanushek, Eric A., and Steven G. Rivkin. 2006. School Quality and the Black-White Achievement Gap. NBER working paper no. 12651. Cambridge, MA: National Bureau of Economic Research.

Hess, Frederick M., ed. 2005. *Urban School Reform: Lessons from San Diego*. Cambridge, MA: Harvard Education Press.

Jacob, Brian A., and Steven D. Levitt. 2003. Rotten Apples: An Investigation of the Prevalence and Predictors of Teacher Cheating. *Quarterly Journal of Economics* 118 (3): 843–77.

Johnson, Susan Moore, Morgean L. Donaldson, Mindy Sick Munger, John P. Papay, and Emily Kalejs Qazibash. 2007. *Leading the Local: Teachers Union Presidents Speak on Change, Challenges*. Education Sector Reports. Washington, DC: Education Sector.

Kemple, James J. 2004. Career Academies: Impacts on Labor Market Outcomes and Educational Attainment. New York: MDRC.

Lavy, Victor. 2007. Using Performance-Based Pay to Improve the Quality of Teachers. *Future of Children* 17 (1): 87–109.

Levy, Frank, and Richard J. Murnane. 2004. *The New Division of Labor: How Computers Are Creating the Next Labor Market*. Princeton, NJ: Princeton University Press.

Loewenstein, George. 1999. Because It Is There: The Challenge of Mountaineering—for Utility Theory. *Kyklos* 52 (3): 315–44.

Murnane, Richard J. 2007. Improving the Education of Children Living in Poverty. *Future of Children* 17, no. 2 (Fall): 161–82.

Murnane, Richard J., and David K. Cohen. 1986. Merit Pay and the Evaluation Problem: Why Most Merit Pay Plans Fail and a Few Survive. *Harvard Educational Review* 56 (1): 1–17.

Murnane, Richard J., and Frank Levy. 1996. *Teaching the New Basic Skills*. New York: Free Press.

Quint, Janet. 2006. Meeting Five Critical Challenges of High School Reform. New York: MDRC.

Reville, S. Paul, ed. 2007. *A Decade of Urban School Reform: Persistence and Progress in the Boston Public Schools*. Cambridge, MA: Harvard Education Press.

Rice, Jacob Mayer. 1969. *The Public-School System of the United States*. New York: Arno Press.

Riis, Jacob A. 1892. *The Children of the Poor*. New York: Scribner's Sons.

Sharkey, Nancy S., and Richard J. Murnane. 2006. Tough Choices in Designing a Formative Assessment System. *American Journal of Education* 112 (4): 572–88.

Sizer, Theodore R. 1968. The Schools in the City. In *The Metropolitan Enigma*, ed. James Q. Wilson, 311–49. Cambridge, MA: Harvard University Press.

TAD Project. 2004. Ready or Not: Creating a High School Diploma That Counts. Executive summary. Washington, DC: Achieve.

U.S. Department of Education, National Center for Education Statistics. 2005. *The Condition of Education, 2005*. NCES 2005-094, table 14.2, 142. Washington, DC: U.S. Government Printing Office.

10

Crime

CRIME IN THE CITY

PHILIP J. COOK

THE GREAT EPIDEMIC of youth violence that swept the nation's cities beginning in the mid-1980s finally crested in 1993, and has largely subsided since then.[1] In many cities, rates of crime and violence are now at levels not seen since the Kennedy era. The remarkable turnaround has contributed to the current golden age in New York, Chicago, and elsewhere.

The epidemic has generated some important lessons. The first is that safe streets are a necessary platform for neighborhood growth and prosperity. Thus the notion that poverty is the mother of crime has been turned on its head. Second, a city's violence rates can be extraordinarily volatile. The homicide victimization rate for young black men increased by a factor of ten in Washington, DC, during the crack era of the late 1980s—not because the city was invaded by violent newcomers but because of the drug-related conflict engendered within the existing population. The traditional "root causes" of crime—poverty, lack of parenting, and limited licit opportunities—were operating in the background, but those factors only created a potential for trouble; the realization of that potential depended greatly on the immediate circumstances. Third, police resources and tactics have a direct effect on the crime rate.

This last lesson is perhaps most surprising and remains contentious. Criminologists and police chiefs had long agreed on one thing: that police bore no responsibility for the everyday violence in the city because they had no way to prevent it. But beliefs have changed. New policing strategies were introduced during the epidemic—most prominently, problem-solving "community" policing and "broken windows" order-maintenance policing—coupled with a new generation of chiefs who have declared they are accountable for lowering crime. And criminologists have provided some systematic evidence in support of their new strategies, although it is less than decisive. The great crime decline of the 1990s made most any intervention look good. In any event, there is solid evidence that more resources devoted to policing are generally productive in reducing crime.

The cities have also benefited from a secular decline in crimes like burglary and motor vehicle theft, for reasons that are even less well understood than the decline of violence. Private self-protection activities may get part of the credit. The private security industry continues to grow faster than public policing. Technical innovations have improved alarm and surveillance systems, which at the same time have become more pervasive. These innovations have the effect of improving the quality of information that private citizens provide law enforcement, and hence increasing the productivity of policing. But there is reason to believe that private cooperation remains a scarce resource, currently undersupplied. One key to more efficient crime control may be enhanced incentives for households and businesses to cooperate with the public aspects of the crime-control task.

The quest for efficiency is motivated in part by the burgeoning costs of the current criminal justice system, especially incarceration. The prison and jail population has quadrupled since 1980, imposing a considerable burden on taxpayers, not to mention the prisoners themselves. For African American males under age forty who lack a high school diploma, imprisonment is almost as prevalent as licit employment. The quest for solutions to this evident failure of social policy can take two obvious directions: improve licit opportunities, or be more parsimonious in the use of prisons. But a third possibility is also promising: namely, finding a more efficient public-private mix in crime control.

Crime Measurement, Patterns, and Trends

This section sets the stage for subsequent analysis by providing a brief introduction to crime measurement, and then characterizing trends and patterns in crime.

Measurement and Data Sources

The volume, trend, and patterns of crime can be measured by the use of three sorts of data. The best-known source is the Federal Bureau of Investigation's (FBI) Uniform Crime Reports (UCR). Thousands of local law-enforcement agencies keep records of crimes reported or otherwise known to them, and of arrests, and compile this information according to definitions and guidelines provided by the UCR system. These compilations are forwarded to the FBI directly or through a state-level agency. Of the various crime categories included in the FBI's crime index, four indicate the volume of serious violence—rape, robbery (muggings, stickups, and other instances of theft through force or threat), aggravated as-

sault (attacks that inflict or threaten serious injury), and criminal homicide. The UCR also tabulates data on reported burglaries (break-ins for
the purpose of theft or other crime), larcenies, and motor vehicle thefts.

Most agencies are quite faithful in tabulating and forwarding UCR
data, but those data are necessarily an incomplete representation of serious crime. While the police are informed about almost all homicides,
the same thing cannot be said about property crimes or even serious
crimes of nonfatal violence, only a fraction of which are ever reported
to the police. To unveil this "dark figure of crime," the U.S. Department
of Justice implemented an alternative system for measuring the volume
of violence and other common crime in 1973. Since then, the National
Crime Victimization Survey (NCVS) has contacted large samples of
households (currently about forty-five thousand) to inquire whether
any members age twelve and over have become crime victims during
the preceding six months, and if so, to request details. The resulting estimates tend to be substantially larger than the UCR counts, and are also
useful in providing the statistical basis for analyzing demographic patterns of violence—both of the victims and the perpetrators (based on
the respondents' reports of their impression of the age, race, sex, and
number of assailants). The limitations of the NCVS data are intrinsic to
the survey approach: the data are too sparse to provide reliable estimates of rates or trends of serious violence at the state or local level, or
to supply sufficient data on rare events to support even national estimates.[2] For that reason and the more obvious one (a survey requires a
live respondent), the NCVS includes no information on homicides.

Fortunately that gap is filled by a third source: the Vital Statistics system. Coroners and medical examiners around the nation report the results of their investigations of deaths, which are compiled at the state
and national level under the aegis of the National Center for Health
Statistics. These mortality data are generally considered the most reliable source of information on homicide-victimization rates and patterns
(Wiersema, Loftin, and McDowall 2000), although they are somewhat
limited—the Vital Statistics provide no information on suspects or the
circumstances of the homicide.

It is possible to estimate trends and patterns in the *commission* rates of
violent crime for different demographic groups, although that is necessarily more speculative. Arrest data provide some guidance, but most
violent crimes do not result in an arrest and there is no reason to believe
that arrestees are a representative sample of perpetrators. The NCVS
data on assault and robbery perpetrators are better in that respect, but
limited by small numbers and the ability of the respondents to recount
the demographic characteristics of their assailant. Perhaps the most
useful information is once again for homicide. Most police departments

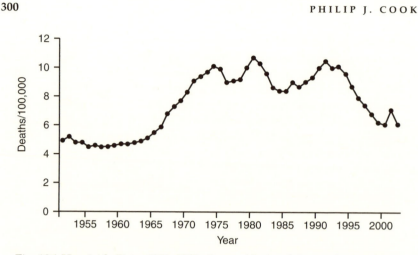

Fig. 10.1 Homicide Rate, 1951–2002. *Source*: National Center for Health Statistics, http://www.ojp.usdoj.gov/bjs/glance/tables/hmrttab.htm.

provide detailed data on homicides as part of the UCR. The Supplementary Homicide Reports include the demographic characteristics of one or more suspects, and these characteristics in the remaining cases can be imputed using reasonable assumptions (Fox 2000; Cook and Laub 2002).[3]

Trends

Homicide rates, the most reliable indicator of violence, have followed a low-high-low pattern during the postwar period (figure 10.1). During the 1950s, homicide rates were about five per hundred thousand residents. In 1964, rates began heading decisively upward, doubling by the end of the Vietnam era. There was some variation off this new high level for the next twenty years, with peaks in 1980 and 1991. A remarkable decline during the 1990s leveled out in 2000 at a rate approaching that of the early 1960s.[4]

For the period since 1973, the NCVS data provide victimization estimates that suggest that nonfatal violence has followed a similar trend. In particular, victimization rates for violent crime varied in a narrow range until 1994, and then dropped to less than half by 2002 (figure 10.2). The UCR robbery rates have followed homicide rates closely throughout this period (Blumstein 2000; Blumstein and Rosenfeld 2007).

The NCVS data for property crime victimization indicate a sustained downward trajectory since 1980; the current rate is just one-third the

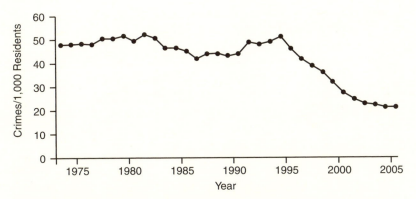

Fig. 10.2 Violent Crime Rate, 1973–2005. *Note*: Violent crimes included are rape, robbery, aggravated and simple assault, and homicide. *Source*: National Crime Victimization Survey, http://www.ojp.usdoj.gov/bjs/glance/tables/viortrdtab.htm.

peak level (figure 10.3). Crime trends based on the UCR police statistics tell a similar story. For example, the NCVS burglary rate per one thousand households declined 70 percent since 1980 (from one hundred to thirty); during the same period, the UCR burglary rate per resident (which includes commercial burglaries) declined 57 percent.

The extraordinary reduction in violent crime during the 1990s has been the object of extensive exegesis, by economists and others (Blumstein and Wallman 2000; Cook and Laub 2002; Zimring 2007; Blumstein and Wallman 2006). No expert predicted this decline, and it remains something of a mystery. Steven Levitt (2004) provides a survey of potential causes. He first notes that the decline was quite universal, affecting all demographic groups and geographic areas. With respect to urbanicity, he observes that the greatest percentage improvements occurred within metropolitan statistical areas and especially among large cities with populations over 250,000. In fact, all the twenty-five largest cities experienced noteworthy declines in homicide rates from their peak year (mostly in the early 1990s) to 2001—declines that ranged as high as 73 percent for New York and San Diego. Based on his analysis, Levitt ends up awarding credit for the crime drop to increases in the number of police, the rising prison population, the receding crack epidemic, and the legalization of abortion through *Roe v. Wade*. His claim for the importance of abortion liberalization is controversial, to say the least (Joyce 2004), but the rest of the list is widely endorsed by experts. His judgment about what is *not* important to the crime drop includes the sustained

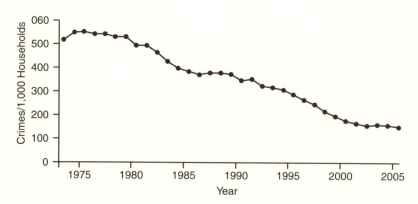

Fig. 10.3 Property Crime Rate, 1973–2005. *Note*: Property crimes include burglary, theft, and motor vehicle theft. *Source*: National Crime Victimization Survey, http://www.ojp.usdoj.gov/bjs/glance/tables/prop trdtab.htm.

economic growth in the 1990s, and the much-ballyhooed innovations in policing in New York and elsewhere.

Crime rates during the period 1984 to 2001 provide a graphic demonstration of their potential volatility, particularly for local areas and specific groups.[5] Most notable was the nationwide epidemic in minority-youth violence that began in the mid-1980s and peaked in 1993, subsiding thereafter. For African American males, homicide commission rates increased by a factor of five for the thirteen to seventeen age group, and by a factor of nearly three for those aged eighteen to twenty-four (Cook and Laub 2002). For individual cities the swings were still larger: homicide involvement by young black men in Washington, DC, increased by a factor of ten during this period. The remarkable conclusion is that similar "fundamentals" of socioeconomic status are compatible with a homicide rate of both X and 10X, given relatively minor changes in circumstances. Franklin Zimring (2007, 206) concludes his analysis of the crime drop by noting, "Whatever else is now known about crime in America, the most important lesson of the 1990s was that major changes in rates of crime can happen without major changes in the social fabric." That observation, reasonable as it sounds, is a rather profound revision of preepidemic conventional wisdom.

Patterns in Urban Crime

Despite the volatility of crime rates, the geography of crime tends to be rather stable and predictable. Any large city's crime map lights up in those neighborhoods that are also characterized by a high concentration of disadvantaged minorities, joblessness, single-parent households, drug abuse, substandard housing, inadequate public services, and high population turnover. It is only reasonable to suppose that this confluence of conditions holds the key to understanding the social and economic conditions that foster crime. Indeed, community characteristics associated with economic and social disadvantage are often seen as the root causes of youth crime and violence.

In the late 1960s, coinciding with the first postwar surge in crime rates, three presidential commissions argued in their final reports that redressing such problems was a necessary precondition for reversing the trend. The first of these, known as the President's Commission on Law Enforcement and the Administration of Justice (1967), opined that "the underlying problems are ones that the criminal justice system can do little about. . . . They concern the Commission deeply, for unless society does take concerted action to change the general conditions and attitudes that are associated with crime, no improvement in law enforcement and administration of justice, . . . will be of much avail." The report of the National Advisory Commission on Civil Disorders, the U.S. Kerner Commission (1968), assigned much of the blame for the urban riots of the 1960s on the effects of racism, with the call for action couched in the now-famous observation that "our nation is moving toward two societies, one black, one white—separate and unequal." One year later, the U.S. National Commission on the Causes and Prevention of Violence (1969, xix) observed that "violence is like a fever in the body politic: it is but the symptom of some more basic pathology which must be cured before the fever will disappear." Further, "the way in which we can make the greatest progress toward reducing violence in America is by taking the actions necessary to improve the conditions of family and community life for all who live in our cities, and especially for the poor who are concentrated in the ghetto slums" (xxi).

Socioeconomic conditions, then, served not only as an explanation for patterns of violence but also as the preeminent candidates for intervention. Reducing disparity and disadvantage was presented as a feasible option, and the *only* approach that could do much good. While the 1960s are long gone, it seems fair to say that this perspective is still influential. These days we may be more sanguine about the ability of the police and prisons to reduce crime, and less sanguine about the feasibility of correcting root cause conditions, but there remains a sense among many social scientists that the community, shaped in part by the larger societal context, is ultimately the right place to look for a satisfactory explanation of crime patterns.

Much of the systematic evidence available on the relationship between crime rates and environmental or "ecological" (the more common term) characteristics derives from multivariate regression analysis

TABLE 10.1

Regression Analysis of Robbery and Homicide Rates/100,000 Residents in the 200 Largest U.S. Counties (48 States), 1990 and 2000

	(All variables are in natural log form)			
Explanatory variable	*Robbery 1990*	*Robbery 2000*	*Homicide 1990*	*Homicide 2000*
Intercept	**–13.402**	–10.57	**–8.937**	–8.174
Population	0.104	0.114	0.061	0.065
Population/square mile	**0.138**	0.079	0.080	0.009
Per capita income	0.466	–0.260	–0.401	–0.761
Income inequality (Gini coefficient)	**1.394**	**1.564**	**1.685**	**1.349**
Female head: % of all families	**1.207**	**1.648**	**1.100**	**1.594**
Black: % of population	**0.328**	0.125	**0.318**	**0.193**
Hispanic: % of population	**0.081**	0.026	0.060	0.025
Movers: % of population that moved in previous 5 years	**1.539**	**1.671**	**1.598**	**1.948**
College: % of population age 25+ with 4 years	–0.466	–0.162	**–0.611**	–0.246
R-squared	80%	51%	76%	62%

Notes: Bold font indicates significantly different from 0 at $p < 5\%$, 2-tailed test. The sample for both 1990 and 2000 consists of the 200-largest counties by population in 1990.

on cross-sections of data on jurisdictions. (The jurisdictions may be anything from states down to Census tracts.) These studies typically include an eclectic list of explanatory factors.[6] A recent example gives the flavor of these studies. Morgan Kelly (2000) analyzed crime rates in 1991 for the two hundred largest U.S. counties, utilizing a variety of demographic and socioeconomic factors as explanatory variables. I have followed his lead, but with some modifications in his original regression specification.[7] The results for robbery and homicide for 1990 and 2000 are reported in table 10.1.

The crime data are derived from the FBI's UCRs, and all other variables are from the decennial Censuses. Since all variables are in log form, the coefficients are conveniently interpreted as "elasticities"—the percentage change in the dependent variable (crime rate) associated with a 1 percent increase in the explanatory variable. Thus, according to these results, a 1 percent increase in the county's population was associated in 2000 with a 0.11 percent increase in the robbery rate, and a 0.06 percent increase in the homicide rate, conditioned on the other explanatory variables.

These results provide general support for the root causes perspective for both the near-peak year (1990) and the postdecline year (2000) of the violence epidemic. Across urban counties, both robbery and homicide rates increase markedly with the prevalence of female-headed (one-parent) families; with population instability (as measured by the percentage of the population that changed addresses in the preceding five years); with income inequality, as measured by the Gini coefficient on household incomes; and with the prevalence of blacks in the population. The weak relationship with population and population density is surprising: contrary to expectation, the effects tend to be quite small and, with one exception, statistically insignificant.[8] As it turns out, one consequence of the differentially paced crime drop during the 1990s was to largely eliminate the long-established association between population size and violent crime rates for cities above 250,000.[9]

This type of study is the statistical equivalent of the crime map, demonstrating that serious violent crime rates tend to be highest in areas with the greatest disadvantage. Beyond that general finding, the results should be taken with a considerable grain of salt. Because different measures of "disadvantage" tend to be highly correlated with each other across jurisdictions, it is difficult to sort out the separate effects of, say, inequality, the prevalence of female-headed households, and the prevalence of those with a college education.[10] And there is a more fundamental problem: a statistical analysis of natural cross-section variation, while suggestive, really says little about causation. (For example, residential turnover may be just as much an effect as a cause of crime.) That fact was largely ignored by those panels of experts from the 1960s quoted above (Wilson 1974).

In any event, the criminogenic factors identified in the cross-section regressions for 1990 and 2000 did not improve during the 1990s. The national income inequality increased markedly, in fact, as did the prevalence of single-parent households. Furthermore, in the two-hundred-county sample, there was little tendency for the counties that showed relative improvement in these factors to exhibit a larger drop in robberies or murders than other counties. When the regression is run on decade-long changes in the variables, the only statistically significant coefficient is for "percent female-headed households" in the case of murder; for robbery there are two marginally significant coefficients, for "percent black" and "percent college." An analysis of changes from 1980 to 1990 also found little in the way of statistical associations.[11]

The 1990s' experience—the large across-the-board reduction in crime without much progress in the socioeconomic fundamentals—is hopeful, in a way. It creates the possibility that crime rates can change dramatically independently of changes in the fundamental socioeconomic conditions. Thus, crime is not only volatile but also potentially malleable, with policies more feasible and immediate than those required to "reshape society."

Costs of Crime

In assessing crime policy, the costs of crime and the costs of crime prevention are equally important (Becker 1968). Reducing the total cost of crime and crime prevention becomes an important public goal, along with the goals of promoting greater justice and equity. Hence, whether it is worthwhile to increase resources devoted to public law enforcement depends in part on whether the projected reduction in crime has value greater than the additional expenditure. Getting the accounting right on the value of crime reduction is vital to setting priorities.

The Public Costs of Crime Prevention

The accounting of relevant crime-prevention costs begins with direct public expenditures. Table 10.2 provides a summary for 2003. In that year the total expenditure was $195 billion ($670 per capita), about half of which was expended by counties and cities. Most local expenditures were for policing ($58 billion), although county governments also have substantial responsibility for courts and jails. When compared with the total expenditures by local governments, including education, transportation, and all else, police services account for about 5 percent.

Figures 10.4 and 10.5 demonstrate the considerable growth in expenditures on criminal justice over the last quarter century. Adjusting for inflation and population growth, the expenditures per capita have grown most rapidly at the federal level (for which the 2004 level was 3.2 times the 1982 level), then the state level (2.3 times), and then the local (1.9 times), trending toward greater parity across the three levels of government. Across functions, the largest growth has been in corrections (where the real expenditure per capita increased by a factor of 2.75), reflecting the burgeoning prison and jail populations.

There appears to be consensus among experts that the extraordinary run-up in the jail and prison population since 1980 (from a half million to over 2.2 million) gets some of the credit for the crime drop (Blumstein and Wallman 2006; Levitt 2004). But that has come at considerable cost, both direct and indirect. The high rates of imprisonment have been a particular burden on the African American community. Steven Raphael

TABLE 10.2
Criminal Justice Expenditures, 2003

| | *$billions* | | | |
	Total	Police	Judicial/legal	Corrections
Local	94	58	18	19
State	66	11	16	39
Federal	35	20	9	6
Total[a]	195	89	43	64

Note: The total entries are computed by summing the column entries. Those sums disagree with the "total" statistics from the *Sourcebook*, which are: total, 185; police, 83; judicial/legal, 42; and corrections, 61.

Source: Bureau of Justice Statistics, *Sourcebook of Criminal Justice Statistics Online,* http://www.albany.edu/sourcebook/pdf/t122003.pdf.

and Melissa Sills (2007, 526) report that roughly 11 percent of black men aged eighteen to forty were imprisoned as of 2000. For high school dropouts in this demographic group, there are almost as many institutionalized as employed; in fact, for those aged twenty-six to thirty, 34 percent were institutionalized compared with 30 percent employed (ibid., 528). The high institutionalization rates for black males leaves a

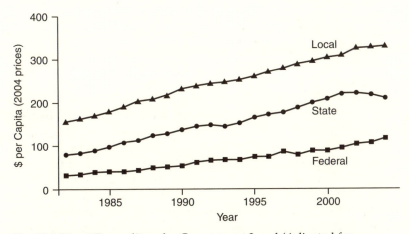

Fig. 10.4 Direct Expenditure by Government Level (Adjusted for Inflation and Population Growth). *Source*: Annual Government Finance Survey and Annual Survey of Public Employment, http://www.ojp .usdoj.gov/bjs/glance/tables/expgovtab.htm.

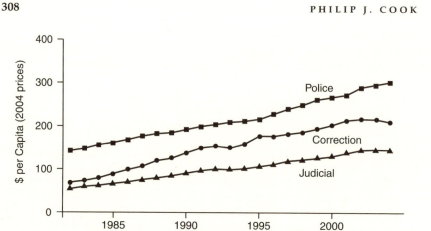

Fig. 10.5 Direct Expenditure by Criminal Justice Function (Adjusted for Inflation and Population Growth) *Source*: Annual Government Finance Survey and Annual Survey of Public Employment, http://www.ojp.usdoj .gov/bjs/glance/tables/exptyptab.htm.

demographic gap in poorer minority communities, with important implications for family and community life. Those who are not actually in prison are likely to have a felony record, limiting their licit employment opportunities (Travis 2005; Western 2006). These ancillary effects of imprisonment should loom large in assessing alternative strategies to control crime.

Economists may debate whether the current level of imprisonment is too high or low, based on a crude comparison between the estimated marginal costs and benefits, but there is no reason to believe that the current allocation of imprisonment is "efficient" from a crime-control perspective. Much of the growth in imprisonment is accounted for by longer sentences (Blumstein and Beck 2005), which have sharply diminishing returns with respect to both deterrence and incapacitation.[12] There is a strong argument to be made for the greater use of "intermediate" sanctions such as fines and intensive supervision in the community (Morris and Tonry 1990). The fact that the seven hundred thousand prisoners released each year usually receive little supervision or support suggests that a larger investment in prisoner reintegration might help reduce the high recidivism rate (about half returned to prison within three years).[13] Furthermore, at the margin there are arguably more cost-effective uses of the corrections budget in prevention, such as preschool education or programs to encourage high school graduation (Donohue and Siegelman 1998; Lochner and Moretti 2004). A worthy quest is to identify and implement an effective crime-control strategy that economizes on the use of prison.

Private Costs of Security, Precaution, and Victimization

The private provision of protection against crime is also costly. The Economic Census (conducted once every five years by the U.S. Census Bureau) provides an estimate of receipts of the private security industry in 2002 as $30 billion, as compared to $80 billion in public expenditures on police protection.[14] (There may be some overlap in these numbers, since governments hire private security for some purposes.) But estimates of the number of employees suggest something closer to parity. According to the Economic Census, there were just over one million police employees in 2002 (of which 75 percent were sworn officers), compared with 754,000 private security employees. In the decade from 1992 to 2002, private security employment grew 34 percent, compared to a 27 percent growth for police employees. Currently, then, there are about as many private security employees as sworn officers.[15]

The costs to businesses, organizations, and households of crime prevention, avoidance, and victimization involve much more than the expenditures on criminal justice programs and private security. Crime and especially the threat of criminal victimization play a pervasive role in the life of the city. Shoplifting and fraud increase the cost of doing business for retailers. Vandalism, open-air drug dealing, prostitution, and loitering by gang members are neighborhood disamenities, with tangible impacts on real estate values and the patronage of local retailers. Perhaps most important is the threat of violence; people who have a choice will avoid dangerous neighborhoods, opting instead to live, work, shop, attend school, and recreate in safer places. In particular, Julie Barry Cullen and Steven Levitt (1999) demonstrated that crime has a powerful effect on residential decisions. For people who do not have the means to relocate from crime-impacted neighborhoods, fear and seclusion may become a fact of life. This point was documented by the Moving to Opportunity experiment (which provided vouchers to low-income families to relocate in Boston and four other cities); by far the most important reason that families signed up for the program was the fear of crime and violence in the housing projects (Katz, Kling, and Liebman 2003).

Estimating the social cost of crime is challenging because so much of it is subjective. One approach to placing a dollar value on commodities like "safety from criminal victimization"—commodities that are not traded in the marketplace—is the contingent-valuation method. Economists have used this method most often in valuing environmental protection, but

Jens Ludwig and I adapted the method to valuing a reduction in the threat of gun assault in a community (Cook and Ludwig 2000; Ludwig and Cook 2001). We asked a nationally representative survey sample a series of questions about how much they would be willing to pay in increased taxes for a program that would reduce interpersonal gun violence in their community by 30 percent. Based on the results, we estimated that the value of a 30 percent reduction to individuals would have been $24 billion in 1995, suggesting that the total burden was about $80 billion. This method has also been used to value general reductions in crime (Cohen 2005).

An alternative approach is to construct an estimate by adding up across the various elements of crime costs, both tangible (expenditures on security or medical costs from assault-related injuries) and intangible, being careful not to double count. A heroic effort to estimate the total for the United States by David Anderson (1999) arrived at an annual figure of $1.1 trillion for the mid-1990s. Included in this figure were the value of risks to life and health from violent crime ($574 billion), time spent securing assets ($90 billion), and "crime-induced production" ($397 billion, covering everything from drug trafficking to small arms purchases to expenditures by Mothers against Drunk Driving). Ludwig (2006) updated this figure using data circa 2004, offering a new total of $2 trillion, over $6,000 per capita.

Violent crime is a prominent component of these estimates, and reducing serious violence deserves correspondingly high priority. It is interesting to place this point in an international context. Compared with other developed nations, the United States has the reputation of having exceptionally crime-ridden cities. But in fact, the United States compares favorably with other countries for common crimes of theft and burglary—it is robbery and assault in which we tend to be relatively high (Zimring and Hawkins 1997). For homicide, the victimization rate in the United States is a multiple of that in other developed nations, combining, as we do, a high assault rate with ready access to guns (Hemenway 2004). An emphasis on violence is also justified by the U.S. public's values. In their contingent-valuation study of a nationally representative sample of Americans, Mark Cohen and his associates (2004) found a greater willingness to pay for a 10 percent reduction in homicide or rape than a 10 percent reduction of the far-more-common crime of burglary.

These attempts at valuation are static, while the effects of crime on a city neighborhood may well evolve over time. Indeed, effective crime control can do much to revitalize a blighted neighborhood. Without a doubt the great crime reduction of the 1990s gets some of the credit for the urban renaissance that occurred in one large city after another beginning in that period, with New York being the most notable case in point (Schwartz, Susin, and Voicu 2003). (President Bill Clinton would not have wanted his office in Harlem back in 1980.) None of the available estimates of the cost of crime successfully captures this dynamic, transformative possibility.

Note that we have now come full circle. The geography of crime is closely linked to socioeconomic disadvantage, as suggested by the regression results in the previous section. It is quite reasonable to believe that income inequality, broken families, and limited education all create fertile ground for criminal activity. But the reverse may also be true. If crime rates are brought down to levels that are more acceptable to middle-class households, then more of them may choose urban over suburban living—a process that will eventually change the socioeconomic makeup in ways associated with lower crime rates.

While crime has a large effect on the standard of living in cities, public responsibility for criminal justice policy is divided between local, state, and federal governments. In particular, courts, prisons, and parole are state and federal matters. The most important city and county responsibility is policing.

Police and Crime Control

Police have the lead responsibility for responding to and preventing crime. Criminologists have traditionally questioned whether the police in fact have much influence on crime rates, and when crime is rising many a chief has blamed youth culture, the breakdown of family life, or unemployment. But a series of innovations in police management and methods, to some extent coincident with the crime drop of the 1990s, have led to a dramatic change in rhetoric. Now, big-city police chiefs publicly embrace responsibility for controlling crime and seek guidance from evaluation research about how best to do so. Criminologists continue to debate best practice, but have become more open to the possibility that policing matters. Understanding just how it matters, and how it can be most effective, requires a strategic analysis of how the police interact with other institutions and the public at large.

More Police, Less Crime

David Bayley (1994), one of the leading academic experts on policing, has opined that "the police do not prevent crime. Experts know it, the police know it, but the public does not know it." As evidence of the public's ignorance in this respect, in 1994 Congress enacted the Violent Crime Control and Law Enforcement Act, which provided funding to local police departments to hire thousands of new police officers. Thanks in part to this federal funding, the number of police did increase substantially during the decade, peaking at 246 police for every 100,000 people in 1999 (Zimring 2007, 178). Along with this expanding work-force came innovations in police deployment and management.

The first question is whether additional resources in policing tend to be deployed effectively, without regard to specific technique or strategy. It has proven difficult to statistically sort out the crime-control effect of police resources, since the causal connection goes both ways—cities may hire additional police *in response* to a crime increase. But several studies have found persuasive ways to isolate the causal effect of police resources on crime. William Evans and Emily Owens (2005) analyzed the effects of the Office of Community Oriented Policing Services (COPS) funding on crime, finding that cities did indeed hire additional police after receiving federal funding, and that the result was reduced crime rates. Another study analyzed variation in police presence in Washington, DC, resulting from changes in the terror alert level, finding that the deployment of additional police reduced crime rates, especially on the National Mall (Klick and Tabarrok 2005). In England and Wales, the Street Crime Initiative provided funding for antirobbery policing in ten of the forty-three police-force areas, with large, statistically discernible effects on robbery rates (Machin and Marie 2005). Other studies have of-fered additional support for the conclusion that extra police suppress crime rates (Levitt 2002; McCrary 2002; Levitt and Miles 2007). The ef-fect sizes are large enough to make a strong case for expanded police funding (Donohue and Ludwig 2007). While the "black box" nature of these estimates is somewhat troublesome—surely it matters how ex-actly the resources are used—it appears true that police departments know how to put additional resources to effective use.

It should be noted that most all the evaluations of increased policing have been incomplete, in the sense that they have failed to measure the ancillary costs and benefits. The expansion of policing may well result in an increase in downstream costs associated with additional arrests, convictions, and incarcerations—but not necessarily, and there is no good evidence on this matter (Levitt and Miles 2007).[16] Furthermore, the increase in public policing may well have an effect on private security and self-protection efforts—an area that has been almost entirely ne-glected in these evaluations.

Innovations in Policing

Surely the crime-control effects of police personnel and expenditures depend on organization and tactics. If so, the answer to the question of whether it is worthwhile to expand policing may well be, "It depends."

The evidence reviewed in the previous section suggests that there are cost-effective uses for additional police resources, and police chiefs typically know enough to make use of them. But there remains a good deal of debate about the *most* efficient use of resources.

A review of the evidence on police practice by an expert panel of the National Academy of Sciences (Skogan and Frydl 2004, 5) defined these innovations relative to the traditional "standard model" of policing, which consists of preventive patrols, rapid responses to 911 calls, follow-up investigations by detectives, and unfocused enforcement efforts. Police departments innovated away from this standard model by adopting more focused tactics designed to address specific problems, such as gun use by drug-dealing gangs or "hot spot" locations where crimes are frequently reported. William Bratton, appointed New York Police commissioner in 1994, took this approach another step by combining focused policing with a new management accountability system, familiarly known as COMPSTAT. In this system, precinct commanders are given considerable authority, responsibility, and discretion over resources, coupled with responsibility for reducing crime in their command areas. Weekly meetings are held at headquarters to discuss solutions to emerging crime problems in each of the precincts, as documented by the COMPSTAT Report (a computerized version of the old pin map), and a wide range of qualitative information at the borough and precinct level. The focus on reducing crime, rather than on process-oriented performance measures (response times to 911 calls, arrest rates, and complaints), is a profound change.

In many departments, proactive, focused policing has been embedded in one of two broad strategies. The first is community policing, in which the police seek to develop a productive working relationship with the community that encourages cooperation in crime prevention, including the identification and solution of neighborhood problems. The traditional emblematic features of community policing were Neighborhood Watch organizations and foot patrol by police in high-crime neighborhoods; more recently, the focus is on information-sharing and problem-specific operational partnerships with community organizations. The 1994 act that provided federal funding for more police also created COPS in the U.S. Department of Justice, thus giving a federal imprimatur to this strategy.

An alternative strategy known as broken windows policing (also known as order-maintenance, "zero-tolerance," and "quality-of-life" policing) has also garnered converts among police departments. The approach has its origin in an essay in the *Atlantic Monthly* by James Q. Wilson and George Kelling (1982). It was adopted by Bratton, and has been credited by him and others with the New York "miracle" (Kelling and Sousa 2001; Bratton and Knobler 1998). The theory behind this approach is that minor social disorder, such as graffiti, litter, public drinking, panhandling, and abandoned buildings, engenders crime by serving as a signal that normal social control has broken down (Harcourt and Ludwig 2006). Its implementation in New York and elsewhere has taken the form of aggressive policing with numerous arrests for public-disorder misdemeanors, sometimes at the cost of good relations with the community.

Objective evaluations of the New York innovations—COMPSTAT and aggressive order-maintenance policing—have reached differing conclusions (Harcourt and Ludwig 2006; Rosenfeld, Fornango, and Baumer 2005; Rosenfeld, Fornango, and Rengifo 2007; Zimring 2007). A broader consensus has emerged supporting the efficacy of concentrating police resources in hot spots, and directing patrols against illicit gun carrying and other criminogenic activities and circumstances (Sherman 2002; Cohen and Ludwig 2003; Braga 2005; Eck and Maguire 2000; Skogan and Frydl 2004). And it is hard to argue with the problem-solving approach embraced by most big-city police departments that seeks to prevent crime by finding ways to intervene where there is an ongoing source of trouble—a rowdy bar, perhaps, or a feud between rival gangs, or a dealer selling guns to youths and criminals. Effective interventions may require bringing in other government agencies (the alcohol licensing authority, for example), or enlisting the help of churches and other groups that have credibility and influence on the street.

No matter how creative the problem solving, though, a zero crime rate is not a realistic goal. Zero tolerance is a myth. Faced with inevitable scarcity of their capacity for effective action and the resulting trade-offs, the police necessarily set priorities with respect to the various services they provide the community and among different crime problems. A case in point is the now-famous Operation Ceasefire, organized by the Boston Police Department working with other law-enforcement agencies and a team of analysts from Harvard. Confronted with a surge in lethal violence by drug-dealing gangs, they announced a program that focused enforcement efforts on the misuse of guns. In the absence of gunplay, gangs could continue dealing drugs subject to no more than the usual enforcement effort, but gang members were informed directly that gunplay by any one member of a gang would result in a heavy police crackdown on all the gang's activities (Kennedy, Piehl, and Braga 1996). The priority on gun misuse is also a long-standing feature of policing in Chicago (Cook et al. 2007). The emphasis on guns over drugs has been widely endorsed by the public. The appropriate priorities are of course a value judgment, which ideally should in some sense represent the interests of the community, diverse though they may be (Moore 2002).

Police chiefs can no longer get away with denying responsibility for crime in their cities. Accountability for crime reduction has stimulated interest in evaluation information about effective approaches to crime control. But reliable information is scarce indeed. The "technology" (if that is the right word) of crime control is as complex as any other social process.

Private Inputs in Crime Control

Private security, and private crime-control efforts more generally, constitute an unwritten chapter in the recent literature on "what works" in crime-control policy. Observed crime rates and patterns reflect private choices regarding cooperation and self-protection (Clotfelter 1977; Cook 1986). A systematic approach to public crime control requires an understanding of the potential interactions between private and public efforts.

A place to begin the discussion of this complex topic is with the private security industry. The current scope of the private security industry is difficult to assess, but as previously recounted, the number of employees is at least as large as the number of sworn officers. It encompasses proprietary (in-house) security, guard and patrol services, alarm services, private investigators, armored car services, and security consultants as well as security equipment (Cunningham, Strauchs, and Van Meter 1990). Private security supplements and in some cases substitutes for public action: for example, businesses in many instances investigate and resolve employee theft and fraud without ever going public. More generally, as noted by Brian Forst (1999, 19), "the central functions of policing—preserving domestic peace and order, preventing and responding to crimes—have always been conducted first, foremost, and predominantly by private means. . . . Most crimes still are not reported to the police."

Private security guards (and police officers who moonlight as private security guards) serve a narrow purpose—namely, to protect the property and people they are hired to protect. The term of art is "situational crime prevention" (Clarke 1983). The guard's job is accomplished if the robbers avoid their bank or the bank's corporate executives are not kidnapped, or rowdy teenagers are successfully kicked out of the guard's shopping mall, or the would-be burglar does not enter the gated community. "Rather than deterring crime through the threat of detection, arrest, and punishment, private policing tries to regulate behavior and circumstances to diminish the possibility that crime will occur" (Bayley and Shearing 2001, 18).

An obvious possibility is that the crime will simply be displaced to other, unguarded victims and places. If private security does not prevent but only redistributes crime, then its public value (as opposed to private) is nil, and it creates serious equity concerns.[17]

While displacement is a legitimate concern, it is not the whole story. Lucrative opportunities, if unguarded, are likely to generate crime that would not otherwise occur. In Isaac Ehrlich's (1974) classic formulation, the supply of offenses is a function of the relative wage rate to licit and illicit activities. An increase in the net return (payoff per unit of effort) to crime will stimulate participation in criminal activity. He postulates that the payoffs to property crimes "depend, primarily, on the level of transferable assets in the community, that is, on opportunities provided by potential victims of crime" (87). But if the most lucrative "transferable assets" are well protected, then the payoffs to crime and crime rates are reduced. Of course, it is the most lucrative targets that do tend to be the best guarded. Banks invest more in security against robbery than, say, travel agencies. Jewelry stores display costume jewelry on open racks, but keep the real thing in glass cases wired with alarms. People with meager assets do not need bodyguards to protect against being kidnapped for ransom. Credit card companies have instituted elaborate systems for preventing fraudulent use.

In fact, there is a reasonable concern that some private precautionary activities are undersupplied due to the moral hazard created by insurance and even the police. For example, a vehicle left unlocked in a public location invites theft, but the owner may be willing to accept that risk knowing that the police will attempt to recover the vehicle at public expense if it is reported stolen—and that in any event, the owner is insured against theft for most of the vehicle's value. The same considerations may dictate against purchasing alarms and other antitheft devices. In response, insurance companies may provide a discount on theft insurance to owners who install such devices, and twelve states mandate these discounts. The mandate reflects a perceived public interest in increasing private precaution in this case.

Not all private actions to prevent or mitigate crime are limited to one's own household or business. The notion of community suggests neighbors looking out for each other, including with respect to crime. A tight-knit community may limit opportunities for crime by controlling the streets and sidewalks, keeping strangers under surveillance, and placing a check on local teenagers. This idea was given a scientific basis utilizing data from the Project on Human Development in Chicago Neighborhoods. A survey-based measure labeled "community efficacy" (a combination of items measuring informal social control and social cohesion) was found to be highly negatively correlated with crime and violence rates, even after accounting for some other features of the neighborhood (Sampson, Raudenbush, and Earls 1997). There is great interest and apparent success in crafting deliberate interventions to strengthen social control through public-private partnerships mobilized to confront chronic youthful offenders (Kennedy 2007).

In sum, private security and precautionary activities reduce crime rates by reducing the quality of criminal opportunities, and in that sense supplement public policing. Both are necessary. Private measures cannot cope efficiently with lawlessness—they need to be backed up by police with their extraordinary power of arrest. Public and private efforts are further interrelated by the fact that effective law enforcement requires close cooperation with the community.

Increasing Private Input to Public Law Enforcement

One important aspect of the police department's mission is to reduce crime. Despite the newfound interest in prevention, much police work remains reactive. Crimes that are not reported to the police by private citizens will never be investigated. If the victim does not cooperate with the investigation, it will likely be dropped, and if witnesses are not cooperative, it is unlikely to go very far. In this set of transactions, we might say that public safety is being produced with inputs of both law-enforcement resources and information from private citizens (Clotfelter 1993). The resulting enhancement of public safety benefits the entire community.

While the police depend on the public to report crimes, assist in investigations, and serve as witnesses in court, these key inputs are uncompensated, and are supplied in some cases at considerable personal cost, inconvenience, and the risk of retaliation. Even victims are unlikely to benefit in any tangible way from cooperation with police, and most victims do not bother to report the crime.[18] In essence, the citizens who become involved in a crime are invited to make a charitable contribution of their time and possibly their safety, in exchange for knowing that they have done a good deed for their community. Better cooperation from victims and other citizens would increase police effectiveness, but it would help to better align private incentives.

A good place to start in eliciting greater cooperation might be reducing the private costs of cooperating. State victim-compensation programs provide some incentive for victims who are injured in violent attacks, since payment is contingent on reporting the crime. (Private insurance policies often stipulate that police be informed of a property theft as well.) Witness coordinators in criminal court can assist victims and other state witnesses in scheduling and understanding court proceedings. Police can offer some protection for witnesses that fear retaliation, although local resources for such efforts tend to be all too meager (Kocieniewski 2007).

In some instances the information needed for a successful investigation of crimes requires some prior action. For example, in the case of motor vehicle theft, it is helpful to investigators to be able to prove the rightful ownership of a vehicle or its constituent parts. Registered vehicle identification numbers (VINs) do not discourage theft directly (since they are hidden) but do facilitate building a legal case against a chop shop owner and others involved in the network. In fact, the federal government requires VINs on various parts of new vehicles. The result is to create a general deterrent to theft—a result that could not be achieved without government regulation. (The self-interested vehicle owner receives little benefit from their own vehicle's VIN, and would not be willing to pay the cost voluntarily.) A similar logic applies to electronic tracking devices such as Lojack. Ian Ayres and Steven Levitt (1998) demonstrated that Lojack has large positive externalities in deterring auto theft. Because much of the benefit is external, the likely result is that too few people will voluntarily equip their vehicles with Lojack.[19]

Information is needed to prevent serious crimes as well as solve them. In the spate of school rampage shootings that culminated in Columbine, one of the commonalities was that the perpetrators had shared their plans with their classmates, and that the classmates had not seen fit to report this information to authorities (Newman 2004). While the causes of these distressing events were multiple and diffuse, a targeted prevention strategy would necessarily give high priority to persuading adolescents to pass on such information. There is a strong parallel here, of course, to terrorist conspiracies of all kinds post–9/11. More mundane is the routine urban problem of gun carrying by dangerous people, where before there is an actual victim there is a possibility of preempting violence by alerting the police. With that thought a number of police departments, including New York's, have established programs that offer a generous reward for a tip leading to the arrest of a gun violator, with guarantees that the tipster remains anonymous.

More broadly, it is important for the police to be viewed as serving the interests of the community. Developing a healthy working partnership between the police and the community is the essence of the community-policing ideal.[20]

Summary and Advice to City Officials

Crime control deserves priority in urban policymaking. High crime rates are a drag on community development and a great burden on households that cannot afford to move out. The successful control of theft, vandalism, public disorder (often associated with drug selling), and especially violence sets the stage for increasing property values, investment, job growth, and a higher standard of living. The fact that most large cities are far safer today than in 1990 has contributed to their growth and prosperity. But crime rates can be remarkably volatile—more so than other social indicators—and require continuing attention.

What recent history teaches us is that large fluctuations in crime rates can occur without much change in the underlying socioeconomic conditions. While crime tends to be concentrated in low-resource neighborhoods year in and year out, crime rates are not uniquely determined by the socioeconomic conditions. That is fortunate. If eradicating entrenched problems of race, class, and culture were a precondition to successful crime reduction, then the crime agenda would have to be put on hold for a generation. But that is clearly not the case. Crime is a problem worth the mayor's attention because there is hope of making progress.

Of course, many of the policies that influence crime rates in a city are not under the control of city government. It is the state legislatures that write the criminal code and establish sentencing rules for judges. Corrections is primarily a state or federal function as well. A host of other state and federal policies and programs outside the criminal justice system arguably affect crime rates—to name a few, those influencing immigration, gun availability, the price of alcohol, mental health treatment, abortion policy, child care, school attendance laws, insurance regulation, and the regulation of violent content in the media. Yet the mayor's portfolio is by no means empty.

Front and center is the police department. One lesson from the crime drop in the 1990s is that police provide an effective deterrent to crime, and that increasing resources in policing has generally reduced crime. Part of the credit may go to innovations in policing tactics and management, although that is not entirely clear. With greater respect for the powers of the police has come a greater demand for evidence on what works in terms of organization and tactics. It is entirely appropriate to hold police chiefs responsible for controlling crime, just as school administrators are now held responsible for improving test scores.

The police operate in the context of the communities they serve. A strategic analysis of crime control should consider ways to encourage the public to do its part to restrict criminal opportunities and increase the strength of the criminal justice deterrent. It cannot be irrelevant that there are as many private security guards as sworn officers nationwide, performing somewhat overlapping functions. Businesses and households make myriad decisions that influence their exposure to criminal victimization and (collectively) the profitability of crime. The criminal justice system certainly has a key role, but it depends to a large extent on the voluntary cooperation of the public. Victims and other members of the public are called on to provide costly and largely uncompensated inputs in producing the public good of safe streets.

It is not easy to translate this discussion into a set of concrete recommendations of general applicability. Here is a rough cut of five broad recommendations that rest in part on the themes of defining public value in crime control, recognizing the importance of private efforts in determining criminal opportunity, and addressing the uncertainties concerning police organization and tactics:

1. Set a high priority on reducing lethal violence. It has deleterious effects on the life of the city that go far beyond the immediate victims.

2. Hold police chiefs accountable for reducing crime, and give them the resources they need, possibly including more officers and the cooperation of other public agencies that may be helpful in problem solving.

3. Pay particular attention to the problems of eliciting voluntary cooperation by the community, and whether police tactics are exacerbating those problems. Seek ways to reduce the costs and risks of cooperation, and experiment with monetary rewards.

4. Move beyond small-scale problem solving to organize higher-level strategic planning exercises in how to address important crime problems, bringing together the relevant private and public parties. Boston's Operation Ceasefire is one model.

5. Stay humble. Crime rates fluctuate in an unpredictable fashion, and crime control is far from an exact science. One long-term goal is to learn more about what works in the city, which requires a capacity to both innovate and evaluate.

Notes

1. Brian Forst, David Kennedy, Jens Ludwig, Michael Tonry, Joel Wallman, and Frank Zimring offered useful suggestions to earlier drafts of this chapter. Erin Hye Won Kim provided excellent research assistance.

2. Surprisingly, the NCVS "uncovers" fewer of the most serious assaults than are known to the police. The NCVS estimate of the number of nonfatal gunshot wounds is low by a factor of three, probably because so many of the victims are beyond the reach of the survey sampling frame—they are hospitalized or incarcerated, or have no fixed address (Cook 1985).

3. The FBI also manages the National Incident-Based Reporting System, in which police departments submit specified data items on each crime incident involving an index crime. This program has a low participation rate, and only covered about 16 percent of the U.S. population in 2003 (http://www.ojp .usdoj.gov/bjs/nibrsstatus.htm).

4. It should be noted that the long-term trend in homicide rates is not an entirely reliable index of criminal behavior. Technological changes in both medical

treatment and weaponry have changed the likelihood that a serious assault will result in the death of the victim. On the one hand, trauma care has improved a good deal, and the current homicide rate would be somewhat higher but for improved emergency medical response and lifesaving procedures for severely wounded victims. On the other hand, the firearms used by assailants have "improved," with increased power and rapidity of fire (Wintemute 2000).

5. Edward Glaeser, Bruce Sacerdote, and Jose Scheinkman (1996, 507) observe that "the high variance of crime rates across time and space is one of the oldest puzzles in the social sciences; this variance appears too high to be explained by changes in the exogenous costs and benefits of crime." They analyze the effects of social interactions as a possible explanation for volatility, finding evidence that such interactions are particularly important for crimes of theft.

6. For a systematic search for structural factors that influence state-level homicide rates, see Land, McCall, and Cohen (1990).

7. In particular, the following changes were made. First, his "percent non-white" was replaced with "percent black" and "percent Hispanic" for the sake of greater specificity. Second, his variable on police expenditures per capita was dropped, since it is plausibly the effect rather than the cause of crime. Third, also dropped was the "percent of population age sixteen to twenty-four"; he included it because that is the most crime-prone age group, but as it turns out its cross-section variation signals which counties have a relatively large population of college students—a group that is not particularly crime prone. He included the male unemployment rate, which did not perform well and was dropped in this specification. Finally, he reports the results of Poisson regression, while the results here are from ordinary least squares—a change that makes little difference in practice.

8. While the unit of observation for these regressions is the county, the characteristics of the state in which the county is located may also be relevant. State governments provide a large share of the funding for the courts and criminal corrections, and differ with respect to criminal law and procedure as it affects robbery and criminal-homicide cases. States also differ with respect to the level of contribution to local finances and service provision. For these reasons, I reran the regressions reported above controlling for the state in which the county is located. The results are similar in all respects to those reported above.

9. Although robbery has long been the quintessential urban crime, in recent years robbery rates are about the same for midsize cities (250,000 to 500,000) and larger cities. The same is true for homicide rates. For an analysis of why crime (used to) increase with the population, see Glaeser and Sacerdote (1999).

10. The right interpretation of these results is also clouded by the aggregation problem. We are either observing the sum of individual propensities or some characteristic that reflects interactions within the community. Robert Sampson, Stephen Raudenbush, and Fenton Earls offered the sociological view that the quality of interactions within the community, and particularly mutual trust, are important. They propose the term "collective efficacy" as a characteristic of communities that predicts the extent of informal social control that limits criminal activity (Sampson, Raudenbush, and Earls 1997; Harcourt and Ludwig 2006).

11. I ran regressions for changes in log crime rates, 1990–2000, as a function

of changes in the independent variables, also in log form. I ran the same regressions for the period 1980–1990. None of the variables "perform" especially well. For robbery, seven of the covariates have estimated coefficients that either switch signs across the two periods or have "perverse" signs in both periods. The "percent black" is significantly positive for the 1990s, but significantly negative for the 1980s. The R2 ranged from 0.4 percent to 7.0 percent for the four regressions.

12. Doubling prison sentences will have an incapacitation effect that is less than double, since criminals tend to "age out" and desist from crime. Doubling prison sentences will have a muted deterrent effect because of the universal tendency to discount the future. The second five years of a ten-year sentence will tend to be heavily discounted relative to the first five years (Cook 1980).

13. A National Research Council (2008, 85) report concluded that there was adequate evidence to support a greater investment in cognitive-behavioral interventions with released prisoners; further, drug treatment coupled with frequent testing, and comprehensive multiservice employment and training programs, were deemed promising.

14. The receipts and employment for the private security industry are taken from the Economic Census for 2002, industry NAICS 5616 (excluding locksmiths). For a complete report, see http://www.census.gov/prod/ec02/ec0256i06.pdf.

15. Two other national surveys also provide estimates of the number of private security employees: the Current Population Survey and the U.S. Census Bureau's County Business Patterns. Estimates for 2002 from the three sources are in rough agreement: 754,000 (Economic Census), 724,000 (Current Population Survey), and 715,000 (County Business Patterns).

16. In principle, the increase in police presence could increase the number of arrests or reduce them, since additional police increase the probability of arrest per crime and reduce the number of crimes. The effect on the number of arrests (the product of the probability per crime and the number of crimes) will depend on the relative proportionate changes in these two variables. Possible relationships between crime, arrest, and policing are explored in Freeman, Grogger, and Sonstelie (1996).

17. Further, there is a danger that affluent people will become less willing to support public policing if they are purchasing private protection (Bayley and Shearing 2001, 30).

18. The National Crime Victimization Survey for 2005 found that 40 percent of property crimes and 47 percent of violent crimes were reported to the police.

19. It should be noted that self-protection activities can have *negative* externalities. Particularly problematic is the inclination to keep and carry firearms for self-protection purposes. Although the matter is hotly contested, the best evidence suggests that a high density of private gun ownership in a community increases both the homicide rate (Cook and Ludwig 2006) and the burglary rate (Cook and Ludwig 2003); the latter is probably due to the fact that firearms are easily fenced loot, so that communities with a high density of gun ownership are relatively lucrative to burglars. For a contrary view, see Philipson and Posner (1996).

20. For example, Durham, North Carolina, has organized the Community Response to Violent Acts for those crimes likely to engender retaliation. The re-

sponse consists of a door-to-door canvasing of the neighborhood where the crime occurred and the victim's residence by the Durham Police Department, partnering agencies and organizations, clergy, and concerned citizens. The canvas is designed primarily to develop investigative leads in the case by asking neighbors to come forward with information that may assist investigators in solving and prosecuting the case.

References

Anderson, David A. 1999. The Aggregate Burden of Crime. *Journal of Law and Economics* 42, no. 2 (October): 611–42.

Ayres, Ian, and Steven D. Levitt. 1998. Measuring Positive Externalities from Unobservable Victim Precautions: An Empirical Analysis of Lojack. *Quarterly Journal of Economics* 113 (1): 43–77.

Bayley, David H. 1994. *Police for the Future.* New York: Oxford University Press.

Bayley, David H., and Clifford Shearing. 2001. The New Structure of Policing: Description, Conceptualization, and Research Agenda. Washington, DC: National Institute of Justice.

Becker, Gary S. 1968. Crime and Punishment: An Economic Approach. *Journal of Political Economy* 76 (2): 169–217.

Blumstein, Alfred. 2000. Disaggregating the Violence Trends. In *The Crime Drop in America*, ed. Alfred Blumstein and Joel Wallman, 13–44. New York: Cambridge University Press.

Blumstein, Alfred, and Allen J. Beck. 2005. Reentry as a Transient State between Liberty and Recommitment. In *Prisoner Reentry and Crime in America*, ed. Jeremy Travis and Christy Visher, 50–79. New York: Cambridge University Press.

Blumstein, Alfred, and Richard Rosenfeld. 2007. Factors Contributing to U.S. Crime Trends. Paper prepared for the National Research Council Understanding Crime Trends workshop, Washington, DC, April 24–25.

Blumstein, Alfred, and Joel Wallman. 2000. *The Crime Drop in America.* New York: Cambridge University Press.

———. 2006. The Crime Drop and Beyond. *Annual Review of Law and Social Science* 2: 125–46.

Braga, Anthony A. 2005. Hot Spots Policing and Crime Prevention: A Systematic Review of Randomized Controlled Trials. *Journal of Experimental Criminology* 1: 317–42.

Bratton, William, and Peter Knobler. 1998. *Turnaround: How America's Top Cop Reversed the Crime Epidemic.* New York: Random House.

Clarke, Ronald V. 1983. Situational Crime Prevention: Its Theoretical Basis and Practical Scope. In *Crime and Justice: An Annual Review of Research, Vol. 4*, ed. Michael Tonry and Norval Morris, 225–56. Chicago: University of Chicago Press.

Clotfelter, Charles T. 1977. Public Services, Private Substitutes, and the

Demand for Protection against Crime. *American Economic Review* (December): 867–77.

———. 1993. The Private Life of Public Economics. *Southern Economic Journal* 59 (4): 579–96.

Cohen, Jacqueline, and Jens Ludwig. 2003. Policing Gun Crimes. In *Evaluating Gun Policy*, ed. Jens Ludwig and Philip J. Cook, 217–39. Washington, DC: Brookings Institution Press.

Cohen, Mark A. 2005. *The Costs of Crime and Justice*. New York: Routledge.

Cohen, Mark A., Roland T. Rust, Sara Steen, and Simon T. Tidd. 2004. Willingness-to-Pay for Crime Control Programs. *Criminology* 42, no. 1 (February): 89–109.

Cook, Philip J. 1980. Reducing Injury and Death Rates in Robbery. *Policy Analysis* (Winter): 21–45.

———. 1985. The Case of the Missing Victims: Gunshot Woundings in the National Crime Survey. *Journal of Quantitative Criminology* 1 (1): 91–102.

———. 1986. The Relationship between Victim Resistance and Injury in Noncommercial Robbery. *Journal of Legal Studies* 15 (1): 405–16.

Cook, Philip J., and John H. Laub. 2002. After the Epidemic: Recent Trends in Youth Violence in the United States. In *Crime and Justice: A Review of Research*, ed. Michael Tonry, 117–53. Chicago: University of Chicago Press.

Cook, Philip J., and Jens Ludwig. 2000. *Gun Violence: The Real Costs*. New York: Oxford University Press.

———. 2003. The Effects of Gun Prevalence on Burglary: Deterrence vs. Inducement. In *Evaluating Gun Policy*, ed. Jens Ludwig and Philip J. Cook, 74–118. Washington, DC: Brookings Institution Press.

———. 2006. The Social Costs of Gun Ownership. *Journal of Public Economics* 90, nos. 1–2 (January): 379–91.

Cook, Philip J., Jens Ludwig, Sudhir A. Venkatesh, and Anthony A. Braga. 2007. Underground Gun Markets. *Economic Journal* 117, no. 524 (November): 588–618.

Cullen, Julie Berry, and Steven D. Levitt. 1999. Crime, Urban Flight, and the Consequences for Cities. *Review of Economics and Statistics* 81 (2): 159–69.

Cunningham, William C., John J. Strauchs, and Clifford W. Van Meter. 1990. *Private Security Trends, 1970 to 2000: The Hallcrest Report II*. Boston: Butterworth-Heinemann.

Donohue, John J., and Jens Ludwig. 2007. More COPS. *Policy Brief #158*. Washington, DC: Brookings Institution.

Donohue, John J., and Peter Siegelman. 1998. Allocating Resources among Prisons and Social Programs in the Battle against Crime. *Journal of Legal Studies* 27: 1–43.

Eck, John, and Edward Maguire. 2000. Have Changes in Policing Reduced Violent Crime? In *The Crime Drop in America*, ed. Alfred Blumstein and Joel Wallman, 207–65. New York: Cambridge University Press.

Ehrlich, Isaac. 1974. Participation in Illegitimate Activities: An Economic Analysis. In *Essays in the Economics of Crime and Punishment*, ed. Gary S. Becker and William M. Landes, 68–134. New York: National Bureau of Economic Research.

Evans, William N., and Emily Owens. 2005. Flypaper COPS. Working paper. University of Maryland, Department of Economics.

Forst, Brian. 1999. Policing with Legitimacy, Efficiency, and Equity. In *The Privatization of Policing: Two Views*, ed. Brian Forst and Peter Manning, 1–48. Washington, DC: Georgetown University Press.

Fox, James Alan. 2000. Demographics and U.S. Homicide. In *The Crime Drop in America*, ed. Alfred Blumstein and Joel Wallman, 288–317. New York: Cambridge University Press.

Freeman, Scott, Jeffrey Grogger, and Jon Sonstelie. 1996. The Spatial Concentration of Crime. *Journal of Urban Economics* 40 (September): 216–31.

Glaeser, Edward L., and Bruce Sacerdote. 1999. Why Is There More Crime in Cities? *Journal of Political Economy* 107, no. 6 (December): 225–58.

Glaeser, Edward L., Bruce Sacerdote, and Jose A. Scheinkman. 1996. Crime and Social Interactions. *Quarterly Journal of Economics* 111 (2): 507–48.

Harcourt, Bernard E., and Jens Ludwig. 2006. Broken Windows: New Evidence from New York City and a Five-City Social Experiment. *University of Chicago Law Review* 73: 278–87.

Hemenway, David. 2004. *Private Guns, Public Health*. Ann Arbor: University of Michigan Press.

Joyce, Theodore. 2004. Did Legalized Abortion Lower Crime? *Journal of Human Resources* 39 (1): 1–28.

Katz, Lawrence F., Jeffrey R. Kling, and Jeffrey B. Liebman. 2003. The Early Impacts of Moving to Opportunity in Boston. In *Choosing a Better Life: Evaluating the Moving to Opportunity Social Experiment*, ed. John Goering and Judith Feins, 177–211. Washington, DC: Urban Institute Press.

Kelling, George, and William H. Sousa Jr. 2001. Do Police Matter? An Analysis of the Impact of New York City's Policy Reforms. Manhattan Institute Civic report, December.

Kelly, Morgan. 2000. Inequality and Crime. *Review of Economics and Statistics* 82, no. 4 (November): 530–39.

Kennedy, David M. 2007. Making Communities Safer: Youth Violence and Gang Interventions That Work. Testimony before the House Judiciary Subcommittee on Crime, Terrorism, and Homeland Security, February 15.

Kennedy, David M., Anne M. Piehl, and Anthony A. Braga. 1996. Youth Violence in Boston: Gun Markets, Serious Youth Offenders, and a Use-Reduction Strategy. *Law and Contemporary Problems* 59 (1): 147–98.

Klick, Jonathan, and Alexander Tabarrok. 2005. Using Terror Alert Levels to Estimate the Effect of Policy on Crime. *Journal of Law and Economics* 48: 267–79.

Kocieniewski, David. 2007. Few Choices in Shielding of Witnesses. *New York Times*, New York region, October 28.

Land, Kenneth C., Patricia L. McCall, and Lawrence E. Cohen. 1990. Structural Covariates of Homicide Rates: Are There Any Invariances across Time and Social Space? *American Journal of Sociology* 95 (4): 922–63.

Levitt, Steven. 2002. Using Electoral Cycles in Police Hiring to Estimate the Effects of Police on Crime: A Reply. *American Economic Review* 92 (4): 1244–50.

———. 2004. Understanding Why Crime Fell in the 1990s: Four Factors That

Explain the Decline and Six That Do Not. *Journal of Economic Perspectives* 18 (1): 163–90.

Levitt, Steven D., and Thomas J. Miles. 2007. The Empirical Study of Criminal Punishment. In *The Handbook of Law and Economics*, ed. A. Mitchell Polinsky and Steven Shavell, 455–95. Amsterdam: Elsevier Science Publishing.

Lochner, Lance, and Enrico Moretti. 2004. The Effect of Education on Crime: Evidence from Prisoner Inmates, Arrests, and Self-Report. *American Economic Review* 94, no. 1 (March): 155–89.

Ludwig, Jens. 2006. The Costs of Crime. Testimony before the U.S. Committee on the Judiciary, September 19.

Ludwig, Jens, and Philip J. Cook. 2001. The Benefits of Reducing Gun Violence: Evidence from Contingent-Valuation Survey Data. *Journal of Risk and Uncertainty* 22 (3): 207–26.

Machin, Stephen J., and Oliver Marie. 2005. Crime and Police Resources: The Street Crime Initiative. IZA discussion paper no. 1853, November.

McCrary, Justin. 2002. Using Electoral Cycles in Police Hiring to Estimate the Effect of Police on Crime: Comment. *American Economic Review* 92, no. 4 (September): 1236–43.

Moore, Mark H. 2002. *Recognizing Value in Policing: The Challenge of Measuring Police Performance*. Washington, DC: Police Executive Research Forum.

Morris, Norval, and Michael Tonry. 1990. *Between Prison and Probation: Intermediate Punishments in a Rational Sentencing System*. New York: Oxford University Press.

National Research Council. 2008. *Parole, Desistance from Crime, and Community Integration*. Committee on Community Supervision and Desistance from Crime. Washington, DC: National Academies Press.

Newman, Katherine S. 2004. *Rampage: The Social Roots of School Shootings*. New York: Basic Books.

Philipson, Tomas J., and Richard A. Posner. 1996. The Economic Epidemiology of Crime. *Journal of Law and Economics* 39 (October): 405–33.

President's Commission on Law Enforcement and Administration of Justice. 1967. *The Challenge of Crime in a Free Society*. Washington, DC: U.S. Government Printing Office.

Raphael, Steven, and Melissa Sills. 2007. Urban Crime, Race, and the Criminal Justice System in the United States. In *Companion to Urban Economics*, ed. Daniel P. McMillen and Richard Arnott, 515–35. New York: Blackwell Publishing.

Rosenfeld, Richard, Robert Fornango, and Eric Baumer. 2005. Did Ceasefire, Compstat, and Exile Reduce Homicide? *Criminology and Public Policy* 4: 419–50.

Rosenfeld, Richard, Robert Fornango, and Andres Rengifo. 2007. The Impact of Order-Maintenance Policing on New York City Robbery and Homicide Rates: 1988–2001. *Criminology* 45 (2): 355–84.

Sampson, Robert J., Stephen Raudenbush, and Felton Earls. 1997. Neighborhoods and Violent Crime: A Multilevel Study of Collective Efficacy. *Science* 277: 918–24.

Schwartz, Amy Ellen, Scott Susin, and Ioan Voicu. 2003. Has Falling Crime Driven New York City's Real Estate Boom? *Journal of Housing Research* 14 (1): 101–35.

Sherman, Lawrence W. 2002. Fair and Effective Policing. In *Crime: Public Policies for Crime Control*, ed. James Q. Wilson and Joan Petersilia, 383–412. Oakland, CA: Institute for Contemporary Studies.

Skogan, Wesley, and Kathleen Frydl. 2004. *Fairness and Effectiveness in Policing: The Evidence*. Washington, DC: National Academies Press.

Travis, Jeremy. 2005. *But They All Come Back: Facing the Challenges of Prisoner Reentry*. Washington, DC: Urban Institute Press.

U.S. National Commission on the Causes and Prevention of Violence. 1969. *To Establish Justice, to Insure Domestic Tranquility: Final Report*. Washington, DC: U.S. Government Printing Office.

U.S. Kerner Commission. 1968. *Report of the National Advisory Commission on Civil Disorders*. Washington, DC: U.S. Government Printing Office.

Western, Bruce. 2006. *Punishment and Inequality in America*. New York: Russell Sage Foundation.

Wiersema, Brian, Colin Loftin, and David McDowall. 2000. A Comparison of Supplementary Homicide Reports and National Vital Statistics System Homicide Estimates for U.S. Counties. *Homicide Studies* 4:317–40.

Wilson, James Q. 1974. Crime and the Criminologists. *Commentary* 58, no. 1 (July): 47–53.

Wilson, James Q., and George L. Kelling. 1982. Broken Windows: The Police and Neighborhood Safety. *Atlantic Monthly*, March.

Wintemute, Garen. 2000. Guns and Gun Violence. In *The Crime Drop in America*, ed. Alfred Blumstein and Joel Wallman, 45–96. New York: Cambridge University Press.

Zimring, Franklin E. 2007. *The Great American Crime Decline*. New York: Oxford University Press.

Zimring, Franklin E., and Gordon Hawkins. 1997. *Crime Is Not the Problem: Lethal Violence in America*. New York: Oxford University Press.

11

Finances

FINANCING CITY SERVICES

ROBERT P. INMAN

FROM THE FIRST records of economic history it has been true that successful, growing cities are those cities that provide quality public services, initially public infrastructure and civil justice, at a fair price. Between 1000 and 1800, cities governed by exploitative rulers languished and died. Those governed by the collective consent of the landowners, guild masters, burghers, and lords of the surrounding feudal estates thrived. Northern Italian cities grew from 1200 to 1500 when governed as independent republics, and stagnated under Habsburg domination after 1550. Similarly, Belgian cities lost population from 1550 onward with the introduction of Spanish absolutism under the Duke of Alva, again part of the Habsburg dynasty. While the population of Paris doubled from 1500 to 1800 under the rule of the Bourbon kings, the population of London increased twentyfold over the same period following the introduction of constitutional rule in 1650. By 1800, London had become the world's dominant trade and commercial center (see De Long and Shleifer 1993; Hohenberg and Lees 1985). In each instance, the key to economic growth was the combination of a strong comparative advantage for the city's location—whether from ports, access to resources, or natural trading routes—plus the rule of law, low taxation, and quality infrastructure. Matters are no different today. Cities only survive and grow *if* they have compelling economic reasons to exist and *if* the city's public finances enhance, rather than encumber, the city's underlying economic advantage.

The recent economic history of Flint, Michigan, illustrates the consequences for city economies and, most important, city residents when the city loses its comparative economic advantage—in this case, the ability to produce quality cars at a low cost. Feeling the competitive pressure from low-cost, high-quality foreign imports, General Motors made the decision in 1978 to significantly scale back and eventually cease the production of Buick cars and parts in Flint. Over the subsequent twenty years, Flint's population declined by 30 percent, from

170,000 residents to 120,000 residents. The residents who left the city were those with the skills and energy to find work elsewhere; Flint's rate of poverty has risen from 12 percent in 1970 to 27 percent today.

Saint Louis has shown similar declines in city population over the same period, but not because of a sudden adverse shock to its local economy. Here the problem was city public finances. Real value public spending increased at an annual rate of 3.4 percent from 1955 to 2000, compared to a national average rate for all large cities of just 2 percent— a growth rate equal to the growth in real incomes. While the share of city spending in resident incomes, and thus city tax rates, remained roughly constant nationally, in Saint Louis these tax rates nearly doubled. The cause of the spending growth was not improved services but growing public employee compensation. City poverty spending was above average as well, required by state and federal mandates to service the nearly 22 percent of city residents with incomes less than the federal poverty standard. The burden of the rising costs of public employees and poverty transfers fell necessarily on the taxpaying middle class and businesses. Facing a significant gap between the taxes paid and the services received, and with an option to move to attractive suburbs, it is no surprise that firms and households left the city. In 1955, Saint Louis had 51 percent of both the region's employment and residents within its border. Today, only 12 percent of area jobs and residents remain within the city. This chapter takes the example of Saint Louis to heart, and examines systematically what we now know about the economic consequences for residents and firms of managing well, or poorly, the finances of city governments.

City Finances and the City's Economy

The single-best metric for how city finances impact a city's economy is the effect of city policies on the market value of city residential and business properties. The logic is straightforward. To live or do business within the city one needs to own city property. If the city is an attractive place to live and work, then new residents and businesses will wish to move in, and current residents will wish to stay. Those who value the city location most will succeed in owning property within the city at a price that reflects the full benefits of the location. An important component of those benefits is efficiently provided public services: good schools, safe neighborhoods, and clean streets for residents, and a trained workforce, secure business sites, and an effective transportation system for city businesses, all offered at competitive tax rates. Paying for city property is equivalent to "buying a ticket" for the right to consume the private

and public amenities of city life. If the quality of city public services declines, or if city taxes rise without an improvement in city services, then
location in the city is less valuable and the price of city property—the cost
of the ticket—falls. Conversely, if the services improve or the taxes fall,
then the city's property values rise. But by how much? Until the extra
amount paid for city property just equals the value to residents and firms
of the additional current and future services supplied or lower taxes paid.

Evidence from city real estate markets supports the theory. Good
fiscal governance improves city property values; bad fiscal governance
lowers values. Table 11.1 shows the impact of city fiscal policies on median residential home values for a national sample of 252 U.S. cities
over the decade 1980–1990, the most recent decade available at the time
of the study. Four measures of a central city's fiscal policy environment
are highlighted: changes in the rate of poverty within the city over the
decade (*Change in city poverty rate*); the presence of strong city public
employee unions as measured by state laws requiring the city to bargain *only* with a worker-approved union (*Strong unions*); weak city governance allocating budgetary responsibility to a city council with a majority elected from neighborhood wards and whose mayor is chosen by
the city council (*Weak governance*); and whether the city is part of a larger
county where the county finances and provides crucial city services, especially welfare services (*County support*). Each variable is statistically
significant and has a quantitatively important effect on property values
in the affected cities.[1]

Increases in the city's rate of poverty is the most damaging to city
home values, and particularly so for central cities in the larger metropolitan areas (with a Metropolitan Statistical Area [MSA] population
greater than 250,000) where the opportunities for residents and firms to
exit to surrounding suburbs is the greatest. An increase in the city's rate
of poverty from the sample mean of 0.15 to 0.18 (a one standard deviation increase over decade of the 1980s) reduces city home values by
$12,000 or about 25 percent over what they might have been without the
poverty increase. The adverse effect of poverty on value in the smaller
MSAs is a bit less than half as large. It is striking to note that in the larger
MSAs, *suburban* home values also *decline* as city poverty rates increase.[2]
Why? One plausible explanation (suggested in Haughwout and Inman
2002) is that the suburbs' economic fortunes are tied to the productivity
of center-city firms and the attractiveness of the city as a center for consumption. If the fiscal and social burden of poverty end up leading city
firms and residents to leave the city, then city productivity and amenity
benefits may decline, and the attractiveness of the region as a whole is
reduced. Both city and suburban home values fall. Interestingly, the
strong positive effect of county fiscal support on home values indicates

TABLE 11.1
City Finances and City Property Values

	Change in city home values. Mean in 1980 = $48,705	Change in suburban home values. Mean in 1980 = $50,590
Change in city poverty rate: Large MSA (= .03)	−$12,345 (2460)**	−$6,696 (2212)**
Change city poverty rate: Small MSA (= .03)	−$4,997 (2512)*	−1,244 (2261)
Strong unions	−$5,358 (1739)**	−$4,047 (1563)**
Weak governance	−$1,948 (1052)*	−$3,035 (946)**
County support	$6404 (2727)**	$1062 (2479)

* Standard errors reported in parentheses. Indicates the estimated effect on home values is statistically significant at the 90 percent confidence interval.

** Standard errors reported in parentheses. Indicates the estimated effect on home values is statistically significant at the 95 percent confidence interval.

Notes: The dollar values that appear in the table have been computed for a sample's one standard deviation increase in the city rate of poverty (= 0.03); the presence of strong public employee unions protected by state duty-to-bargain rules; the presence of weak city governance as measured by city council control of city budgets with council members elected from neighborhood (ward) districts; and the presence of county fiscal support for some local services, most notably for welfare spending.

Source: Haughwout and Inman (2002, tables 5 and 6).

that these adverse effects of poverty will be muted for cities where suburbs help to fund poverty services—a point I stress below (see table 11.5) as part of the guidelines for well-run city finances.

Strong public employee unions also damage city home values. Cities in states with "duty-to-bargain" rules face, in effect, a monopoly supplier of city public services. Like any monopolist, unions will seek to raise their prices, and if possible sell more of their product at the higher price. Here that means higher wages and the use of more workers than might be efficient at the higher wage. The wider empirical evidence studying the effect of strong unions on city budgets indicates that both effects occur.[3] Further, there is no compelling evidence that strong unions provide a compensating increase in worker productivity (see Freeman 1986; Eberts 2007). It is no surprise, then, that home values in cities—and again in their surrounding suburbs—are lower in cities facing strong unions protected by state duty-to-bargain laws. Residents pay more and get less for their dollars. As a consequence home values decline.

So too does weak governance depress city property values. City government typically takes either of two forms: legislative-only or *council government*, or elected executive or *strong mayor government*. Council governance has a problem, however: policy gridlock. City council members who differ on how best to spend city money may never be able to reach a majoritarian agreement. A majority of the legislators can always team up to disadvantage a minority, but then those in the excluded minority have a strong incentive to offer a slightly better deal to one of the majority members to form a new majority. But then the new minority can respond with a new budget proposal, undo the new majority, and so it goes. The risk is that no budget gets approved. To avoid gridlock, legislators may vote to include *all* new initiatives. Such budgeting is likely to be inefficient, though—much like what happens when a group of friends agrees to share the dinner check. Why order salad when you share the costs of everyone else's steak and lobster? At the end of the evening the dinner bill is expensive, and for the same reasons, so too will be the city's budget. One way to avoid cycling, gridlock, and the inefficient incentives of the shared fiscal check is to independently elect someone to dictate the final budget. This is a strong mayor elected at large with the powers to set budgets and veto amendments. Does it make a difference? The results in table 11.1 show cities run by weak governance rules have significantly lower home values, by perhaps as much as 4 percent (= −$1,948/$48,705).[4]

Finally, table 11.1 shows that increased outside aid to cities improves city home values, measured here by the institutional variable, *County support*, representing the joint city-suburban funding of county services, the most important of which is welfare services for suburban *and* city residents. Such support is a fiscal redistribution from suburban to city taxpayers. City home values rise, but interestingly, suburban home values do not fall as one might expect. The estimated effect of providing fiscal support for the city is slightly positive, though not statistically different from zero. There must be some offsetting benefit for suburban residents from sending money to support city finances, most likely from the economic spillover benefits to suburban residents from being close to a strong city economy.[5]

Tables 11.2 and 11.3 provide a more nuanced look at exactly what it is in city budgets that determines a city's long-run economic vitality. It will be no surprise to learn that improved personal safety, better schools, and lower taxes all enhance city home values. While this conclusion is now well documented generally, the results in tables 11.2 and 11.3 are unique in that they provide estimates of the impact of fiscal

TABLE 11.2
Philadelphia Finances and City Property Values

	Change in city home values Mean in 2000 = $74,119
Change in effective tax rate (= .01)	−$11,829 (3489)*
Change in precinct murder rate (1 murder/precinct)	−$428 (110)*
Change in own block crime rate (= .01)	−$834 (277)*
Change in neighboring block crime rate (= .01)	−$1140 (285)*
Change in neighborhood school test score (= 10%)	$2816 (670)*

* Standard errors reported in parentheses. Indicates the estimated effect on home values is statistically significant at the 95 percent confidence interval.

Notes: The dollar values that appear in the table have been computed for a 1 percent (= 0.01) increase in the city's effective property tax on the home; the effect of an increase in one murder within the home's police precinct raising the average precinct's murder rate from 0.0002 to 0.000217; a 0.01 increase in the home's own block total crime rate (includes robbery, aggravated assault, burglary, theft, and auto theft) from the sample mean crime rate of 0.06; a 0.01 increase in the home's neighboring block total crime rate (includes robbery, aggravated assault, burglary, theft, and auto theft) from the sample mean crime rate of 0.06; and a 10 percent improvement in the math and reading fifth-grade test scores for the home's neighborhood school.

Source: Estimates in table 11.2 are the author's calculations based on results presented in Russo (2008), chapter 1, tables 1 and 3.

policies for individual cities over time.[6] Table 11.2 reports estimates from Karl Russo (2008) of the effects of neighborhood variation in taxes, school performance, and crime rates on home values within Philadelphia. Russo's study uses a sample of sixty-two thousand arm's-length sales of single-family homes in Philadelphia for the years 2000 to 2004. In estimating the effects of fiscal policies on home values, he controls for a long list of house attributes, and by looking at the effects of changes in taxes, crime rates, and school performance within small city neighborhoods over time, he obtains far more precise estimates than usually available. Table 11.3 reports estimates by Andrew Haughwout and his colleagues (2004) of the effects of changes in city average tax rates on changes in city home values and jobs for Houston, Minneapolis, New York City, and Philadelphia separately for the years 1969 to 2000.

From Russo's study of Philadelphia home values, homes whose effective property tax rate rises by 1 percent (approximately a 40 percent increase from the average rate of 2.5 percent) will see their values fall by almost –$12,000 or 16 percent (= –$11,829/$74,119; see table 11.2). Neighborhood crime also lowers home values in Philadelphia. An increase in a police precinct's murder rate by one murder per year reduces the home value in that precinct by $428. This is a reasonable number. It implies a value of a *statistical life* of about $8.2 million, close to the value now used by the Environmental Protection Agency (EPA) to measure the benefits of environmental policies generally.[7] An increase in the rate of nonmurder crimes both within one's own block and on neighboring blocks—crimes such as robberies, assaults, burglaries, and thefts—also depress home values. An increase in the local crime rate of 0.01 from its Philadelphia mean of 0.06 lowers home values from $800 to $1,100. Better neighborhood schools, however, raise home values. In Philadelphia, homes near schools with 10 percent higher test scores are worth $2,816 or 4 percent more on average.

From the study by Haughwout and his colleagues (2004), summarized in table 11.3, we learn that in the four sample cities, higher taxes depress city property values and reduce jobs within the city, *even allowing for the possibly positive effect of increased revenues on city services*. The analysis is specified so that the effect of taxes on the tax base includes any offsetting effects added revenues might have from allowing more spending on valued city services. If taxpayer benefits exceed the revenues paid, then the estimated effects on values and jobs could be positive. This favorable outcome is not observed for the four cities in table 11.3, though. The estimated elasticities of property values and city jobs with respect to city taxes—$\varepsilon_{B,t} = (\Delta B/B)/(\Delta t/t)$—is negative and statistically significant. Higher taxes cost these cities taxpaying residents and firms, and conversely, lower taxes return taxpayers to the city.[8] And interestingly, when the authors tested for a separate positive effect of having a "superstar" mayor—for example, Rudy Giuliani in New York and Ed Rendell in Philadelphia—neither mayor impacted the city tax base favorably, beyond the effects arising from their sound fiscal policies. It is policies that matter, not personalities.

The damage to the private economy of a higher city tax rate is greatest in Houston and smallest in Minneapolis. The estimated negative effect of taxes on property values suggests there is a "fiscal gap" between the costs of the taxes paid and the benefits received by those buying property in the city. It is significant. Haughwout and his colleagues (2004) estimate that Houston and New York City property owners receive *no* additional benefits from the last dollar of property taxes paid. Philadelphia and Minneapolis property owners receive, respectively, an

TABLE 11.3
City Taxes and the City Economy

	Houston's tax base elasticity	Minneapolis' tax base elasticity	New York City's tax base elasticity	Philadelphia's tax base elasticity
Change in the property tax rate	−1.00 (.33)*	−.19 (.06)*	−.75 (.10)*	−.43 (.07)*
Change in the local sales tax rate	—	—	−.49 (.11)*	−.19 (.04)*
Change in the local income or wage tax rate	—	—	−.50 (.15)*	−.06 (.07)
			New York City's job base elasticity	Philadelphia's job base elasticity
Change in the local income or wage tax rate	—	—	−.16 (.05)*	−.36 (.11)*

* Standard errors reported in parentheses. Indicates the estimated effect on home values is statistically significant at the 95 percent confidence interval.

Notes: Rows (1)–(3) present estimates of the elasticity of each individual tax base with respect to its own tax rate. Estimates less (negative) than (−) 1 imply the city is on the rising portion of its revenue hill. Row (5) presents estimates of the city's job tax base with respect to the city's income (NYC) or wages-only (Philadelphia) tax rate. The Philadelphia tax rate includes a tax on commuters. A (—) indicates that the city did not use the tax as a significant revenue source.

Source: Estimates are from Haughwout et al. (2004, tables 4 [controlling for economic and policy shocks] and 5).

estimated $.43 and $.77 in added benefits from their last dollar of city taxes.[9] If this last dollar is not providing sufficient benefits to taxpayers to justify its cost, where does the new tax money go?

Returning to the evidence in table 11.1 provides an answer. There we saw the major fiscal causes of low city home values were high rates of city poverty, strong public employee unions, and inefficient city governance. It should come as no surprise to learn that Houston, Minneapolis, New York, and Philadelphia each has a high rate of city poverty, must bargain with a strong public employee union, and must budget using relatively weak fiscal institutions. Rather than to taxpayer services, it appears the incremental tax dollar goes to support required increases in poverty spending, public employee wages above improved worker productivity, and politically useful yet economically inefficient public projects.

To ensure our cities can reach their full potential as centers of economic activity, cities must efficiently manage their poverty budgets, public employee labor contracts, and spending on neighborhood projects. These are the central tasks for efficient city public finance.

Efficient City Finances

Three conditions must be met for efficient city public finance. *First*, we must get city fiscal responsibilities right. City governments should be asked to provide only those services they can do well. *Second*, we must be sure city governments have the fiscal tools necessary to meet their service responsibilities at the lowest cost possible—a cost that includes the economic costs of taxation. *Third*, the institutions of city governance must offer incentives for elected officials to supply the efficient services using the efficient taxes.

Getting Fiscal Responsibilities Right

What public services should the efficient city government provide? Successful cities require public services and infrastructure that complement private capital and labor in production, and that create the physical and social environments valued by the cities' residents. City services should focus on city residents and be provided to the efficiently sized city population. Services with significant spatial spillovers should be financed by higher levels of government, as should services such as national security with significant economies of scale ("publicness") in production. Candidate city services will include access and neighborhood roads, public transit, trash collection, parks and recreation, public health including sewer and water infrastructure, libraries and cultural centers, police and fire services, courts and prisons, and education.

What city governments should *not* do, at least from their own tax resources, is redistribute incomes from city taxpayers to poor residents beyond what taxpayers themselves might prefer. Table 11.1 has shown city property values fall significantly if the city is required to address the fiscal and social problems associated with large poverty populations. The burden of city poverty on city taxpayers is twofold. First, a large poverty population implies a potentially large tax burden on middle-income households and firms. Table 11.4 shows the direct fiscal cost of cities' own poverty spending on median household incomes for a sample of large U.S. cities. Poverty spending per capita is significant, and the implied increase in the middle-class taxes needed to fund such expenditures can be as large as 2 to 3 percent of a city's median family

TABLE 11.4
Poverty Spending by U.S. Cities

	1982	1992	2002
Large cities			
Spending/resident (stand. dev.)	$476	$590	$667
	(649)	(973)	(1039)
"Tax" on median family income	.033	.035	.032
Medium cities			
Spending/resident (stand. dev.)	$185	$238	$250
	(162)	(268)	(298)
"Tax" on median family income	.013	.016	.011
Small cities			
Spending/resident (stand. dev.)	$164	$184	$223
	(175)	(212)	(257)
"Tax" on median family income	.011	.011	.011

Notes: Poverty spending by U.S. cities measured in 2006 dollars per resident. The estimated "tax" on median family income is computed as [(Spending/resident) $\times$ 3]/median family income in each year. The sample cities have been grouped by their 1960 populations. Large cities: Los Angeles, San Diego, San Francisco, Washington, DC, Chicago, New Orleans, Boston, Baltimore, Detroit, Saint Louis, Buffalo, New York City, Cincinnati, Cleveland, Philadelphia, Pittsburgh, Dallas, Houston, San Antonio, Seattle, and Milwaukee. Medium cities: Birmingham, Phoenix, Oakland, Denver, Atlanta, Indianapolis, Louisville, Minneapolis, Saint Paul, Kansas City (MO), Omaha, Newark, Rochester, Columbus, Toledo, Oklahoma City, Portland, Memphis, Fort Worth, and Norfolk. Small cities: Tucson, Sacramento, San Jose, Jacksonville, Miami, Tampa, Honolulu, Des Moines, Wichita, Charlotte, Jersey City, Albuquerque, Akron, Dayton, Tulsa, Nashville, Austin, Corpus Christi, El Paso, and Richmond.

income. This added tax burden is likely to drive middle-class families and firms from the city. Second, city poverty implies a possible increase in the costs of providing public services to city residents. K–12 education (Dunscombe and Yinger 1997) and resident safety (Glaeser and Sacerdote 1999) are the services whose costs are most likely to be increased by large poverty populations. Either city spending must rise or service quality must decline. Again, resident taxpayers and city firms will be tempted to leave the city. Their exit will undermine the city's consumption and production agglomeration advantages. As the city's private sector economic performance declines, city and perhaps suburban property values fall. Outside grants to pay the costs of federal and state service

TABLE 11.5

Regional Financing for Regional Poverty in Philadelphia

Policy reforms	2000 city house value (% change from status quo) (1)	2000 suburban house value (% change from status quo) (2)	Total value of regional houses (% change from status quo) (3)
No reform: Status quo	$59,700 (–)	$157,836 (–)	$111.66 Billion (–)
"No strings attached"	$59,855 (0.26%)	$157,741 (–0.06%)	$111.99 billion (0.03%)
Uniform wage tax cut	$60,787 (1.82%)	$157,773 (–0.04%)	$112.21 billion (0.50%)
Nonresident wage tax cut	$60,960 (2.11%)	$160,614 (1.76%)	$113.74 billion (1.87%)

Source: Inman (2003a, table 3).

mandates for lower-income families as well as aid for the added costs of service provision because of large concentrations of lower-income families are the appropriate policy responses. Removing the responsibility for city poverty from the city's budget is an important first step toward greater city fiscal efficiency.

Table 11.5 illustrates the potential economic benefits to one regional economy of such a reform. In a study of Philadelphia's poverty spending, I (2003a) ask, What would happen to city and suburban home values if Philadelphia and the region's suburban counties shared the responsibility for the region's poverty spending using a uniform proportional tax on all regional residents' incomes? The four suburban counties have 25 percent of the region's poor, and Philadelphia has 75 percent. Holding fixed poverty services per poor person at the current levels in all counties but equalizing service financing would transfer $191 million annually from suburban residents to the city budget, worth about $125 per every Philadelphia resident. Table 11.5 shows the predicted change in city and suburban home values following the transfer. The predictions are based on a regional fiscal model allowing households and firms to move freely between Philadelphia and its suburbs to maximize firm profits or household welfare. The model is calibrated to match the prereform city and suburban populations, average home values, and average incomes of the Philadelphia metropolitan economy.

Three conclusions are evident. First, and not surprisingly, city home values always rise. Second, it matters how the money is transferred for

the overall effectiveness of the reform. The "no-strings-attached" reform allowing the city to allocate the suburban transfer between tax
cuts and government spending as in the past has only a small impact on
city values and a negative final impact on suburban values. The region
as a whole gains only three-tenths of 1 percent in added homeowner
wealth. Requiring the transfer to be targeted toward a proportional cut
in both the city's resident and commuter wage taxes further improves
city values while softening the loss to suburban homes. The component
of the city's wage tax that is most damaging to city jobs, and thus to city
agglomeration economies, is the commuter tax. Targeting reform aid to
be spent totally on cutting the city's nonresident commuter wage tax offers the biggest improvement in home values, now 1.9 percent for the
region as a whole. Third, all residents of the region share these efficiency gains, even those suburbanites who pay for the fiscal transfer to
the city's poverty budget. By getting fiscal responsibilities right, city
home values have the potential to rise by 2.1 percent and suburban
home values increase by 1.8 percent.[10]

Getting Fiscal Tools Right

Getting fiscal responsibilities correct is an important first step, but using
the right fiscal tools to meet those responsibilities is crucial too. We saw
in table 11.5 that the benefits of poverty funding reform was greatest
when the reform required the city to spend all of its poverty aid to lower
the inefficient nonresident (commuter) wage tax. To achieve fiscal efficiency, elected officials must have the spending tools and tax instruments
needed to maximize service benefits and minimize financing costs.

SERVICES

Labor is the most significant input for providing city services, and the
key spending tool for fiscal efficiency is the right to hire, assign, and if
necessary, fire public employees as effective service provision requires.
The major impediment to effective public labor management is *state-
imposed* duty-to-bargain laws requiring city governments to bargain
with their employees over all aspects of the employment contract.
Duty-to-bargain rules give the recognized city public employee unions
the right to veto any city labor contracts, including those with nonunion
providers. In effect, such unions have a monopoly right to provide public services.

So empowered, one would expect union member wages to exceed
their competitive market alternative—they do—and for the level of employment at those noncompetitive wages to exceed the efficient level—it

does. The best studies, those that control for individual worker characteristics, find union wages are from 5 to 15 percent higher than what
that worker might have earned in their most likely alternative position,
and that health care and pension benefits are significantly higher for
union than nonunion public employees as well. There is no evidence
that unionized workers' higher wages and benefits can be justified by a
compensating increase in worker productivity.[11] Further, holding wages
fixed, strong public employee unions are able to negotiate a larger public employee workforce than taxpayers would prefer had union negotiations not been required.[12] There is "featherbedding" in duty-to-bargain
cities (see Inman 1981, 1982; Zax and Ichniowski 1988). Typically, the increase in employment in strongly unionized city services is achieved at
the expense of nonunionized services—often redistributive services for
lower-income households (see Freeman and Valletta 1988). The end results are excessive wages, inefficient employment, and consistent with
the results reported in table 11.1, significantly lower resident home values in strong union, duty-to-bargain cities.[13]

Twenty-four states now have strong duty-to-bargain laws imposed
on their local governments, almost all approved over the decade 1965–
1975, and arising from organized public employee political action and
private sector union support at the state level (see Ichniowski 1988). Because of the significant fiscal implications of these rules, public employees had to develop broad-based, statewide political support for their
approval. Reform no doubt will require an equal political effort by taxpayers.[14] Worth doing, but perhaps not easily achieved.[15]

Facing duty-to-bargain rules, what then can city residents do on their
own? In two words: bargain tough. The union should be made aware of
the long-run economic consequences of excessive labor contracts. For
cities near the peak of their local revenue hill, as Houston, New York
City, and Philadelphia are, there simply may not be sufficient resources
to support a high-cost labor contract. Fiscal crises may result as in New
York City in 1974 and Philadelphia in 1991 (see Shefter 1992; Inman
1995). Union officials must be made to appreciate the realities of this *economic constraint*. This position was the foundation for Mayor Rendell's
successful negotiations with Philadelphia's public unions at the time of
the city's 1991 fiscal crisis; the unions understood, and agreed to two
years of no wage increases along with significant benefit and work-rule
givebacks.[16]

In cities where the peak of the revenue hill does not limit bargaining
offers, elected officials must be made to feel, and then urged to convey,
the realities of their *political constraint* that voters will require public employees to provide service benefits commensurate with wages paid.

Higher wages must be matched by productivity increases, most easily achieved with relaxed work rules and layoffs, if necessary. Or if jobs are to be protected, then there must be concessions on wages and benefits. A failure to balance extra costs with extra benefits must mean a mayor's defeat in the next election. There is no better signal of taxpayer support, and hence of the high cost of accepting an inefficient contract, than the willingness by citizens to take a strike.[17] This was Mayor Michael R. Bloomberg's strategy in his most recent and, as generally viewed, successful negotiations with New York City's public unions.[18]

Conveying the importance of management's economic and political constraints is no less critical when compulsory arbitration becomes the bargaining option of last resort, as is required in twenty-two states for essential city services (education, police, and fire). Arbitrators typically set awards as a weighted average of what they view as a "fair award" and an average of management's and labor's last best offers. Typically, the fair award depends on the arbitrator's perception of the city taxpayers' ability to pay ("economic wealth"), the pay of city employees relative to a sample of their national peers, and the difficulty and danger of the job. Last offers are conditioned by the underlying political and economic realities of elected officials and union leaders, and their aversion to receiving a damaging award. The more risk averse is a bargainer, the less demanding will be their final offer, and thus the less favorable to their position will be the arbitrator's final award.[19] Secure union leaders and mayor's confident of taxpayer support will be less risk averse with respect to the outcomes of any one bargain, and therefore will do better for their constituents. Here again, building a taxpayer coalition in support of efficient labor contracts is a city's best response to duty-to-bargain requirements.

FINANCING

The efficient financing of city services requires that today's services be financed by today's taxes and user fees, and that future services be financed by future period taxes and user fees facilitated through the issuance of public debt. Economists identify two forms of taxation: *source-based taxation* that taxes factors of production where they are employed and taxes goods and services where they are purchased, and *resident-based taxation* that taxes factors of production by owners' residences and taxes goods and services by consumers' residences. To the extent that a city resident is both a producer and a consumer of a city good or service, then any city tax on that good or service will be, by definition, both a source- and resident-based tax. The taxation of resident-owned city housing is the important example. Efficient city financing should pick that mix of taxes that maximizes the profitability of city firms and the welfare of city residents.

Most taxes are either source- or resident-based, however. Prominent source-based city taxes include: taxes on city employees' wages regardless of residence (e.g., a commuter tax); taxes on city firms' capital or profits (e.g., commercial-industrial property taxes); taxes on local retail sales; and taxes on city firms' total sales (e.g., a gross receipts tax or turnover tax). Prominent resident-based city taxes include: taxes on residents' wages or more generally all income, and as mentioned, a tax on resident-owned properties.

Most cities use source-based taxes for two quite understandable reasons. First, they are easy to administer as the collecting agent is typically a firm or business located within the city, and second, at least initially, a significant share of the burden of such taxes may fall on nonvoting taxpayers residing outside the city. Unfortunately, source-based taxes often have large negative effects on the overall economic performance of the city's private economy (see table 11.3). Commercial-industrial property taxes, the taxation of commuter workers, and the taxation of firm output or sales all reduce firm profitability at the taxing location. Unless the resulting reduction in firm profits is matched by at least a fully compensating profit increase from added city services, the firm, constrained to earn the competitive rate of return, must leave the city. From the perspective of economic efficiency, there is little to recommend source-based taxation.

Efficient financing recommends user fees and resident-based taxation for residential services, and user fees and business-based land-value taxes for business services. The resident tax might be a tax on residential property or resident wage or income, with the latter administered as a locally decided additional tax rate (called "piggybacking") applied to all, or perhaps just a locally decided portion, of the state or federal income tax base. Business should be charged a combination of user fees for the use of city services (e.g., water, trash, and parking fees) and then a tax on the value of business land when the administration of user fees is not possible (e.g., for police and fire services along with general infrastructure maintenance). Pittsburgh and Queensland (Australia) have both successfully administered a business land tax (see Oates and Schwab 1997).

Finally, nonresidents who use city services—commuters and tourists—should contribute toward the costs of the services they use. But there are more efficient ways to charge those visitors for city services than broadly assessed source-based taxation such as sales or commuter taxes. User fees and excise taxes such as beach fees, parking fees, airport fees, tolls at bridges and center-city access points, and hotel and entertainment taxes can be targeted at outsiders' for their use of city infrastructure and services, with residents exempted through rebates and discounts.

For the financing of the construction costs of city infrastructure—schools, public transit, waterworks, airports, communication networks, major access roads, prisons and courts, and waste-treatment facilities—economic theory is clear: tax payments should be smoothed over the productive life of the government asset through the use of long-term borrowing (see Barro 1979). Ideally, taxes on the resulting improvement in the value of city land should then be used to repay the debt's principal and interest as well as all ongoing costs of maintenance (see Rangel 2005). The now common use of "tax increment financing"(aka TIFs) for city capital projects illustrates the feasibility this approach (see Brueckner 2001). If such assessments prove difficult, however—what is the "reach" of economic benefits from the new sports stadium or museum?—then citywide taxes on residential incomes or property should be used to fund borrowing for residential projects, and similarly, citywide taxes on business land should be used to fund business-related projects. Debt for projects that benefit both residents and businesses should be repaid by such citywide taxation on both resident and business tax bases.

To ensure fiscal accountability, cities should not be allowed to use city long-term debt to finance an annual shortfall between current spending and current revenues by borrowing "off the books" through special project accounts, reclassifying current period expenditures such as janitor salaries as "capital outlays" (once a New York City favorite), underfunding defined-benefit public employee pensions, or just "rolling over" last year's deficit into this year's budget (see Inman 1983). Undetected deficit financing imposes either of two damaging effects on the private economy. First, if city taxpayers repay the debt, as was the case for New York City and Philadelphia deficits, city property values then fall by the discounted present value of all required taxes. Hidden city deficits create asset value uncertainty for new investors—uncertainty that may discourage future investment in an otherwise productive city's economy. Second, if deficits are not repaid by city residents but rather covered by state or national governments (a "bailout")—as in cases of Camden, New Jersey, and Washington, DC—then the deficit acts as an implicit subsidy to current accounts spending. Such bailouts create incentives for excessive city spending (see Inman 2003b). To control the first inefficiency, reputable accountants should actively monitor city deficits using "generally accepted accounting practices" (GAAP) and the city's surplus or deficit position should be made known to all potential investors in city properties. Investors will then be able to discount ("capitalize") future taxes less benefits into the price they pay for city assets. Lacking reputable monitoring, though, deficit regulation through balanced budget rules may be needed (see Bohn and Inman 1996). To control the second inefficiency, the national government must adopt a credible position against city government bailouts, much like President Gerald R. Ford's response when New York City requested federal assistance following its 1974 fiscal crisis ("Ford to City: Drop Dead," *New York Daily News*, October 29, 1975). City borrowing is an important tool for efficient city financing, but it must be watched, publicized, and if necessary, regulated.

Getting Fiscal Incentive Right

The last condition necessary for an efficient public budget are institutions and rules of governance that align the interests of elected city officials with the long-run economic interests of city residents and firms. City officials will first need to know the costs and benefits of city services, and then given the costs and benefits, design budgets that maximize the net economic gains to taxpayers.

While the costs of government services are generally well-known, the benefits are not. If asked, residents have an incentive to overstate their benefits from those services they value and understate their benefits from those they do not. Either of two institutions may be used to extract more truthful information about how citizens feel about receiving more, or less, city services. When services are shared and exclusion is difficult, as with police and fire protection, public health, roads, and parks, then citizens can vote directly for their preferred level—a referendum—or a representative(s) who will decide service levels on their behalf. When services can be targeted and exclusion from use is possible, as for water, electricity, libraries, education, and trash pickup, then a market process can be used and prices charged. Both politics and markets have key roles to play in providing city services.

POLITICS

While there is no guarantee that politics will find the efficient allocation of government services, there are circumstances when it may come close. As long as the efficient tax structure applies, all citizens vote, citizen preferences for services are separable in the sense that the chosen level of one service (e.g., education) does not influence the preferred level for another service (e.g., police protection), and the distribution of preferences for any public service is not "too badly skewed," then the majority rule outcome for each public service will approximately satisfy efficiency's requirement that the social marginal benefits equal the social marginal costs. It does not matter if the budget is set by a referendum for each public service or by elected representatives. In both cases, budget outcomes converge toward the overall median allocation (see Shepsle 1979). If preferences are close to normally distributed, then these median allocations will approximate what the average voter, and thus the sum of all voters, will prefer.[20]

When preferences are not separable—and this is the most likely case—then the ordering of voting on the issues can affect the chosen allocation. In this case, the agenda matters, and the one who sets the agenda can dictate the political outcomes. It is therefore essential that the citizens elect the agenda–setter. Now city budgets are best decided not issue by issue but rather by representative government. Representative city government can take either of two forms: *city council government* or *strong mayor government*.

Council governance has a problem, however: policy gridlock. One way to escape gridlock is through legislative logrolling, allowing each legislator to submit their most favored project for inclusion in the budget.[21] To avoid gridlock and the risk of no new spending, legislators may choose to vote to include *all* new initiatives via a legislative logroll. Such budgeting is likely to be inefficient, however, and the more so the more legislators who share the cost of services.[22]

The strong executive form of governance—a citywide elected executive granted broad agenda-setting powers and a line-item veto—is a preferred alternative. *If* the elected mayor is rewarded for adopting and implementing efficient city budgets, then any project whose benefits do not exceed its costs will not make the budget agenda, or if it does, it will be vetoed. As a consequence, city spending should be more efficient in strong mayor cities than in cities run by council government alone. As fiscally more efficient cities are more attractive cities, city property values should be higher in cities with a strong mayor form of governance. This is exactly what we have seen in table 11.1, where homes in weak governance cities sell at a 4 percent discount.[23]

MARKETS

Even in strong mayor cities, elected officials must embrace fiscal efficiency as their goal for city budgeting. Here markets play their crucial role. In private business, we seek to align management incentives to constituent (shareholder) long-run interests by giving management a stake in the *long-run* profitability of the firm. Such a strategy has worked in U.S. suburbs too, where elected local mayors and the members of school boards are also homeowners (shareholders, again) with an economic stake in the long performance of their community. The empirical evidence suggests these suburban communities do in fact adopt fiscal strategies that maximize resident home values, and that those strategies are fiscally efficient.[24] In U.S. suburbs, fiscal incentives have been aligned to citizen interests for two reasons: elected officials own property, *and* property owners are a voting majority.

Will such a direct market-based incentive structure work to promote fiscal efficiency in large cities? Probably not. In large cities, the market incentive for fiscal efficiency is diluted by the fact that city mayors are most likely career politicians rewarded more directly by reelection and higher office than by home-value appreciation. Further, politically decisive voters that determine election outcomes in large and especially poorer cities are often renters, not homeowners.[25]

Market-driven incentives to adopt efficient budgets can restored, however, through the creation of business and neighborhood improvement districts (BIDs and NIDs, respectively) within the city. BIDs and NIDs are associations of property owners within a geographic subdivision of the city, sanctioned by state law to provide services paid for by taxes and debt for the benefit of district businesses and residents (see Briffault 1999; Ellickson 1998). BIDs and NIDs can be the sole provider of district services, replacing city provision, or more likely they can offer supplemental services above the common level provided by the city government to all city neighborhoods.

A board elected by property owners within the district and administered by an appointed BID/NID director determines the level of these services. The property owners within the BID/NID solely finance the services; all owners within the district are required to contribute to the cost of service provision. For economic efficiency within NIDs, residents should pay for services by a residential property or income tax, assessed as a supplement to the citywide property or residential income tax. For economic efficiency within BIDs, businesses should pay for services by user fees or a piggybacked property—ideally land—tax.[26] Candidate services for BID or NID provision are those that can be efficiently provided to relatively small populations—say, twenty thousand residents or less, located within a relatively tight geographic area. K–12 education, neighborhood police patrols and fire protection, trash collection, street and sidewalk maintenance, parks and recreation, and libraries are all services that can be efficiently supplied at this scale. Where economies of scale or spatial spillovers are more significant—for example, water and electric services, telecommunications, trash and waste disposal (but not collection), public health, welfare services, public transportation, museums and stadiums, higher education, courts, and prisons—then citywide provision will be appropriate.

Beyond motivating more efficient service provision within their own district, BIDs and NIDs may also offer two additional efficiency benefits for the wider city economy. First, successful BIDs and NIDs will demonstrate to firms and residents in other city neighborhoods how public services might be more efficiently financed and provided. Successful strategies can then be demanded by residents of, and replicated in, other city neighborhoods.[27] Second, if BIDs and NIDs are more efficient providers of public services, then firms and middle-class residents may return to the city, and because of agglomeration economies, stimulate additional private sector production and consumption benefits for the city's economy. Through BIDs and NIDs, the efficiency gains from fiscal competition enjoyed by suburban residents might come to benefit central-city residents as well.[28]

Equitable City Finances

Most standards of fiscal fairness will require all citizens of equal economic circumstances to be treated equally (horizontal fairness), and between citizens of different circumstances, those with the lesser economic opportunity and resources to be favored in the distribution of public services and taxation (vertical fairness). How much the poor should be favored will depend on one's motivating sense of economic justice. City governments should strive to ensure horizontal fairness among their citizens, but because of the mobility of middle- and upper-income households and firms, they will be limited in their ability to implement a standard of vertical fairness much beyond that preferred by the least generous of their taxpaying residents. As tables 11.1, 11.3, and 11.5 make clear, any city acting alone in its desire to help its poor residents will drive out less sympathetic residents and profit-maximizing firms, undermine city production and consumption efficiency, and reduce city property values. Even within these economic constraints, however, there are fiscal policies that mayors can pursue to help their lower-income residents.

SERVICE EQUITY

Efficient city governments have more resources than their less efficient rivals, and if the politically decisive voter approves, these extra resources can be allocated to improve the current and future economic prospects of lower-income families, particularly young children in poverty. Prenatal care funded by Medicaid, nursing home visit following the birth of the child, and preschool programs with a strong emphasis on school readiness skills not just day care have all been shown to be effective in preparing lower-income children for K–5 schooling. "Ready" lower-income children learn more and reduce the spillover costs of poverty when providing education to all children in the classroom. What might cities do for older, lower-income children? Programs that link schooling directly to job skills through workplace internships show a significant positive impact on future earnings.[29] For poor adults, one of the least expensive and most successful strategies is to offer assistance in applying for federal transfers through the Earned Income Tax Credit. Finally, and perhaps most important, cities should lower the costs to eligible families of accessing federal, state, and city programs. Just as efficient cities provide "one-stop shopping" for firms wishing to locate in their boundaries, the efficient city should offer similar services for lower-income families applying for poverty assistance. It makes little policy or fiscal sense to erect, as did New York City under Mayor Giuliani, administrative barriers to poor families applying for federal and state programs. Poor families may be "off the rolls," but they are, most likely, still "on the streets," and federal and state monies that could be leveraged for the benefit of poor city residents only go unused.

FINANCING EQUITY

More efficient city financing—resident taxes for resident services, business taxes for business services (table 11.3), and regional, state, and federal financing of city poverty (table 11.5)—provide benefits that can be reallocated to improve the welfare of the poor. Efficient city finances attract firms back into the city, and this means greater job access for poor city residents and higher average city wages. Unfortunately, city land prices and rents rise too, but at least for one large city (Philadelphia) it is likely that the increase in average wages is enough to cover the increase in average housing costs (Haughwout and Inman 2001).[30] But for many newly employed poor families, the large gains in income more than exceed the average rise in rents, and they are unambiguously better off. Moreover, city land values are higher by the gains in citywide economic efficiency. A city land tax on business properties could capture some of those gains, and the proceeds could then be allocated to supply valued education and health care services to lower-income families. If so, then everyone wins with more efficient city financing.

Finally, the extensive use of NIDs and BIDs will introduce financing and service disparities across city neighborhoods as richer neighborhoods have the ability to pay for, and most likely will demand, greater neighborhood services. But here too wider city fiscal policies can restore fairness and then tax the economic surplus from increased efficiency to improve overall fiscal equity. First, *inter*neighborhood equalization aid administered by the city government can be designed to restore fiscal equity without undoing the initial gains in city fiscal efficiency. The city, for example, can ensure a common citywide service minimum while still allowing richer neighborhoods to "top up" above the minimum. Or the city can allocate revenues directly to approved BIDs and NIDs in lower-income neighborhoods to equalize the ability of all neighborhoods to provide meritorious local services.[31] Second, to the extent that BIDs and NIDs plus equalization aid lead to improved fiscal efficiency in the city as a whole, there will be an additional margin of economic "surplus" capitalized into city property values that can be taxed to support services for lower-income families. Significantly, city fiscal efficiency need not be antithetical to greater fairness in the provision of city services.

Conclusion

Our urban centers are vital contributors to the economic success of the U.S. economy. Proximity fosters productive idea sharing and innovation, facilitates the efficient use of locationally specific productive assets, and provides consumers with wider choice through product variety. But for these advantages of spatial proximity to be realized, cities must offer complementary public services: roads and bridges for access, police and fire services for property protection, education for a quality labor force, and sanitation, sewerage, and clean water for a healthy environment. It is the task of city government to finance and provide these services efficiently. Table 11.6 summarizes what we have learned here about how this might best be done.

Cities should be fiscally responsible for those services whose benefits are spatially contained within the cities' boundaries and whose technology allows the desired level of service quality to be provided to an efficient scale of city population. The responsibility for services with spatial spillovers, such as clean air and water, or that require large populations to be efficiently provided, such as highways, telecommunication networks, and electric generation infrastructure, should be shared with or provided by an encompassing larger government such as a region or state. Importantly, services and income support for a city's lower-income population above that preferred by the city's taxpayers should be fully financed by the city's region or the state.

Assigned city services should be supplied at the efficient scale, and governed by a political process best able to reflect the preferences of the

TABLE 11.6
Financing City Services

Local service	Responsibility of	Provided by
Poverty services: Transfers and services	Region or state	State or city
Residential services: K–12 education	City	Neighborhood council (NIDs) with an option to contract to a private firm
Residential services K–12 equalization aid	City	City mayor
Residential services: Police/fire patrols	City	Neighborhood council (NIDs)
Residential services: Trash collection, parks and recreation, libraries	City	Neighborhood council (NID's) with an option to contract to a private firm
Residential services: Courts and prisons	City and region	City mayor
Residential services: Higher education, water/electricity, public health	City and region	City mayor with an option to contract to a private firm
Residential Infrastructure: Research, library/museums, concert hall/sports stadiums	City and region	City mayor with an option to contract to a private firm
Business Services: Police/fire patrols	City	Business improvement district (BIDs)
Business services: Trash collection, open spaces, maintenance	City	Business improvement district (BIDs) with an option to contract to a private firm
Shared infrastructure: Roadways and parking, water, sewer, electricity, telecommunications, airports and ports	City and region or state	City mayor with an option to contract to a private firm

TABLE 11.6 *(cont.)*

Governed by	*Financed by*
Governer or Mayor	State income tax
Majority rule in NID elected by one person, one vote from neighborhood residents	Neighborhood residential property or income taxation *or* resident user fees
Strong city mayor elected by one person, one vote of city residents	City tax on residential property or income taxation
Majority rule in NID elected by one person, one vote from neighborhood residents	Neighborhood residential property or income taxation
Majority rule in NID elected by one person one vote from neighborhood residents	Neighborhood residential property or income taxation *or* resident user fees
Strong city mayor elected by one person, one vote of city residents	City tax on residential property or income taxation
Strong city mayor elected by one person, one vote of city residents	City tax on residential property or income taxation *plus* user fees
Strong city mayor elected by one person, one vote of city residents	City debt financed by tax on residential property or income *plus* user fees
Majority rule in BID council elected by voting allocated in proportion to business land values	Business district land taxes *or* business user fees
Majority rule in BID council elected by voting allocated in proportion to business land values	Business district land taxes *or* business user fees
Strong city mayor elected by one person, one vote of city residents in consultation with business district representatives	Citywide debt financed by city tax on residential property and business land tax *plus* user fees

residents and firms who benefit from the services being provided. For residential services that can be offered efficiently to relatively small populations (say, twenty thousand residents)—K–12 education, police and fire patrols, trash collection, parks, and libraries—consideration should be given to having neighborhood councils (NIDs) decide the service levels, most sensibly as incremental spending above some city-wide foundation or "floor." The increments should be fully financed by the residents of the neighborhood. Similarly, business services that can be efficiently provided in concentrated spatial areas—police and fire patrols, trash collection, and street beautification—should be supplied and financed by local business districts (BIDs). Yet residential and business services that require larger populations or spatial areas for efficient provision—courts and prisons, higher education, water and electricity distribution, public health including trash disposal and sewerage treatment, roads and public transit, and airports—and the citywide equalization of meritorious neighborhood services (K–12 education) should all be provided by the city, but with a strong mayor form of governance to avoid the inefficiencies of decentralized city politics. Finally, NIDs, BIDs, and the city itself must retain the right to contract for services with the most efficient high-quality provider, not just from a monopoly (duty-to-bargain) public employee union. Of course, current public employees should be allowed to bid for such contracts.

The financing of city services should be designed to match the costs paid to the benefits received. A useful rule of thumb is this: residential taxes for residential services; business taxes for business services; and deficit financing for infrastructure services only. Good residential taxes include the property tax using market-value assessment or a residential income tax administered as a surcharge (called piggybacking) on the state income tax. Commuter taxes must be avoided as this tax is shifted back to business as a tax on workers hired; the logical consequence is that firms leave the city and the city's economy suffers. Visitors to the city and suburban commuters should pay for the city services they consume, most efficiently through the use of user fees, and then, if necessary, through taxes on parking, hotels, and perhaps restaurant dining. The best business taxes will be user fees when possible and a tax on the market value of land employed by the firm as necessary. Deficit financing for current services including public employee pension underfunding should be avoided as it creates incentives to overspend today and, if unchecked, lays open the risk of a future fiscal crisis.

Assigning cities their appropriate fiscal responsibilities, giving city officials the right tools to meet those responsibilities, and finally, designing the structure of governance so as to motivate elected officials to provide services efficiently leads to a larger city economy, a larger city tax base, and potentially more economic benefits for everyone, rich and poor alike.

Notes

1. The study (Haughwout and Inman 2002) on which the results in table 11.1 are based addresses the important issue of whether the estimated effects in that table measure a causal relationship *from* poverty, unions, governance, and fiscal aid *to* home values. First, the institutional variables representing unions (state bargaining laws), governance (city council seats and mayoral powers), and county support (county borders) have all been in place long before the period of study—1980–1990. Governance rules and county-city borders came with the city's home charter (typically before 1950). Union bargaining laws were set in the 1960s. Given this history, each institutional variable is arguably exogenous to changes in city home values twenty to thirty years later. Instrumental variable estimation is used to control for the possible joint determination of changes in city home values and city poverty rates by using *predicted* changes in city poverty in the change in home value equation. Exogenous predictors of the change in the city's rate of poverty include regional fixed effects, the lagged racial composition of the city, and crucially, the percent of the city's 1980 housing stock built before 1939. See Gyourko's chapter in this volume.

2. Also included in the suburban home value equation as controls are the change in the suburban rate of poverty, the number of suburban school districts, strong teacher unions, the presence of airline hubs and interstate highways, suburban population density, weather, and the log value of 1980 suburban home values (see Haughwout and Inman 2002).

3. For evidence that public employee wages and employment both have risen with strong unions, see Freeman (1986); Zax and Ichniowski (1988).

4. Further, the more legislative seats on a city council, the larger the city spending per resident (see Baqir 2002).

5. These results suggest poverty funding need not be a zero-sum game in the urban economy. The potential source of the economic surplus that arises from the suburban sharing of city poverty spending is from improved agglomeration economies within the city economy. This is modeled explicitly in table 11.5 below.

6. These within-city estimates of the effects of city fiscal policies avoid a potential weakness of many cross-city comparisons, where the measured impacts of weak finances on home values may include important omitted city effects (e.g., a historically declining economy) that independently depress home values, raise taxes, and also harm the provision of city services.

7. One additional murder in a precinct raises the average number of murders in a sample year from twelve to thirteen murders in a precinct. On average, there are sixty thousand residents in each precinct. Thus, the risk to a typical precinct resident rises from 0.0002 to 0.000217, or by 0.000017. Each home has three residents, on average. Hence, each person would be willing to pay about $140 (= $428/three) to avoid this increase in risk. The implied value of a statis-

tical life arising from this increased risk is approximately $8.2 million ($140/ 0.000017). The EPA currently values a statistical life saved by lowering environmental risk at $6.94 million. Russo's larger estimates for the benefits of a lower risk of death are not surprising, given that Russo's analysis includes not just current but all future generations of residents. EPA estimates are for only the current, now alive, person at risk.

8. The estimated elasticities reported in table 11.3 also tell us if a higher tax can bring in additional revenues. If $0 > \varepsilon_{B,t} > -1$, say, $\varepsilon_{B,t} - 0.50$, then a 10 percent increase in the tax rate only lowers the tax base by 5 percent, so more city revenues result when the rates are increased. If $\varepsilon_{B,t} = -1$, then a 10 percent increase in the city tax rate lowers the tax base by 10 percent and no new revenues are raised. Lastly, if $-1 > \varepsilon_{B,t}$, then a 10 percent increase in the city tax rate lowers the tax base by more than 10 percent and the city actually raises less money at the higher tax rates. In this case, the city is "over the top" of its revenue hill. From table 11.3, we see Houston is at the top of its property tax revenue hill, while Minneapolis, New York City, and Philadelphia are all still on the rising portions of their hills.

Finally, it is reassuring that the implied elasticity from Russo's study of the response of individual home values to changes in their individual tax rates gives an implied tax base elasticity of $-.40 = (-0.16/0.40$; see above at table 11.2's discussion) that is virtually the same as the estimated elasticity of Philadelphia's average property value with respect to average property tax rates ($= -0.43$) obtained from the historical time series regression of Haughwout and his colleagues, reported in table 11.3. The microeconomic and macroeconomic evidence support each other.

9. To estimate the marginal benefit from the last dollar of taxation, Haughwout and his colleagues (2004) proceed as follows: the market value is the discounted stream of future rents: $MV = R/r$; rents are approximated by the sum of private benefits (R_{pr}) plus the value (υ per dollar) of public spending (G) less the taxes paid (T): $R = R_{pr} + \upsilon G - T$; local taxes translate directly into local government services as: $G = \Phi T$, so that $R = R_{pr} + (\upsilon\Phi - 1)T$; a small increase in the local property tax rate (τ) will generate an initial revenue of $\Delta T = \Delta\tau\cdot MV_0$; and therefore, $\Delta MV = [(\upsilon\Phi - 1)/r]\cdot\Delta\tau\cdot MV_0$. Knowing $\Delta MV/\Delta\tau$ from their estimates of the cities' revenue hills, r and MV_0, they can estimate ($\upsilon\Phi - 1$), where $\upsilon\Phi$ measures the annual economic benefits of an additional dollar of property taxation. The estimates above assume $r = 3.00$ percent and MV_0 equal to each city's mean property value over the sample period. For Houston $\upsilon\Phi = -0.03$ (s.e. $= 0.36$); New York City $\upsilon\Phi = -0.16$ (s.e. $= 0.16$); Philadelphia, $\upsilon\Phi = 0.43$ (s.e. $= 0.11$); and Minneapolis, $\upsilon\Phi = 0.77$ (s.e. $= 0.08$).

10. Showing there are potential gains from cooperation between the central city and its suburbs does not mean that a cooperative agreement to realize those gains will be forthcoming. For a thorough discussion of the difficulty in fostering city-suburban cooperation and possible ways to facilitate such agreements, see Gillette (2005).

11. For a review, see Freeman (1986); for recent evidence, see Eberts (2007).

12. In duty-to-bargain cities, both wages and employment will be negotiated as well as enforced by a contract that requires, for example, a minimal number

of police officers or firefighters in a station, or a maximal class size in a school. Since union preferences will typically allow a trade-off of higher employment (job security) for lower wages or conversely, the mutually preferred bargain must be where this trade-off of wages for jobs is respected. If so, then city taxpayers must also be in a bargaining range where higher employment will only be accepted if wages are reduced, or again, conversely. But if taxpayers will only accept the extra benefits of more employees if the marginal costs of those employees are reduced, then it must be true that those extra benefits fall below the current marginal costs. Thus, city employment is too large relative to its overall economic efficient level. The cause of the problem is duty-to-bargain rules requiring both wages and employment to be jointly negotiated. This argument is presented formally in Inman (1981).

13. In duty-to-bargain cities, public employee wages and benefits are typically 5 to 15 percent higher than in cities free of this labor requirement. Wages and benefits are typically 70 percent of aggregate city expenditures and taxes. Thus, residents of duty-to-bargain cities can expect to pay from 3.5 percent $(= 0.05 \times 0.70)$ to 10.5 percent $(= 0.15 \times 0.70)$ more in taxes for comparable levels of city services. For the sample (Haughwout and Inman 2002) in table 11.1, the average annual tax payment was about $5,000 per household. Families in the duty-to bargain cities in this sample are therefore estimated to pay an additional $175 $(= 0.035 \times \$5,000)$ to $525 $(= 0.105 \times \$5,000)$ per year in taxes for the same level of services. Capitalizing these extra tax payments at a real interest rate of 0.05, home values should decline by $3,500 $(= \$175/0.05)$ to $10,500 $(= \$525/0.05)$ per year. This is exactly the range of home value loss reported in table 11.1 for duty-to-bargain cities (as estimated by Haughwout and Inman 2002). Other studies have found similar effects of strong unions on home values (Gyourko and Tracy 1989). Importantly, the results from the microeconometric studies of public employee bargaining are fully consistent with the results from the macroeconometric studies of strong unions' effects on city home values.

14. The political histories behind the final acceptance of duty-to-bargain rules in Ohio and Illinois are instructive for how a reform might be fashioned (see Saltzman 1988). In both instances, all parties involved in the legislation understood the large fiscal consequences of the rules, and therefore broad-based political support was required for final approval. In Ohio, a Republican governor successfully vetoed the duty-to-bargain bills; only in 1982 with the election of a Democratic governor was a bill passed and signed. In Illinois, the initial barrier to the passage of a duty-to-bargain bill was the Democratic state legislature, controlled by the political machine of Chicago's Mayor Richard M. Daley. The reason for the machine's opposition was simple. As part of its patronage system, the Daley machine used outside contractors for the provision of many city services. This system for political compensation would be undermined if city unions controlled who received, or not, the right to provide services. Only as the political influence of the Daley machine eroded could the bill have a chance of state approval. This occurred in 1983, after Harold Washington, Chicago's first African American mayor, actively supported the duty-to-bargain bill. Why? Washington's patronage ran through the public sector, and many of Chicago's public employees were themselves African Americans. The Democratic

state legislature approved the duty-to-bargain bills and then overrode the Republican governor's veto.

15. This recommendation to remove duty-to-bargain requirements is *not* a recommendation to remove public employee unions altogether. Quite the contrary, unions have been valuable in representing worker rights on grievances, and ensuring equal pay between men and women employees for equal skills and work (see Freeman 1986). It is only the duty-to-bargain requirement that is objectionable on efficiency grounds.

16. In a meeting with all city union leaders, Mayor Rendell made it clear that raising taxes was not an option: "We are losing our middle class, our working class, to other places. We have to increase our tax base, or we are finished." Rendell viewed raising taxes as the equivalent of placing a gun to the city's forehead and pulling the trigger. See Bissinger (1997, 131), including the chapters on the city's labor negotiations.

17. Below, I advocate the expanded use of business improvement districts (BID) and neighborhood improvement districts (NID) as a way to improve management incentives for efficient service provision. BIDs and NIDs also give city officials organized alternative providers of certain city services in the case of a city strike.

18. See the sequence of *New York Times* articles covering the two-year-long labor negotiations: *New York Times*, "To Move Ahead, Each Side's Negotiators Had to Loosen Grip on the Past," December 18, 2000; *New York Times*, "Bloomberg and City Unions Draw the Lines, Far Apart," August 19, 2003; and *New York Times*, "No Raises without Concessions, Bloomberg Tells Unions," September 15, 2003.

19. Henry Farber (1981) presents the theory, and then he and Max Brazerman (1986) and David Bloom (1988) provide the evidence. Final arbitrator outcomes are nearly identical for conventional and final offer arbitration.

20. The intuition of this conclusion is straightforward. Cities should balance the sum of the extra benefits created to the cost of each extra dollar they spend: $\sum MB = MC$. Dividing both sides by the number of residents redefines the efficiency condition in per capita benefits and costs as: $mb = mc$. That is, for efficiency the marginal benefit of city services to the average citizen should equal the marginal cost to the average citizen. Competitive, majority rule voting ensures that the median, or fiftieth percentile, voter determines the policy outcome. If the median voter is also the average voter, as will be the case when voter preferences are normally distributed, then the median voter will prefer the efficient ($mb = mc$) budget. This efficiency case for majority rule democracy was first made by Howard Bowen (1943) and was formalized by Ted Bergstrom (1979). For some empirical evidence that competitive local politics may give the efficient outcome, see Bergstrom et al. (1989).

21. An alternative to logrolling for council governments is to form two strong political parties so that the majority party can hold together its winning coalition through the party discipline of each council member who threatens to defect. Unfortunately, party discipline does not appear to be an effective constraint on council behavior in large U.S. cities (see Ferreira and Gyourko 2007).

22. This is what Reza Baqir (2002) finds in his study of city spending and city governance for a sample of 1,420 U.S. cities for the decade of the 1990s. The elas-

ticity of city spending with respect to the size of a city council, holding fixed city population and other important attributes of the local economy, is 0.20; doubling the size of a city council leads to a 20 percent increase in city spending per resident. In Inman (1995), I provide confirming evidence from a "natural experiment" involving the changes in the structure of a city council in Philadelphia in 1980. In 1979, the leadership of Philadelphia's then nearly all white city council (there was one black councilperson) got caught seeking bribes in the federal government's Abscam sting operation. Six of seventeen council members were either convicted or forced to resign, and all just before the city's November election. As a result, six new black and Hispanic members were elected to the city council. It is fair to think of this result as a 33 percent increase in effective council representation of neighborhoods. The budgetary consequence of this change was a permanent 25 percent increase in citywide spending on neighborhood services and a 5 percent increase in overall city spending. The implied elasticity of overall city spending with respect to the "increase" in de facto council representation is 0.15 (= 0.05/0.33) and within the range of Baqir's cross-city estimates.

23. Again, the microeconometric evidence studying how fiscal policy is set is consistent with the more aggregative evidence presented in table 11.1. Baqir's (2002) study of city fiscal policymaking finds strong mayors with veto powers neutralize the excessive spending by large city councils. The average city in Baqir's sample spent approximately $2,400 per family, and the mean size of a city council was seven representatives (s.d. = three representatives). A one standard deviation increase in council size would increase the number of representatives to ten or by about 40 percent. Without a strong mayor, Baqir estimates that city spending would rise by 8 percent (= 0.2 × 40 percent) or roughly $200 per family. A strong mayor successfully vetoes this spending increase. What is the gain in economic efficiency from the reduction in $200 per family in city spending? From the results in Haughwout and his colleagues (2004), a plausible middle estimate might value the benefit of each marginal dollar of city spending at $.50. If so, then the $200 per family reduction in spending costs $100 per family in lost service benefits, but saves $200 per family in taxes. With strong mayor governance, therefore, families are better off by about $100 per family annually. The discounted present value of this annual efficiency gain will be $2,000, capitalized at a 5 percent real rate of interest (= $100/0.05). This result is strikingly close to the loss in home value reported in table 11.1 from the presence of weak governance.

24. For the empirical evidence, see Brueckner (1983); for a full treatment of the argument, and further review of the anecdotal and econometric evidence, see Fischel (2001).

25. Renters will bear the burden of the property tax in higher rents, but forward shifting on to higher rents will be less than 100 percent if the supply curve of rental housing is less than perfectly elastic. Wallace Oates (2005) estimates the effect of renters on overspending to be from 5 to 10 percent for the average community where renters represent 25 percent of the residents. In the typical large U.S. city, the share of residents who are renters is closer to 50 percent.

26. By arguments similar to those developed for efficient corporate gover-

nance, votes proportional to the market value of land held within the district will typically be the efficient voting rule for BIDs and NIDs (see Harris and Raviv 1988). This voting rule will likely survive court review for BIDs, but will violate the Supreme Court's requirement of one person, one vote for residential services, and thus is likely to be disallowed for NIDs. The alternative is to draw the boundaries for NIDs to ensure a coincident of economic interests for residents—say, by setting NID boundaries to ensure common home values within the district.

27. Such demonstration effects are common among state governments (see Besley and Case 1995).

28. For evidence that BIDs are more efficient, see Brooks (2006); and that such efficiency gains lead to higher property values, see Ellen, Schwartz, and Voicu (2006).

29. The chapters by Janet Currie and Richard Murnane in this volume provide excellent overviews of programs that work for addressing poverty in our cities.

30. The chapter by David Card in this volume on the effects of increased city immigration also finds higher average wages offset higher rents.

31. Several studies (Inman 1978; Inman and Rubinfeld 1979; Nechyba 1996) look at the efficiency and equity performance of a variety of alternative revenue-sharing formulas, including those that ensure a foundation (minimum) for service provision and those that equalize taxing capacity across local voting jurisdictions.

References

Baqir, Reza. 2002. Districting and Government Overspending. *Journal of Political Economy* 110 (December): 1318–54.

Barro, Robert J. 1979. On the Determination of Government Debt. *Journal of Political Economy* 87 (October): 940–71.

Bergstrom, Ted C. 1979. When Does Majority Rule Supply Public Goods Efficiently? *Scandinavian Journal of Economics* 81 (2): 216–26.

Bergstrom, Ted C., Judy Roberts, Dan Rubinfeld, and Perry Shapiro. 1989. A Test for the Efficiency in the Supply of Public Education. *Journal of Public Economics* 35 (April): 289–308.

Besley, Timothy, and Anne Case. 1995. Incumbent Behavior, Vote-Seeking, Tax-Setting, and Yardstick Competition. *American Economic Review* 85 (March): 25–45.

Bissinger, Buzz. 1997. *A Prayer for the City*. New York: Random House.

Bloom, David E. 1988. Arbitrator Behavior in Public Sector Wage Disputes. In *When Public Sector Workers Unionize*, ed. Richard B. Freeman and Casey Ichniowski, 107–24. Chicago: University of Chicago Press.

Bohn, Henning, and Robert P. Inman. 1996. Balanced Budget Rules and Public Deficits: Evidence from the U.S. States. *Carnegie Rochester Conference Series on Public Policy* 45 (December): 13–76.

Bowen, Howard R. 1943. The Interpretation of Voting in the Allocation of Economic Resources. *Quarterly Journal of Economics* 58 (February): 27–48.

Briffault, Richard. 1999. A Government for Our Time? Business Improvement Districts and Urban Governance. *Columbia Law Review* 99 (March): 365–476.

Brooks, Leah. 2006. Volunteering to Be Taxed: Business Improvement Districts and the Extra-Governmental Provision of Public Safety. Working paper, McGill University.

Brueckner, Jan K. 1983. Property Value Maximization and Public Sector Efficiency. *Journal of Urban Economics* 14 (February): 1–15.

———. 2001. Tax Increment Financing: A Theoretical Inquiry. *Journal of Public Economics* 81 (August): 321–43.

De Long, J. Bradford, and Andrei Shleifer. 1993. Princes and Merchants: European City Growth before the Industrial Revolution. *Journal of Law and Economics* 36 (October): 671–702.

Dunscombe, William, and John Yinger. 1997. Why Is It So Hard to Help Central City Schools? *Journal of Policy Analysis and Management* 16 (Winter): 85–113.

Eberts, Randall W. 2007. Teacher Unions and Student Performance: Help or Hindrance? *Future of Children* 17 (Spring): 178–200.

Ellen, Ingrid Gould, Amy Ellen Schwartz, and Ioan Voicu. 2006. The Impact of Business Improvement Districts on Property Values: Evidence from New York City. Working paper, Wagner School of Public Policy, New York University.

Ellickson, Robert C. 1998. New Institutions for Old Neighborhoods. *Duke Law Journal* 48 (October): 75–110.

Farber, Henry S. 1981. Splitting-the-Difference in Interest Arbitration. *Industrial and Labor Relations Review* 35 (October): 70–77.

Farber, Henry S., and Max H. Bazerman. 1986. The General Basis of Arbitrator Behavior: An Empirical Analysis of Conventional and Final-Offer Arbitration. *Econometrica* 54 (July): 819–44.

Ferreira, Fernando, and Joseph E. Gyourko. 2007. Do Political Parties Matter? Evidence from U.S. Cities. Working paper, Zell/Lurie Real Estate Center, Wharton School.

Fischel, William A. 2001. *Homevoter Hypothesis: Home Values' Influence on Local Government Taxation, School Finance, and Land-Use Policies*. Cambridge, MA: Harvard University Press.

Freeman, Richard B. 1986. Unionization Comes to the Public Sector. *Journal of Economic Literature* 24 (March): 41–86.

Freeman, Richard B., and Robert G. Valletta. 1988. The Effects of Public Sector Labor Laws on Labor Market Institutions and Outcomes. In *When Public Sector Workers Unionize*, ed. Richard B. Freeman and Casey Ichniowski, 81–103. Chicago: University of Chicago Press.

Gillette, Clayton P. 2005. The Conditions for Interlocal Cooperation. *Journal of Law and Politics* 21 (Spring): 365–95.

Glaeser, Edward L., and Bruce Sacerdote. 1999. Why Is There More Crime in Cities? *Journal of Political Economy* 107 (December): S225–58.

Gyourko, Joseph, and Joseph Tracy. 1989. Local Public Sector Rent-Seeking and Its Impact on Local Land Values. *Regional Science and Urban Economics* 19 (August): 493–516.

Harris, Milton, and Artur Raviv. 1988. Corporate Governance: Voting Rights and Majority Rule. *Journal of Financial Economics* 20 (January–March: 203–35.

Haughwout, Andrew F., and Robert P. Inman (2001), "Fiscal Policies in Open Cities with Firms and Households," *Regional Science and Urban Economics*, Vol. 31 (April), 147–180.

———. 2002. Should Suburbs Help Their Central City? *Brookings Wharton Papers on Urban Affairs*, 45–88. Washington, DC: Brookings Institution Press.

Haughwout, Andrew F., Robert P. Inman. Steven Craig, and Thomas Luce. 2004. Local Revenue Hills: Evidence from Four U.S. Cities. *Review of Economics and Statistics* 86 (May): 570–85.

Hohenberg, Paul, and Lynn Lees. 1985. *The Making of Urban Europe: 1000–1950*, Cambridge, MA: Harvard University Press.

Ichniowski, Casey. 1988. Public Sector Union Growth and Bargaining Laws: A Proportional Hazards Approach with Time-Varying Treatments. In *When Public Sector Workers Unionize*, ed. Richard B. Freeman and Casey Ichniowski. 19–38. Chicago: University of Chicago Press.

Inman, Robert P. 1978. Optimal Fiscal Reform for Metropolitan Schools. *American Economic Review* 68 (March): 107–22.

———. 1981. Wages, Pensions, and Employment in the Local Public Sector. In *Public Sector Labor Markets*, ed. Peter Mieszkowski and George Peterson, 11–57. Washington, DC: Urban Institute.

———. 1982. Public Employee Pensions and the Local Labor Budget. *Journal of Public Economics* 19 (October): 49–72.

———. 1983. Anatomy of a Fiscal Crisis. *Business Review: Federal Reserve Bank of Philadelphia* (June): 15–22.

———. 1995. How to Have a Fiscal Crisis: Lessons from Philadelphia. *American Economic Review* 85 (May): 387–83.

———. 2003a. Should Philadelphia's Suburbs Help Their Central City? *Business Review: Federal Reserve Bank of Philadelphia* (June): 24–36.

———. 2003b. Transfers and Bailouts: Enforcing Local Fiscal Discipline with Lessons from U.S. Federalism. In *Fiscal Decentralization and the Challenge of Hard Budget Constraints*, ed. Jonathan A. Rodden, Gunnar S. Eskeland, and Jennie Litvack, 35–83. Cambridge, MA: MIT Press.

Inman, Robert P., and Daniel L. Rubinfeld. 1979. The Judicial Pursuit of Local Fiscal Equity. *Harvard Law Review* 92 (June): 1662–1750.

Nechyba, Thomas J. 1996. A Computable General Equilibrium Model of Intergovernmental Aid. *Journal of Public Economics* 62 (November): 363–98.

Oates, Wallace E. 2005. Property Taxation and Local Public Spending: The Renter Effect. *Journal of Urban Economics* 57 (May): 419–31.

Oates, Wallace E., and Robert M. Schwab. 1997. The Impact of Urban Land Taxation: The Pittsburgh Experience. *National Tax Journal* 50 (March): 1–21.

Rangel, Antonio. 2005. How to Protect Future Generations Using Tax-Base Restrictions. *American Economic Review* 95 (March): 314–46.

Russo, Karl. 2008. What Makes a Neighborhood: Essays in Local Public Finance. PhD diss., Wharton School, University of Pennsylvania.

Saltzman, Gregory M. 1988. Public Sector Bargaining Laws Really Matter: Evidence from Ohio and Illinois. In *When Public Sector Workers Unionize*, ed. Richard B. Freeman and Casey Ichniowski, 41–78. Chicago: University of Chicago Press.

Shefter, Martin. 1992. *Political Crisis, Fiscal Crisis: The Collapse and Revival of New York City*. New York: Columbia University Press.

Shepsle, Kenneth A. 1979. Institutional Arrangements and Equilibrium in Multidimensional Voting Models. *American Journal of Political Science* 23 (February): 27–59.

Zax, Jeffrey, and Casey Ichniowski. 1988. The Effects of Public Sector Unionism on Pay, Employment, Department Budgets, and Municipal Expenditures. In *When Public Sector Workers Unionize*, ed. Richard B. Freeman and Casey Ichniowski, 323–61. Chicago: University of Chicago Press.

Author Index

Note: **Boldfaced** page numbers refer to reference lists at the end of each chapter.

Subject Index